P9-DET-355

Modern European
Intellectual History

Modern European Intellectual History

REAPPRAISALS AND NEW PERSPECTIVES

Edited by

DOMINICK LaCAPRA AND
STEVEN L. KAPLAN

CORNELL UNIVERSITY PRESS

Ithaca and London

Copyright © 1982 by Cornell University Press

All rights reserved. Except for brief quotations in a review, this book, or parts thereof, must not be reproduced in any form without permission in writing from the publisher. For information address Cornell University Press, 124 Roberts Place, Ithaca, New York 14850.

First published 1982 by Cornell University Press.
Published in the United Kingdom by Cornell University Press Ltd.,
Ely House, 37 Dover Street, London W1X 4HQ.

International Standard Book Number (cloth) 0-8014-1470-9
International Standard Book Number (paper) 0-8014-9881-3
Library of Congress Catalog Card Number 82-7418
Printed in the United States of America
Librarians: Libraryof Congress cataloging information
appears on the last page of the book.

The paper in this book is acid-free and meets the guidelines for permanence and durability of the Committee on Production Guidelines for Book Longevity of the Council on Library Resources.

Contents

5

CONTENTS

Preface

For at least a decade, intellectual historians have had a grow-ing belief that their field is undergoing a far-reaching change. The direction of the change is still difficult to discern. But the recent invasion of new theoretical perspectives and research practices from Europe has agitated the whole realm of historical studies. In part because of the very nature of the material with which they work, intellectual historians are especially sensitive barometers of change within the profession. Indeed, they face a peculiar problem compara-ble to that confronted by anthropologists. To what extent should they "go native" and come to resemble that often disconcerting tribe they try to scrutinize in scholarly fashion, the intellectuals themselves?

The essays in this book focus upon modern European intellectual history, but, explicitly or implicitly, they raise broad issues of method and approach that go beyond the boundaries of specific periods or topics. It might not be an exaggeration to say that the book is a manifesto—a manifesto not in the sense of delivering a shared mes-sage or program but in that of disclosing a set of common questions and concerns. Let us consider some of the most prominent among these.

What is the relevance to research in intellectual history of Critical Theory, hermeneutics, structuralism, and post-structuralism? One of the more significant claims of figures who belong to these "schools" of thought (for example, Jürgen Habermas, Hans-Georg Gadamer, Michel Foucault, and Jacques Derrida) is that their reconceptualiza-tion of problems has important implications for the understanding of the historical process and for the writing of history itself. Often prac-ticing historians dismiss these claims for a number of reasons: the difficulty or obscurity of the works in which they are formulated; the

7

elusiveness of their import for actual historical research; the false or objectionable nature of their assumptions or implications. How can these claims be elucidated, related to one another, critically evaluated, and employed in research? Are older critical approaches, such as Marxism and psychoanalysis, still viable? More generally, what is the nature of description, interpretation, and explanation in intellectual history? What is the bearing upon the field of recent tendencies in semiotics and the general theory of language? Does intellectual history have any broad implications in terms of ethics, social action, or politics?

What is the relation of intellectual history to contemporary social history? Within the profession, it is social history that has posed the greatest challenge to intellectual history—a challenge that can be seen in a variety of ways. Statistical research may reveal that the number of courses offered under the label "intellectual history" has remained constant in the recent past.[1] But the relative growth and the absolute excitement often seem to have passed to social history. And, within intellectual history itself, a reorientation in the direction of social and cultural history seems to have taken place. Are there problems or methods specific to intellectual history, for example, with reference to the interpretation of difficult texts and other artifacts of "high culture"? What types of problem require research at the intersection of intellectual and social history? In more substantive terms, what is the relation between elite and popular culture? How does it vary over space and time? What are the consequences of variations in the relation of elite and popular culture for methodological perspectives? What is alive and what is dead in the heritage of the *Annales* School, which has done so much to reshape our understanding of historical inquiry? Does the entire problem of the relations among intellectual, cultural, and social history have to be rethought from the ground up?

In presenting this volume to the reader, we cannot pretend that all these questions have been answered or even addressed to our satisfaction. And, needless to add, the book does not represent the positions of all those doing modern European intellectual history—much less intellectual history in general—at the present time.[2] But we think that we have a good cross section of critical opinion, especially with respect to those who are in the liminal position of younger older (or

[1]See Robert Darnton, "Intellectual and Cultural History," in *The Past before Us: Contemporary Historical Writing in the United States*, ed. Michael Kammen (Ithaca, 1980).

[2]For the representation of some other perspectives, see, for example, *New Directions in American Intellectual History*, ed. John Higham and Paul K. Conkin (Baltimore, 1979).

older younger) scholars. In asking Hayden White to provide a concluding reflection for the volume, we requested that he refer to specific
contributions as he deemed fit in raising what he saw as the important
issues for the future of the discipline. The result was both a remarkable assessment and a substantial offering in its own right—a contribution that readers might take as a point of departure for their own
thoughts.

Most of these papers were first presented at a conference held at
Cornell University on April 24–26, 1980. We thank the National
Endowment for the Humanities and the Cornell Society for the Hu-
manities, as well as the Cornell Western Societies Program and History
Department, for funds that made the conference possible.

DOMINICK LACAPRA
STEVEN L. KAPLAN

Ithaca, New York

Modern European

Intellectual History

CHAPTER ONE

Intellectual History or Sociocultural History? The French Trajectories

ROGER CHARTIER

Posing the problems of intellectual history is surely one of the most difficult things in the world to do for several reasons. The first is a matter of vocabulary. In no other branch of history does there exist such a national specificity of terms used and such a difficulty in introducing them, indeed in simply translating them, into another language and another intellectual context.[1] American historiography claims two categories, whose links are nowhere plainly specified and thus always problematical. First, there is intellectual history, which appeared with the "new history" at the beginning of the century and was constituted as a particular field of research by the work of Perry Miller. Second, there is the history of ideas, developed by A. O. Lovejoy as a discipline having its own objective, program, and research procedures, and its own institutional locus (the *Journal of the History of Ideas*, which Lovejoy founded in 1940). But in the various European countries, neither of these categories has gained much of a foothold: in Germany, *Geistesgeschichte* dominates; in Italy, *Storia intellectuale* does not appear, even in the work of Delio Cantimori. In France, *histoire des idées* hardly exists, either as a notion or as a discipline (in fact, it has been historians of literature such as Jean Ehrard who have laid claim to the term, albeit cautiously and with reservations). "Intellectual history" as a label seems to have arrived too late to take the place of the traditional terms (philosophical history, literary history, art history, and the like) and has had no impact

[1]See Felix Gilbert, "Intellectual History: Its Aims and Methods," *Daedalus* 100 (Winter 1971), 80–97, esp. 80–84.

on a new vocabulary forged essentially by the *Annales* historians: *histoire des mentalités, psychologie historique, histoire sociale des idées, histoire socio-culturelle*, and so on. This coin has its obverse, however, since the term "history of mentalities" is difficult to export, seems awkward in languages other than French, and remains the source of considerable confusion. We are forced to leave the expression untranslated and thus to recognize the inevitable rigidity of a given nation's way of considering historical questions. To the lexical certainties of the other kinds of history (economic, social, political), intellectual history thus opposes a double uncertainty in the vocabulary that describes it: each national historiography possesses its own conceptualization, and in each one different ideas enter into play, each indistinguishable from the next to foreign eyes.

But behind the words that seem to differ so radically, are the concepts similar? Or, to state it differently, is the object that they represent so diversely, merely one unique and homogeneous idea? Nothing seems more unlikely. Consider, for example, two attempts at taxonomy: for Jean Ehrard, the "history of ideas" includes three kinds of history—"individualistic history of the great world systems, history of the collective and diverse reality represented by opinion, and structural history of forms of thought and feeling."[2] For Robert Darnton, "intellectual history" includes "the history of ideas (the study of systematic thought usually in philosophical formulations), intellectual history proper (the study of informal thought, climates of opinion and literary movements), the social history of ideas (the study of ideologies and idea diffusion), and cultural history (the study of culture in the anthropological sense, including world-views and collective *mentalités*."[3] Using different vocabularies, these definitions actually say the same thing: that the field of so-called intellectual history covers, in fact, the totality of the forms of thought and that its object or objective has no more precision a priori than that of social or economic history.

Much more important than classifications and definitions are the way or ways in which historians, at any given moment, categorize this immense and vague territory and how they treat the units of observation thus constituted. Caught in the center of oppositions that are intellectual as well as institutional, each of these diverse cate-

[2]Jean Ehrard, "Histoire des idées et histoire littéraire," *Problèmes et méthodes de l'histoire littéraire*, Publications de la Société d'Histoire Littéraire de la France (Paris, 1974), 68–80.
[3]Robert Darnton, "Intellectual and Cultural History," in *The Past before Us: Contemporary Historical Writing in the United States*, ed. Michael Kammen (Ithaca, 1980), 337.

gories determines its own object or objective, its conceptual tools, its methodology. Nonetheless, explicitly or not, each one embodies a representation of the totality of the field of history and delimits the place it claims to occupy in history as well as the places it leaves aside or denies to others. The uncertainty and the compartmentalization of specific vocabularies doubtless relate to intra- or interdisciplinary struggles whose characteristics are peculiar to each field of intellectual forces and whose stakes are a hegemonic position—above all a lexical hegemony. So we shall turn to some of the oppositions that have shaped and divided French intellectual history. I suggest these tentatively, all the while being conscious of a double limitation: on the one hand, owing to lack of research on this topic, I cannot fully explain the institutional or political stakes of the methodological confrontations; on the other hand, I want to stress certain debates, in particular those focused around the *Annales* from 1930 to the present, thus perhaps distorting the whole picture.

The First *Annales* Generation and Intellectual History

In the twentieth century, the trajectory of intellectual history in France (in the double meaning of its thematic or methodological mutations and of the displacement of its positions in the disciplinary field of history) has largely been controlled by a discourse exterior to itself: that held by the historians between the wars who instituted a different way of writing history. We must begin from there and try to understand how the *Annales* and particularly its first directors, Lucien Febvre and Marc Bloch, thought intellectual history ought to be constituted. This is important not for some kind of retrospective celebration, but because their approach to the history of ideas has become dominant, to the extent that it is followed by the historical community somewhat presumptuously called the *Annales* "School."[4]

For Febvre, to examine intellectual history is first and foremost to react to the way in which that history is written in one's own time. From this point of view, there is great continuity between the first reviews he published in Henri Berr's *Revue de Synthèse Historique* before 1914 and those he contributed to the *Annales* during and after

[4]Cf. Jacques Revel, "*The Annales*: Continuities and Discontinuities," *Review: Journal of the Fernand Braudel Center for the Study of Economies, Historical Systems, and Civilizations* I (Winter-Spring 1978), 9–18, and "Histoire et sciences sociales: Les paradigmes des *Annales*," *Annales E.S.C.* 34 (1979), 1360–1376.

the Second World War. Consider, for example, the two long reflections published in Berr's journal in 1907 and 1909 and devoted respectively to Louis Delaruelle's book on Budé and to Edouard Droz's on Proudhon. Two questions are raised there which will lay the groundwork for his great books, *Luther* in 1929 and *Rabelais* in 1942. First of all, can one reduce the frequently contradictory, often composite, and at any rate always changing ideas of a man or a milieu to the traditional categories used by the history of ideas (renaissance, humanism, reformation, and the like)? Such retrospective and classifying terms are bearers of contradictions, and they are not faithful to the lived psychological and intellectual experience of the time. "Thus, for example, by terming 'Reformation' those efforts of religious renewal and Christian renaissance undertaken by Lefèvre and his disciples at the beginning of the sixteenth century, are we not falsifying the psychological reality of that epoch?"[5] By getting rid of labels which, while pretending to identify former ways of thinking, in fact disguise them, the task of the "historians of the intellectual movement" (Febvre wrote) is above all to relocate the originality—impossible to reduce to an a priori definition—of each system of thought in all its complexity and its vicissitudes.

The second preoccupation expressed by Febvre even before 1914 is the effort to examine the relationship between ideas (or ideologies) and social reality with the use of categories other than those of influence or determinism. Consider this text from 1909 on Proudhonism: "There are no 'creative' theories, properly speaking, because as soon as an idea, as fragmentary as it may be, has been realized, however imperfectly, in the domain of facts, it is no longer the idea that counts and acts, it is the institution situated in its place, in its time, incorporating within itself a complicated and protean network of social facts, producing and enduring in turn a thousand diverse actions and a thousand reactions."[6] Even if the procedures for the "incarnation" of ideas are more complex than Febvre would have us believe, it is nonetheless true that he clearly affirms his desire to break with a whole tradition of intellectual history (the inverted counterpart of a simplified Marxism) which deduced from a few volontarist thoughts all of the processes of social transformation. For him, the social

[5]Lucien Febvre, "Guillaume Budé et les origines de l'humanisme français. A propos d'ouvrages récents," *Revue de Synthèse Historique* (1907), reprinted in *Pour une histoire à part entière* (Paris, 1962), 708.

[6]Lucien Febvre, "Une question de l'influence: Proudhon et les syndicalismes des années 1900–1914, *RSH* (1909), reprinted in *Pour une histoire à part entière*, 785.

structure could never be dissolved in the ideologies wishing to shape it. Febvre thus established, in these youthful texts, a double split: on the one hand, between the old ways of thinking the past and the categories, for the most part poor, in which historians intended to catalog them; on the other hand, between those old ways of thinking and the social terrain in which they are inscribed. Lucien Febvre indicated the appropriate direction for a historical analysis that took as its model the descriptions of *faits de mentalité*, such as the Durkheimian sociologists or ethnologists following in the path of Lévy-Bruhl then construed them.

Forty years later, Febvre's tone was more critical and biting in protesting against a history of ideas that he perceived as petrified in its abstractions. In 1938, he chastised the historians of philosophy in the following terms:

> Of all the workers who cling to the generic title of historian, there is only one group that cannot in some way justify it in our eyes. They are those who, applying themselves to rethink for their own purposes systems that are sometimes several centuries old, and without the slightest care to show the links with other manifestations of the epoch which saw them come into being, end up doing precisely the opposite of what a historical method demands. They engender concepts from disincarnated minds which live their lives beyond time and space. Historians who deal with them forge strange chains whose links are at the same time unreal and closed.[7]

The criticism leveled against the intellectual history of the time is thus twofold: because it isolates the ideas or the systems of thought from the conditions that authorized their production, because it separates them radically from the forms of social life, this disincarnated history institutes a universe of abstractions where thought seems limitless since it depends on nothing. Reviewing Etienne Gilson's book *La philosophie du Moyen Age* with admiration, Febvre returned in 1948 to this central idea: "We must not underestimate the role of ideas in history. Nor may we subordinate them to the action of [personal] interests. We must show that a Gothic cathedral, the marketplace of Ypres and one of those great cathedrals of ideas such as those Etienne Gilson describes to us in his book—are daughters of a single epoch, sisters reared in the same household."[8] Without making it explicit or

[7] Lucien Febvre, "Leur histoire et la nôtre," *Annales d'Histoire Economique et Sociale* (1928), reprinted in *Combats pour l'histoire* (Paris, 1953), 278.

[8] Lucien Febvre, "Doctrines et societés. Etienne Gilson et la philosophie du XIV⁰ siécle," *Annales E.S.C.*3 (1948), reprinted in *Combats pour l'histoire*, 288.

mapping out its theory, Febvre suggests here a reading that postulates for a given epoch the existence of "structures of thought" (the term is not his), which are determined by the socioeconomic evolutions that organize intellectual constructions, such as artistic productions, and collective practices, such as philosophical thoughts.

Architecture and scholasticism: Febvre's very words prompt a comparison between his approach and Erwin Panofsky's contemporary work, *Gothic Architecture and Scholasticism* (the subject of a series of lectures in 1948, published in 1951).[9] Both of them, in parallel fashion and quite probably without reciprocal influence, were attempting in the same period to equip themselves with the intellectual means to conceptualize this "spirit of the times," this "Zeitgeist"— which is, among other things, the basis for Burckhardt's entire enterprise but which, for Panofsky as for Febvre, is much more what must be explained than what explains. In so doing, each in his own way kept a distance from the principles that up to that point implicitly upheld all the works of intellectual history, namely: (1) the postulating of a conscious and transparent relationship between the intentions of the intellectual producers and their products; (2) the ascription of intellectual or aesthetic creation uniquely to individual inventiveness or freedom—an idea that leads to the notion of precursor, a notion cherished by a certain kind of history of ideas; (3) the explanation of the agreements noted among the different intellectual (or artistic) productions of a time, whether it be by borrowing or by influence (more key words of intellectual history), or by the return to a "spirit of the times," the latter being a composite of philosophical, psychological, and aesthetic characteristics. To conceptualize these different relationships otherwise (that is, between the work and its creator, between the work and its time, between different works of a given period) required the forging of new concepts: in Panofsky the concepts of mental habits (*habitus*) and of a habit-forming force, and in Febvre, that of mental equipment (*outillage mental*). Both of them, owing to new approaches, could take a distance from the standard procedures in intellectual history and, as a result, its object or objective was itself displaced.

In his *Rabelais*, published in 1942, Febvre does not define mental equipment, but characterizes it as follows: "Each civilization has its own mental tools; and furthermore, each epoch of a given civilization, each bit of progress, be it in techniques or sciences—requires a re-

[9]Erwin Panofsky, *Architecture gothique et pensée scolastique*, prefaced by *L'abbé Suger de Saint Denis*, tr. and end comments by Pierre Bourdieu (Paris, 1967).

newed set of tools, more highly developed for certain needs, less for others. This civilization, this epoch, is not guaranteed to transmit such mental equipment, integrally, to the civilizations and epochs that will follow; the equipment may undergo mutilations, regressions, deformations of considerable consequence. Or, on the contrary, progress, enrichment, new complications. It is valid for the civilization that is able to forge it; it is valid for the epoch that really uses it; it will not endure through eternity, nor is it relevant to all humanity: not even during the limited course of an internal evolution of civilization."[10] This characterization meant essentially three things: first, following the Lévy-Bruhl of *La mentalité primitive* (1922), it sees the categories of thought as not universal and therefore not reducible to those set forth by the people of the twentieth century; next, ways of thinking depend above all on material instruments (the techniques) or conceptual instruments (the sciences) that make them possible; finally—in contrast to a naive evolutionary theory—there is no continual and necessary progress (defined as a passage from the simple to the complex) in the succession of different kinds of mental tools. To understand what Febvre means by the very notion of mental tools, we can call upon two texts: one, in the first volume of the *Encyclopédie française*, published in 1937, the entry "l'outillage mental. Pensée, langage, mathématique"; the other, the second book of the second part of *Rabelais*. What defines mental equipment in these pages is the state of language, its lexicon, its syntax, the scientific language and instruments, and also the "sensitive support of thought" represented by the system of perception, whose variable economy determines the *structure* of affectivity: "So close to us in appearance, the contemporaries of Rabelais are really far away by dint of their intellectual beliefs. And even their *structure* was not ours"[11] (my italics). In any given epoch, the crisscrossing of these various fulcrums (linguistic, conceptual, affective) determines certain "ways of thinking and feeling" that categorize specific intellectual configurations (for example, the limits between the possible and the impossible or the boundaries between the natural and the supernatural).

The primary duty of the historian, as of the ethnologist, is then to reconstruct these earlier representations in their irreducible specificity, without either shrouding them in anachronistic categories or measuring them against the standards of the twentieth century's mental equip-

[10]Lucien Febvre, *Le problème de l'incroyance au XVIe siècle. La religion de Rabelais* (1942; rpt. Paris, 1968), 141–142.
[11]Ibid., 394

ment, which appears implicitly as the necessary result of continual progress. On this point also, Febvre joins Lévy-Bruhl in warning against an erroneous reading of the old way of thinking. For proof we have only to note the similarity between the opening pages of Lévy-Bruhl's *La mentalité primitive* and Febvre's *Amour sacré, amour profane. Autour de l'Heptaméron* (1944). Lévy-Bruhl tells us: "Instead of imaginatively substituting ourselves for the primitive peoples whom we study, and thereby having them think as we would if we were in their place, which could only lead to hypotheses that are plausible but nearly always false, let us, on the contrary, force ourselves to block out our own mental habits and try to discover primitive man's way of thinking by analyzing his collective representations and the connections among these representations."[12] Compare this with Febvre's strictures: "To cordially attribute to these ancestors factual knowledge—and therefore idea materials—which we all possess, but which was, for the wisest among them, impossible to procure; to imitate all those good missionaries who used to return from the islands all agog because the savages they had encountered believed in God, another tiny step and they would be true Christians; to endow, in a boundlessly generous way, the contemporaries of Pope Leo with conceptions of the universe and life that our knowledge has forged for us and that are such that none of their elements, or hardly any, ever inhabited the mind of a Renaissance man—one can count the historians, whom I would call the shrewdest, who recoil before such a deformation of the past, such a mutilation of humanity in its evolution. And all this, most likely, for lack of having asked the question we asked earlier, the question of intelligibility. Indeed, a man of the sixteenth century must be intelligible not in relationship to us, but in relationship to his contemporaries."[13]

Febvre's notion of mental equipment differs in a number of ways from the idea that Panofsky developed at about the same time. First of all, the very word equipment (*outillage*) and the expression *outils mentaux* that Febvre sometimes used—which suggest the quasi-objective existence of a panoply of intellectual instruments (words, symbols, concepts, and so on) at the disposition of thought—contrast with Panofsky's manner of defining the mental habit, the group of unconscious schemes, of internalized principles that give their unity to an epoch's ways of thinking no matter what the object of thought

[12]Lucien Lévy-Bruhl, *La mentalité primitive* (1922; rpt. Paris, 1976), 41.

[13]Lucien Febvre, *Amour sacré, amour profane. Autour de l'Heptaméron* (1944; rpt. Paris, 1971), 10.

might be. In the twelfth and thirteenth centuries, for example, these are the principles of clarification and conciliation of opposites, which constitute a scholastic *modus operandi* whose application is not limited to theological construction. From this first discrepancy emerges a second. For Febvre, the intellectual equipment that men of a certain time can handle is considered a storehouse of "idea materials" (to use his expression). From that time on, what principally distinguishes the mentalities of social groups is the more or less extensive use they make of the available "tools": the wisest will put into play the quasi-totality of existing words or concepts while those less well equipped will use only the most minute part of the mental equipment of their time, thus limiting, in comparison to their contemporaries, what it is possible for them to think. Panofsky's stress is different (and paradoxically more social). In fact, for him, mental habits point back to their conditions of inculcation, thus to the "habit-forming forces"—for example, the institution of the school in its different modalities. From thence it is possible to understand, in the unity of their production, the homologies of structure existing among different intellectual "products" of a given milieu and also to conceptualize the variations among groups as differences in systems of perception and appreciation, themselves issuing from differences in modes of education or formation. It is just such a conception that Marc Bloch approaches when, in the chapter from *La société féodale* entitled "Ways of Feeling and Thinking," he sets forth a hierarchy of levels of language and cultural universes in terms of the conditions of intellectual training.[14] There is nonetheless lacking here, as with Febvre, an analysis of the mechanism (a central item in Panofsky) by which categories of fundamental thought become, in a given group of social agents, internalized and unseen schemas structuring all the particular thoughts or actions.

Despite this theoretical limitation, it is quite clear that the position of historians belonging to the first *Annales* generation heavily influenced the evolution of French intellectual history. It has, in fact, changed the basic question: what is important to understand is no longer the audacities of thought but the limits of what is thinkable. To an intellectual history of unbridled minds and ideas without support structure is opposed a history of collective representations, of intellectual equipment and categories available and shared at a given epoch. In Lucien Febvre's work, it is just such a project that establishes the primacy accorded to biographical study. Luther in 1928,

---

[14]Marc Bloch, *La société féodale* (1939; rpt. Paris, 1968), 115–128.

Rabelais and des Périers in 1942, Marguerite de Navarre in 1944: all of them so many case studies from which to log how, for the people of the sixteenth century, the perception and representation of the world are organized, how the limits of the "thinkable" are defined, how relationships among religion, science, and morality appropriate to the epoch are constructed. Thus the individual is returned to his time since, whoever or whatever he may be, he cannot exempt himself from the determinations that control his contemporaries' ways of thinking and acting. Intellectual biography as done by Febvre is then, in fact, a history of society since it locates its heroes simultaneously as witnesses and as products of the collective conditioning that limits free and individual invention. The path was thus opened (once Febvre's personal bent for biography was bypassed) toward a history of systems of beliefs, of values and representations appropriate to an epoch or a group, designated in French historiography by an expression all the more encompassing to the extent that its conceptual content remains blurred, namely "history of mentalities." It is this notion that we must now examine.

History of Mentalities/History of Ideas

As of the 1960s, the notion of *mentalité* became essential to French historiography in characterizing a history that proffers as its object neither the ideas nor the socioeconomic foundations of societies. More practiced than theorized about, this history of mentalities "à la française" is informed by several conceptions more or less shared by its users.[15] First, the definition of the word as suggested by Jacques Le Goff: "the mentality of an individual, although he may be a great man, is what he has in common with other men of his time." Or: "the level of the history of mentalities is that of daily life and habits; it is what escapes the individual subjects of history because it reveals the impersonal content of their thoughts." Thus there is constituted as a

---

[15]See Georges Duby, "L'histoire des mentalités," *L'histoire et ses méthodes*, ed. Charles Samaran (Paris, 1961), 937–966; Robert Mandrou, "L'histoire des mentalités," in *Encyclopedia Universalis*, vol. 8 (1968), 436–438; Georges Duby, "Histoire sociale et histoire des mentalités. Le Moyen Age: Entretien avec Georges Duby" (1970) in *Aujourd'hui l'histoire: Enquête de la nouvelle critique* (Paris, 1974), 201–217; Jacques Le Goff, "Les mentalités. Une histoire ambigue," *Faire de l'histoire*, ed. Jacques Le Goff and Pierre Nora, 3 vols. (Paris, 1974), 3:76–94; Philippe Ariès, "L'histoire des mentalités," in Jacques Le Goff et al., *La nouvelle histoire* (Paris, 1978), 402–423; Roger Chartier, "Outillage mental," in *La nouvelle histoire*, 448–452.

fundamental historical object the very opposite of the object of classical intellectual history: to the idea, the conscious construction of an individualized mind, is opposed, term for term, the always collective mentality that regulates, without their knowing it, the representations and judgments of social subjects. The relationship between consciousness and thought is therefore posed in a new way, close to the formulation of sociologists in the Durkheimian tradition, placing the accent on the schemas or the contents of thought which, even if they are expressed in the style of the individual, are, in fact, the "unthought" and internalized conditionings that cause a group or a society to share, without the need to make them explicit, a system of representations and a system of values.

Another common point is a very broad conception of the field covered by the notion of *mentalité,* which includes, as Robert Mandrou writes, "what is conceived and felt, the field of intelligence and of emotion (*affectivité*)." Starting from that shared concept, attention is directed toward psychological categories at least as much as and probably more than toward intellectual categories: hence a supplementary distinction between a history of mentalities identified with historical psychology and intellectual history in its traditional definition. The identification with psychology is very evident in Febvre, who was an attentive reader of Charles Blondel (*Introduction à la psychologie historique,* 1929) and of Henri Wallon (*Principes de psychologie appliquée,* 1930)[16] and in his successors (Mandrou, for example, whose book *Introduction à la France moderne,* published in 1961, was subtitled *Essai de psychologie historique*). This identification is also at the very core of the work of Ignace Meyerson, whose importance has been paramount for the transformation of Greek studies.[17] Well beyond the project of reconstituting the sentiments and sensibilities belonging to the people of a certain time period (which is essentially Febvre's project), Meyerson's enterprise concerns the essential psychological categories—those at work in the construction of time and space, in the production of the imaginary, in the collective perception of human activities—which he places at the center of observation and captures in their precise historical specificity. For example, the notion of person as it is treated by Jean-Pierre Vernant, following

[16]Cf. the following three articles: "Méthodes et solutions pratiques. Henri Wallon et la psychologie appliquée," *Annales d'Histoire Economique et Sociale* 3 (1931); "Une vue d'ensemble. Histoire et psychologie," in *Encyclopédie française* (1938); and "Comment reconstituer la vie affective d'autrefois? La sensibilité et l'histoire," *Annales d'Histoire Sociale* 3 (1941), reprinted in *Combats pour l'histoire,* 201–238.

[17]Ignace Meyerson, *Les fonctions psychologiques et les oeuvres* (Paris, 1948).

Meyerson: "there is not, there cannot be, a person-model beyond the course of human history, with its vicissitudes, its variety from place to place, its transformations from era to era. The investigation does not intend to establish whether Greece had the concept of the person, but to discover what the ancient Greek person is, how he differs from today's person, in the multiplicity of his traits."[18] Starting from a similar intellectual position Alphonse Dupront proposed to constitute the history of collective psychology as a specific discipline in the field of the human sciences, and to do this by giving it maximal extension since it included "the history of values, mentalities, forms, symbols, and myths."[19] In fact, under the guise of a definition of collective psychology, he suggested a total reformulation of the history of ideas. One of the major objects of the history of collective psychology is constituted by the idea-forces [idées-forces] and the concepts that make up what Dupront calls the mental collectif of the people of an epoch. Grasped through the circulation of the words that designate them, located in their social roots, considered as much in terms of their affective or emotional charge as of their intellectual content, ideas become, like myths or complexes of values, one of these "collective forces by which men live their time" and thus one of the components of the "collective psyche" of a civilization. Therein one can see something like the fulfillment of the Annales tradition, both in the fundamentally psychological characterization of the collective mentality and in the redefinition of what the history of ideas must be, reinserted into an inquiry into the whole of the mental collectif.

It is clear, moreover, that the history of mentalities (considered as a part of sociocultural history), having as object the collective, the automatic, the repetitive, can and must employ quantitative methods: "The history of collective psychology needs series that are, if not exhaustive, at least as broad as possible."[20] We see then what this approach owes to the history of economies and societies which, spurred on first by the great crisis of the 1930s, then by the post-World War II crisis, became the "heavy" sector (by number of collective investigations and the striking successes of some of them) of historical research in France. When in the 1960s cultural history emerged as the most popular and the most innovative domain in

---

[18]Jean-Pierre Vernant, Mythe et pensée chez les Grecs. Etudes de la psychologie historique (Paris, 1967), 13–14.
[19]Alphonse Dupront, "Problèmes et méthodes d'une histoire de la psychologie collective," Annales E.S.C. 16 (1961), 3–11.
[20]Ibid., 8.

history, it did so by taking up and then transposing the problematics and the methodologies that assured the success of socioeconomic history. The project is simple, as stated a posteriori by Pierre Chaunu: "The problem consists of attaining the third level [the level of the affective and mental] with the help of the techniques of regressive statistics, that is, with the help of the mathematical analysis of the series and of the double interrogation of the document, first of all in itself, then in relation to its position in the midst of the homogeneous series in which the fundamental information is integrated. It amounts to as complete an adaptation as possible of the methods that were perfected first by historians of the economy, then by social historians."[21]

This preeminence accorded to the series, and therefore to the collection and to the treatment of homogeneous, repeated, and comparable givens, has several implications. The most important is the central position bestowed upon the massive documentary collections, widely representative socially and allowing the categorization of multiple data over the long run. This orientation leads to the rereading and the exploitation of sources classically used in social history (for example, the notarial archives). It also results in the invention of new sources that permit the reconstitution of ways of thinking or feeling. Beyond the methodological similarity, Chaunu's "serial history of the third level" shares a double problematic with the history of economies and societies. The first is that of duration: how to articulate together and reconcile the mentalities of the long run, which tend to be more or less immobile, with the brusque changes and transfers of belief and sensibility of the short run. This issue (posed, for example, about the dechristianization of France) prefigures the central question of Braudel's *Méditerranée*: how to conceptualize the formation of hierarchies, the articulation and imbrication of different durations (short time, *conjoncture*, long run) of historical phenomena.[22]

The second problematical inheritance, a bequest of cultural history, is found in the manner of conceiving the relationship between social groups and cultural levels. In fidelity to the work of Ernest Labrousse and the French "school" of social history, the categorizations elaborated in order to classify facts of *mentalité* are always those resulting

[21]Pierre Chaunu, "Un nouveau champ pour l'histoire sérielle: Le quantitatif au troisième niveau," in *Mélanges en l'honneur de Fernand Braudel*, 2 vols. (Toulouse, 1973), 2: 105–125.

[22]Fernand Braudel, *La Méditerranée et le monde méditerranéen à l'époque de Philippe II*, 2 vols. (2d ed.; Paris, 1966), 1:16–17, and "Histoire et sciences sociales. La longue durée," (1959) in *Ecrits sur l'histoire* (Paris, 1969), 41–83.

from a social analysis that places levels of fortune in a hierarchy, distinguishes types of revenues, and classifies professions. It is then on the basis of this social and professional grid that the reconstitution of different systems of thought and of cultural behavior can take place. There results a necessary commensurability between the intellectual or cultural divisions on the one hand and the social boundaries on the other, whether it be the frontier that separates the little people from the notables or the dominated from the dominating, or the gradations that mark a social ladder. This almost tyrannical preeminence of the social dimension, which initially defines cultural cleavages that subsequently have only to be characterized, is the clearest trace of the dependence of cultural on social history that marks postwar French historiography. (We can note, moreover, that this dependence does not exist in the work of Febvre or Bloch, both of whom were more sensitive either to categories shared by all the people of a time period, or to differential usages of available intellectual equipment.)

It is upon these methodological bases, affirmed or unconscious, that the history of mentalities has developed in French historiography during the past fifteen years. Indeed, it has responded much more tellingly than intellectual history to French historians' new levels of awareness. Of these the most significant is the recognition of a new equilibrium between history and the social sciences. Contested in its intellectual and institutional primacy, French history reacted by annexing the terrains and the modes of questioning of neighboring disciplines (anthropology, sociology) that challenged its domination. Attention was thereby displaced toward new objects or objectives (collective thoughts and gestures vis-à-vis life and death, beliefs and rituals, educative models, and so on) which until then had belonged to ethnological investigation, and toward new questions, largely foreign to social history, which were principally concerned with ranking the constitutive groups of a society. Second, there was the recognition that social differentiations cannot be conceptualized solely in terms of fortune or dignity, but are either produced or mediated by cultural differences. The unequal division of cultural competencies (for example, reading and writing), cultural goods, (for example, books), and cultural practices (attitudes toward life or death) becomes the central object or objective of multiple inquiries conducted according to quantitative procedures and aiming to provide another sort of content for social hierarchies, without placing these hierarchies in question. Finally, there was the realization that, for taking on these new domains, classical methodologies did not suffice: consequently, as we have seen, historians have recourse to serial analysis where testamentary formulas, iconographic motifs, and the printed word replaced the price of wheat, and we witness the flowering of work on historical language or languages, from the description of semantic fields to the analysis of "énoncés."[23] Therefore, because it transposed the approaches and the problems that belonged to socioeconomic history as part of a far-reaching transformation of the historical problematic, the history of mentalities (as part of sociocultural history) was able to occupy the front of the intellectual stage and seem (as Dupront implicitly suggested) to reformulate—and thereby disqualify—the old way of doing the history of ideas.

But such a reformulation was also undertaken within the field of intellectual history, and resulted in positions completely contradictory to those of historians of mentalities. The major work here—which was, incidentally, well received by the *Annales*—is Lucien Goldmann's.[24] At the outset, a similar distance from the traditional modalities, biographical and positivistic, of the history of ideas seems to mark Goldmann's project. As with Febvre, and as in the history of mentalities, the question was first and foremost one of investigating the articulation between thoughts and the social world. The concept of "vision of the world," borrowed from Lukács, is the instrument that makes such an approach possible. Defined as "the ensemble of aspirations, sentiments and ideas that unite the members of a given group (most often of a social class) and oppose them to other groups,"[25] it makes possible a threefold operation: to assign a defined social significance and a defined social position to literary and philosophical texts, to understand the kinships between works of opposing forms and natures, and to discriminate within an individual work the "essential" texts (Goldmann's adjective), constituted as a coherent whole, to which each individual work must be related. For Goldmann the concept of world vision has simultaneously the functions of Febvre's mental equipment and the "habitus" of Panofsky (and Pierre Bourdieu). The *Dieu caché* gave an application, debatable but exemplary, of these propositions, construing Pascal's *Penseés* and nine of Racine's tragedies, from *Andromaque* to *Athalie*, as the corpus expressing most coherently "a tragic vision of the world," identified with Jansen-

[23]Compare Régine Robin, *Histoire et linguistique*, (Paris, 1973).

[24]Lucien Goldmann, *Le dieu caché. Etude sur la vision tragique dans les Pensées de Pascal et dans le théâtre de Racine* (Paris, 1955), and Robert Mandrou, "Tragique au XVIIe siècle. A propos de travaux récents," *Annales E.S.C.* 12 (1957), 305–313.

[25]Goldmann, *Le dieu caché*, 26.

ism, and connecting this collective conscience to a particular group, that of the officials of the robe dispossessed of their political power, and hence of their social leverage, as a consequence of the construction of the absolutist state.

Whatever may be the historical validity of such an analysis, it brought out one crucial idea that is the complete opposite of one of the postulates of the history of mentalities: it is the "great" writers and philosophers who depict with the greatest coherence, throughout their essential works, the conscience of the social group of which they are members; it is they who attain "the maximum possible consciousness of the social group they represent." Hence the primacy accorded to the major texts (defined in a new way, by their relationship to a vision of the world), and hence its corollary: suspicion, if not outright refusal, of quantitative approaches in the field of cultural history. Well before the present-day mistrust of such approaches, nourished by an anthropological conception of culture, Goldmann's kind of intellectual history first alerted us to the illusions of quantification. "A sociological history of literature owes it to itself to privilege the study of the great texts," wrote Jean Ehrard.[26] That meant, on the one hand, that it is in the singularity of these texts that shared ideas are to be found most clearly and completely, and, on the other hand, that the counting of words, titles, and collective representations is literally "insignificant," that is, incapable of reconstituting the complex, conflicting, and contradictory significance of collective thought. This sort of numerical collection of the superficial, the banal, and the routine is not representative, and the collective conscience of the group (which is collective "unconsciousness" for the greatest number) can be read only in the imaginative or conceptual work of the few authors who carry it to its highest degree of coherence and transparency.

The debate joined here touches upon the very definition of intellectual history, thus upon the constitution of its proper object or objective. In 1961, Dupront pleaded against the history of ideas as follows: "The history of ideas, as ever amorphous and capable of absorbing, a bit like a thirsty sponge, everything that traditional history cared so little about treating, leans too far toward pure intellectuality, the abstract life of the idea, often isolated beyond proportion from the social milieux where it takes root and which give varying expression to it. . . . What is as important as the idea and maybe even more important is the embodiment of the idea, its significance, the use one makes of

[26]Jean Ehrard, "Histoire des idées et histoire littéraire," 79.

it."[27] From this attitude emerges the call for a social history of ideas, taking as its object the implantation and circulation of ideas. In a text published ten years later, Franco Venturi challenges the pertinence of such a project which, for him, misses the essential point: "The risk of the social history of the Enlightenment, as we see it practiced today, especially in France, is that of studying ideas when they have already become mental structures without ever grasping the creative and dynamic moment of their birth, and of examining the whole geological structure of the past without investigating the soil itself from which fruits and plants grow."[28] Ideas against mental structures: the opposition clearly shows the location of the divergences and the rejection of the supposed reductionism of the social (therefore quantitative) history of intellectual production. Moreover, this reductionism has two faces. The first is sociological, viewing the significance of ideas in terms of their foundation, whether it be indicated by the position of the individuals or the milieux that produce them, or by the social field of the reception of ideas.[29] It should be noted that this criticism, directed against the undertakings of cultural sociology, does not impugn Goldmann's perspective, but in reality is situated in his own tradition. Without conflating the two questions, the notion of the world vision enables one to relate the significance of an ideological system, described in its own terms, to the sociopolitical conditions that cause a well-defined group or class, in a given historical moment, more or less to share, consciously or unconsciously, this ideological system. We are here far from the summary characterizations that sacrifice the ideological to the social, for example, by viewing the Enlightenment as simply bourgeois on the pretext that the philosophes and their readers were for the most part bourgeois themselves. Confronted with the ideas, or better, with the concepts utilized by the people of a specific time in a specific sense, the historian of ideas then has as his task "to abandon the search for a determination in favor of the search for a function," a function that can make sense only if one takes into account the entire ideological system of the epoch in question.[30]

Criticism addressed to the social history of ideas has recently aimed at another target and denounced another form of reductionism. Under attack is no longer the reduction of an idea or an ideology to its

[27]Dupront, "Problèmes et méthodes d'une histoire de la psychologie collective."

[28]Franco Venturi, *Utopia e riforma nell'Illuminismo* (Turin, 1970), 24.

[29]Jean Ehrard, "Histoire des idées et histoire sociale en France au XVIIIe siècle: Réflexions de méthode," in *Niveaux de culture et groupes sociaux*, Actes du colloque réuni du 7 au 9 mai 1966 à l'Ecole Normale Supérieure (Paris, 1967) 171–178.

[30]Ibid., 175, and the comments of Jacques Proust, 181–183.

conditions of production or reception, but the assimilation of thought contents to cultural objects through a process of reification. "Serial history of the third level" carries such a reduction in its enterprise, since its quantifying vocation supposes either that the analyzed cultural and intellectual facts are from the outset coherent universes of objects (for example, books whose subjects can be treated statistically or pictures whose themes can be inventoried) or that collective thoughts, captured in their most repetitive and least personal expression, can be "objectified," that is to say, reduced to a limited number of formulas that need only to be studied in terms of their differential frequency in the diverse groups of a population. The sociological temptation here consists then of considering the words, the ideas, the thoughts, the representations as simple objects to be counted in order to bring out their unequal distribution. This is tantamount to ejecting the subject (individual or collective) from the analysis and denying any importance to the personal or social relationships that social agents entertain with cultural objects or thought contents. A study that focuses exclusively on distribution perforce fails to take into account the fact that any use or appropriation of a product or an idea is an intellectual "work": "with respect to the quantitative history of ideas only an awareness of the historical and social variability of the figure of the reader can truly establish the bases of a history of ideas that is also qualitatively different."[31] As Carlo Ginzburg has shown, what readers make of their readings in an intellectual sense is a decisive question that cannot be answered either by thematic analyses of printed production, or by analysis of the social diffusion of different categories of works. Indeed, the ways in which an individual or a group appropriates an intellectual theme or a cultural form are more important than the statistical distribution of that theme or form.[32]

Sure of their quantitative methodology, united in a definition of the history of mentalities less blurred than has been supposed, French historians have long remained deaf to these sharp challenges. Implicitly their representation of the field of intellectual history reduced these criticisms to so many rearguard battles in the name of a worn-out tradition. They envisioned the absorption of the history of ideas into a broader categorization that could be baptized sociocultural history or history of mentalities or history of collective psychology or social history of ideas. We can see today that according to this way of

[31]Carlo Ginzburg, *Il formaggio et i vermi. Il cosmo di un mugnaio del' 1500* (Turin, 1976), xxi–xxii.
[32]Pierre Bourdieu, *La distinction. Critique sociale du jugement* (Paris, 1979), 70–87.

thinking, nothing had changed since the thirties in the domain of intellectual history. The French historians have been guilty twice over of neglect or misunderstanding. First of all they paid no attention to the models that the epistemologies of Gaston Bachelard, Alexandre Koyré, and Georges Canguilhem offered for any undertaking in intellectual history. It is symptomatic to encounter in the *Annales* only a single review devoted to Bachelard (two pages by Lucien Febvre in 1939 on the *Psychanalyse du feu*) and none on the works of Canguilhem or Koyré (the only article published by Koyré in the *Annales* did not appear until 1960). This extraordinary blindness is laden with consequences. It deprived French historians of a whole world of concepts that might have put them on guard against the overly rough certainties drawn from statistical inquiry. These concepts might have permitted them to substitute for a nonarticulated description of the cultural products or thought contents of an epoch (such as quantitative research presents), a comprehension of the relations that exist, at a given moment, among the different intellectual fields. This approach would have made it possible to think in terms inaccessible to quantitative inquiry. First one could examine the bonds of reciprocal dependence that unite the representations of the world, the technologies, and the state of development of different branches of knowledge. Then, by using an insightful idea such as the notion of epistemological obstacle (which brings out in another way what is the sharpest idea in mental equipment), one could explore the articulation among common representations (the accumulated fund of sensations, images, theories) and the progress of knowledge designated as scientific.[33] Had they listened to the epistemologists, the French historians might also have learned a different way to pose the problem on which all history of mentalities stumbles, that of the reasons for and modalities of the passage from one system to another. There, too, the quantitative lenses through which one perceives major changes are radically unable to pick up the deep processes of transformation, which can be understood only by examining together the dependence and autonomy of the different fields of knowledge, as Koyré has done. The passage from one system of representations to another can, from this perspective, be understood at the same time as a drastic break (in branches of knowledge but also in the very structures of thought) and as an itinerary composed of hesitations, of steps backward, of roadblocks.[34]

[33]Gaston Bachelard, *La formation de l'esprit scientifique. Contribution à une psychanalyse de la connaissance objective* (Paris, 1939).
[34]Alexandre Koyré, *From the Closed World to the Infinite Universe* (Baltimore, 1957).

In addition to their failure to appreciate epistemology, which has deprived them of the intellectual instruments capable of articulating what the social history of ideas allowed them only to observe, historians have been guilty of another: the failure to consider the new manner of conceptualizing the relations between works (in the broadest sense) and society, proposed by historians of literature and ideas. The familiar historical problematic was modified by this manner of conceptualizing in two senses: first by suggesting a nonquantitative conception of representativeness and second by dislocating the ideological systems of the society whose conflicts they were supposed to reflect or continue or translate. This dislocation does not mean affirming the absolute independence of the ideological systems vis-à-vis the social domain, but rather posing this relationship in terms of structural homologies or global connections. Today, historians of mentalities are rediscovering the validity of this line of inquiry, heretofore neglected. Having renounced the project of a total history, they now pose the problem in terms of articulations between intellectual choices and social position on the scale of well-defined segments of society or even on the scale of the individual.[35] It is on this reduced scale, and probably only on this scale, that we can understand, without deterministic reduction, the relationships between systems of beliefs, of values and representations on one side, and social affiliations on another. Techniques of analysis fashioned for a history of ideas from above, at the summit, are thus transposed to another terrain, in order to grasp how an "ordinary" man appropriates for himself and in his own way (which risks deforming or mutilating) the ideas or beliefs of his time. Far from being drained, intellectual history (understood as the analysis of "work" done on specific ideological material) then annexes the terrain of popular thought that seemed to be the domain *par excellence* of quantitative history. The relationship between the history of mentalities and the history of ideas must thus be conceptualized in an infinitely more complex way than that characteristic of the French historians of the 1960s.

Categorization in Question: Popular and Learned, Producing and Consuming, Reality and Representation

Beyond methods of analysis or disciplinary definitions, the fundamental issues of today's debates concern the essential categories

[35]For example, see the above-cited work of Carlo Ginzburg, concerning the cosmology of a miller; see also the essays of Natalie Z. Davis, which, on the basis of several case studies,

that until recently have been accepted by everyone. These primordial distinctions, expressed most often by binary oppositions (learned/popular, creation/consumption, reality/fiction, and so on) served as the common and nonproblematic basis of the diverse ways of treating the objects of intellectual or cultural history. For several years now, however, these categories have come under attack from convergent if not identical sources. Little by little, historians have in fact become aware that the categories which structured the field of their analysis (with a clarity so evident that it most often went unperceived) were, just like those categories whose history they were writing, the products of changing and temporary divisions. That is why attention is presently being given (in this text but also from many other vantage points in the historical discipline) to a critical reevaluation of distinctions which are taken as self-evident but which are, in fact, those that must be questioned.

(1) The first traditional division is that which opposes *savant* and *populaire*, high culture and popular culture. Presented as obvious, this division carries with it a whole series of methodological corollaries whose rationale John Higham expressed in 1954: "the internal analysis of the humanist applies chiefly to the intellectual elite, it has not reached very far into the broad field of popular thought. The blunter, external approach of the social scientist leads us closer to collective loyalties and aspirations of the bulk of humanity."[36] In numerous texts in France and the United States we find this same opposition between, on the one hand, the culture of the greatest number, which must be apprehended by means of an external approach, collective and quantitative, and, on the other hand, the intellectuality of the elites' ways of thinking, susceptible only to an internal analysis, individualizing the irreducible originality of ideas. Clearly or not, it is upon this distinction that historians desiring to explore the vast territory of popular culture based their enterprise. Popular culture has been the privileged object of the history of mentalities in France and of a cultural history inspired by anthropology in the United States.

Let us take the French example. Popular culture (which could also be designated as what the field of intellectual history considers popular) has been characterized by two associations. First, it has been identified with a universe of texts—those booklets sold by peddling and known under the generic term of *bibliothèque bleue*. Second, it

---

poses the problem of the connections between religious choice and social rank, in *Society and Culture in Early Modern France* (Stanford, 1975).

[36] John Higham, "Intellectual History and its Neighbors," *The Journal of the History of Ideas* 15, no. 3 (1954), 346.

has been identified with a group of beliefs and gestures considered to constitute a popular religion. In both cases the popular element is defined by its difference vis-à-vis something it is not (scholarly and literate literature or the normative Catholicism of the Church). In both cases the historian ("intellectual" or "cultural") has before him a well-classified corpus whose themes he must inventory.

But it is precisely this categorization that causes the problem. First, the social attribution of cultural practices that until recently were classified as popular is now conceptualized in a more complex manner. Is "popular" religion the religion of the peasants, of the world of the dominated (as opposed to the elites), of the totality of laics (as opposed to the clerics)? Does "popular" literature nourish the reading (or listening) of peasant society, or of a public situated midway between the illiterate people and the slim minority of scholars? Or does it constitute a reading shared by a whole society—a reading that each group decodes in its own way, from simply spotting signs to fluent reading? These are difficult questions that indicate that it is not easy to identify a cultural or intellectual level representing the little people, on the basis of an ensemble of objects or practices. Second, all the cultural forms in which historians recognize the culture of the people always appear today as compound worlds that bring together, in a virtually inextricable mixture, elements of very diverse origins. The literature of the *bibliothèque bleue* is produced by professional writers and printers, but it draws from themes or processes of composition that belong to the oral literature of popular circulation. And by dint of more or less massive purchasing, the readers state their preferences. Thus their tastes are in a position to influence the production of the texts themselves. In an inverse sense, folkloric culture, which has its base in the religion of the greatest number, has been profoundly "worked over" in each epoch by the norms or the interdictions of the ecclesiastical institution. To ask whether we must label as popular what is created by the common people themselves or what is contrived for their use is, then, to pose a false problem. The most important thing is to identify the way that, in practice, the representations or the productions crisscross and imbricate different cultural figures.

Despite appearances, these statements do not lead us away from intellectual history. It is clear that the elite culture is itself constituted in large measure by an operation on materials that do not properly belong to it. It is also a very subtle game of appropriations, of reusages, of misappropriations, that establishes, for example, the relationships between Rabelais and the "popular culture of the public square"[37] or between the Perrault brothers and oral literature.[38] The relationship thus established between the elite culture and what it is not concerns the forms as well as the content, the codes of expression as well as the systems of representation, therefore the entire field recognized as intellectual history. These intersections must not be understood as relations of exteriority between two juxtaposed but autonomous worlds (one scholarly, the other popular), but rather as producers of cultural or intellectual "alloys" whose elements are as solidly incorporated in each other as in metal alloys. According to Bakhtin, for certain epochs (such as the Renaissance), it was in works of literate or scholarly culture that popular culture proclaimed itself with maximum coherence and revealed its very principles most completely. He writes: "To help us penetrate the very depth of this matter, Rabelais is unique. In his creative world, the inner oneness of all the heterogeneous elements emerges with extraordinary clarity. His work is an encyclopedia of folk culture."[39] "Encyclopedia": that is to say that beyond the utilization of words, images, or forms of the "popular" comic culture, the whole text turns on a conception of carnivalesque culture, posited as the matrix of all popular expression.

Moreover, to make the popular/scholarly division problematical is at the same time to annul the methodological differences postulated as necessary for the treatment of each of these domains. The "popular" is not by nature reserved for the quantitative and external analysis of the social scientists. Indeed, as Carlo Ginzburg shows us, when the documents authorize it, it is entirely permissible to explore, as through a magnifying glass, the way a man of the people can think and use the sparse intellectual elements that reach him from literate culture by means of his books and the reading he gives them. Here Bakhtin is turned upside down, since a system of representations is constructed from fragments borrowed from scholarly and bookish culture, giving them another meaning because in the system's foundation there is another culture: "Behind the books pondered by Menocchio we have discovered a reading code; and behind this code, a whole stratum of oral culture."[40] We cannot then postulate as necessary the connection established by Felix Gilbert, between the social broadening of the field of research in intellectual history and the recourse to statistical

[37]Cf. Mikhail Bakhtin, *Rabelais and His World*, tr. Hélène Iswolsky (Cambridge, Mass., 1968).
[38]Marc Soriano, *Les contes de Perrault. Culture savante et traditions populaires* (Paris, 1968).
[39]Bakhtin, *Rabelais*, 58.
[40]Ginzburg, *Il formaggio et i vermi*, 80.

procedure.[41] In fact, if under certain conditions the quantitative approach (internal or external) of the most elaborate texts can be accepted as legitimate, conversely, when the archives permit it, the intellectual work of the most anonymous of readers may be amenable to the analytical procedures ordinarily reserved for the "greatest" thinkers.

(2) The doubts I have raised concerning the scholarly/learned coupling lead us to question another set of distinctions that historians, be they historians of ideas or of mentalities, hold as fundamental: the opposition between creation and consumption, between production and reception. From this primordial distinction again unfolds a whole series of implicit corollaries. In the first place, it establishes a representation of cultural consumption which is opposed term for term to that of intellectual creation: passivity against invention, dependence against liberty, alienation against consciousness. The intelligence of the "consumer" is (to borrow a metaphor from ancient pedagogy) like soft wax on which is inscribed quite legibly the ideas and images forged by intellectual creators. This leads to another corollary, a necessary disciplinary division between the study of intellectual diffusion, which would be the province of a retrospective cultural sociology, and the study of intellectual production, which would follow from an aesthetic approach to forms and a philosophical comprehension of ideas. This radical separation between production and consumption leads us then to postulate that ideas or forms have an intrinsic significance, totally independent of their appropriation by a subject or a group of subjects. Through this separation, the historian usually surreptitiously insinuates his own "consumption" and erects it, without realizing it, into a universal category of interpretation. To act as if texts (or images) had autonomous internal significance, beyond the readings that construct them, forces us, whether we like it or not, to trace the texts back to our own intellectual (and sensorial) field. Thus, we are led to decode them through categories of thought whose historicity is never perceived and which present themselves implicitly as being permanent.

To restore their historicity demands first of all that cultural or intellectual "consumption" be itself taken as a form of production, which, while it certainly manufactures no object, does constitute representations that are never identical to those that the producer, the author or the artist, has implanted in his work. That is why it is

[41]Gilbert, "Intellectual History: Its Aims and Methods," 92.

probably necessary to accord a general resonance to Michel de Certeau's definition of the mass cultural consumption that characterizes Western societies today: "To a rationalized and expansionist production which is likewise centralized, clamorous, and spectacular, there corresponds *another* production, qualified as 'consumption.' The latter is sly, it is dispersed, but it insinuates itself everywhere, silent and quasi-invisible, since it is not recognizable by its products *per se* but by ways of using the products imposed by a dominant economic order."[42] To do away with the split between producing and consuming is first of all to affirm that the work acquires meaning only through the strategies of interpretation that construct its significances. The author's interpretation is one among several, and it does not monopolize the supposedly unique and permanent "truth" of the work. In this way a just place can probably be restored to the author, whose intention (clear or unconscious) no longer contains all possible comprehension of his creation, but whose relationship to the work is not, for all that, ignored.

Defined as "another production," cultural consumption—for example, the reading of a text—can thus escape the passivity that is traditionally attributed to it. Reading, viewing, and listening are, in fact, so many intellectual attitudes which, far from subjecting the consumer to the omnipotence of the ideological or aesthetic message that is supposed to condition him, make possible reappropriation, misappropriation, defiance, or resistance. This observation should lead to a reexamination of the relation between a public referred to as popular and the historically diverse products (books and pictures, sermons and speeches, songs, photo-novels, and television programs) offered for its consumption. "Oblique attention," which, for Richard Hoggart, characterizes the contemporary popular decoding of these materials,[43] is one of the keys enabling us to grasp just how the culture of the greatest number can at any epoch make a place for itself or establish proper coherence in the models that are imposed upon it willy-nilly by the dominant groups or powers. Such a perspective leads us to provide a counterweight to the one that stresses the discursive or institutional apparatuses in a society that aim to block off times and places, to discipline bodies and practices, to shape conduct and thoughts by the regulated ordering of space. These technologies of surveillance and inculcation must in fact come to terms with the tactics of con-

---

[42]Michel de Certeau, *L'invention du quotidien*, I, *Arts de faire* (Paris, 1980), 11.
[43]Richard Hoggart, *The Uses of Literacy* (London, 1957).

sumption and utilization of those whom they are supposed to condition.

These remarks challenge a whole list of implicit postulates in contemporary French sociocultural history (concerning particularly the interpretation of the Catholic Reformation, whose effects are supposed to have totally annihilated an old folkloric culture). Do they also estrange us from intellectual history strictly defined? It does not seem so, to the extent that they incite us to situate all texts in the reading relationships that are entangled with them. Against the conception dear to historians of literature or philosophy, according to which the meaning of a text can be hidden within it like a vein of mineral in stone (criticism thus becoming the operation that brings this hidden sense to the surface), we must recall that any text is the product of a reading, a construction by its reader: "The reader takes neither the place of the author nor an author's place. He invents within the text things other than what was the author's 'intention.' He detaches them from their origin (lost or incidental). He combines the fragments and he creates the unknown in the space that their capacity to permit an indefinite plurality of meanings organizes."[44] Conceived as space open to multiple readings, texts (and all categories of images) cannot then be apprehended either as objects whose distribution it would suffice to catalog, or as entities whose significance could be spoken of in universal terms. Rather, the texts must be confronted in the contradictory network of utilizations that constituted them historically. All of which obviously poses two questions: What to read? How to restore the old readings? Answers are hardly guaranteed, but it is clear that intellectual history cannot avoid searching for them much longer. Provisionally, it is probably good method not to refuse any of the insights that allow the reconstitution, at least in part, of what readers did with their readings: the direct confrontation by means of a confession, written or oral, voluntary or extorted; the examination of the facts of rewriting and intertextuality where the classical break between writing and reading is annulled, since here writing is itself a reading of another writing;[45] finally the serial analysis of closed corpuses to the extent that the crystallization of the themes within a given genre (for example, the *livrets de civilité* or the preparation for death) occurs at the intersection of an intention—that of the pro-

---

[44]Certeau, *L'invention du quotidien*, 285–286, and ch. 8, "Lire: Un braconnage," 279–296.

[45]On the notion of intertexuality see Julia Kristeva, *Semiotikè*, (Paris, 1969); "Intertexualités," *Poetics* 27 (1976); and Hans Robert Jauss, *Pour une esthétique de la réception* (Paris, 1978).

ducers of texts—and of a reading—that of their public.[46] Without reducing that relationship to a place in a history of the social diffusion of ideas, intellectual history must then present as the central idea the relationship of the texts to the individual or collective readers who, each time, construct them (that is, decompose them in order to recompose them).

(3) But what is the nature of these multiple texts that intellectual history takes on as the object of its analysis? Traditionally, their very function is supposed to give them unity: all, in fact, are supposed to constitute representations of a reality they strive to apprehend in different ways, philosophical or literary. The opposition between reality and representation is thus presented as primordial, at the same time distinguishing types of history and discriminating between types of texts. Contrasted to the historian of economies and societies who reconstitutes what was, is the historian of mentalities or ideas whose objectives is not the real, or reality, but the ways in which people consider it and transpose it. To this division of historical work apparently corresponds a division of materials appropriate to each field. To the "documentary" texts, which when subjected to a just criticism reveal what ancient reality was like, are opposed "literary" texts whose status is that of fiction and which thus cannot be held as witnesses of reality. This fundamental split has been altered neither by the construction of old "documents" in the form of statistical series, which only accentuates their truth value, nor by the historical use of literary texts that reduces them to the status of documents, admissible because they state in another way what social analysis has established by its own procedures. The individual text thus becomes a "lived" illustration of the laws of quantity.

It is these oversimplified divisions that historians who have been listening to contemporary literary criticism or sociology are challenging today.[47] It is immediately clear that no text, even the most apparently documentary, even the most "objective" (for example, a statistical table drawn up by an administration), entertains a transparent relationship with the reality that it apprehends. Never can the literary or documentary text deny itself as a text—that is, as a system constructed according to categories, schemas of perception and appreciation, rules of functioning that go back to the very conditions of its production. The relationship of the text to the real (which one can

[46]Compare the views of Daniel Roche in "Histoire littéraire et histoire globale," *Problèmes et méthodes de l'histoire littéraire*, Colloque 18 (November 1972), 89–101.

[47]Jean-Marie Goulemot, "Histoire littéraire," in *La nouvelle histoire*, 308–313.

perhaps define as what the text itself poses as real in constituting it as a referent situated beyond itself) is constructed according to discursive models and intellectual categories peculiar to each writing situation. This leads one to avoid treating fictional works as simple documents, realistic reflections of a historical reality. Instead, one should pose their specificity as texts situated in relation to other texts and whose rules of organization as formal elaborations aim to produce something other than a description. This leads next to considering that "document-materials" also obey construction procedures in which the concepts and obsessions of their producers are invested and the rules of writing peculiar to the genre of the text are marked. These categories of thought and these principles of writing must be brought to light before one attempts any "positive" reading of the document.[48] The real then takes on a new meaning: what is real, in fact, is not (or is not only) the reality aimed at by the text, but the very manner in which the text aims at it in the historicity of its production and the strategy of its writing.[49]

If instead of texts taken in isolation or in reduced corpuses, intellectual history examines the ideological system of a period or of a group in a period, it finds itself face to face with a similar difficulty in articulating the representations and the social reality that they represent. For simplistic readings, postulating the absolute autonomy of ideology or, conversely, attributing to it a function of social reflection, there must be substituted another sort of comprehension, whose principles Pierre Bourdieu has defined.[50] On the one hand, by postulating that the schemas of perception and appreciation that constitute the totality of representations of a group are the product of an internalization of the most fundamental oppositions of the social world, he permits a conceptualization of a relation between the principles of division or classification and the social divisions themselves: "The cognitive structures that social agents put to work in order to know the social world in a practical way are incorporated social structures."[51] But, on the other hand, the relationship thus established is not one of

---

[48]See, for example, Michelle Perrot, "Délinquance et système pénitentiaire en France au XIXᵉ siècle," *Annales E.S.C.* 30 (1975), 67–91; and Roger Chartier, "The Two Frances: The History of a Geographical Idea," *Social Science Information* 17, nos. 4–5 (1978), 527–554, and "La 'monarchie d'argot' entre le mythe et l'histoire," *Les marginaux et les exclus dans l'histoire* (Paris, 1979), 275–311.

[49]See the remarks of Jean-Marie Goulemot in his introduction to Valentin Jamerey Duval, *Mémoires: Enfance et éducation paysanne au XVIIIᵉ siècle* (Paris, 1980).

[50]Pierre Bourdieu, "Conclusion: Classes et classements," in *La distinction*, 543–564.

[51]Ibid., 545.

dependence of the mental structures on their material determinations. The representations of the social world themselves are the constituents of social reality. Instruments of power, the stakes of struggles as fundamental as economic struggles, the systems of classification or images of social order are all transformers of this very order: by modifying the demands (of fortune, of title, of comportment) attached to some position or another; by shifting the frontiers between groups, first in the imaginary realm and then in the factual; even by bringing into existence new groups or new classes.[52] Thus, "the negotiations among groups of opposing interests have the virtue of recalling the incessant struggles over the classifications that contribute to producing these classes, although the classifications are the product of struggles between classes, and they depend on relations of force that have emerged between them."[53]

Has this sociological detour once again diverted us from intellectual history? No, if we admit that the decoding of texts or of discursive compositions that make possible the reading of an ideology courts the same risks as the decoding of social facts, namely the negation of representations in "objective reality" which they are supposed to reflect, or the identification of the reality of the social world exclusively with its representations by the elimination of any referent situated beyond the ideological field.[54] It is this double stumbling block that historians of ideas have often not known how to avoid for lack of having posed as central the reciprocal relationships that conceptual systems and social relations entertain in a given historical moment. From this point of view a study like the one Georges Duby devoted to the trifunctional image of eleventh- and twelfth-century society is an excellent case in point. The model of the three orders, as it functions within a number of different texts, is understood in its relation to the social or political evolutions that justify its construction or its reuse and in the use, polemical or legitimating, simultaneous or successive, that the different classes or the powers (the bishops, the king, the aristocracy) make of it.[55] The social "imaginary" of a time is thus

---

[52]Luc Boltanski, "Taxonomies sociales et luttes de classes: La mobilisation de la 'classe moyenne' et l'invention des 'cadres,'" *Actes de la Recherche en Sciences Sociales* 29 (1979), 75–105.

[53]Bourdieu, *La distinction*, 561.

[54]Cf. Pierre Bourdieu, *Le sens pratique* (Paris, 1979), esp. ch. 9, "L'objectivité du subjectif," 233–247.

[55]Georges Duby, *Les trois ordres ou l'imaginaire du féodalisme* (Paris, 1978), and Jacques Le Goff, "Les trois fonctions indo-européenes: L'historien et l'Europe féodale," *Annales E.S.C.* 35 (1980), 1187–1215.

constituted as a basic mental structure, as a system of representations whose genealogy must be worked out, and as a reality as real as the concreteness of the relations within a society.

Conclusion?

Do not expect to find here, despite the imperatives of the genre, propositions stating what intellectual history must now be, as opposed to what it must no longer be. As well as being presumptuous, such a conclusion would be incommensurate with the current state of collective reflection. We are scarcely beginning to pose problems in a different way: no longer across disciplinary confrontations, where the explicit debates about labels and definitions implicitly bespeak conflicts over institutional divisions in the university field, but by considering as problematical the categories and classifications that heretofore have been taken for granted. What is placed in question is no longer the competence or the methodology of such and such a discipline, but rather the fundamental concepts that all disciplines share. By modifying our manner of posing questions in such a way, today's debates come to possess the means of avoiding the formalism and the vain imbroglios arising from confrontations of definitions while permitting the reintroduction of intellectual history into the field of the social sciences. To conceptualize the relationships between the learned and the popular or between the real and its representations is not, in fact, an affair for specialists, but a challenge for the sociologist and the ethnologist as well as for the historian. Intellectual history must therefore come out of its ghetto, gilded or not, to take part in the common discussion and question the distinctions on which its analyses are founded (and of which it has not always been aware), in the light of the doubts raised about those distinctions in the neighboring social sciences.

The only definition of intellectual history presently admissible is probably that given by Carl Schorske, to the extent that he assigns it neither particular methodology nor obligatory concepts but only indicates the double dimension of a task: "The historian seeks to locate and interpret the artifact temporally in a field where two lines intersect. One line is vertical, or diachronic, by which he establishes the relation of a text or a system of thought to previous expression in the same branch of cultural activity (paintings, politics, etc.). The other is horizontal, or synchronic; by it he assesses the relation of the content of the intellectual object to what is appearing in other branches or aspects of a culture at the same time."[56] Hayden White appears to have a similar conception of the intellectual historian's task, proposing a double model and double problematic: "Gombrich and Kuhn have given us models of how to write the histories of genres, styles and disciplines; Goldmann shows us how to unite them on the broader canvases provided by social, political, and economic historians."[57] Without necessarily saying so, those in France who attempt to understand "intellectual objects" (to use Schorske's term) concur in this definition of cultural space (and therefore of the very terrain of their study) as two-dimensional, which permits us to conceptualize an intellectual or artistic production at once in the specificity of the history of its genre or discipline, in its relation to other contemporaneous cultural productions, and in its relations with different referents situated in other fields of the social totality (socioeconomic or political). To read a text or decode a system of thought means, then, to embrace together these different questions that constitute, in their articulation, what we can consider to be the very object or objective of intellectual history.

Behind its apparent power, however, such a definition sets still more traps. Two concepts generate trouble here and risk leading us astray: that of the "intellectual object" and that of culture.

After Foucault, it is quite clear in fact that we cannot consider these "intellectual objects" as "natural objects" that change only in the historical modalities of existence. Madness, medicine, and the state are not categories that can be conceptualized in terms of universals whose contents each epoch particularizes. Behind the misleading permanence of a vocabulary like ours, we must recognize not objects, but objectifications that construct an original figure each time. As Paul Veyne aptly writes: "In this world, we do not play chess with eternal figures like the king and the fool: the figures are what the successive configurations on the playing board make of them."[58] It is thus the relations to objects that constitute the latter in a way that each time is specific and in accordance with groupings and distributions that are always unique. Intellectual history must not let itself get caught in the trap of words which can give the illusion that different

---

[56]Carl Schorske, *Fin-de-Siècle Vienna: Politics and Culture* (New York, 1980), 21–22.

[57]Hayden V. White, "The Tasks of Intellectual History," *The Monist* 53 (October 1969), 626.

[58]Paul Veyne, "Foucault révolutionne l'histoire," *Comment on écrit l'histoire suivi de Foucault révolutionne l'histoire* (Paris, 1978), 236.

fields of discourse or practices are constituted once and for all, categorizing objects whose contours, if not contents, do not vary. Quite to the contrary, it must depict as paramount the discontinuities that cause knowledge and deed to be labeled and categorized in different or contradictory ways according to the epoch. *That* is its very object, namely "to relate the so-called natural objects to the dated and rare practices that objectivate them and to explain these practices, not on the basis of a single moving force, but on the basis of all the neighboring practices on which they are anchored."[59] This means reconstituting, beneath visible practices or conscious discourses, the "hidden or submerged grammar" (as Veyne expresses it) that does justice to them. It is in identifying the divisions and the relations that have constituted the object that history wants to apprehend, that history (of ideas, of ideological formations, of discursive practices—the label is of no importance) will be able to consider that object without reducing it to being only a detailed figure of a supposedly universal category.

The concept of culture is as parlous as the concept of intellectual object. This is not the place for a full-fledged discussion of it. At most one can note that a common representation, found in the practice of "serial history of the third level," constructs culture as an instance of social totality, situated "above" the economic and the social domains supposedly constituting the first two levels of the scaffolding. This tripartite division, used as a shorthand convenience by quantitative historians to point out different fields of application for the serial treatment, in fact reproduces Marxist categorizations as Louis Althusser has systematized them. This schema, which postulates, on one hand, that one of the elements—the economic—is determinant and, on the other hand, that the cultural or ideological forms a level apart (clearly identifiable and confined within recognizable limits) from the social totality, no longer seems admissible. In fact, what one must consider is how all the relationships, including those that we call economic or social relations, are organized according to various logics that put into play the schema of perception and appreciation of different social subjects, therefore the representations that comprise what one can call a "culture," be it common to the whole of a society or peculiar to a limited group. The most worrisome thing in the habitual acceptance of the word "culture" is not so much that it generally covers only the intellectual or artistic productions of an elite, but that it leads us to believe that the "cultural" invests itself only in a particular

[59]Ibid., 241.

44

field of practices or productions. To conceptualize culture, and therefore the field of intellectual history itself, differently, demands that we conceive of it as an ensemble of meanings that emerge from the apparently "least cultural" discourses and behaviors, as Clifford Geertz does: "The culture concept to which I adhere . . . denotes an historically transmitted pattern of meanings embodied in symbols, a system of inherited conceptions expressed in symbolic forms by means of which men communicate, perpetuate, and develop their knowledge about and attitudes towards life."[60] But as he shows in his essay "Ritual and Social Change: A Javanese Example," the risk of denying the representations of a society as a totality structured in hierarchical layers is that of a dissolution of the social domain in the meanings that are given it by social actors through the theoretical or practical knowledge that they have of it.[61] It is thus a new articulation between "cultural structure" and "social structure" that must be created without projecting either the mirror image, which makes one the reflection of the other, or that of the gearbox, which constitutes each instance as one of the wheels of a system, all echoing the primordial movement affecting the first link of the chain.

Even if it cannot escape these theoretical questions, intellectual history finds itself in practice placed before a multiplicity of objects (or objectifications). Each one of them implies the constitution, the categorization of a corpus presented as that which must be analyzed, a procedure of analysis and, at the end, the production of another discourse, the one by which the historian attempts to explain the complexity of the object or objective that he confronted at the outset. What remains beyond his grasp, if not beyond his ambition, is the fabrication of a totalizing discourse that would permit him to account for all possible objects or objectives at the same time. Intellectual history, or any other history, is this very tension between a "belief"— one can conceptualize the past—and an infirmity—to conceptualize an object cut out of the past implies that one cannot simultaneously conceptualize all objects. This is how we arrive at this "splintered" history, which is not so much the unfortunate result of a methodological drift as the very translation of the laws that regulate the production of historical discourse: we must conceptualize together the king and the fool and the space of their linked displacements. But that is precisely what is impossible. In the awareness of this impossibility can perhaps be inscribed a reciprocal tolerance among the different

[60]Clifford Geertz, *The Interpretation of Cultures* (New York, 1973), 89.
[61]Ibid., 142–169.

methodologies that would no longer be constituted in irreducible pairs of oppositions. Such tolerance requires that we postulate that the analyses produced by these diverse methodologies not be taken as the pieces of a mosaic that we insist can be completed.

Translated by Jane P. Kaplan

CHAPTER TWO

Rethinking Intellectual History and Reading Texts

DOMINICK LaCAPRA

> But if we see this circle as a vicious one and look out for ways of avoiding it, even if we just 'sense' it as an inevitable imperfection, then the act of understanding has been misunderstood from the ground up.
>
> Heidegger, *Being and Time*

Over the last decade, intellectual historians have come increasingly to believe that their field is undergoing a crisis significant enough to reopen the question of the field's nature and objectives. Whatever the presumed causes of this sense of crisis (for example, the rapid rise of social history), one of its beneficial effects is the pressure it places upon practitioners to be more articulate about what they are doing and why. In response to this pressure, I shall attempt to define and to defend in relatively theoretical terms the approach to the field, and specifically, to modern European intellectual history, that I have come to find most fruitful. In setting forth this approach, I shall stylize arguments to bring into prominence a number of controversial issues. At times I shall be forced not to practice what I preach, for I shall selectively treat the texts of other historians or theorists in order to highlight problematic positions as well as possible directions for inquiry.

In the course of its own history in this country, intellectual history has often patterned itself on the approaches of other branches of the discipline, taking a framework of significant questions from somewhere else to orient and organize its research. The desire to adapt to

Except for a few changes and additions, this essay appeared in *History and Theory* 19 (1980), copyright © 1980 by Wesleyan University, 245–276.

modes of inquiry immediately intelligible to some important set of historians, if not to all historians, has characterized perspectives that are frequently seen as competing or opposed options: the internal or intrinsic history of ideas (exemplified in the works of A. O. Lovejoy); the extrinsic or "contextual" view of intellectual history (exemplified in the works of Merle Curti); and the attempted synthesis of internal and external perspectives that has most often taken the form of a narrative of "men and ideas" (for example, in the works of Crane Brinton or H. S. Hughes). The problems generated by these options have become increasingly evident, and I shall return to some of them. They are exacerbated by intellectual history's tendency either to become narrowly professional and even antiquarian by applying the internal method to increasingly insignificant problems, or to become fixated more or less permanently at a popularizing and introductory level in narrating the adventures of "men and ideas." The more recent elaboration of a social history of ideas has seemed to offer an answer to these problems, for in its rigor and methodological sophistication it goes beyond the older forms of contextualism, and it promises to give intellectual history access to the remarkable achievements of modern social history. Undoubtedly, certain questions that earlier intellectual historians addressed impressionistically can be cogently investigated only through the techniques of modern social history. But intellectual history should not be seen as a mere function of social history. It has other questions to explore, requiring different techniques, and their development may permit a better articulation of its relationship to social history. It may even suggest areas in which the formulations of social history stand in need of further refinement.

In the pages that follow, an obvious "territorial imperative" is at work, modified by an active awareness of both the limits of intellectual history and its relations to other perspectives. Thus my argument is not motivated by the desire to establish a specious autonomy for intellectual history within historiography or within the disciplines in general. On the contrary, it is informed by an understanding of the subdiscipline of intellectual history that is in important respects transdisciplinary, and it defends what may be called the relative specificity of intellectual history. It also urges the intellectual historian to learn of developments in other disciplines addressing the problem of interpretation, notably literary criticism and philosophy. In fact, the argument I shall put forth constitutes a new twist to a rather traditional view of things—but one that involves a sometimes disorienting critique and rethinking of tradition through an insistence upon problems and interests that have been obscured in more traditional approaches. The concern I want to reanimate centers around the importance of reading and interpreting complex texts—the so-called "great" texts of the Western tradition—and of formulating the problem of relating these texts to various pertinent contexts. This is a concern that, I think, does not have the place it deserves in historiography today, including intellectual history, which would seem to be its "natural home." The approach I shall discuss does not, however, aim solely at returning these texts to their rightful place. It also critically raises the question of why these texts are often objects of excessively reductive interpretation even when they are centers of analysis and concern. The primary form of reduction I shall discuss arises from the dominance of a documentary conception of historical understanding, because I believe that it is most prevalent in the historical profession today. But the implications of my argument extend to all extreme derogations of the dialogue between past and present, dialogue that requires a subtle interplay between proximity and distance in the historian's relation to the "object" of study. (This dialogical relation between the historian or the historical text and the "object" of study raises the question of the role of selection, judgment, stylization, irony, parody, self-parody, and polemic in the historian's own use of language—in brief, the question of how the historian's use of language is mediated by critical factors that cannot be reduced to factual predication or direct authorial assertion about historical "reality." Significant in this respect is the manner in which the historian's approach to the "object" of study is informed or "influenced" by the methods and views of other historians or "speakers.") In addition, the approach I shall defend is not motivated exclusively by the attempt to find order in chaos by familiarizing the unfamiliar; it is also sensitive to the ways in which the ordinary format for the acquisition of knowledge may be placed in question as the familiar is made unfamiliar, especially when it is seen anew in significant texts.

What is meant by the term "text"? It may initially be seen as a situated use of language marked by a tense interaction between mutually implicated yet at times contestatory tendencies. On this view, the very opposition between what is inside and what is outside texts is rendered problematic, and nothing is seen as being purely and simply inside or outside texts. Indeed the problem becomes one of rethinking the concepts of "inside" and "outside" in relation to processes of interaction between language and the world. One of the more challenging aspects of recent inquiries into textuality has been the investigation of why textual processes cannot be confined within the bindings of the book. The context or the "real world" is itself "textualized" in a variety of ways, and even if one believes that the point of criticism is to change the world, not merely to interpret it, the process and results of change themselves raise textual problems. Social and individual life has in part a textual structure and is involved in textual processes that are often more complicated than the historical imagination is willing to allow. In addition, the attempt to relate texts to other "symbolic," "representational," or "expressive" media (music, painting, dance, gesture) raises the problem of the interaction among signifying practices—the problem of translating from medium to medium in a process that entails both losses and gains in "meaning." To the extent that the historian or critic employs language to effect this translation, he or she confronts the issue of textuality writ large. More generally, the notion of textuality serves to render less dogmatic the concept of reality by pointing to the fact that one is "always already" implicated in problems of language use as one attempts to gain critical perspective on these problems, and it raises the question of both the possibilities and the limits of meaning. For the historian, the very reconstruction of a "context" or a "reality" takes place on the basis of "textualized" remainders of the past. The historian's position is not unique in that all definitions of reality are implicated in textual processes. But the issue of historical understanding is distinctive. The more general problem is to see how the notion of textuality makes explicit the question of the relationships among uses of language, other signifying practices, and various modes of human activity that are bound up with processes of signification. The more distinctive issue in historiography is that of the relationship between documentary reconstruction of, and dialogue with, the past.[1]

To the extent that the relationship between the documentary and the dialogical is a problem relevant to all historiography, the argument I shall develop is not restricted to intellectual history. I shall generally

[1]This paper is best read in conjunction with the works of Hayden V. White, notably *Metahistory* (Baltimore, 1973) and *Tropics of Discourse* (Baltimore, 1978). White's work has been of immense importance in generating the current debate about approaches to historiography. My own discussion agrees with White's critique of conventional narrative and a narrowly documentary approach as inadequate to the tasks of intellectual history. But it is critical of the more "presentist" and "constructivist" tendencies that at times emerge in White's works, and it tries to provide a different way of understanding intellectual history as in part a dialogue with the past. For a discussion of White's *Tropics of Discourse*, see my review in *Modern Language Notes* 93, no. 5 (1978), 1037–1043. For a discussion of related problems as they arise in the interpretation of the works of Jean-Paul Sartre, the reader is referred to my *Preface to Sartre* (Ithaca, 1978).

forego extended discussion of the larger issues I may evoke, however, in order to focus on the limited topic of the relation of a "textual" problematic to intellectual history, and I shall concentrate on the even more limited topic of written texts and, within this topic, on the problem of reading and interpreting the "great" texts of the tradition. These texts are not absolutely unique, and the processes they disclose are not altogether peculiar to them. But two reasons for focusing intellectual history on these texts are that the study of them tends not to be emphasized in contemporary historiography and that in them the use of language is explored in an especially forceful and critical way—a way that engages us as interpreters in a particularly compelling conversation with the past.[2]

It is important to argue over the question of what works are to be considered great and to reevaluate the "canon" of works to which we devote special attention. I even see value in the argument that our understanding of a canon has been too ethnocentric in its confinement of the text to the book and in its exclusion of texts from other traditions and cultures. Indeed it is important to examine critically the very notion of a canon and certain of the functions it may serve. But I must confess that most often I agree with traditional authorities in identifying works to be included in any necessary but not sufficient list of especially significant texts. What puzzles me at times, however, is the way these works are interpreted, for the interpretations may have little correspondence to the judgment that the work is great or at least of special significance. Here one may wonder whether something is elided in the passage from the judgment that identifies a great work to the discourse that interprets it, for interpretations often treat these texts in terms that domesticate them by emphasizing their commonality with lesser works or with ordinary beliefs, desires, tensions, and values. Such treatment begs a number of crucial questions. Are great texts of special interest not in their confirmation or reflection of common concerns but, to paraphrase Nietzsche, in the exceptional way in which they address commonplace themes?[3] Do they often or even

[2]The notion of historical understanding as a conversation with the past is developed in the works of Heidegger and in those of his more conservative disciple, Hans-Georg Gadamer. See especially Heidegger's "Onto-theo-logical Constitution of Metaphysics" in *Identity and Difference*, tr. Joan Stambaugh (New York, 1969) and Gadamer's *Truth and Method*, tr. Garrett Barden and John Cumming (New York, 1975) and *Philosophical Hermeneutics*, tr. David E. Linge (Berkeley, 1976).

[3]See especially Nietzsche's *Use and Abuse of History*, tr. Adrian Collins (Indianapolis, 1957), 39. For Nietzsche's argument that the renunciation of interpretation and the restriction of scholarship to pure "truth" in its residual form as "truth to facts" constitute an expression of the ascetic ideal, see *On the Genealogy of Morals*, tr. Walter Kaufmann (New

typically engage in processes that employ or refer to ordinary assumptions and simultaneously contest them, at times radically? Is the judgment of greatness at times related to the sense that certain works both reinforce tradition and subvert it, perhaps indicating the need for newer traditions that are more open to disconcerting modes of questioning and better able to withstand the recurrent threat of collapse? Do certain works themselves both try to confirm or establish something—a value, a pattern of coherence, a system, a genre—and call it into question? Is there something sensed in judgments that is perhaps not said in reductive interpretations that make certain works all too familiar? Are processes of contestation often or typically more powerful in certain kinds of texts—for example, literary or poetic texts—than in philosophical or historical ones? How watertight are these higher-order forms of classification in relation to the actual use(s) of language in texts? What does a less reductive, normalizing, or harmonizing mode of interpretation require of the reader?

These are the types of question raised in what Heidegger calls "thinking the unthought" of tradition and Derrida, "deconstruction." (What I take to be especially valuable in the approaches to textuality developed by Heidegger and Derrida is critical inquiry that tries to avoid a somnambulistic replication of the excesses of a historical tradition by rehabilitating what is submerged or repressed in it and entering the submerged or repressed elements in a more even-handed "contest" with tendencies that are damaging in their dominant forms.)

I want to begin to address these questions by distinguishing between documentary and "worklike" aspects of the text.[4] The documen-

---

York, 1969), 151. For a more general discussion of Nietzsche's "genealogical" understanding of history, which combines the documentary and the critically reconstructive in a polemical pespective, see Michel Foucault, "Nietzsche, Genealogy, History," in *Language, Counter-Memory, Practice*, tr. Donald F. Bouchard and Sherry Simon (Ithaca, 1977), 139–164. (The essays collected in this book represent an often critical supplement to the more well-known and somewhat doctrinaire "structuralist" positions that Foucault—despite protestations to the contrary—often develops in his principal works.)

[4]The notion of the "worklike" is of course indebted to Heidegger's discussion in "The Origin of the Work of Art" in *Poetry, Language, Thought*, tr. Albert Hofstadter (New York, 1975), 15–87. It does not exlude receptivity and should not be interpreted in a narrowly "productivist" sense. The distinction between the documentary and the worklike may also be compared to J. L. Austin's distinction between the "constative"—the descriptive statement that is measured against the criteria of truth and falsehood in"corresponding" to facts—and the "performative"—the doing of things with words that brings about a change in the situational context. On the approach I am suggesting, the constative and the performative are best seen not as generic types or sets of speech acts ("realms of discourse") but as more or less pronounced aspects of speech acts (or texts) that may be conceptually elaborated into analytic distinctions, ideal types, or heuristic fictions.

tary situates the text in terms of factual or literal dimensions involving reference to empirical reality and conveying information about it. The worklike supplements empirical reality by adding to, and subtracting from, it. It thereby involves dimensions of the text not reducible to the documentary, prominently including the roles of commitment, interpretation, and imagination. The worklike is critical and transformative for it deconstructs and reconstructs the given, in a sense repeating it but also bringing into the world something that did not exist before in that significant variation, alteration, or transformation. With deceptive simplicity, one might say that while the documentary marks a difference, the worklike makes a difference—one that engages the reader in recreative dialogue with the text and the problems it raises.

I shall return to this distinction and its implications in a somewhat different light. What I stress here is that the documentary and the worklike refer to aspects or components of the text that may be developed to different degrees and related to one another in a variety of ways. We usually refer to *The Brothers Karamazov* and *The Phenomenology of Mind* as works, and to a tax roll, a will, and the register of an inquisition as documents. But the work is situated in history in a way that gives it documentary dimensions, and the document has worklike aspects. In other words, both the "document" and the "work" are texts involving an interaction between documentary and worklike components that should be examined in a critical historiography. Often the dimensions of the document that make it a text of a certain sort with its own historicity and its relations to sociopolitical processes (for example, relations of power) are filtered out when it is used purely and simply as a quarry for facts in the reconstruction of the past. (A register of an inquisition, for example, is itself a textual power structure with links to relations of power in the larger society. How it functions as a text is intimately and problematically related to its use for the reconstitution of life in the past.) Conversely, the more documentary aspects of a work are neglected when it is read in a purely formalistic way or as an isolated source for the recovery of past meaning. Clearly, the larger questions at issue turn on the relations between documentary and worklike aspects of the text and between the correlative ways of reading it.

A dialogue with an "other" must have a subject matter and must convey information of some sort. But, as Weber and Collingwood have observed, a fact is a pertinent fact only with respect to a frame of reference involving questions that we pose to the past, and it is the ability to pose the "right" questions that distinguishes productive scholarship. Heidegger has emphasized that these questions are themselves situated in a "context" or a "life-world" that cannot be entirely objectified or fully known. For Heidegger, moreover, it is only by investigating what a thinker did not explicitly or intentionally think but what constitutes his still question-worthy "unthought" that a conversation with the past enters into dimensions of his thinking which bear most forcefully on the present and future. Here anachronism is an obvious danger, but an imaginative and self-reflective kind of comparative history inquiring into the unrealized or even resisted possibilities of the past is nonetheless an important supplement to more empirical kinds of comparison in the dialogue between past and present. (Weber himself, it may be recalled, argued that the attribution of causal weight to an event or phenomenon depended upon its comparison with an imaginative rethinking of the historical process in which it figured. Only by hypothesizing what might have come to pass given the absence or significant variation of an event or phenomenon could one arrive at the understanding of transformational possibilities that enabled one to appreciate the fact that something occurred in the form it actually took.) Indeed, insofar as it is itself "worklike," a dialogue involves the interpreter's attempt to think further what is at issue in a text or a past "reality," and in the process the questioner is himself questioned by the "other." His own horizon is transformed as he confronts still living (but often submerged or silenced) possibilities solicited by an inquiry into the past. In this sense, the historicity of the historian is at issue both in the questions he poses and (*pace* Weber) in the "answers" he gives in a text that itself reticulates the documentary and the worklike. It may, finally, be argued that the interaction between documentary and worklike tendencies generates tension, and this tension is neutralized only through processes of control and exclusion. These processes may operate both in the text being interpreted and in the text interpreting it. In intellectual history, they tend to operate more in our interpretations or uses of the texts of primary interest than in those texts themselves.[5]

A documentary approach to the reading of texts has predominated in general historiography and, in important respects, it has also characterized intellectual history. If the dominance of this approach is open to question in other areas of historiography, it is perhaps even

[5]This theme has been especially important in the works of Foucault and Derrida. For an application of it to the interpretation of Rousseau, see Jacques Derrida, *Of Grammatology* [1967], tr. Gayatri C. Spivak (Baltimore, 1976).

more questionable in intellectual history, given the texts it addresses.[6] For certain texts themselves explore the interaction of various uses of language such as the documentary and the worklike and they do so in ways that raise the issue of the various possibilities in language use attendant upon this interaction. The Menippean satire is a manifest example of a type of text openly exploring the interaction or dialogue among uses of language.[7] But this issue may be raised in relation to any text in a manner that both opens it to an investigation of its functioning as discourse and opens the reader to the need for interpretation in his or her dialogue with it. Indeed there would seem to be something intrinsically wrongheaded in the idea of a purely or even predominantly documentary approach to a markedly worklike and internally "dialogized" text making claims on its readers that are not met by documentary understanding alone.

The predominance of a documentary approach in historiography is one crucial reason why complex texts—especially "literary" texts—are either excluded from the relevant historical record or read in an extremely reduced way. Within intellectual history, reduction takes the form of synoptic content analysis in the more narrative method and the form of an unproblematic identification of objects or entities of historical interest in the history of ideas.[8] These entities are, of

[6]A critique of an exclusively or even predominantly documentary conception of historiography in general is developed by Hayden V. White in *Tropics of Discourse*. See especially the introduction and chapters 1–4. Curiously, White in this book does not explore the more specific applications of his arguments to intellectual history.

[7]For an illuminating discussion of Fernand Braudel's *Mediterranean and the Mediterranean World in the Age of Philip II* as a Menippean satire, see Hans Kellner, "Disorderly Conduct: Braudel's Mediterranean Satire," *History and Theory* 18 (1979), 197–222. Kellner, however, does not address two important issues: (1) the role of scientific discourse in Braudel's work and the problem of how it relates to other uses of language, and (2) the way the "Menippean satire" is not simply a category that allows one to identify the genre of a work, but a multivalent use of language that may test the limits of genre classifications. These issues arise in a pointed way when one attempts to relate Northrop Frye's classical understanding of the menippea to the more carnivalized notion of Mikhail Bakhtin (notably in *Problems of Dostoevsky's Poetics*, tr. R. W. Rotsel [Ann Arbor, 1973], 92–100). On Bakhtin, see Julia Kristeva, "Le mot, le dialogue et le roman," in *Semiotikè* (Paris, 1969), 143–173, and Tzvetan Todorov, *Mikhail Bakhtine: Le principe dialogique* (Paris, 1981).

[8]I shall not further discuss synoptic content analysis, which is both necessary and limited as a method of analyzing complex texts. But for one of the most successful and perspicuous narratives relying essentially on synoptic methods, see Martin Jay, *The Dialectical Imagination: A History of the Frankfurt School* (Boston, 1973). In an extremely ambitious and intelligent work, Mark Poster, with some misgiving, also practices intellectual history as a narrative relating synopses or paraphrases of the arguments in texts to contextual developments (*Existential Marxism in Postwar France: From Sartre to Althusser* [Princeton, 1976]). For an attempted analysis and critique of the role of the synoptic method in contextualist

course, "ideas" ("unit-ideas" in the work of A. O. Lovejoy) or "structures of consciousness" or of "mind" (for example, in the work of Ernst Cassirer). Ideas or structures of consciousness are abstracted from texts and related to comprehensive, formalized modes of discourse or symbolic forms (philosophy, literature, science, myth, history, religion). How these structures actually function in complex texts is often not asked or is given only marginal attention. The ideas or structures (for example, the idea of nature or the great chain of being) may then be traced over time and used to distinguish between periods. This approach is criticized as excessively detached—a form of history of ideas "in the air"—from a more socially oriented perspective.[9] But, on a very basic level, the social history of ideas often shares the assumptions of the approach it criticizes. For it too may take ideas, structures of consciousness, or "mentalities" as relatively unproblematic entities and not raise the question of how they function in texts or actual uses of language—looking instead into the causes or origins of ideas and their impact or effect in history. In brief, social history often adjusts a history of ideas to a causal framework and a conception of the social matrix without critically investigating what is being caused or having an impact.[10] It may also lead to the idea that the only things worth studying are those that had a social impact or effect in their own time, thereby depriving historiography of the need to recover significant aspects of the past that may have "lost out."

A different understanding of intellectual history as a history of texts

---

interpretation, see my "Reading Exemplars: *Wittgenstein's Vienna* and Wittgenstein's *Tractatus*," *Diacritics* 9 (Summer 1979), 65–82.

[9]See the critique of Cassirer in Peter Gay, "The Social History of Ideas: Ernst Cassirer and After," in *The Critical Spirit: Essays in Honor of Herbert Marcuse*, ed. Kurt H. Wolff and Barrington Moore, Jr. (Boston, 1967), 106–120. Gay nonetheless praises Cassirer for his emphasis upon structure and his ability to find order in seeming chaos. Gay does not raise the question of the extent to which the order thus found is limited or even specious. (The point of this remark is to suggest that the imposition of "order and perspicuity"—in one of Gibbon's favorite phrases—upon the historical record is misleading and that the objective of the historian should rather be to explore critically the ways in which the interaction between order and its contestatory "others" takes place.)

[10]For an extremely successful example of this approach, inspired by the methods of the *Annales* School, see Daniel Roche, *Le siècle des lumières en province: Académies et académiciens provinciaux, 1680–1789*, 2 vols. (Paris, 1978). Roche's approach to the texts of Rousseau, of which he does not provide an extended critical analysis, may be contrasted with that of Derrida in *Of Grammatology*. There are, however, signs at present that those affiliated with the *Annales* School are developing an expanded notion of "*le travail du texte*" that reveals the limitations of narrowly documentary readings. See, for example, Michel de Certeau, *L'absent de l'histoire* (Paris, 1973) and Jacques Le Goff and Pierre Nora, *Faire de l'histoire* (Paris, 1974).

may permit a more cogent formulation of problems broached by established approaches and a more mutually informative interchange with the type of social history that relates discourse and institutions. On this understanding, what was taken as an assumption or elided in the perspectives I have mentioned becomes a problem for inquiry. One such problem at the very crossroads of the documentary and the dialogical is the precise nature of the relation between texts and their various pertinent contexts. I will break this problem down into six partially overlapping areas of investigation and, in discussing them, stress certain points that are often neglected at present.

It may be helpful if I first make my own objective clear. My list is not exhaustive, and my point is that, in treating the relation of texts to contexts, what is often taken as a solution to the problem should be reformulated and investigated as a real problem itself. An appeal to the context does not *eo ipso* answer all questions in reading and interpretation. And an appeal to *the* context is deceptive: one never has—at least in the case of complex texts—*the* context. The assumption that one does, relies on a hypostatization of "context," often in the service of misleading organic or other overly reductive analogies. For complex texts one has set of interacting contexts whose relations to one another are variable and problematic and whose relation to the text being investigated raises difficult issues in interpretation. Indeed, what may be most insistent in a modern text is the way it challenges one or more of its contexts. In addition, the assertion that a specific context or subset of contexts is especially significant in a given case has to be argued and not simply assumed or surreptitiously built into an explanatory model or framework of analysis. With these caveats in mind, the six "contexts" I shall single out for attention are intentions, motivations, society, culture, the corpus, and structure (or analogous concepts).

(1) *The relation between the author's intentions and the text.* I would not deny the importance of intentions and of the attempt to specify their relationship to what occurs in texts or in discourse more generally. But speech-act theory has lent support to the extreme belief that the utterance and, presumably by extension, the text derive their meaning from the author's intentions in making or writing them. Quentin Skinner has argued forcefully that the object of intellectual history should be the study of what authors meant to say in different historical contexts and communicative situations.[11] This view tends to

[11]See especially Skinner's "Meaning and Understanding in the History of Ideas," *History and Theory* 8 (1969), 3–53. For a defense of authorial intention as providing the criterion

assume a proprietary relation between the author and the text as well as a unitary meaning for an utterance. At best it permits an overly simple idea of divisions or opposing tendencies in a text and of the relationships between texts and analytic classifications of them. By presenting the text solely as an "embodied" or realized "intentionality," it prevents one from formulating as an explicit problem the question of the relationship between intentions, insofar as they can be plausibly reconstructed, and what the text may be argued to do or to disclose. This relationship may involve multiple forms of tension, including self-contestation. Not only may the intention not fill out the text in a coherent or unified way; the intention or intentions of the author may be uncertain or radically ambivalent. Indeed the author may in good part discover his or her intentions in the act of writing or speaking itself. And the "reading" of intentions poses problems analogous to those involved in the reading of texts.

It is significant that an intention is often formulated retrospectively when the utterance or text has been subjected to interpretation with which the author does not agree. The first time around, one may feel no need to make one's intentions altogether explicit, or one may feel that this is impossible, perhaps because one is writing or saying something whose multiple meanings would be excessively reduced in the articulation of explicit intentions. Along with the "projection" of a goal that in part directs the writing process, an intention is a kind of proleptic reading or interpretation of a text. A retrospectively formulated intention is more manifestly a reading or interpretation, for it is rarely a transcription of what the author meant to say at the "original" time of writing. Insofar as there is a proprietary relation between the author and the text, especially in cases where the author's responsibility is at issue (for example, in cases at law), one may want to give special weight to statements of intention, at least to the extent that they are plausible interpretations of what actually goes on in a text. But even if one is content merely to extend the relevant analogy, one can argue that, to some significant extent, tradition expropriates the author. For the texts of the tradition have entered the public domain. Here the intentions of the author have the status of either aspects of

---

of valid interpretation, see E. D. Hirsch, Jr., *Validity in Interpretation* (New Haven, 1967), and *The Aims of Interpretation* (Chicago, 1976). For a critique of Hirsch, see David C. Hoy, *The Critical Circle* (Berkeley, 1978). Hoy's book is a good introduction to the works of Gadamer, who offers an extensive criticism of the attempt to center interpretation on the *mens auctoris*. A more fundamental critique is provided by Jacques Derrida, notably in "Signature Event Context," tr. Samuel Weber and Jeffrey Mehlman, *Glyph* 1 (1977), and "Limited Inc. abc," tr. Samuel Weber, *Glyph* 2 (1977).

the text (for example, when they are included in a preface) or interpretations of it which the commentator should certainly take into account but whose relation to the functioning of the text is open to question.

The idea that authorial intentions constitute the ultimate criterion for arriving at a valid interpretation of a text is motivated, I think, by excessively narrow moral, legal, and scientific presuppositions. Morally and even legally, one may believe that a person should bear full responsibility for utterances and have a quasi-contractual or fully contractual relation to an interlocutor. Scientifically, one may seek a criterion that makes the meaning of a text subject to procedures of confirmation that leave minimal room for disagreement over interpretation. At times responsibility may be great enough to meet moral or legal demands, although this eventuality would satisfy neither the theoretical nor the practical conditions for *full* freedom or intentionality. In any case, to believe that authorial intentions fully control the meaning or functioning of texts (for example, their serious or ironic quality) is to assume a predominantly normative position that is out of touch with important dimensions of language use and reader response. The scientific demand is closely related to the moral one. It might be acceptable if it were applicable. To insist upon its applicability is to sacrifice more dialogical approaches and to obscure the role of argument in matters of interpretation, including the interpretation of intentions themselves. It is, moreover, commonplace to observe that a sign of a "classic" is the fact that its interpretation does not lead to a definitive conclusion and that its history is very much the history of conflicting or divergent interpretations and uses of it. It is less commonplace to apply this insight to the process of argument that engages its interpreters. Insofar as an approach supplements the documentary with the dialogical, informed argument in it is to be seen not merely as an unavoidable necessity but as a valuable and stimulating activity bound up with the ways interpretation may be related to forms of renewal, including the renewal of beliefs to which one is deeply committed. The point here is to do everything in one's power not to avoid argument but to make argument as informed, vital, and undogmatically open to counterargument as possible.

These considerations bear upon the question of criteria for a "good" interpretation. The latter should of course resolve documentary matters that are amenable to ordinary procedures of verification, and it should seek mutual understanding on larger issues of interpretation. But, equally important, it does not settle once and for all the question of how to understand a work or a corpus. A "good" interpretation reactivates the process of inquiry, opening up new avenues of investigation, criticism, and self-reflection. This is not to say that one should make a fetish of the new or become a slave to current ideas about what is interesting. But it is to say that basic differences in interpretation (or mode of discourse) rarely turn on simple matters of fact—and that on certain levels these differences may have a value that is not entirely subordinated to the ideal of consensus in interpretation. For they may relate to processes of contestation that have a critical role at present and that one would want to retain in some form in any social context.

(2) *The relation between the author's life and the text.* This approach is inspired by the belief that there may be relations between life and text that go beyond and even contradict the author's intentions. What is sought in a psychobiographical perspective is the motivation of the author, which may be only partly known to him or her or even unconscious. A difficulty analogous to that with the intentionalist view arises, however, when there is an assumption of full unity or identity between life and texts that allows both to be situated in parallel or homologous fashion in a cycle of development or a pattern of breakdown.[12] The temptation is then to see the text as a sign or symptom of the life process even when the resultant understanding of their relationship is left on the level of suggestion rather than elaborated into a full-blown causal or interpretative theory.

Here again, what is taken as a solution should be posed as a problem. There may of course be symptomatic aspects of texts. But life and text may also be both internally marked and related to each other by processes that place identity in question. A text or a life may question itself in more or less explicit ways, and each may question the other. Insofar as they are distinguishable, life and text may be characterized by patterns of development or by forms of repetition that are not simply coincident and that may even challenge one another. A problem common to a written text and a lived "text" may be worked or played out differently in each, and these differential relations pose important problems for interpretation. And we read significant written texts not only because they are compensatory but also because they are supplementary: they add something to the ordinary life that as a matter of (perhaps unfortunate) fact might not exist without them.

In addition, for a writer who takes what he or she is doing seriously (an attitude not necessarily divorced from a view of art or even of

---

[12]This assumption and the difficulties attendant upon it affect even so careful and well-documented a study as Jerrold Seigel's *Marx's Fate: The Shape of a Life* (Princeton, 1978).

writing in general as a form of serious play or of jesting in earnest), writing is a crucial way of life. At times the writer may be more willing to defend the writings than other dimensions of the life. One may find this attitude in certain ways objectionable or "alienated," but one has to take it into account. It may (as with Kierkegaard) be proffered not to establish the innocence of the writings or to promote a vision of art for art's sake but to articulate a situation of which the writer is himself critical. In other words, the writer too may want a world in which writing is less distinctive because the text of life is itself "written" in a better way.

The general problem for an attempt to relate life and texts is to arrive at an understanding of the "text" of a life and of the use of language in texts, and of the relation between these signifying practices, that is sufficiently nuanced to do justice to them. To believe that a relatively simple idea of identity or of breakdown does justice to a life may at times be plausible, although certain lives are rather complex. To believe that a relatively simple understanding of "real-life" problems provides the causal or interpretative key to the meaning of the texts or to the interaction between life and texts is altogether implausible. This belief almost invariably prefaces an excessively reductive interpretation of the texts and their relation to life. By contrast, the investigation of the relation between life and texts does more to complicate the problem of interpretation than it does to simplify it. For it supplements the difficulty of interpreting demanding texts with the difficulty of cogently relating them to existential processes. The text to be interpreted then becomes larger and probably more intricate, for it includes the written texts, in cases where writing itself may be a highly existential process, and other dimensions of the life that are not simply external to these texts. Simplification occurs only to the extent that it is plausible to read texts, or aspects of texts, as secondary elaborations or projective rationalizations. And here there is always the possibility that a psychobiography will tell us more about its author than about the author being studied.[13]

(3) *The relation of society to texts.* At this point the intersecting

---

[13]This problem may arise in a rather subtle form. The psychohistorian may make a dichotomous opposition between fully logical or rational arguments and illogical or irrational arguments in the text and assert that psychohistorical methods apply only to the interpretation of the latter. For a well-reasoned and careful exposition of this view, see Gerald Izenberg, "Psychohistory and Intellectual History," *History and Theory* 14 (1975), 139–155. The problem here is whether this extremely neat opposition applies to the text in question or whether it reflects the perspective of the analyst. In any case, it obviates inquiry into the interaction between the "logical" and the "illogical" in the functioning of the text itself.

nature of the categories I am using becomes evident. One cannot discuss the individual life without significant reference to society and vice versa. But I shall attempt to focus on problems that have been taken to be more specifically social or sociological in nature. (And I shall do so not from the perspective of a social history that inquires into the uses of texts for the empirical reconstitution of past society but from the complementary perspective of an intellectual history that inquires into the relationship between social processes and the interpretation of texts.) These problems have often been seen in terms of the "before" and "after" of the text: its genesis and its impact.

I have already indicated that the problem often elided or not emphasized in a social history of ideas is that of the relation of social to textual processes—a relation that notions of "genesis" and "impact" may be inadequate to formulate. Foucault, aware of this problem, has elaborated a notion of discursive practice which signals the interaction between institutions and forms of discourse. But he has not altogether succeeded in relating the discursive practice to the significant text or, even more generally, in articulating the relationship between more or less formalized modes of discourse and written or lived "texts." For he often treats written texts and other phenomena in a similar manner by falling back on the notion that they are instances or tokens of the discursive practice—signs of the times. In certain respects, this understanding may be accurate. A text may exemplify discursive practices or modes of discourse in a relatively straightforward way. Marxist interpretation has often seen a similar relationship between ideology and text, and while Foucault's notion of discursive practice is more comprehensive than the notion of ideology as false consciousness, it relies on an understanding of relationship comparable to the more orthodox Marxist type.

But in both Foucault and in certain Marxists a different possibility at times arises. The text may then be seen not only to exemplify discursive practices or ideologies in a relatively straightforward way but also to engage in processes that, whether consciously or not, render them problematic, at times with critical implications. The question then becomes how precisely the discursive practice, deep structure, or ideology—even the prejudice—is situated in the text other than in terms of instantiation or simple reflection. The *locus classicus* of this kind of inquiry may still in certain respects be Lukács's investigation of the relationship between conservative ideology and what the text discloses about social processes in the works of Balzac.[14] But

[14]See his *Studies in European Realism* (New York, 1964).

in Lukács the understanding of language use and textual process was often not subtle or searching enough to account for the interaction between text and society. The almost Platonic vehemence of his condemnation of modernist literature not only illustrates this point; it points to problems that are intimated in Lukács's texts themselves but in a manner that remains "unthought" or not rendered explicit.

This is where Derrida's work may hold out possibilities for the type of inquiry into the interaction between text and social process that Derrida himself rarely seems to undertake overtly. His elaborate critique of Foucault's reading of Descartes in *Histore de la folie* should not, I think, be seen as a simple rejection of Foucault's interpretation.[15] Rather it directs attention to the question of precisely where and how the exclusion of madness takes place in Descartes's text and whether that text may be understood as a straightforward sign of the times. Derrida's argument in "*Cogito* et histoire de la folie" must be seen in the broader context of his understanding of the long and tangled tradition constituting the history of metaphysics. It must also be seen with reference both to the problem of relating a text to its times and to the way texts may place in radical question their own seemingly dominant desires and themes.

The manifest division between Derrida and Foucault takes place over the local interpretation of a passage in Descartes's first *Meditation*. Where Foucault locates the exclusion of madness that inaugurates or confirms its status in the classical age, Derrida sees a "pedagogical" and dialogical discursive process that instead includes madness in a movement of increasing hyperbole. Derrida in effect gives a new turn to the very classical argument that one cannot take the passage in question out of context but must relate it to the overall movement of the text. Given the uncertainty in the passage concerning whether

---

[15]Michel Foucault, *Folie et déraison: Histoire de la folie à l'âge classique* [1961] (Paris, 1972) with an appendix in which Foucault responds to Derrida. For Derrida's essay, published in French in 1967, see *Writing and Difference* (Chicago, 1978), 31–63. In "The Problem of Textuality: Two Exemplary Positions," *Critical Inquiry* 4 (1978), 673–714, Edward Said argues that Derrida's "deconstructive" criticism remains within the text while Foucault's history of discursive practices takes one into "thick" historical reality where various "discourses of power" and related dominant institutions have ruled the production of texts. In a valid attempt to stress the political importance of Foucault's concerns, Said ignores Derrida's extension of "textuality" beyond the confines of the book, and he fails to see how Foucault's view at times tends to reduce the complex text to a token of a mode of discourse. Nor does Said pose the problem of how the complex text may both "reflect" or inscribe dominant modes of discourse and also challenge them, at times with significant critical effects. The view of modern history that emerges from this perspective veers toward a rather monochromatic story of repression in which the contestatory role of certain texts is not investigated. The consequences of this limited view mark Said's own *Orientalism* (New York, 1978).

Descartes is speaking in his own voice, it may be impossible to decide whether Derrida or Foucault gives the better account. There is something to be said for both—and that may be the thought-provoking feature of the passage in question.

A more forceful moment in Derrida's analysis comes when he discusses the point of hyperbolic doubt in Descartes, which seems to be open to the possibility of madness and to occur on a level that undercuts the opposition between madness and reason. But this point of extreme hyperbole is almost immediately followed in Descartes by a gesture that seems definitively to exclude madness and to establish a firm foundation for reason. Thus for Derrida, Descartes also excludes madness, but in a manner that repeats in modified form both the traditional philosophical desire for a firm and fully unified foundation for reason and the hyperbole that, at least momentarily, seems to subvert or contest that desire. In fact, in Descartes the moment of hyperbolic doubt and radical contestation is more explicit than it is in many other philosophers as Derrida himself interprets them. The larger question raised in Derrida's analysis is that of relating long and intricate traditions, such as the history of metaphysics, the specific period or time (including some delimited structural or epistemological definition of it), and the specific text. The attempt to delineate the mode of interaction among them requires an interpretation of the text in all its subtlety, and it indicates the importance for historical understanding of a notion of repetition with variation over time. In this respect, the relation among long tradition, specific time, and text cannot be determined through a notion of either simple continuity or discontinuity. Nor can the text be seen as a simple instantiation or illustration of either the long tradition or the specific time. Rather the problem becomes that of the way long tradition, specific time, and text repeat one another with variations, and the matter for elucidation becomes the degree of importance of these variations and how to construe it. The text is seen as the "place" where long tradition and specific time intersect, and it effects variations on both. But the text is not immobilized or presented as an autonomous node; it is situated in a fully relational network.

This network is the context for one of the most difficult issues for interpretation: that of how the critical and the symptomatic interact in a text or a work of art. Only by exploring this issue in a sustained way can one avoid the one-sidedness of analyses that stress either the symptomatic and representative nature of art (as did even Lukács and Lucien Goldmann, for whom art was critical solely as an expression of larger forces) or the way "great" art is itself an exceptional critical force for constructive change (as those affiliated with the Frankfurt School tended to argue). Stated in somewhat different terms, the issue is the extent to which art serves the escapist function of imaginary compensation for the defects of empirical reality and the extent to which it serves the contestatory function of questioning the empirical in a manner that has broader implications for the leading of life. One might suggest that texts and art works are ambivalent with respect to this issue, but that they differ in how they come to terms with the ambivalence. A criterion of "greatness" or at least of significance might well be the ability of certain texts or works of art to generate a heightened sense of the problematic nature of this ambivalence and yet to point beyond it to another level of ambivalence where the very opposition between escapism and criticism seems to become tenuous—indeed where oppositions in general founder and emerge in the passage between radical hyperbole and delimited structures. There is no ready formula for "decoding" the relations among the symptomatic, the critical, and what Derrida terms the "undecidable," but the attempt to interpret significant modern works forces one to confront the problem of what to make of these relations.

The question of "impact" is best seen in terms of complex series of readings and uses which texts undergo over time, including the process by which certain texts are canonized. Any text reaches us overlaid and even overburdened by interpretations to which we are consciously or unconsciously indebted. Canonization itself is a procedure not only of selection but of selective interpretation, often in the direction of domestication. We as interpreters are situated in a sedimented layering of readings that demand excavation. But the process of gaining perspective on our own interpretations does not exclude the attempt to arrive at an interpretation we are willing to defend. Indeed the activity of relating the existing series of interpretations, uses, and abuses of a text or a corpus to a reading that one tries to make as good as possible is essential to a critical historiography. Of course, this is not to say that the interpretation one offers is definitive and exhaustive. Not only is it open to revision through argument and reconsideration. It may actively address the issue of how the text itself resists the "closure" of definitive and exhaustive interpretation. And it should be agitated by the realization that we are inevitably blind to certain limitations of our own perspective. But we interpret nevertheless And, unless we interpret, our reference to a text becomes purely nominal, and we trace the movement of an "I-know-not-what" across time. To proceed in this manner is to abandon all hope of attaining a critical understanding of what is involved in the "impact" of texts. Indeed one might well argue that what is needed at present at the intersection of intellectual and social history is precisely an approach that relates an informed interpretation of complex texts to the problem of how those texts have been adapted to—and in certain ways have allowed—important uses and abuses over time. The cases of Marx, Nietzsche, and Heidegger call for treatment of this kind.[16]

One important area for the study of impact that has not been sufficiently investigated is that of the readings texts receive at trials. The trial serves as one instance of social reading that brings out conventions of interpretation in an important social institution. It is significant that in their basic assumptions about reading, the prosecution and the defense may share a great deal, and what they share may be quite distant from, or even placed on trial in, the work itself. (One thing a trial must repress is the way style, as Flaubert realized, may be a politically subversive or contestatory force, more unsettling than the

[16]George Steiner's *Martin Heidegger* (New York, 1978) is one of the best short introductions to Heidegger's thought, and it raises the problem of the relation between that thought and Heidegger's life. But the way Steiner addresses the latter issue is too summary and extreme to be altogether acceptable. He asserts an "organic" relation between the "vocabulary" of *Being and Time* (especially its later sections) and Heidegger's addresses of 1933 as well as "instrumental connections" between the "language" and "vision" of Heidegger's treatise and Nazi ideology (121–123). The mixing of metaphors to designate the nature of the relationships at issue itself indicates that they demand a more careful and extensive investigation than Steiner allows. He provides some crucial steps in this investigation by stressing the dangers of the more mesmeric sides of Heidegger's thought and the combination in it at times of near total criticism of the present and vague apocalyptic hope for the future. These aspects of Heidegger's thought may well have helped to induce the belief that the Nazis were the bearers of the fundamental change in modern civilization that Heidegger desired. And Steiner is, I think, justified in insisting upon the question of why Heidegger after 1945 remained publicly silent about his brief affiliation with the Nazis. What is also significant is that Steiner, in spite of his strictures about Heidegger's relation to the Nazis, wants to argue that Heidegger's work remains a basic and valuable contribution to modern thought. But the elucidation of the relation of that thought (notably *Being and Time*) to Nazi ideology and to Heidegger's own brief participation in politics requires an interpretation that inquires into the question of how the "same" themes or "ideas" function differently (or even in opposed ways) in different texts and contexts and how they may be both used and abused, not only by others but by the author himself in certain circumstances. Steiner does not provide this extremely difficult kind of interpretation. His own categorical response not only creates unexamined divisions in his own account (for Steiner himself argues that certain discussions in *Being and Time* constitute a radical critique of totalitarianism). It also leads him to the extremely dubious and unsupported assertion that the later sections of *Being and Time* (the ones presumably closer to Nazi ideology) are less persuasive and more opaque than the earlier portions of the text. The specious but useful separation between "good" and "bad" parts of the text is, I think, too simple an answer to the admittedly intricate question that Steiner has the merit of raising.

revolutionary message packaged in conventional forms.) In the modern West, it is writers of "literature" who have been placed on trial for their writings. This may be one sign of the more contestatory character of literature in comparison with other varieties of "high" culture in modern society, at least on levels where a more general public may sense that something disconcerting is happening—although the reasons given for trial often neutralize this sense by appealing to very conventional criteria of judgment, for example, "prurient interest." Writers of "theoretical" or philosophical works in the West are tried more informally through critical responses to their works. This has happened to Nietzsche, Heidegger, Derrida, and even Wittgenstein—philosophers who have perhaps gone farthest in challenging traditional understandings of philosophical discourse. In this sense, the history of critical response, including the book review, is an important chapter in the history of social impact, especially with reference to the constitution and development of disciplines. One can often learn more about the operative structure of a discipline from its book reviews and their distribution in different sorts of journals than one can from its formal institutional organization.

(4) *The relation of culture to texts.* The circulation or noncirculation of texts among levels of culture is an intricate problem, and difficulties arise even at the stage of deciding how to identify "levels." The approach to intellectual history I have been defending is directed at what has been traditionally (and now is often derogatorily) called "high" or "elite" culture. The dissemination of the "great" texts of at least the modern period to a larger audience is frequently at best a desideratum. At times it is actively opposed by important writers and intellectuals, although one may wonder to what extent this reaction is a defense against rejection, for modern texts often make demands upon the reader that few readers—even those in the so-called educated class—are willing to accept. One crucial function of a more "recuperative" or domesticating kind of intellectual history has been to disseminate these texts to the "generally educated" class in a "digestible" or "assimilable" form that may have little in common with the texts themselves and may even function as an excuse not to read them. Here I would note a general difference between a documentary and a dialogical approach to history. Insofar as an approach is documentary, it may validly function as a processing of "primary source material" that enables the nonexpert reader not to go to the sources or the archives themselves. But the very point of a dialogical ap-

proach is to stimulate the reader to respond critically to the interpretation it offers through his or her own reading or rereading of the primary texts.

To the extent that a text is not a mere document, it supplements existing reality, often by pointing out the weaknesses of prevailing definitions of it. In a traditional context, texts may function to shore up norms and values that are threatened but still experienced as viable. For example, Chrétien de Troyes had the quests of his knights test and ultimately prove the validity of courtly values that were threatened in the larger society.[17] In a revolutionary context, texts may help to break down the existing system and suggest avenues of change. But it is at times difficult to distinguish clearly between the traditional and the revolutionary context. And any text that pinpoints weaknesses in a system has an ambivalent function, for it may always be read against its own dominant tendency or authorial intention—a "conservative" text being used for "radical" purposes or vice versa. The fate of Marx in the hands of his liberal and conservative critics—or even certain of his putative followers—is illustrative in this respect.

Most modern writers of note have seen their period as revolutionary or at least as "transitional." Indeed they have often been "alienated" from what they perceive as the dominant society and culture. Even significant conservatives, such as Burke and Maistre, do not simply defend a status quo, but often inveigh against it in defense of values they believe to be under full siege and rapidly disappearing. They may advocate a context in which the attachment to values, norms, and communal groups is prereflective or quasi-instinctive, but they are forced to become highly reflective intellectuals in spite of themselves. More often than not, the modern conservative is a divided self who may even harbor rather radical tendencies. This tension is quite evident in Dostoevsky and Balzac. And, for conservatives and radicals alike, the very notion of a popular culture to which they might relate arose largely as an ideal, a critical fiction, or a goal to be opposed to "modern" forces that jeopardized those at times vestigial forms of popular culture they judged to be desirable.

One might argue that the global society or culture is too large and undifferentiated a unit for the investigation of the most relevant community of discourse for intellectuals. The more delimited school, movement, network of associations, or reference group would seem to

[17]The example of Chrétien de Troyes is discussed by Wolfgang Iser in *The Act of Reading* (Baltimore, 1978), 77–78.

provide the more immediate complex of shared assumptions or pertinent considerations that operate, tacitly or explicitly, to shape the
intellectual's sense of significant questions and modes of inquiry.
Hence intellectual history should be a history of intellectuals, of the
communities of discourse in which they function, and of the varying
relations—ranging in often complicated ways from insulation to openness—they manifest toward the larger culture. Thinkers as diverse
as T. S. Kuhn, Quentin Skinner, R. G. Collingwood, and Michel Foucault may be drawn upon in the attempt to elaborate and apply this
view. This approach has much to commend it, but I want to point out
at least two problems it sometimes generates.

First, it may be used to restrict historical inquiry to the historicist
and documentary attempt to recreate the dialogue of others, prohibit-
ing the extension of that dialogue to include the interpretations of
the historian, perhaps on the grounds that epochs are primarily if
not exclusively dissociated in their forms of understanding. (Those
grounds give rise to damaging aporias that are too well known to be
rehearsed here.) Even more often, the assumption is made that historical understanding itself is (or should be) purely "objective" and that
the very notion of an informed dialogue with the past is absurd or at
least nonhistorical. This position not only identifies the historical with
the historicist and the documentary. It may also construe the notion of
dialogue in a simplistic way (for example, in terms of drawing immediate lessons from the past or projecting our own particular or
subjective concerns onto it). One may, however, argue that the reconstruction of the dialogues of the dead should be self-consciously combined with the interpretative attempt to enter into an exchange with
them that is itself dialogical only insofar as it actively recognizes the
difficulties of communication across time and the importance of understanding as fully as possible what the other is trying to say. To the
extent that the past is investigated in terms of its most particularized
aspects, dialogue with it becomes minimal. But the subsequent question is whether historical research should be directed primarily to
aspects of this sort, which restrict the historian's use of language to
predominantly informational and analytic functions. When it is applied to the works of major figures, an approach that attempts to be
exclusively documentary is often deadly in its consequences. And
when we historians who are trained to believe in the primacy of the
documentary ideal do venture to put forth interpretations or critical
judgments, the latter may well be of little interest, for they are not the

products of a rich and varied discursive background. Here, of course, we face the traditional problem of how the educator is himself to be educated.

Second, the focus on communities of discourse must be cogently related to the problem of textual interpretation. It is not enough to establish influence or the existence of a shared "paradigm" through the enumeration of common presuppositions, questions, themes, or arguments. One must elucidate in a more detailed way how the borrowed or the common actually functions in the texts in question. To document common assumptions or lines of influence may suffice to debunk the myth of absolute originality. But this procedure easily gives rise to its own forms of self-deception or even mindless chronicling when debunking goes to the extreme of not recognizing why there is, for example, a major difference between a Fliess and a Freud. Influence studies are of minor interest unless they address the issue of how common ideas function differentially in different texts and corpuses, and even the attempt to dethrone a reigning "great" must face up to the problem of interpreting his works in their complexity. All too often the focus on the community of discourse leads the historian to limit research to minor figures or to highly restricted and unsituated aspects of the thought of a major figure (for example, Nietzsche's elitism, Marx's utopianism, or Freud's biologism). In addition, the delimited "communities" in which important modern intellectuals participate may themselves be made up more of the dead or absent than of the living or present. The most significant reference group may prominently include dead or distant (even future) "others" who become relevant largely through their works, which the "creative" intellectual helps bring to life in his or her own works through emulation, selective appropriation, parody, polemic, anticipation, and so forth. The contemporary person-to-person group may have a lesser significance for the actual production of "ideas," and in any case its role is always supplemented by relation to others through their texts or other artifacts. The dialogue with the text may even be experienced as more immediate and engrossing than most conversations. Indeed one of the re-creative implications of reading might well be to attempt to create social and cultural conditions in which the literal conversation and the general text of life are more like the processes stimulated by an encounter with a great text.

This last consideration provides a limited avenue of reentry into the question of the relation between "great" texts and general or popular culture. The processes that Mikhail Bakhtin discusses in terms of "carnivalization" help to identify at least one kind—or one vision—of popular culture activated or reactivated in the texts of many significant modern writers and often desired by them as the larger context to which their writings might relate. "Carnivalization," in Bakhtin's own normative, indeed visionary conception, is epitomized in carnival as a social institution but not confined to it. In its larger sense, "carnivalization" is an engaging process of interaction through which seeming opposites—body and spirit, work and play, positive and negative, high and low, seriousness and laughter—are related to each other in an ambivalent, contestatory interchange that is both literally and figuratively "re-creative." It is set within an encompassing rhythm of social life, and one might argue that its nature and functions depend upon that larger setting. While Bakhtin provides little description or analysis of actual carnivals, he does note broad variations in the role of carnival in society and of carnivalization in literature, and he stresses the importance of the carnivalesque as a vital dimension of life itself.

According to Bakhtin, a lively interchange among carnival as a social institution, popular culture, and high culture existed in Rabelais's Renaissance. While aspects of elite culture were closed to the common people (for example, works written in Latin), the elite participated in popular culture, and aspects of that culture affected high culture. Thus, with some underemphasis of their erudite and esoteric side, Bakhtin can interpret the works of Rabelais as drawing upon, and feeding into, a rich and vital popular culture. The modern period witnessed the decline of carnival, the separation of the elite from popular culture, and the detachment of processes of carnivalization in literature from significant public institutions. Indeed great literature is for Bakhtin the primary repository of the modern carnivalesque in its more restricted but still potent state. Social forms of carnivalization have tended to be appropriated for official political purposes, as in the parade and the pageant, or to withdraw to the private sphere, for example, in the domestic celebration of holidays. And the modern literary carnivalesque has itself often gravitated toward more reduced extremes, such as largely negative irony and hysterically shrill laughter. Bakhtin's analysis of the works of Dostoevsky, however, itself indicates the more re-creative possibilities of carnivalization and "grotesque realism" in modern literature.[18]

[18]See Mikhail Bakhtin, *Rabelais and His World* [first submitted as a dissertation in 1940], tr. Hélène Iswolsky (Cambridge, Mass., 1968), *Problems of Dostoevsky's Poetics* [1929], tr. R. W. Rotsel (Ann Arbor, 1973), and *The Dialogic Imagination*, tr. Caryl Emerson and

The decline of carnival was directly related to religious reform and indirectly related to the multiple processes gathered together under the label of "modernization." The withdrawal of the elites from popular culture was a long-term process extending from 1500 to 1800, and what had been everyone's second culture was rediscovered as an exotic residue of the past. In the nineteenth century, the turn toward folklore and other forms of popular culture was often one aspect of various responses to the perceived "excesses" of the Enlightenment. In post-Enlightenment writing, there is often, moreover, an adversary relation to the dominant society in which "carnivalization" is underplayed or repressed. Here, for example, we have one basis for Nietzsche's critique of positivism as a eunuchlike flight from carnivalesque contestation—the Nietzschean version of the "betrayal of the intellectuals." We also have one way of viewing Flaubert's "postromantic" notion of art as an ironic and stylistically insurrectionary variant of the transformed carnivalesque. More generally, the notion of carnivalization provides one way of interpreting the contestatory styles with political overtones that have been so characteristic of modern writing. Indeed, official resistance to carnival-type behavior may stem from political and cultural insecurity. And processes of carnivalization can themselves be related to social action in part inspired by a desire for a context of "lived experience" more open to revitalizing, contestatory forms. One need not look to the distant past for examples of these phenomena. Not only may aspects of the work of recent French figures (for example, Foucault, Deleuze, Sollers, Kristeva, and Derrida) be seen in terms of processes of carnivalization. But the events of 1968 in France have been interpreted in this way, often with the term "carnival" being used in a pejorative sense by opponents and at times with the vision of "carnivalization" becoming a pretext for romanticization in defenders of the *événements*.[19] The larger problem

---

Michael Holquist (Austin, 1981). For an application of certain of Bakhtin's views, see Natalie Z. Davis, *Society and Culture in Early Modern France* (Stanford, 1975).

[19]For a treatment of early modern culture (or cultures), with a discussion of the role of carnival, its decline over time, and the withdrawal of the elites from popular culture, see Peter Burke, *Popular Culture in Early Modern Europe* (New York, 1978). For a study of French culture emphasizing the problem of carnivalization, including its role in 1968, see Maurice Crubellier, *Histoire culturelle de la France* (Paris, 1974). A more detailed discussion of the history of the carnivalesque and its relation to various writers would require qualifications and discriminations that I have not provided. For an analysis of Flaubert and carnivalization, see Arthur Mitzman, "Roads, Vulgarity, Rebellion, and Pure Art: The Inner Space in Flaubert and French Culture," *Journal of Modern History* 51 (1979), 504–524. It must, however, be noted that the danger in Flaubert is that the leveling tendency he saw operating in modern culture affected his own approach in an uncritical way, leading him at

these considerations bring out is that of the way innovatory "elite" responses in the modern period may appeal to more or less transfigured versions of older "popular" culture in the radical critique of what is perceived as the dominant sociocultural context.

(5) *The relation of a text to the corpus of a writer*. The notion of context provided by other texts is itself apparently textual in nature (although one must recall that "corpus" here may also mean "body"). And it raises the problem of the relationship between a text and the texts of other writers as well as other texts of the same writer. For what is at issue here is precisely the unity or identity of a corpus. Often the corpus is seen in one of three ways: continuity among texts ("linear development"); discontinulty among texts (change or even "epistemological break" between stages or periods); and dialectical synthesis (the later stage raises the earlier one to a higher level of insight). The corpus is thus unified in one way or another (developmental unity, two discrete unities, higher unity) and, so seen, it is like a single text writ large, for the single text may be interpreted through the use of these categories. The question, however, is whether these categories are too simple for interpreting the functioning of both a complex text and the corpus of complex texts. The relation among aspects or elements of a text, and a fortiori among texts in a corpus, may involve uneven development and differing forms of repetition or displacement that put in question simple models of intelligibility. Indeed the "corpus" of a writer may be at least partially dismembered, sometimes in ways that are intended or explicitly explored by the writer himself. Carnivalization as described by Bakhtin involves dismemberment or creative undoing that may be related to processes of renewal. One strategy of dismemberment is the use of montage and quotation through which the text is laced or even strewn with parts of other texts—both written texts and elements of social discourse. In Flaubert, for example, the text is punctuated with parodic citations

---

times to a homogenized and nearly nihilistic condemnation of both modern society and humanity in general. In his most lapidary and famous formulations of the ideal of "pure art," Flaubert "sublimated" the carnivalesque into its opposite: an ascetic negation of reality and an attempt to transcend it into an inviolate sphere of beauty or absolute style. The more compelling and subtle dynamic in his stories is that whereby a vision of pure art is not simply exemplified but contested and even "carnivalized," notably through the treatment of analogous forms of the quest for the absolute and the empathetic-ironic modulations of narrative voice in the so-called "free indirect style." In general, art was for Flaubert the most important commitment in the world and the work of a clown. It is important to recognize that he affirmed both these conceptions with great intensity and that there is in his works a variable tension between a pathos of belief and critical forms such as irony, parody, and self-parody. On these issues, see my *"Madame Bovary" on Trial* (Ithaca, 1982).

from other novels and from the clichés of daily life. In Mann and Joyce, the montage technique assumes panoramic proportions in its ability to piece or graft together various uses of discourse. In Sollers and Derrida, dismemberment (involving textual distribution of the "self") at times seems to attain Dionysian heights or depths. The larger question raised by these strategies is that of the interaction between the quest for unity, which may continue to function in direct or parodic ways, and challenges to that quest operative or experimented with in the texts themselves. The texts, however, do not become hermetically closed upon themselves: they differ from and also defer to other texts both written and lived.

(6) *The relation between modes of discourse and texts.* In the recent past, considerable attention has been paid to the role of more or less formalized modes of discourse, structures of interpretation, and conventions or rules. Many theorists have argued that writing and reading are informed by structures or conventions that should be a primary, if not an exclusive, center of critical interest.[20] Hayden White has attempted to arrive at a level of deep structure that undercuts the opposition between literature and history to reveal how modes of emplotment inform all coherent narratives and how tropes construct the linguistic field. He has also indicated that figurative uses of language connect the levels of description and explicit interpretation or explanation in prose narratives. This last point serves to raise again a question that has been insufficiently explored in structuralist accounts of discourse: the question of how various modes of discourse, rules, or conventions actually function in texts or extended uses of language. In this regard, the reading of "minor" texts is certainly important for the attempt to establish what the dominant rules or conventions of a genre were at a given time. But the relation of a "great" text to genres—both the ones it is placing in question and the ones it is helping to establish—is always problematic, and even a "minor" text may hold out some surprises here. Often, however, it is assumed that this relation is one of coverage on the part of structures and instantiation on the part of texts. This view (which may actually be held by theorists who in other respects criticize the subordination of the humanities to "positivism" with its "covering laws") leads to the belief that there are unproblematic realms of discourse, illustrated by texts that fall within them.

---

[20]For one especially forceful elaboration of this view, see Jonathan Culler, *Structuralist Poetics* (Ithaca, 1975). For an equally forceful exploration of some of its limitations, see Culler, *Flaubert: The Uses of Uncertainty* (Ithaca, 1974).

This view is misleading as it relates to the status of analytic distinctions or structural oppositions and to the question of how these distinctions or oppositions function in texts.[21] Analytic distinctions such as those drawn between history and literature, fact and fiction, concept and metaphor, the serious and the ironic, and so forth, do not define realms of discourse that unproblematically characterize or govern extended uses of language. Instead, what should be taken as a problem for inquiry is the nature of the relationships among various analytically defined distinctions in the actual functioning of language, including the use of language by theorists attempting to define and defend analytic distinctions or oppositions in their conceptual purity. To say this is neither to advocate the obliteration of all distinctions nor to offer a purely homogeneous understanding of a mysterious entity called the "text." It is rather to direct attention to problems that are obscured when one relies uncritically on the concept of "realms of discourse." For example, it is common to distinguish history from literature on the grounds that history is concerned with the realm of fact while literature moves in the realm of fiction. It is true that the historian may not invent his facts or references while the "literary" writer may, and in this respect the latter has a greater margin of freedom in exploring relationships. But, on other levels, historians make use of heuristic fictions and models to orient their research into facts, and the question I have tried to raise is whether historians are restricted to the reporting and analysis of facts in their exchange with the past. Conversely, literature borrows from a factual repertoire in multiple ways, and the transplantation of the documentary has a carry-over effect that invalidates attempts to see literature in terms of a pure suspension of reference to "reality" or transcendence of the empirical into the purely imaginary. Even when literature attempts to "bracket" empirical reality or to suspend more ordinary documentary functions, it engages in a self-referential work or praxis through which the text documents its own mode of production. The very prevalence of literature about literature or art about art raises the question of how to interpret self-referential activity with respect to a larger historical context. Thus there certainly are distinctions to be drawn, but the problem is the manner in which these distinctions function in texts and in our reading or interpretation of them.

In the last-mentioned respect, there are different possibilities, ranging from the dominance of a given analytic distinction or type to more

---

[21]I try to develop this assertion with reference to the thought of Jürgen Habermas in "Habermas and the Grounding of Critical Theory," *History and Theory* 16 (1977), 237–64.

open interplay and contestation among various uses of language. But dominance implies some form of subordination or exclusion, and how this relationship is established must be investigated. Any critique of pure identities, pure oppositions, and attendant hierarchies must pay close attention to the way these categories function, for they have indeed been of decisive importance in thought and in life. One has certainly witnessed a quest for pure fact, pure fiction, pure philosophy, pure poetry, pure prose, and so forth. For those committed to some variant of it, the quest is taken at face value and defended. It may also be institutionalized in disciplines that organize themselves around conventions and rules that restrict language to certain uses and prohibit or sanction the attempt to raise questions that problematize these restricted uses. One of the largest of these questions is whether the quest for purity and the direct projection of analytic categories onto "reality" are related to a "metaphysics of the proper" whereby one's own identity, propriety, or authenticity is established through the identification of a totally different "other," an outsider who may even become a pariah or scapegoat. In any case, the problem is how seeming purity (or unmarked identity and unity) is established and whether the quest for it in language use is contested by other aspects of the text or more general linguistic context in which this quest takes place. A text itself may of course seek purity by engaging in procedures of exclusion or domination that tend to neutralize or reduce its more disconcerting or contestatory movements. These procedures provide points of entry for interpretations or entire disciplines that "found" themselves upon the purity and autonomy of "realms of discourse" putatively emanating from certain master texts. But complex texts may well involve other movements that test the desire for unity in a variety of ways. Indeed certain texts that seem to rely exclusively on one function or analytic dimension of language—for example, analytic dissociation or simulated denotative usage and attendant metaphoric deprivation in Beckett—may involve parody and stimulate in the reader an awareness of other possible uses of language. In fact the question is whether any text that seems successful in the sustained reliance on one function or analytic aspect of language, for example, the accumulation of facts or of theoretical reflections, is engaged in intentional or unintentional parody or self-parody, or at least may always be so read.

These points indicate that analytic distinctions are useful for purposes of clarification and orientation as pursued on an ideal level in their pure or "laboratory" form, but that they never function "as such" in actual discourse or in texts. When they do seem to be used purely as such, other processes are at work or at play. The critique of these processes is perforce prone to its own excesses (discursive delirium, political quietism, anomic disorientation, the quest for full liberation either of or from libidinal demands). At its best, however, this critique may raise the problem of a more viable interaction between forms of language and forms of life. The exploration of this problem in the great texts of the tradition constitutes an especially engaging adventure that at times involves a strangely disconcerting way of making us think seemingly alien thoughts that are in fact within us and that may well return in unmitigatedly destructive ways when they are simply repressed or excluded. This problem may not be seen or appreciated when texts are read in an excessively reductive way or delegated exclusively to discrete disciplines. No discipline has the imperial right to dominion over a Freud, Marx, Nietzsche, or Joyce. (The practical advantage of intellectual history in this respect is that it can, without excuse or subterfuge, explore the problem of reading various texts together and thus raise questions about their functioning as language that might not otherwise be apparent.) Indeed, as I have already intimated, a discipline may constitute itself in part through reductive readings of its important texts—readings that are contested by the "founding" texts themselves in significant ways.[22] These readings render the texts less multifaceted and perhaps less critical but more operational for organized research. Here the decisive role of certain disciples and practitioners lies not in the fine-tuning of a paradigm enunciated in "founding" texts but in the active reduction of those texts to their paradigmatic level.

The "great" texts should be part of the pertinent record for all historians. They are certainly part and parcel of a general historical culture. Something excessively reductive has already taken place when they are assigned to the subdiscipline of intellectual history, which may then function as a park or reserve for them. But at least within that subdiscipline, they should be read with an eye for the broader and occasionally uncanny processes they engage and that engage us. One such process is precisely the interaction between the desire for unity, identity, or purity, and the forces that contest it. The investigation of this process does not imply a simple rejection of conceptions of unity or order in a mindlessly antinomian celebration of chaos and dismemberment. What it calls for is a rethinking of the

[22]This view motivates my study of Durkheim in *Emile Durkheim: Sociologist and Philosopher* (Ithaca, 1972).

concept of unity and its analogues in more workable and critical terms. It also requires a sensitivity to the way these concepts are related to their "adversaries" in the texts we study and in our own attempts at theoretical self-understanding. One practical implication of these considerations is the possibility of reconstructing norms and conventions in forms that may be more durable precisely because they enable us to contend better with criticism and contestation. In this respect, a function of dialogue with the past is to further the attempt to ascertain what deserves to be preserved, rehabilitated, or critically transformed in tradition.

I want to conclude by returning to the distinction I drew between intellectual history as a reconstruction of the past and intellectual history as a dialogue or conversation with the past—a distinction that should not be taken as a purely dichotomous opposition. The reconstruction of the past is an important endeavor, and reliable documentation is a crucial component of any approach that claims to be historical. But the dominance of a documentary conception distorts our understanding of both historiography and the historical process. Indeed I have tried to suggest that a *purely* documentary conception of historiography is itself a heuristic fiction. For description is never pure, in that a fact is relevant for an account only when it is selected with reference to a topic or a question posed to the past. The simplest fact—a dated event—relies on what is for some historians a belief and for others a convenient fiction: the decisive significance of the birth of Christ in establishing a chronology in terms of a "before" and "after." Yet a purely documentary conception may function as an unexamined assumption or it may give rise to a paradoxically self-conscious and sophisticated defense of a "naive" idea of the historian's craft—a defense that may border on anti-intellectualism. In any case, insofar as it achieves a position of dominance, a documentary conception is excessively restrictive, especially in the results it yields in the analysis of significant texts. And it obscures the problem of the interaction between description and other uses of language in an account. The idea of a purely descriptive, objective rendering of the past can allow for uses of language that escape it only in terms of the exiguous category of unavoidable bias or particularistic subjectivity. This category may apply to certain aspects of historiography. But the simple opposition between self-effacing objectivity and subjective bias fails to accommodate the range of language uses in any significant history.

The purely documentary view of historiography often coincides with a historicist definition of the historical that identifies the object of study as changing "particulars" in contrast with extratemporal or synchronic types or universals. This venerable view ignores the historical process of repetition with variation or change that functions to mitigate the analytic opposition between the particular or unique and the typical or universal. Yet it is this historical (and linguistic) process that is operative in the past and that raises the problem of the historicity of the historian in his or her attempt to come to terms with it. A documentary historiography that tries to exclude interpretation or to see it only in the guise of bias, subjectivity, or anachronism also has a bizarre consequence. It presents historical truth in an essentially nonhistorical way. For, by attempting to restrict historiography proper to the description and analysis of verifiable facts (ideally in the form of a definitive and exhaustive account), it strives for an unchanging representation of changing "particulars" that would itself transcend the historical process. As the work of Ranke amply documents, the narrowly historicist and the ahistorical are extremes that meet in the ideal of a purely documentary historiography. And the desire to transcend history reappears in a form that may be invisible precisely because it has become so familiar. Indeed, a belief that historiography is a purely documentary or descriptive reconstitution of the past may be prone to blind fictionalizing because it does not explicitly and critically raise the problem of the role of fictions (for example, in the form of models, analytic types, and heuristic fictions) in the attempt to represent reality. The result is often a tacit reliance upon the most conventional narrative structures to combine documented fact, *vie romancée*, and unsubstantiated judgments about the past or flimsy analogies between past and present.

With specific reference to intellectual history, I would argue for a more "performative" notion of reading and interpretation in which an attempt is made to "take on" the great texts and to attain a level of understanding and perhaps of language use that contends with them. This notion, which valorizes the virtuoso performance in reading, is easily abused when it becomes a license for reducing the text to little more than a trampoline for one's own creative leaps or political demands. Certainly, the act of interpretation has political dimensions. It is not an autonomous hermeneutic undertaking that moves on the level of pure meaning to establish a "fusion of horizons" assuring authoritative continuity with the past. In some relevant sense, interpretation is a form of political intervention that engages the historian in a critical process that relates past, present, and future through complex modes of interaction involving both continuities and discontinuities. But it is misleading to pose the problem of understanding in terms of either of two extremes: the purely documentary representation of the past and the "presentist" quest for liberation from the "burden" of history through unrestrained fictionalizing and mythologizing. In relation to both these extremes (which constitute parts of the same complex), it is necessary to emphasize the status of interpretation as an activity that cannot be reduced to mere subjectivity. A significant text involves, among other things, creative art, and its interpretation is, among other things, a performing art. But art is never entirely free, and the art of the historian is limited in specific ways. He must attend to the facts, especially when they test and contest his own convictions and desires (including the desire for a fully unified frame of reference). And even when he attempts to think further what is thought in a text, he cannot reduce the text to a pretext for his own inventions or immediate interests. The belief in pure interpretation is itself a bid for absolute transcendence that denies both the finite nature of understanding and the need to confront critically what Freud discussed in terms of "transference."

The genuine alternative to a purely documentary and contemplative conception of the past "for its own sake" is not its simple opposite: the futile attempt to escape the past or to identify it through projection with the present. Rather, texts should be seen to address us in more subtle and challenging ways, and they should be carried into the present—with implications for the future—in a dialogical fashion. Historiography would be an exercise in narcissistic infatuation if it amounted to a willful projection of present concerns upon the past. The notion of "creative misreading" (or active "rewriting") is itself misleading when it legitimates one-sided, subjectivist aggression that ignores the ways texts may actually challenge the interpreter and lead him to change his mind. Even if one accepts the metaphor that presents interpretation as the "voice" of the historical reader in the "dialogue" with the past, it must be actively recognized that the past has its own "voices" that must be respected, especially when they resist or qualify the interpretations we would like to place on them. A text is a network of resistances, and a dialogue is a two-way affair; a good reader is also an attentive and patient listener. Questions are necessary to focus interest in an investigation, but a fact may be pertinent to a frame of reference by contesting or even contradicting it. An interest in what does not fit a model and an openness to what one does not expect to hear from the past may even help to transform the very questions one poses to the past. Both the purely documentary and the "presentist" extremes are "monological" insofar as they deny these possibilities. Indeed the seeming anomaly should be seen as having a special value in historiography, for it constrains one to doubt overly reductive interpretations and excessively "economical" shortcuts from understanding to action.

The conception of the field that I have tried to defend complicates the task of the intellectual historian. But it also keeps intellectual history in touch with questions that are raised in "great" texts and that are forever old and new in a manner that cannot be reduced to some *philosophia perennis* or to a subjectivistic relativism. And it defines intellectual history more in terms of a process of inquiry than in terms of rules of method or of a body of information about the past. This is the most fruitful kind of "definition" possible for an approach that both addresses historical problems and understands itself as historical. The demand for documentation serves to keep responsive interpretations from becoming irresponsible. But to use this demand to attempt to escape our own dialogical relation to the past is to attempt to escape our own historicity. We need to understand more clearly what is involved in a relationship that is dialogical and historical without being either "historicist" or "presentist." The historian who reads texts either as mere documents or as formal entities (if not as Rorschach tests) does not read them historically precisely because he or she does not read them as texts. And, whatever else they may be, texts are events in the history of language. To understand these multivalent events as complex uses of language, one must learn to pose anew the question of "what really happens" in them and in the reader who actually reads them. One of the most important contexts for reading texts is clearly our own—a context that is misconstrued when it is seen in narrowly "presentist" terms. I have only alluded to ways in which this context involves the reader in an interaction among past, present, and future having a bearing on both understanding and action. But it is precisely here that intellectual history opens out to other modes of interpretation and practice. This "opening" relates to the way the power of dialogue and of reflection is itself effective only when it comes with the "working through" of existential problems that are perforce also social and political problems.[23]

---

[23]I will simply mention one limited way in which intellectual history should address this issue. The intellectual historian should, I think, recognize his or her audience as a tensely divided one made up of both experts and a generally educated public. The intellectual historian is required to come as close as possible to an "expert" knowledge of the problems

I shall here append a few observations that have a specific bearing upon this volume (and the conference from which it stemmed). Our over-all purpose is to arrive at some conception of where our subdiscipline finds itself at present and where it should be going. I want to emphasize that my own paper is largely programmatic. It tries to raise questions about existing approaches and to sketch alternative ways of addressing issues. It does not itself show how to practice the approach it somewhat presumptuously defends on a relatively theoretical level. Only in footnotes do I attempt to indicate possible approaches to reading and interpretation that relate to the more general issues.

I nonetheless think that there is a need today for more programmatic and relatively theoretical statements in the field of intellectual history. This need is conjunctural, and my insistency in urging it is to some extent transitional. At issue is the process of recognition and even of naming with respect to various approaches to history. One important question facing us is that of the type of research that should be called intellectual history, indeed that of the type of research to be recognized as historical. We are, I think, in a situation analogous to that about which Confucians spoke in terms of the issue of a "rectification of names."

The idea that the mansion of history has many chambers or that we should not build walls between approaches bespeaks a false generosity insofar as there exists a hierarchy among various perspectives and even an unwillingness to recognize certain approaches as validly historical. The issues of recognition and naming relate to practical as well as cognitive matters, for example, job placement. Material interests are involved in processes of recognition and nonrecognition. These interests cannot be separated from questions of professional or disciplinary politics. When a position in intellectual history is to be filled and candidates with different perspectives apply for it, what approach to research will be considered relevant and which candidates will be accorded preferential treatment? I think that there is at present an excessive tendency to give priority to social or sociocultural approaches

---

being investigated. But a goal of intellectual history should be the expansion of the "class" of the generally educated and the generation of a better interchange between them and the "experts." This means helping to put the generally educated in a position to raise more informed and critical questions. It also means attempting to prevent expertise from becoming enclosed in its own dialect or jargon. In these senses, intellectual history faces complex problems of "translation," and its own concerns bring it into contact with larger social and cultural questions. One such question is how to resist the establishment of common culture on a relatively uncritical level and to further the creation of a more demanding common culture that, within limits, is genuinely open to contestation.

and to downgrade the importance of reading and interpreting complex texts. The recent shift from the more statistical methods of the earlier version of *Annales* historiography to a concern with problems of social and cultural "meaning" does not remedy the problem, for it often leads to a definition of intellectual history as retrospective symbolic or cultural anthropology. This definition frequently brings about what might be called an anthropological bulldozer effect, whereby the significance and the specificity of interpreting complex texts is plowed under in the attempt to reconstruct a common or collective "discursive culture." But certain cultures provide "mechanisms" for the preservation and reinterpretation of their exceptional products; intellectual history is one of these "mechanisms."

Let me immediately add that I recognize the importance of reconstituting institutional practice and social discourse. But I must also stress that the focus upon this problem often involves a very restricted interpretation of complex texts (when the latter are considered at all). Conversely, the focus on the understanding of complex texts may bring certain losses in the more general reconstitution of institutionalized or shared social discourses in various classes, groups, or occupations. The comprehensive problem is to understand how complex texts relate to their various contexts and vice versa—and this problem itself involves an appreciation of the losses and gains attendant upon a research strategy. Without more programmatic or even polemical statements, studies employing certain research strategies may easily be written off as beyond the pale of historiography or merely marginal to its main concerns. In an ideal world, each historian would be responsible for the treatment of all problems from the most comprehensive of all possible perspectives. In the real world, certain choices must be made. Only when these choices are self-conscious and thought out can genuine cooperation among historians with different emphases be undertaken in a noninvidious spirit. My concern is that the specific problems involved in the understanding of complex texts are becoming radically deemphasized in intellectual history and that the latter is being defined in ways that obscure or avoid these problems.

In the most general terms, where does the perspective on intellectual history that I have tried to elaborate lead? What implications does it have for the relation between past and present and between "theory and practice"? The field of humanistic studies today seems increasingly divided by two opposed tendencies. One tendency attempts, more or less self-consciously, to rehabilitate conventional approaches to description, interpretation, and explanation. It stresses the need to discover or perhaps to invent, on some decisive level, unity and order in the phenomena under investigation and, by implication, in one's own life and times. It may recognize chaos or disorder in phenomena, but its overriding goal is to uncover order in chaos, for example, through delimitation of topics, selection of problems, empirical and analytic procedures of investigation, and perhaps even synthesis of results by means of causal or interpretative models. In the reading of texts, it emphasizes the importance of determining central arguments, core meanings, dominant themes, prevalent codes, world views, and deep structures. In relating texts or other artifacts to contexts, it seeks some comprehensive, integrative paradigm: formally, by arguing that once texts "internalize" contexts, the latter are subjected to procedures "internal" to the text; causally, by arguing that the very problems or, indeed, the formal procedures operative in texts are themselves "caused" or generated by changes in the larger context; or structurally, by arguing that both texts and contexts attest to the agency of deeper forces homologous to them. A single account may variously employ all three of these paradigms of integration, or it may seek to include them in some higher "order of orders."

The other tendency tries to bring out the ways in which debates that agitate those taking the first approach actually rest on common assumptions, and it points to the limitations of those assumptions. What is assumed in conventional approaches is the priority, perhaps the dominance, of unity or its analogues: order, purity, closure, undivided origin, coherent structure, determinate meaning at least at the core, and so forth. Those working within the other, more "experimental" tendency (often identified, at times misleadingly, as "deconstructive") will thus stress the importance of what is marginal in text or life as seen from the conventional view—what is uncanny or disorienting in terms of its assumptions. But the danger in this other tendency is that it will remain fixated at the phase of simple reversal of dominant conventional assumptions and replace unity with disunity, order with chaos, center with absence of center, determinacy with uncontrolled plurality or dissemination of meaning, and so forth. In so doing, it may aggravate what its proponents would see as undesirable tendencies in the larger society, become symptomatic where it would like to be critical, and confuse ordinary equivocation and evasiveness—or even slipshod research—with the kind of transformative interaction between self and other (or language and world) it would like to reactivate.

Reversal may be necessary as a type of shock therapy that enables a critique to register, but its inadequacies are blatant, especially when it has become familiar and fails to shock. What is then needed is a general rethinking of problems, including a modulated understanding of the relation between tradition and its critique. Involved in this process of rethinking is the realization that both full unity and full disunity (or their analogues) are ideal limits more or less approximated in language and life. The general problem then becomes that of how precisely these limits have been related in texts and contexts of the past and how they should be related in the present and future. An informed dialogue with the past, which investigates significant texts and their relations to pertinent contexts, is part of an attempt to come to terms with this problem. It is premised upon the conviction that the intellectual historian is both intellectual and historian and that he or she, as intellectual, does not simply cease being a historian. Indeed, the relationship between the "critical" intellectual and the "scholarly" historian (or traditional *érudit*) is essential for the internalized dialogue that marks the intellectual historian.

CHAPTER THREE

Should Intellectual History Take a Linguistic Turn? Reflections on the Habermas-Gadamer Debate

MARTIN JAY

When the intellectual historians of the next century come to write their accounts of our own, they will inevitably remark on the dramatic quickening of interest in virtually all disciplines in the question of language. Although anticipations of this change can be discerned in literature before 1900, an obvious example being the poetics of Mallarmé, the twentieth century dawned with the long-standing assumption still widely unshaken that language is an essentially transparent medium for the expression of ideas and emotions or the description of an external world. Private mental reflection was thus taken to be prior to public, intersubjective discourse. Generally accompanying the equally time-honored notion that truth is an adequate expression of objective reality, this concept of language can be traced at least as far back as Plato's denigration of Sophistic rhetoric and the poetical ambiguities of the Homeric epic.[1] Perhaps its most exaggerated manifestation in the Western philosophical tradition was Spinoza's attempt to negate linguistic mediation entirely by casting philosophy in the form of geometric proofs. In the early twentieth century, its greatest exemplar was Wittgenstein's *Tractatus* with its

[1]For a general history of philosophies of language, see Ernst Cassirer, *The Philosophy of Symbolic Forms*, tr. Ralph Manheim, vol. I (New Haven, 1953), 117–176. Cassirer's survey is, to be sure, selective and ignores figures like Nietzsche who anticipated the twentieth-century linguistic turn. See also Ian Hacking, *Why Does Language Matter to Philosophy* (Cambridge, 1975), and Richard Rorty, *Philosophy and the Mirror of Nature* (Princeton, 1979).

contention that language provides *Bilder* (pictures or models) of a real external world.[2]

Although, to be sure, there were isolated exceptions, such as the antischolastic rhetoricians of the Italian Renaissance, most notably Lorenzo Valla and Mario Nizolio, and the later, relatively isolated figures of Vico and Hamann, it was not really until our own century that mainstream Western philosophy took a decisive linguistic turn. Why this occurred, whether or not it was a product of the crisis in signification in later bourgeois culture, cannot concern us now. What is important to note instead is that the linguistic turn in philosophy affected many other disciplines and came in several different forms. It is now even threatening to penetrate the defenses of that most conservative of cultural enterprises, the study of history, through the opening provided by intellectual historians who have allowed what they examine to influence how they examine it.

Before speculating on the wisdom of following their example, one must determine which theory of language is being employed, for the rejection of the older descriptive model has taken several forms. Despite certain examples of cross-fertilization to be noted below, until very recently there has been a remarkable degree of insularity along national lines. In England, the linguistic turn was taken in the interwar era by Wittgenstein at Cambridge and J. L. Austin and Gilbert Ryle at Oxford.[3] Very schematically put and bracketing the differences among them, these philosophers understood language less as a neutral medium of expression or representation than as a complex human activity. Language was first of all speech, which was a central component of what Wittgenstein called a form of life. Accordingly, the philosopher's task was not to construct an ideal metalanguage neutralizing the concrete mediation of the speaker, but rather to examine and clarify ordinary language within specific social contexts. Understanding the meaning of a word as its specific use, the ordinary language philosopher directed his attention to the performative as well as descriptive function of language, at sentences as speech acts (promises, assertions, commands, questions, and so on) as well as propositions

---

[2]Wittgenstein's fidelity to this view of language in the actual writing of the *Tractatus* has, however, itself been called into question. See Dominick LaCapra, "Reading Exemplars: *Wittgenstein's Vienna* and Wittgenstein's *Tractatus*," *Diacritics* 9 (Summer 1979), 65–82.

[3]Wittgenstein's later philosophy was preeminently expressed in his posthumously published *Philosophical Investigations* (New York, 1955); Austin's major work is *How to Do Things with Words* (Cambridge, 1962); Ryle's is *Concept of Mind* (London, 1949). For a general comparison of ordinary language philosophy and hermeneutics, see Gerard Radnitzky, *Contemporary Schools of Metaphysics*, 3d ed. (Chicago, 1973).

about the world. In Austin's terminology, such speech acts have three dimensions: a locutionary one, which conveys their propositional content; an illocutionary one, which conveys their force (the "I promise you that" or "I command you to"); and a perlocutionary one, which is actually what is done after the utterance is made. Because of their illocutionary force in particular, speech acts are to be understood essentially as communication between or among speakers, as intersubjective dialogues. In other words, language is an eminently social practice.

In France, linguistic philosophy has generally meant something very different than in England or Germany.[4] Here the turn came a generation later than in England. After the waning of existentialism, which at least in its Sartrean form paid little attention to language,[5] French culture discovered the revolution in linguistics begun by Ferdinand de Saussure before World War I and combined it with the ethnological speculations of Marcel Mauss to create the explosive movements that have become familiar to us as semiotics, structuralism, and post-structuralism. Abandoning the descriptive view of language, the proponents of these movements did not, however, embrace the English alternative of language as speech and intersubjective communication. Rather than focusing on meaning or intentionality, on the illocutionary dimension of utterances or speech acts, they explored what they saw as the deeper level of structural regularities that constitute language as an unintended and arbitrary system of diacritical signs, what in Saussure's now familiar terminology is the level of *langue* rather than *parole*. Interested less in the historical development of a linguistic system than in its synchronic relations, they tended to dismiss historical consciousness itself as a fictional construct no different from the other codes used in the present to order reality. The repetition of or transformations within a given set of relations interested them far more than change or process.

Although Saussure himself had seen speech as the basis of language, more recent post-structuralists, and here the obvious figure is

[4]The qualifier "generally" is necessary because there were and are French philosophers whose view of language is closer to German hermeneutics than to structuralism, i.e., Paul Ricoeur, Maurice Merleau-Ponty, and George Gusdorf.

[5]For a discussion of Sartre's relative neglect of language, see Dominick LaCapra, *A Preface to Sartre* (Ithaca, 1978), 26, and Joseph R. Fell, *Heidegger and Sartre: An Essay on Being and Place* (New York, 1979), 268f. It should be noted that in the decade before his death in 1961 Merleau-Ponty discovered Saussure and began to reflect on his importance in *Le visible et l'invisible*, published posthumously in 1964. For a discussion, see Albert Rabil, Jr., *Merleau-Ponty: Existentialist of the Social World* (New York, 1967), 197–204.

Jacques Derrida, have emphasized the primacy or at least the equivalent status of writing. With its unspecified audience and absent author, writing suggests the autonomous nature of language as a system beyond human subjectivity. In the name of an impersonal play of intertextuality rather than intersubjectivity, they have systematically deconstructed all received notions of the subject, argued against reducing meaning to the intention of original authors, and inflated the role of the critic or philosopher into that of a godlike producer of new combinations of linguistic signs. Stressing the silences and absences in language, they have sought to unmask the ways language disingenuously hides from itself its inability to represent anything outside its own boundaries.

In the hands of the most historically concerned of the post-structuralists, Michel Foucault, intellectual history has been turned into an archaeology of past discourses whose diachronic transformation into each other is virtually ignored. Grounded in a view of language as more like an archive or library—impersonal, self-referential, and beyond subjective mastery—than an intersubjective dialogue, Foucault's alternative to traditional intellectual history eliminates concern over the issues of origin, cause, source, influence, and purpose. Instead, it concentrates on discontinuities and ruptures, remaining radically hostile to any teleological or causal view of the course of history. Although Foucault's position has evolved somewhat over the years, some would say in a direction closer to hermeneutics,[6] and while he has by no means been universally accepted by all post-structuralists, as his widely discussed polemic with Derrida demonstrates,[7] his anti-subjectivist concept of language can be taken to represent the general French attitude of the past two decades.

In Germany, on the other hand, a very different linguistic turn occurred. To understand its roots would require a discussion of German cultural history as far back at least as the Reformation, when Protestants needed to find a way to interpret scripture once the authority of the Catholic Church was no longer binding. The resulting practice of biblical exegesis became known as hermeneutics in the middle of the seventeenth century, following J. C. Dannhauer's use of the

---

[6]See David C. Hoy, "Taking History Seriously: Foucault, Gadamer, Habermas," *Union Seminary Quarterly Review* 34 (Winter 1979); and the forthcoming book on Foucault by Hubert Dreyfus and Paul Rabinow.

[7]Derrida began the quarrel with an attack on Foucault's *Folie et déraison* (Paris, 1961) in *L'ecriture et la différence* (Paris, 1967). For an excellent account of their differences, see Edward W. Said, "The Problem of Textuality. Two Exemplary Positions," *Critical Inquiry* 4 (1978).

word in a book title.[8] Originally a Greek term, it referred to the god Hermes, the sayer or announcer of divine messages—often, to be sure, in oracular and ambiguous form. Hermeneutics retained its early emphasis on saying as it accumulated other meanings such as interpreting, translating, and explaining. Christianity had, of course, long emphasized the importance of the Word, Saint Paul having claimed that salvation comes through the ears. The sacramental character of speech continued to inform later hermeneutic theory as it widened beyond biblical exegesis. The *Sturm und Drang* philosopher Johann Georg Hamann, who shared with Vico a belief in the priority of poetry over prose, saw nature as the embodiment of a divine word that spoke to man.[9] Language and thought, he claimed against Kant and the Enlightenment, were one; abstractions violated the natural and sacramental character of the concrete word.

Although Kant and his successors in the idealist movement had little use for Hamann's irrational hermeneutics,[10] it was preserved and extended by the romantics, most notably the theologian Friedrich Schleiermacher. For Schleiermacher, all cultural creation and reception had to be understood as a process of continuous interpretation. His general hermeneutics went beyond the purely religious, legal, and philological uses to which it had previously been put. The understanding that marked everyday human interaction was hermeneutic in nature; all thought, Schleiermacher contended at an early stage in his career, was linguistic. Later he moved toward what might be called a more psychologistic version of hermeneutics in which the meaning to be recaptured was the original intention of a text's author, or even more fundamentally, his actual life experience. This latter assumption was also adopted later in the century by Wilhelm Dilthey in his attempt to ground the *Geisteswissenschaften* in a method of reexperiencing original intentionality. Under the impact of Husserl, Dilthey shifted away from a psychologistic version of hermeneutics in the last years of his life, but the concept of hermeneutics as the recovery of an

[8]J. C. Dannhauer, *Hermeneutica sacra sive methodus exponendarum sacarum litterarum* (1654). See the discussion in Richard Palmer, *Hermeneutics: Interpretation Theory in Schleiermacher, Dilthey, Heidegger, and Gadamer* (Evanston, 1969), 34.

[9]On Hamann's views of language, see James C. O'Flaherty, *Unity and Language: A Study in the Philosophy of Johann Georg Hamann* (Chapel Hill, 1952); and Harold Stahmer, *Speak That I May See Thee* (New York, 1968).

[10]Although idealism was antihermeneutic, its proponents did not lack an interest in language. Hegel, in particular, was concerned with its importance. See Daniel J. Cook, *Language in the Philosophy of Hegel* (The Hague, 1973). It should also be noted that Wilhelm von Humboldt's very influential theory of language was in part indebted to Kant. See the discussion in Cassirer, 155f.

original authorial intention of life experience has continued to influence later thinkers such as Emilo Betti, E. D. Hirsch, and, to some extent, Quentin Skinner.[11]

In certain circles, hermeneutics also preserved its links with its religious origins. Twentieth-century theologians like Martin Buber, Franz Rosenzweig, Friedrich Ebner, and Eugen Rosenstock-Huessy continued to share with Hamann a belief that divine revelation came through speech.[12] Committed to what the French post-structuralists would later damn as the "metaphysics of presence," they stressed the power of spoken language to unite subjects in a meaningful dialogue of common understanding, what Buber made famous as an "I Thou" relationship. In Paul Ricoeur's well-known terms, they practiced hermeneutics as a recollection of primal meaning, a recognition of an original message, rather than as an exercise in suspicion to demystify illusion.[13] The latter, Ricoeur contended, was best exemplified by Marx, Freud, and Nietzsche, none of whom is normally seen as primarily within the hermeneutics tradition.

Within the more secularized variants of modern German hermeneutics, however, it is possible to see the effects of both tendencies, often in uneasy tension within the same thinker's work. In two recent traditions particularly, that of *Existenzphilosophie* and Critical Theory, both impulses have been operative. Although Martin Heidegger's central preoccupation was the restoration of Being, his later work after his celebrated "turn" emphasized the extent to which language is prior to human intentionality and subjectivity.[14] The demystifying potential in this latter argument has been recognized by no less a deconstructionist than Derrida, who has turned it with Nietzschean ruthlessness against the nostalgic yearnings for wholeness in Heidegger's quest for Being.[15] In Critical Theory, similar yearnings can be discerned in Wal-

[11]Emilo Betti, *Teoria generale della interpretazione*, 2 vols. (Milan, 1955); E. D. Hirsch, Jr., *Validity in Interpretation* (New Haven, 1967); Quentin Skinner, "Motives, Intentions and the Interpretation of Texts," *New Literary History* 4 (Winter 1972), and "Hermeneutics and the Role of History," *New Literary History* 8 (Autumn 1975). For critiques of Betti and Hirsch from a Gadamerian standpoint, see Palmer, *Hermeneutics*, and David C. Hoy, *The Critical Circle: Literature and History in Contemporary Hermeneutics* (Berkeley, 1978).

[12]For a discussion of their work, see Stahmer, *Speak That I May See Thee*.

[13]Paul Ricoeur, *Freud and Philosophy. An Essay on Interpretation*, tr. Denis Savage (New Haven, 1970), 26f.

[14]For a discussion of Heidegger's philosophy of language, see Palmer, *Hermeneutics*, chapters 9 and 10; and the essays in Joseph J. Kockelmans, *On Heidegger and Language* (Evanston, 1972).

[15]Derrida's critique of Heidegger comes in his discussion of Heidegger's reading of Nietzsche in "La question du style," in *Nietzsche aujourd'hui* (Paris, 1973). See the discussion in Gayatri C. Spivak's translator's preface to Jacques Derrida, *Of Grammatology* (Baltimore,

ter Benjamin's speculations on a primal *Ursprache* and Jürgen Habermas's notion of an ideal speech situation, to which we will return shortly. But insofar as Critical Theory has been concerned with the unmasking of ideology, carried to its extreme in the antinomian moments of Theodor Adorno's negative dialectics, it must also be understood as practicing a hermeneutics of suspicion and demystification.

The tensions between the two impulses are in part responsible for the continued fecundity of the two traditions. Indeed, it might be said that the cutting edge of contemporary German hermeneutics is precisely where *Existenzphilosophie* and Critical Theory intersect, for it is here that the implications of the two types of hermeneutics have been most profoundly exposed. The central site of this intersection has been the ongoing debate between Habermas and the major disciple of Heideggerian hermeneutics, Hans-Georg Gadamer. Sparked in 1967 by Habermas's review of Gadamer's *magnum opus, Truth and Method*, the debate has gone through several cycles and generated a flood of secondary comment.[16] It is of particular importance for historians because Habermas specifically extended the scope of hermeneutics beyond philosophy and cultural criticism to the study of society itself. Like Peter Winch, A. R. Louch, and Hanna Pitkin in the ordinary language tradition,[17] and a host of authors in the structuralist

---

1976). It should be noted that Derrida's reading of Nietzsche is more radical than Ricoeur's in that he denies a desire for ultimate truth beneath Nietzsche's hermeneutics of suspicion. For Derrida, Nietzsche posits an infinite play of metaphoricality.

[16]Habermas, *Zur Logik der Sozialwissenschaften* (Frankfurt, 1970); tr. in *Understanding and Social Inquiry* ed. Fred Dallmayr and Thomas McCarthy (South Bend, Ind., 1977). Habermas's critique was aimed at Gadamer's *Wahrheit und Methode* (Tübingen, 1965); tr. as *Truth and Method*, by Garrett Barden and John Cumming (New York, 1975); several further exchanges are collected, with other contributions, in *Hermeneutik und Ideologiekritik* (Frankfurt, 1971). An English translation of one of Gadamer's replies can be found in his *Philosophical Hermeneutics*, tr. and ed. David E. Linge (Berkeley, 1976); another, with a rebuttal by Habermas, appeared in *Continuum* 8 (1970). The third edition of *Wahrheit und Methode* (1975) contains yet another reply.

The debate has stimulated widespread discussion; see Albrecht Wellmer, *Critical Theory of Society*, tr. John Cumming (New York, 1971); Karl-Otto Apel, *Transformation der Philosophie* (Frankfurt, 1973); Paul Ricoeur, "Ethics and Culture: Gadamer and Habermas in Dialogue," *Philosophy Today* 17 (Summer 1973); Dieter Misgeld, "Critical Theory: The Debate between Habermas and Gadamer," in *On Critical Theory*, ed. John O'Neill (New York, 1976); Anthony Giddens, *Studies in Social and Political Theory* (London, 1977); Thomas McCarthy, *The Critical Theory of Jürgen Habermas* (Cambridge, Mass. 1978); Hoy, *The Critical Circle*; and Jack Mendelson, "The Habermas-Gadamer Debate," *New German Critique*, 18 (Fall 1979). See also the special issue of *Cultural Hermeneutics* 2 (February 1975) devoted to the hermeneutics–Critical Theory controversy, which contains an extensive bibliography of relevant works.

[17]Peter Winch, *The Idea of a Social Science and Its Relation to Philosophy* (London, 1958); A. R. Louch, *Explanation and Human Action* (Berkeley, 1969); Hanna F. Pitkin,

and post-structuralist movement, he has speculated on the implications of a linguistic turn for social theory. Although the debate has not focused specifically on the issue of intellectual history, its implications are no less suggestive here than in other fields. Set against the hastily sketched backdrop of the other linguistic turns mentioned above and discussed elsewhere in this book, an examination of the confrontation between Habermas and Gadamer will help us to understand the opportunities and dangers latent in a basically linguistic approach to intellectual history.

Habermas's interest in hermeneutics was itself stimulated by Gadamer's work, so it is not surprising that they share a number of fundamental assumptions. Both reject the traditional philosophical view of language as a disinterested description of the real world, agreeing instead that it is a practical, intersubjective activity. Both see language, as Gadamer put it, as the "self-estrangement of speech," rather than a derivative of writing.[18] And both are interested more in the level of *parole* (or what the Germans call *Rede*) than *langue* (or *Sprache*). In Habermas's words,

> This abstraction of *language* from the use of language in *speech* (*langue* versus *parole*), which is made in both the logical and structuralist analysis of language, is meaningful. Nonetheless, this methodological step is not sufficient reason for the view that the pragmatic dimension of language from which one abstracts is beyond formal analysis. . . . not only language but speech too—that is, the employment of sentences in utterances—is accessible to formal analysis.[19]

Although the precise nature of this formal analysis in Habermas's work is not equivalent to Gadamer's hermeneutics, both thinkers reject the view that linguistic philosophy should study only underlying structures as synchronic diacritical systems. By emphasizing the rhetorical and pragmatic dimension of language as communication, they introduce an inevitable historical moment into their theories, which sets them apart from their French counterparts.

Gadamer, however, was a student of Heidegger's in Marburg dur-

---

Wittgenstein and Justice (Berkeley, 1972); for a critique of the work of Winch and Louch in particular, see Richard J. Bernstein, *The Restructuring of Social and Political Theory* (Philadelphia, 1978).

[18]Gadamer, *Truth and Method*, 354–355.

[19]Habermas, *Communication and the Evolution of Society*, tr. Thomas McCarthy (Boston, 1979), 6. Habermas's confidence in the formal analysis of language's pragmatic dimension seems to stem from the early work of Searle, who has more recently retreated from this position.

ing the 1920s, and remains indebted to a number of his major premises. Many of these were anathema to Habermas's mentors in the
Frankfurt School, and although he revised Critical Theory in several
crucial ways,[20] Habermas inherited their distrust of Heidegger's project.[21]
Gadamer's residual Heideggerianism has thus been at the heart of the
debate. Following his teacher, Gadamer has extended the scope of
hermeneutics beyond that of a method of the cultural sciences in
Dilthey's sense. Endorsing Heidegger's celebrated contention that
"language is the house of Being,"[22] Gadamer sees hermeneutics as
fundamentally ontological. That is, all human reality is determined by
its linguisticality (*Sprachlichkeit*). To understand any of it, therefore,
is to engage in a process, an endless process, of interpretive reflection. Because human beings are thrown into a world already linguistically permeated, they do not invent language as a tool for their own
purposes. It is not a technological instrument of manipulation. Rather,
language is prior to humanity and speaks through it. Our finitude as
human beings is encompassed by the infinity of language.

The second lesson Gadamer learned from Heidegger follows from
this ontological premise. Because humans are always in the midst of a
pregiven linguistic context, they can never achieve a transcendental
vantage point outside it. There can be no presuppositionless knowledge, no point of absolute origin. Knowledge can be gained only
experientially, through what Aristotle called *phronesis*, or practical
wisdom. It cannot be achieved by adopting the method of the natural
sciences in which a neutral observer confronts an objective world,
which he passively records. Method (that is, scientific method) is not
the way to truth. The "alienating distanciation"[23] of the sciences must
be replaced by a participatory involvement in the dialectics of subject
and subject and subject and object. Only by acknowledging one's
place in an already given interpretative context, the so-called hermeneutic circle in which parts illuminate wholes and vice versa, can one
correctly approach truth.

[20]For a discussion of Habermas's departures from classical Critical Theory, see Axel
Honneth, "Communication and Reconciliation: Habermas' Critique of Adorno," *Telos* 39
(Spring 1979).

[21]For Habermas's criticisms of Heidegger, see *Philosophisch-politische Profile* (Frankfurt,
1971). Gadamer, it should be noted, also differed with Heidegger on certain issues. For an
illuminating discussion of some of them, see Hubert L. Dreyfus, "Holism and Hermeneutics," *Review of Metaphysics* 34 (September 1980).

[22]Heidegger, *Platons Lehre von der Wahrheit: Mit einem Brief über den "Humanismus"*
(Bern, 1947), 53.

[23]This term is Ricoeur's: see his "Ethics and Culture," 156.

The third implication Gadamer drew from Heidegger's philosophy is that the scientific method was grounded in the untenable subjectivism that had dominated Western metaphysics since Plato. This subjectivism, which reached its apogee with Descartes, assumed that the individual subject could gain knowledge of reality, either deductively or inductively, through a monological act of consciousness. Instead, Gadamer contends, understanding is inevitably an intersubjective process in which the participants carry out an endless dialogue, an infinite translation. Because each participant is thrown into this flux, he is never able to achieve knowledge totally by himself or without the cultural presuppositions that inform his thought.

Finally, Gadamer learned from Heidegger to repudiate the premise underlying hermeneutics from the later Schleiermacher to the early Dilthey, and revived in our own day by Betti, Hirsch, and Skinner, the premise that interpretation means recovering the intentionality of the original author of a cultural product. "The meaning of a text," he insists, "surpasses its author not occasionally, but always. Thus understanding is not a reproductive procedure, but rather always a productive one."[24] Because it is impossible to suspend one's own linguistic presuppositions and cancel out one's own historical context, it is equally impossible to enter into the mind of another human being, especially one from an earlier era. "The meaning of hermeneutical inquiry," Gadamer argues, "is to disclose the miracle of understanding texts or utterances and not the mysterious communication of souls. Understanding is participation in the common aim."[25] Dilthey's belief that total empathetic reexperiencing is possible in fact betrayed a subtle capitulation to the Cartesian subjectivism of the scientific method, because it showed that he felt the present situation of the historian could be bracketed and the distance between the past and present nullified.

That distance, Gadamer claims, is less a source of error than a ground of truthfulness. For truth can be achieved only through what Gadamer calls the "fusion of horizons" between the original thinkers or texts and their historical interpreters. Defining horizon as "the range of vision that includes everything that can be seen from a particular vantage point," he contends that individual horizons are always partial.[26] Like language itself, truth transcends the particular

[24]Gadamer, *Truth and Method*, 264.
[25]Gadamer, "The Problem of Historical Consciousness," in *Interpretative Social Science: A Reader*, ed. Paul Rabinow and William M. Sullivan (Berkeley, 1979), 147.
[26]Gadamer, *Truth and Method*, 269.

95

horizon of any one participant in the hermeneutic process. It is rather a mediation of past and present, an "application" of the text to the contemporary situation, never an allegedly objective view of the past "in itself." History is thus neither a Rankean recovery of the past "as it actually was," nor a Crocean reduction of the past to contemporary consciousness, but instead an integration of the two.

Here parenthetically, one might note an important parallel, not always acknowledged,[27] between Gadamer and the antipsychologistic structuralists and post-structuralists who also fulminate against the reduction of meaning to intention. In fact, one recent observer has argued that Derrida, whose debt to the later Heidegger I have already mentioned, complements rather than contradicts Gadamer because of their common denial of objective knowledge, disdain for authorial presence, rejection of totalized experiences, and Nietzschean love for interpretive play.[28] The essential differences, of course, are that Gadamer has not gone as far as the post-structuralists in decentering the subject or replacing intersubjectivity by intertextuality. Nor has he argued, as has Foucault, for radical discontinuities in history, preferring instead to emphasize the possibility of fusing past and present. The characteristic violent gesture of *découpage* or rupture, which Edward Said has identified as common to many structuralists and post-structuralists,[29] is totally absent from Gadamer's approach. Although he clearly rejects the traditional philosophical view of language as transparent, he avoids the other extreme of assuming its perfect opacity. Language, as Heidegger stressed, is the site of disclosure, of "unhiddenness." While meaning may exist where it is not intended, it also may appear where it is. Even the texts of the past should be treated as potential partners in a process of dialogic communication, not merely as dead things to be decoded. Hermeneutics, in short, need not be reduced to a process of infinite demystification; meaning, if not simply recovered, can be produced.

Gadamer's hermeneutics is even more obviously comparable to the ordinary language philosophy of the later Wittgenstein. Both share a view of language as a practice or a game whose rules and procedures can be learned only experientially. But whereas Wittgenstein isolates his language games from each other as distinct forms of life, Gad-

---

[27]See, for example, the mistaken equation of Gadamer and Dilthey by Sande Cohen, "Structuralism and the Writing of Intellectual History," *History and Theory* 17 (1978), 176–177.

[28]Hoy, *The Critical Circle*, 77–84.

[29]Said, *Beginnings: Intention and Method* (Baltimore, 1975), 324.

amer, more universalistic in his approach, argues for the potential translatability of one game into another. Similarly, he contends that hermeneutic interaction begins only between already mastered primary languages, while Wittgenstein focuses instead on the acquisition of language through a process of socialization into a form of life. For Gadamer, discourse is more like a dialogue or translation than a process of socialization; it is the fusion of already given horizons, rather than the achievement of an initial horizon *ex nihilo.*

But perhaps most important for our purposes, Gadamer, unlike Wittgenstein, contends that preconceptions, which he provocatively calls prejudices, play an inevitable role in the process of understanding. Indeed, he claims that it is only through our prejudices that our horizons are open to the past. Because Gadamer stresses the impossibility of presuppositionless knowledge, history plays a role in his hermeneutics that it never plays in English ordinary language philosophy. "Understanding," he argues, "is essentially, an effective-historical relation."[30] By "effective-historical" (*Wirkungsgeschichtliche*), Gadamer means that each text has accumulated a history of effects or interpretations that are a constituent part of its meaning for us. It is thus impossible to cancel out the intervening mediations, suspend our own historicity, and recuperate the initial meaning of a cultural phenomenon. The "correctness" of an interpretation is thus not a function of its fidelity to an imagined pure reading of a text; truth, as we have seen, is a historical fusion of horizons.

Moreover, Gadamer contends, an awareness of the effective-historical dimension of understanding helps to denaturalize our own given perspectives:

> Only by virtue of the phenomenon and clarified concept of "temporal distance" can the specifically *critical* task of hermeneutics be resolved, that is, of knowing how to distinguish between blind prejudices and those which illuminate, between false prejudices and true prejudices. We must raise to a conscious level the prejudices which govern understanding and in this way realize the possibility that "*other* aims" emerge in their own right from tradition—which is nothing other than realizing the possibility that we can understand something in its *otherness.*[31]

Because of this avowed critical aim, Gadamer's position can be seen to have some resemblance to Ricoeur's hermeneutics of suspicion, for

---

[30]Gadamer, *Truth and Method*, 266.
[31]Gadamer, "The Problem of Historical Consciousness," 156.

he distrusts both the text and the interpreter. At the same time, however, he is clearly concerned as much with the achievement of new truths as with the destruction of illusion, and is thus never as radically suspicious as Derrida.[32] Whether or not Gadamer provides a viable criterion by which to test true and false prejudices is a question to which we will return shortly.

Because Gadamer links truth and historicity so strongly, and argues for the dialectical overcoming of the gaps between language games, it is tempting to see an affinity to Hegel in his thought.[33] But in several crucial ways he remains closer to Heidegger. Although his view of the critic and philosopher is less passive than Heidegger's, he shares with his teacher an aversion to Hegel's metasubjectivism, preferring instead a concept of linguisticality that is prior to the distinction between subject and object. More important, he denies the Hegelian idea of an absolute, rational *logos* underlying the historical process as a whole. Stressing the finitude of human experience, he rejects the omniscient claims of Hegel's *Wissenschaft*. In fact, in Hegel's terms, Gadamer's untotalized infinity of perpetual translation would be called a "bad infinity" because of its resistance to closure. In opposition to Hegel, Gadamer elevates the power of authority and tradition to a place in knowledge denied them ever since the Enlightenment, except by romantics and conservatives. For Gadamer, tradition furnishes the flow of ideas and assumptions within which we must stand; even reason, he argues, is encompassed by tradition, rather than superior to it.

It was precisely on this issue that Habermas's quarrel with Gadamer was first joined in 1967. Although by no means a simple neo-Hegelian, Habermas was and remains anxious to retain Hegel's emphasis on rationality and his belief that history as a whole is potentially coherent. In fact, as Rudiger Bübner has argued, Habermas was even closer to Hegel than were Adorno and Horkheimer because of his desire to construct the synthetic speculative system that negative dialectics had denied was possible.[34] Although a major component of

[32]For an interpretation suggesting Gadamer's allegiance only to the hermeneutics of recollected meaning, see David Halliburton, "The Hermeneutics of Belief and the Hermeneutics of Suspicion," *Diacritics* 6 (Winter 1976), 9.

[33]Gadamer has, in fact, written extensively on Hegel. See his *Hegel's Dialectic: Five Hermeneutic Studies*, tr P. Christopher Smith (New Haven, 1976). For a brief discussion of his affinities to Hegel, see Palmer, *Hermeneutics*, 215–216.

[34]Rudiger Bübner, "Theory and Practice in the Light of the Hermeneutic-Criticist Controversy," *Cultural Hermeneutics* 2 (February 1975). Bübner contends that Adorno's negative dialectics should properly be called reflection rather than theory, because the latter implies system.

the eclectic system that he has constructed is indebted to Gadamer's hermeneutics, Habermas was compelled to challenge the ontological reading of hermeneutics Gadamer had derived from Heidegger. While agreeing that it had a practical dimension ignored by Dilthey, he nonetheless returned to the more modest Diltheyan notion of hermeneutics as a method of the cultural sciences. In somewhat traditional terms, he has argued that natural scientific knowledge is based on a nonhermeneutical, instrumental use of language, which is appropriate to the subjective domination of a natural object. More important, Habermas claims that in understanding society as well, hermeneutics can take us only so far. "This metainstitution of language as tradition," he writes, "is evidently dependent in turn on social processes that are not exhausted in normative relationships. Language is *also* a medium of domination and social power."[35] By grounding reflection entirely in the context-dependent understanding of the participants in the linguistic tradition, Gadamer had provided no way to go beyond their everyday consciousness. By stressing the prejudgmental nature of all understanding, he has proscribed calling into question the legitimacy of the conclusions reached by hermeneutical discourse. In other words, Gadamer lacks the means to uncover or criticize the socially determined distortions in communication which may produce an irrational or illegitimate consensus. What in the Marxist lexicon is commonly known as ideology critique is thus impossible on Gadamer's premises, because he fails to distinguish between authority and reason. Lacking a standard of criticism, he is too tolerant of and too receptive to the voices of the past. The emancipatory impulse of the Enlightenment, the generalizable interest in liberation from illegitimate structures of authority, is thus lost to Gadamer's theory, whose implications are inherently conservative.

It is perhaps indicative of Gadamer's impact on Habermas that in trying to overcome the weaknesses of a pure hermeneutics, Habermas resorts in large measure to a linguistic theory of his own.[36] But it is a theory tied less to the explication of the past than to the possibilities of the future. In ways that are too complicated to spell out now in any

[35]Habermas, *Zur Logik der Sozialwissenschaften*, 287. In stressing the extralinguistic existence of power, Habermas is making a criticism of Gadamer similar to that of Derrida made implicitly by Foucault.

[36]In *The Critical Circle*, Hoy goes so far as to argue that "Habermas's own later shift toward a linguistic theory of communication as the basis for a *universal* hermeneutics vindicates Gadamer's reply" (124). What should, however, be added is that Habermas does not rely on his universal pragmatics alone to ground his emancipatory interest, but integrates it with several other theoretical schemes which are nonhermeneutically defended.

detail, Habermas argues for what he calls a "universal pragmatics" based on the implicit norm of perfect communication contained, to be sure counterfactually, in every intersubjective utterance.[37] Drawing on the Austinian distinction between the locutionary and illocutionary dimensions of speech acts, further developed in the work of John Searle,[38] Habermas contends that even without the idealist fiction of an a priori transcendental subject,[39] it is possible to isolate a normative telos in speech. In pragmatic terms, this telos is the rational testing of truth claims in an ongoing process of critical clarification. *"In the final analysis,"* he contends, *"the speaker can illocutionarily influence the hearer and vice versa, because speech-act-typical commitments are connected with cognitively testable validity claims*—that is, because the reciprocal bonds have a rational basis."[40]

Translated into social terms, this rational validity testing can take place only between or among equal subjects in nonhierarchical relationships. But because such social arrangements have rarely prevailed,

---

[37]Habermas, "What Is Universal Pragmatics?" in *Communication and the Evolution of Society.* For good accounts of Habermas's intentions, see McCarthy, *The Critical Theory of Jürgen Habermas*, 272f., and Albrecht Wellmer, "Communications and Emancipation: Reflections on the Linguistic Turn in Critical Theory," in *On Critical Theory*, ed. O'Neil.

[38]Searle, *Speech Acts*, (Cambridge, 1969).

[39]In earlier versions of Habermas's position, the transcendental nature of the anthropological interests he posited (an instrumental interest in the mastery of nature, a hermeneutic interest in linguistic consensus, and an emancipatory interest in liberation from illegitimate authority) was such that a number of critics argued that he had returned to Kant. In the introduction to a later edition of *Theory and Practice*, tr. John Viertel (Boston, 1973), he modified this position somewhat: "As long as these interests of knowledge are identified and analyzed by way of a reflection on the logic of inquiry that structures the natural and the human sciences, they can claim a transcendental status; however, as soon as they are understood in terms of an anthropology of knowledge, as results of natural history, they have an 'empirical' status." And in "What Is Universal Pragmatics?" he specifically distanced himself from Apel's "transcendental hermeneutics" for two reasons: "The idea underlying transcendental philosophy is—to oversimplify—that we constitute experiences in objectivating reality from invariant points of view. . . . However, I do not find any correspondent to this idea under which the analysis of general presuppositions of communication might be carried out. Experiences are, if we follow the basic Kantian idea, constituted; utterances are at most generated. . . . Moreover, adopting the expression *transcendental* could conceal the break with apriorism that has been made in the meantime" (p. 24). Despite these disclaimers, some Gadamerian critics continue to talk of Habermas's "transcendental narcissism." (See Hoy, "Taking History Seriously" 94.) Although this epithet, which is actually from Foucault's *Archaeology of Knowledge*, seems to me unwarranted, it is nonetheless true that Habermas's attempt to find a quasi- or nontranscendental vantage point is not without its problems. As McCarthy puts it, "the spectre of ultimate foundations still haunts the theory of cognitive interests; Habermas is not unaware of the problem but seems to feel that it can be remedied (if at all) only to the extent that the future progress of science leads to a unified theory of nature and society" (*The Critical Theory of Jürgen Habermas*, 403).

[40]Habermas, "What Is Universal Pragmatics?," 63.

the linguistic telos of undistorted communication has not hitherto been generally realized in history. Gadamer's purely linguistic focus cannot account for this situation for two reasons: first, because it lacks a criterion of rational discourse based on nonhierarchical relations, and second, because it cannot provide a causal analysis of social relations, which emerge as much from the dialectic of instrumental reason, or labor, as from that of symbolically mediated interaction.[41] Thus, despite his anti-idealist intentions, Gadamer falls back into an idealized model of always possible perfect communicability. He has no sense of the need for an institutionally secured public sphere in which discourse can take place undistorted by inequalities of power.[42] As a result, he implicitly considers ideology to be caused merely by linguistic misunderstanding rather than by the interaction of linguistic, power, and economic factors.

In order to engage in an effective ideology critique, Habermas contends, it is necessary to employ both hermeneutic reflection and the type of scientific methodology used to examine natural phenomena. As Georg Lukács pointed out in *History and Class Consciousness*, society under capitalism is experienced as if it were a "second nature." Although on the deepest level this is an illusion because society is historically mutable, it is an illusion that can not simply be dispelled by seeing through it, for it is rooted in social institutions and relations. In Habermas's early work, especially *Knowledge and Human Interests*, psychoanalytic therapy was offered as a model for the kind of combined hermeneutic and explanatory method necessary to emancipate men from the thrall of illegitimate authority. The hermeneutic dimension of therapy is crucial in relieving the patient's neurotic symptoms, which are essentially forms of distorted communication within the psyche; nonetheless, the therapist has to draw upon a theoretical framework that transcends his interaction with the patient. Although the ultimate justification for that theory is the patient's emancipation from his discursive blockages, the theory itself is grounded in a nonhermeneutic explanatory epistemology.

While he does not completely abandon the psychoanalytic model in his more recent work, Habermas has turned more to the develop-

[41]Habermas's distinction between these two dialectics was developed in one of his earliest works, *Technik und Wissenschaft als 'Ideologie'* (Frankfurt, 1968), as a corrective to the collapse of symbolically mediated interaction into the dialectic of labor in Marx.

[42]Habermas's first complete book, *Strukturwandel der Öffentlichkeit* (Neuwied, 1962), dealt with the concept of the public sphere and its historical implementation. His later work on language clearly follows from this early interest in public discourse. See the discussion in Jean Cohen, "Why More Political Theory?" *Telos* 40 (Summer 1979).

mental theories of Jean Piaget and Lawrence Kohlberg, the systems theory of Talcott Parsons and Niklas Luhmann, and the theory of historical evolution in Marx, all to be sure with revisions, to provide the extrahermeneutic criteria by which social and linguistic distortion can be measured. Whether or not these theories are themselves valid or can be integrated in a fruitful way is, of course, highly problematic. What must, however, be understood is Habermas's continuing effort to find a critical vantage point outside the hermeneutic circle by which to avoid the conservative implications of Gadamer's position. If we are to be paroled—no pun intended—from what Nietzsche called the "prison-house of language,"[43] it is to such efforts that we must turn.

For Gadamer, however, Habermas's attempts to get outside the hermeneutic circle have been in vain. In several replies to his challenge, Gadamer asserted once again the ontological quality of linguisticality. "There is no societal reality," he contended, "with all its concrete forces that does not bring itself to representation in a consciousness that is linguistically articulated. Reality does not happen 'behind the back' of language."[44] In other words, the dialectics of instrumental reason, labor, and social institutions cannot be examined without the inevitable mediation of language. There is no way to find an Archimedean point outside the hermeneutic circle.

Moreover, Gadamer contended, Habermas too hastily equates openness to the authority of the past with blind, dogmatic submission to tradition. For authority, which is not automatically wrong, may be willingly accepted through increased insight into its validity. In fact, he argued, "authority can rule only because it is freely recognized or accepted. The obedience that belongs to true authority is neither blind nor slavish."[45] Nor is it possible to hold all of our opinions up to the test of rationality at once; there is inevitably a measure of rhetorical persuasion involved in any of our beliefs. To think that reason can be opposed to tradition in every case is to posit an "anarchistic utopia" or a Robespierrean dictatorship of the *soi-disant* rational.

Finally, Habermas's specific attempt to find an extrahermeneutic vantage point in Freudian theory is misleading. The psychoanalytic encounter is between two individuals who share an a priori interest in the resolution of the neurotic symptoms of one of them. The analyst is

---

[43]Quoted in, and used as the inspiration for the title of, Fredric Jameson, *The Prison-House of Language; A Critical Account of Structuralism and Russian Formalism* (Princeton, 1972).
[44]Gadamer, *Philosophical Hermeneutics*, 35.
[45]Ibid., 34.

thus able, at least in theory, to bracket his own interests and work toward the common goal. Social interaction, in contrast, is among many different individuals or groups whose concrete, material interests may objectively clash. Possibly no amount of rational validity testing will lead to a perfect consensus. There is thus no necessary link between the ideal speech situation and the resolution of power-related material conflicts.

Recent defenders of Gadamer have added that his variety of hermeneutics is by no means as lacking in a critical dimension as Habermas has charged. Hermeneutics aims at the exposure of preunderstandings and prejudices in order to denaturalize the given perspectives of nonreflective participants in the linguistic process. In David Hoy's words:

> Criticism implies distance, and the distance introduced by the generality of philosophical reflection makes possible the negative move essential to criticism. But criticism must also be able to return constructively, and here greater methodological self-awareness makes actual interpretations more self-consistent and hence more legitimate. Finally, hermeneutics also contributes a basis for arbitration between different interpretations by demanding that the extent to which the interpretation has clarified its own assumptions and scope—and has remained consistent with those assumptions and within that scope—be made a further test for the interpretation.[46]

All of these criteria—self-consistency, clarification of assumptions, methodological self-awareness—are, however, internal to the interpretation itself and have little to say about the fit between the interpretation and its object, let alone the criterion of rationality. Even if one admits that the object of interpretation is a construct created by the fusion of horizons, there is still the problem of how one decides which fusion is superior. One possible answer, which is implied by Gadamer's undefended assumption of the universality of hermeneutic discourse, is that the more encompassing the interpretation, the better it is. But contained in this view is the harmonistic belief that horizons can be fused into bigger and better wholes, a notion that calls to mind

[46]Hoy, *The Critical Circle*, 130. It should also be noted that Gadamer strongly rejects the accusation that his position is relativistic in its refusal to seek absolutes outside of the hermeneutic circle. Following Heidegger, he sees hermeneutic reflection as allowing truth to be disclosed, contending that "the anticipation of perfect coherence presupposes not only that the text is an adequate expression of a thought, but also that it really transmits to us the *truth*" ("The Problem of Historical Consciousness," 154). But how perfect coherence and the disclosure of truth are to be verified Gadamer does not convincingly say.

Karl Mannheim's belief in a "relationist" totalization of conflicting views by the free-floating intelligentsia.[47] As the Frankfurt School showed in its frequent critiques of Mannheim, there may well be unharmonizable dissonances between different positions which resist fusion, at least until social conditions themselves are noncontradictory.[48] In other words, the reproach Gadamer made against Habermas's reliance on psychoanalysis as a model of social and linguistic totalization can be turned against his own optimistic assumption of fused horizons.

That Habermas's own notion of an undistorted speech situation may in general be open to this same charge is undeniable, but at least it is cast counterfactually as a future possibility, a kind of regulative ideal, rather than a present and past reality. Other questions about Habermas's own solutions may, of course, be easily raised, and they have been, especially by those beholden to other linguistic traditions. Aside from the objections made by contemporary defenders of a positivist view of language, such as Hans Albert, followers of French trends have introduced a number of troubling criticisms. Lacanians such as Samuel Weber, himself a former advocate of Critical Theory, have questioned the possibility of a fully rational discourse among subjects whose inherent capacity for reason can by no means be simply assumed.[49] Criticizing Habermas's reliance on an ego psychologistic reading of Freud, they have argued that the unconscious, understood in Lacanian terms as a perpetually decentering engine of desire, cannot allow the type of undistorted communicative discourse Habermas posits as the telos of language. The ideal speech situation is thus another form of that logocentric desire for perfect presence which dominated Western metaphysics for millennia. Derrideans like Dominick LaCapra have added that, lacking a concept of supplementarity, Habermas posits rigidly categorical distinctions that reproduce, against his

[47]For a comparison of Gadamer and Mannheim, see A. P. Simonds, *Karl Mannheim's Sociology of Knowledge* (Oxford, 1978), 92–96. Hoy, however, warns against too harmonistic an interpretation of Gadamer's position: "The term 'fusion' *(Verschmelzung)* is indeed misunderstood if it is believed, as some accounts of Gadamer seem to indicate, that the fusion is a *reconciliation* of the horizons, a flattening out of the perspectival differences. Although Gadamer does claim that a *single* horizon results . . . it must be remembered that a horizon is in flux and that the hermeneutic consciousness maintains a *tension* between the historical consciousness (of the past) and the strictly present horizon *(Gegenwartshorizont)*."

[48]For a discussion of their criticisms, see Martin Jay, "The Frankfurt School's Critique of Karl Mannheim and the Sociology of Knowledge," *Telos* 20 (Summer 1974).

[49]Samuel Weber, *Rückkehr zu Freud, Jacques Lacans Ent-stellung der Psychoanalyse* (Frankfurt, 1978). For a discussion of this and other Lacanian critiques of Habermas, see Rainer Nägele, "The Provocation of Jacques Lacan: Attempt at a Theoretical Topography apropos a Book about Lacan," *New German Critique* 16 (Winter 1979).

intentions, a hierarchical structure of domination.[50] Defending the inevitability of ambiguity in terms Gadamer would approve, LaCapra suggests that "from the perspective of ordinary and literary language, the ideal speech situation might in one sense appear to be a technocratic fantasy."[51] Even those who generally support Habermas have acknowledged certain unresolved questions in his critique of Gadamer. As Thomas McCarthy concludes in his admirable summary of Habermas's work, "the shadow of the hermeneutic circle (in its Gadamerian, neo-Wittgensteinian, Kuhnian form) has by no means been finally dispelled."[52] And Jack Mendelson, who is also a partisan of Habermas in the debate with Gadamer, follows Paul Ricoeur in arguing for at least a partial return to the earlier Frankfurt School's notion of an immanent critique in which the truth claims of a society's ideology are compared with its practice. This return is necessary, he contends, to avoid the overly abstract and ahistorical nature of the perfect speech situation:

> While in a sense the ideal of rational consensus may be immanent in language *per se* and not simply an external standard, in most societies it is bound to remain unarticulated in the actual culture. It becomes politically relevant as an ideal to be consciously striven for only in societies which have begun to approach it on the level of their own cultural traditions.[53]

Habermas's explication of his universal pragmatics is still very much in progress, so it is possible that he may yet meet some or all of these objections. In any event, it would be difficult to render a final judgment on the viability of his critique of Gadamer in the scope of this paper, even assuming I were fully equipped to do so. Instead, I would like to conclude with some observations about the relevance of the debate for the practice of intellectual history, in particular the issue of whether or not it should take a linguistic turn.

Most obviously, the Habermas-Gadamer debate reinforces the lesson learned from the ordinary language and structuralist critiques of the traditional notion of language as a transparent medium of expression and description. If language inevitably mediates meaning, indeed if it plays a constituent role in the creation of meaning, intellectual

[50]LaCapra, "Habermas and the Grounding of Critical Theory," *History and Theory* 16 (1977).

[51]Ibid., 263.

[52]McCarthy, *The Critical Theory of Jürgen Habermas*, 353.

[53]Mendelson, "The Habermas-Gadamer Debate," 73.

historians will have to pay some attention to the linguistic dimension of the texts they examine. How suggestive such an approach may be has already been shown by the pioneering efforts of Hayden White in *Metahistory* and *Tropics of Discourse*.[54] Although the boundaries between literary criticism and intellectual history need not be entirely dissolved, we have much to learn from our more theoretically self-conscious colleagues in that discipline.

The Habermas-Gadamer debate also draws our attention, however, to the fact that the intellectual historian who does want to incorporate linguistic insights into his work need not rely on only one paradigm of language to do so. Linguistic turns, as we have seen, may take very different directions. It may, in fact, be possible to integrate some of them, as Habermas's indebtedness to Austin and Searle and the common Heideggerian roots of Gadamer and Derrida suggest, but a fusion of the horizons of each is clearly no easy task. Choices, therefore, will have to be made. Because the tradition of hermeneutics has been most keenly interested in the question of history and has included historicity in its very definition of language, one can at least argue that it will be the most fruitful to follow. At the same time as it resists the naturalization of historical consciousness produced by a naively objectivist view of the past, it also avoids reducing history to an arbitrarily constructed fiction of the present.

Moreover, by jettisoning the earlier hermeneutic goal of perfect empathetic understanding of an authorial mind, Gadamerian hermeneutics frees us from the illusion that texts are merely congealed intentionalities waiting to be reexperienced at a later date. But at the same time, by resisting the radical antihumanism of structuralist and post-structuralist criticism, it reminds us that subjectivity, however that concept may be defined, can in fact be objectified, if in an inevitably mediated and imperfect way. Even if our intercourse with the past is through documents in the present, there is a dialogic component in that intercourse that cannot be put aside. Although it may well be that there is no perfectly centered subject lurking behind these texts, a subject which itself needs no further interpretation, it is nonetheless equally questionable to flatten out the distinction between subjectivity and objectivity to the point where no differences remain. Gadamerian hermeneutics, while avoiding what the New Critics W. K. Wimsatt

[54]Hayden White, *Metahistory: The Historical Imagination in Nineteenth-Century Europe* (Baltimore, 1973), and *Tropics of Discourse; Essays in Cultural Criticism* (Baltimore, 1978). See also the suggestive use of Saussure's notion of syntagmatic relations in George Armstrong Kelly, *Hegel's Retreat from Eleusis* (Princeton, 1978).

and Monroe Beardsley called the "intentional fallacy," also resists what might be termed the "anti-intentional fallacy" of the structuralists and post-structuralists.

Another critical insight in Gadamer's account of interpretation arises from what he calls the effective-historical dimension of all understanding. The historical fate of a work should be included in the meaning of the work for us. What Gadamer's student Hans Robert Jauss calls a "reception aesthetics" suggests that the reproduction as well as production of a text must be taken into account in its interpretation.[55] The history of a text's effects may well be more a chronicle of successive misunderstandings than perfect reproductions, that "map of misreadings" suggested by Harold Bloom,[56] but the potential for the specific distortions that do occur can be understood as latent in the original text. Thus, while it may be questionable to saddle Marx with responsibility for the Gulag Archipelago or blame Nietzsche for Auschwitz, it is nonetheless true that their writings could be misread as justifications for these horrors in a way that, say, those of John Stuart Mill or Alexis de Tocqueville could not.

One final implication of Gadamer's hermeneutics that merits comment concerns the notion of a fusion of horizons. Putting aside its problematic harmonistic implications, what this fusion suggests is, first, that historians themselves must be aware of their own historicity and, second, that they are themselves irrevocably changed by their reflective involvement with the past. Although it would be wrong to characterize this involvement simply as a form of surrender,[57] it is nonetheless more ambiguous in this regard than either the outmoded positivist objectification of the past or the more recent structuralist version of the historian as a detached decoder of the synchronic relations of the past preserved in the present.[58] Gadamer's defense of prejudice may well have conservative implications, but it reminds us that we delude ourselves if we think our present vantage point is somehow

[55]Hans Robert Jauss, *Literaturgeschichte als Provokation* (Frankfurt, 1970); for a discussion of Jauss's debt to Gadamer, see Hoy, *The Critical Circle*, 150f.

[56]Harold Bloom, *The Anxiety of Influence: A Theory of Poetry* (New York, 1973), 152. For a comparison of Bloom and Gadamer, see Hoy, *The Critical Circle*, 159f.

[57]Gadamer argues for a kind of surrender when he claims that "understanding involves a moment of 'loss of self' that is relevant to theological hermeneutics and should be investigated in terms of the structure of the game" (*Philosophical Hermeneutics*, 51).

[58]Lévi-Strauss once acknowledged that structure could be grasped only from the outside, whereas process and change can never be understood in this way ("La notion de structure en ethnologie" in *Sens et usages du terme structure* [The Hague, 1962], 44–45). It is thus highly questionable to assume the role of a detached anthropologist in examining the history of one's own tradition. See the discussion in Said, *Beginnings*, 335.

outside of history. Participation as well as distanciation is necessary to our understanding of the past. It is impossible, as some of the French post-structuralists seem to imply, to criticize the Western tradition from a position external to it.

Turning to Habermas's critique of Gadamer, there are two major lessons to be learned. First, Gadamer's Heideggerian ontologization of language need not be accepted without reservation.[59] As Ricoeur puts it in support of Habermas, "language is only the locus for the articulation of an experience which supports it. . . . everything consequently, does not arrive *in* language, but only comes *to* language."[60] Because certain social forms can be read as if they were languages, there is no reason to suppose their linguisticality exhausts their being. However one may wish to chastise Habermas for failing to see the supplementary ambiguities of his categorical distinctions, it is equally unwise to collapse the dialectic of labor completely into the dialectic of symbolically mediated interaction. Indeed, to understand and expose the distortions in the latter, one must have a grasp of the contradictions in the former. Intellectual historians must, therefore, continue to probe the interaction between texts and contexts through a combination of hermeneutic understanding and causal explanation. Even if the contexts themselves can be read as texts, as Ricoeur has suggestively argued,[61] here too a combination of *Verstehen* and *Erklärung* is necessary to make sense of the dynamics of their interaction with the texts themselves. Only by so doing will we be able to combine an effective hermeneutics of suspicion with one of recollected meaning, which seems to me the most fruitful way to enrich our intercourse with the past.

The second lesson suggested by Habermas's challenge to Gadamer concerns the critical implications of a method combining hermeneutic and nonhermeneutic insights. Habermas, as we have seen, faults Gadamer for his uncritical tolerance of tradition and prejudice as standards of judgment. Although Gadamer and his supporters have responded that hermeneutics does in fact contain critical standards by which to separate true from false prejudices, these have been relatively empty, imprecise, and self-referential. And as David Hoy has admitted, the central assumption of the universality of hermeneutic

[59]The same objection might be made against some of the post-structuralists—such as Derrida, who, in Hayden White's words, "is the minotaur imprisoned in structuralism's hypostatized labyrinth of language" (*Tropics of Discourse*, 280).

[60]Ricoeur, "Ethics and Culture," 162.

[61]Ricoeur, "The Model of the Text; Meaningful Action Considered as a Text," in *Interpretative Social Science*, ed. Rabinow and Sullivan.

discourse, which separates Gadamer from Wittgenstein, is itself incapable of being grounded hermeneutically.[62] What, moreover, is the hermeneutic justification for that "anticipation of perfect coherence" which Gadamer insists is "always at work in achieving understanding"?[63] Habermas has confronted this problem with great candor and struggled to find more rational criteria linking language and society, without, however, falling back into a discredited transcendentalism. He has remained true to the classical Frankfurt School insight that critique and rationality are intimately linked. Whether or not he has fully succeeded in demonstrating the nature of that link, of course, is still very much in dispute.

But what does seem to me indisputable is the need to pursue such a search. There are, to be sure, some commentators who would equate rational criteria with the establishment of hierarchy, which in turn becomes an excuse for domination. Gadamer himself darkly warns against the Robespierrean danger in Habermas's fetish of reason.[64] To avoid this implication, it has sometimes seemed necessary to go to the opposite extreme of embracing what Edward Said has called the "nihilistic radicality" of Derrida's infinite play of dissemination and supplementarity.[65] It is, however, an illusion to think that in so doing, hierarchy is somehow avoided. For as Hayden White has acutely noted in his discussion of the "absurdist moment" in recent criticism, the result of so total a rejection of reason, totalization, and coherence is to privilege nature over culture, and in fact nature in its most demonic forms.[66] Habermas, to be sure, may have underestimated the costs of his own choice, as critics of his ego psychologistic model of the psyche have contended. The older Frankfurt School theme of the domination of nature has, in fact, been relatively muted in his revision of Critical Theory.[67] But he has certainly remained faithful to his mentors' concern for the dangers of an irrationalist celebration of the natural.

Intellectual history is, of course, filled with unattractive examples of rationally judgmental readings of the past—Lukács' notorious *Die*

[62]Hoy, "Taking History Seriously," 94.
[63]Gadamer, "The Problem of Historical Consciousness," 153.
[64]Gadamer, *Wahrheit und Methode*, 3d ed., 534.
[65]Said, *Beginnings*, 343. LaCapra argues that "Derrida's approach does not sterilize utopian hope" (*A Preface to Sartre*, 224), but it is difficult to see how his nihilism avoids just this sterilization.
[66]White, *Tropics of Discourse*, 269.
[67]For an acute discussion of Habermas's attitude toward nature, see Joel Whitebook, "The Problem of Nature in Habermas," *Telos* 40 (Summer 1979).

Zerstörung der Vernunft comes to mind as a particularly insensitive case—and one would certainly not want a revival of Enlightenment historiography at its most naive. But in turning too eagerly to linguistic philosophy in any of its various guises and making it the sole or even primary source of our method, we risk losing the critical edge that rationalism, defended by Habermasian or other means, can provide. To avoid that risk, we must, to be sure, distinguish among various types of rationality—substantive, formal, objective, subjective, instrumental, technological, practical, and so on—in order to rebut the identification of reason with only one of its variants. Too often, in fact, such a reduction occurs, with the result that reason is rejected out of hand.

This sequence has perhaps been followed by certain contemporary linguistically inclined philosophers, Gadamer generally equating reason with the monological "subjectivism" of the scientific method and Derrida associating it with the logocentric desire for perfect presence underlying Western metaphysics. Because they are able to expose the vulnerabilities of these variants of reason, they move, perhaps too quickly, to a denigration of reason *per se*. Habermas's defense of reason as an intersubjectively generated quasi-regulative ideal entailed in discourse itself shows that these reductions of reason by no means exhaust its meaning. Indeed, the extraordinarily rich and fecund tradition of rationalism, in all its forms, is part of that "effective-historical consciousness" which constitutes the horizons of contemporary men and women. Intellectual historians ignore at their peril its power to give our intercourse with the past a valuable critical dimension.

To defend a rational moment in our method is not, however, to deny the importance of the recent turn in philosophy to linguistic issues. Just as the alternative between seeing language as either perfectly transparent or totally opaque is too rigidly posed, so too the opposition between a linguistically informed intellectual history and one indebted to traditional (or in Habermas's case, nontraditional) concepts of rationality is unnecessarily extreme. Whether the two horizons can be perfectly fused or must remain forever in a supplementary interaction is impossible to say. But without some dialogic play between them, our reading of the past will remain either anachronistic, in the sense of being indifferent to the liveliest philosophical currents of our day, or, what is worse, incapable of providing a critical perspective on the past and present in the name of a more attractive future.

CHAPTER FOUR

Triangular Anxieties:
The Present State of European
Intellectual History

HANS KELLNER

> When I contemplate the present age with the eyes of some remote
> age, I can find nothing more remarkable in present-day humanity
> than its distinctive virtue and disease which goes by the name of
> "the historical sense."
>
> Nietzsche, *The Gay Science*

I

> The historian looks backward; eventually he also believes back-
> wards.
>
> Nietzsche, *Twilight of the Idols*

When historians ponder the future, even the future of their own trade, the time is, at least in some small and very literal sense, out of joint; the future, that great generator of insecurity, must be defused, turned into a special variety of the past, a new sourcebook in the "lessons of history." Since the question "Where are we going?" almost invariably covers the question "Where are we?"—itself a surrogate for the question "Where have we just been?"—our logic or direction of inquiry will doubtless bear out the truth of Nietzsche's sarcasm about believing backwards.

The origin of inquiry into the future of anything is found in an apprehensive desire to grasp something that seems to be unraveling or slipping away; and concern for the future of academic disciplines is not to be found in a merely healthy curiosity about the opinions of one's colleagues. But what precisely is the nature of these anxieties? What are their origins? What forms do they assume? How do changes in the way intellectual historians perceive the challenges to their traditional tasks influence the kind of intellectual history that is being written? To ask such questions is to suggest a unanimity of voice and direction among historians which is clearly nonexistent. Furthermore, it is all too clear that to label a group of thinkers as the vanguard is to assume as proven the case one is about to test. Nevertheless, certain trends are becoming apparent. The pages that follow will focus on some of the issues that European intellectual history is addressing at present and will increasingly address in the future.

Areas of formal study are, in my view, complexes of defenses against particular anxieties, anxieties whose kaleidoscopic changes shape and blur the entire discourse of the field. This assertion can be made as relevant to biochemistry or astrophysics as to historical study, but it is the latter which is the subject here. The classic theory of anxiety, scattered and developed throughout Sigmund Freud's writings, follows the course of many of his ideas, from an early hydraulic model of sexual disorders to the later psychological subtleties of defenses and defenses against defenses. A brief survey of his notions on this matter will provide a clue to the problem at hand in intellectual history.

In an early undated draft, Freud speaks of anxiety as a "damming-up" of accumulated sexual tension, which is converted into a neurosis resembling coitus in its symptoms.[1] Soon after, he noted that the "psyche finds itself in the *affect* of anxiety if it feels unable to deal by appropriate reaction with a task (a danger) *approaching from outside*."[2] This "affect," however, may lead either to an anxiety attack as described above, or it may become a neurotic symptom, usually a phobia. The function of the symptom, Freud added in *The Interpretation of Dreams*, is "to avoid an outbreak of anxiety; the phobia is erected like a frontier fortification against the anxiety."[3] Anxiety is a response to the *perception* of external danger, of an "expected and foreseen" injury. As such it is related to instincts of flight for self-preservation, but it is by no means merely a fearful response to

[1] Sigmund Freud, "Extracts from the Fliess Papers," in *The Standard Edition of the Complete Psychological Works of Sigmund Freud* (London, 1966), 1:191, 195.

[2] Freud, "On the Grounds for Detaching a Particular Syndrome from Neurasthenia under the Description 'Anxiety Neurosis,'" *Standard Edition*, 3:122.

[3] Freud, *The Interpretation of Dreams*, in *Standard Edition*, 5:581.

imaginary troubles. Although Freud points out that there *is* an anxiety based upon ignorance, such as a savage's fear of solar eclipses, there is also an anxiety based upon "superior knowledge," such as the same savage's terror of the signs of a wild animal on a trail, signs that would tell a civilized observer nothing.[4] He concludes that the preparedness for anxiety—the apprehension that leads to action—is the expedient element, while the generation of anxiety—the onset of the attack itself—is inexpedient.[5] To abbreviate Freud's lengthy discussion of anxiety in the *New Introductory Lectures* of 1933, we note that the origin of anxiety, in his late opinion, is the fear of castration.[6] It is worth noting here that while the older Freud criticizes Otto Rank's notion that the act of birth was "the model of all later situations of danger,"[7] he had put forth such a notion himself—no mention of Rank—in his discussion of anxiety in the *Introductory Lectures on Psycho-Analysis* of 1916–1917. In sum, anxiety is *both* the prophylactic defense against a psychic attack *and* the attack itself, should the defense fail; it is also the general term for the condition under which the anxiety-as-neurotic-defense and the anxiety-as-hysterical-attack may take place. The etiology is a fear of castration, the loss of identity and definition provided by differentiation—and, lingering beside it perhaps, in Freud's mind, a repressed birth trauma. Anxieties about identity and origins, the sublimated descendants of castration and birth traumas, haunt intellectual history today.

Harold Bloom has described the "anxiety of influence" experienced by the poet who fears that competition with the great poetic fathers will render him speechless, without an identity.[8] Intellectual historians face a different problem. In a sense, the historian's anxiety today is "an anxiety in expectation of *being flooded*," to cite Bloom—flooded not by the past, but by the methodological competitors of our own day. Questions arise without answers; new developments seem only to confuse matters. Yet repression, the continuation of old ways, seems increasingly ineffective, that is to say, unrewarding. Adaptations must be made.

The traditional problem of intellectual history has been that almost none of its subject matter has ever been peculiar to it. While geneti-

[4]Freud, *Introductory Lectures on Psycho-Analysis*, in *Standard Edition*, 16:594.
[5]Ibid., 595.
[6]Freud, *New Introductory Lectures on Psycho-Analysis*, in *Standard Edition*, 22:86–87. The position developed in the later set of lectures is largely that of *Inhibitions, Symptoms and Anxiety* (1926).
[7]Freud, *New Introductory Lectures*, 88.
[8]Harold Bloom, *The Anxiety of Influence: A Theory of Poetry* (New York, 1973).

cists study genes, political theorists study governments, epigraphers study epigraphs, intellectual historians study . . . what? Not ideas as such, for these are the traditional fiefs of the philosophers. With one exception, intellectual historians have had to study the ideas of members of other discourses, whether philosophers, witch-hunters, or poets. The exception has traditionally been the study of historians themselves; that is, historiography has "belonged" to historians, if only as a questionable form of inbreeding. Recently even this preserve has been lost, as literary critics, theorists of narrative, poeticians of prose, and the like have begun to swarm over nonfiction texts of all sorts, spoiling the last refuge of "proper intellectual history"—that is, the historian writing about another historian's writing. In the hands of critics like Roland Barthes, Lionel Gossman, and Linda Orr, the historical text becomes a text among others, to be studied for the art of its composition, the devices required by the discourse of historical writing, and the means by which it claims to represent reality.[9] Historical writing thus becomes an instance of *writing*, historical representation an instance of *representation* in general, historical truth an instance of rhetorical *figuration*. The "historical" identity of the text becomes as secondary as that of a patient in a hospital gown; the name may be on the wristband, but what matters is on the chart. If, at the level of language, there is nothing to differentiate the historical text from other forms of "realistic" representation, the problem of identity becomes even more perplexing.

This question of identity—perhaps legitimacy is a better word— was recently taken up by Leonard Krieger in an article called "The Autonomy of Intellectual History."[10] Although the title suggests Louis Mink's essay "The Autonomy of Historical Understanding,"[11] Krieger

---

[9]See Roland Barthes, "Le discours de l'histoire," *Social Science Information* 6, no. 4 (1967); Lionel Gossman, "Augustin Thierry and Liberal Historiography," *History and Theory*, Beiheft 15 (1975); and Linda Orr, *Jules Michelet: Nature, History, Language* (Ithaca, 1976). Certain recent trends in historical poetics are discussed in Hans Kellner, "Le langage et la structure de l'histoire," in *Bulletin 2: Société des Professeurs Français en Amérique* (1977), 51–60, and in Kellner "Review Essay—Linda Orr, *Jules Michelet: Nature, History, Language*," in *History and Theory* 16 (1977), 217–229.

A linguistic approach to these matters is Roberto Miguelez, "Théorie du discours et théorie de l'histoire," *Dialogue* 13, (1974), 53–70. See also the literary critics on historical writing: Geoffrey H. Hartman, "History-Writing as Answerable Style," in *The Fate of Reading and Other Essays* (Chicago, 1975), 101–113; Paul Hernadi, "Clio's Cousins: Historiography as Translation, Fiction, and Criticism," *New Literary History* 7 (1976), 247–250; and J. Hillis Miller, "Narrative and History," *English Literary History* 41, (1974) 455–473.

[10]Leonard Krieger, "The Autonomy of Intellectual History," *Journal of the History of Ideas* 34 (1973), 499–516.

[11]In *History and Theory* 5 (1966), 24–47.

hardly inspires confidence in the assertion of his own title by calling intellectual historians "cuckoos in the historical nest," nor by displaying a bewildering series of enumerations of schools of intellectual history past and present, varieties of method, divergent definitions, and so forth. The confidence of the essay's tone is undercut by the briar-patch complexity of its structure. If intellectual history is "autonomous"—that is, possesses the right to make its own laws—Krieger has, quite correctly, noted the absence of a definable polity. In fact, in his recent study of Ranke, he suggests, on the basis of some comments on the role of ideas in the *History of the Popes*, that the "ostensibly scientific and political Ranke, then, leaves us with the intriguing thought that the only scientific universal history is intellectual history."[12] To cite Ranke as an unexpected ancestor in the family tree of intellectual history is to suggest that the lineage is as insecure as are the current family relationships, since Ranke has long been conventionally considered the founder of an archive-centered study of diplomatic politics.

While Krieger's essay was optimistic in its positive tone, but depressing in its elusive content, Hayden White in a 1969 article addressed the same subject in a funereal voice, only to find a new source of hope for intellectual history outside the "profession." Noting that "as historical reading, intellectual history is rather like vicarious sex; neither satisfying nor, ultimately, very helpful as a guide to action,"[13] White states quite bluntly that the most fruitful intellectual history of recent times has been done by philosophers, art historians, literary critics, scientists—scholars, like E. H. Gombrich, Thomas Kuhn, Michel Foucault, Roland Barthes, or Lucien Goldmann.[14] White, who has written some of the most significant work to date on the nature of historical discourse, now calls his own field "cultural criticism," and he directs a program in the "history of consciousness." Similarly, a thesis on, say, Diderot and Hegel is today more likely to be written in a department of comparative literature than in a department of history; and one may pick a book with the title *Gödel, Escher, Bach*, written by a professor of computer sciences.

Yet another indication of this loss of definition is the emergence of new journals to prominence, journals which are by no means historical in the traditional academic sense, yet which publish some of the best thought today about figures of long-standing canonical interest to intellectual historians. Titles such as *Diacritics, New Literary History,*

[12]Leonard Krieger, *Ranke: The Meaning of History* (Chicago, 1977), 158.
[13]Hayden White, "The Tasks of Intellectual History," *The Monist* 53, no. 4 (1969), 608.
[14]Ibid., pp. 616–623.

New German Critique, and *Telos*, to name but a few, are much more likely, in any given issue, to provide fresh insight into major cultural texts than is the true blue *Journal of the History of Ideas* or the true but no longer blue *American Historical Review*.

The traditional rhetorical figure of intellectual history has been periphrasis, the circumlocution of an essential position. Central to this tactic is the prior extraction of a vital core in the text or corpus of texts to be studied, and the focusing of all aspects of these texts back upon this core. This assumption of unity, which has been just as tyrannical for historians as it *used* to be for critics, dominates the method of intellectual history; it is not easy to conceive of an intellectual history without it. In approaching a figure like Rousseau—a figure whose stature is preselected and focused by that great lens, the canonical tradition—we assume a fundamental meaning, an *Ur-Rousseau*, which must be found either in the texts or, more likely, in the tradition of Rousseau scholarship. Once this center has been hypothetically identified, the *possibility* of "reading" Rousseau is secure despite the variety of available strategies:[15] the center may be questioned by revisionists; or isolated aspects of Rousseau's corpus may be found to contradict it; or certain divergences from the core meaning may be posited either before or after the core in the form of developmental stages or degenerative lapses; or the meaning of the core itself may be found to be demonstrably ambiguous, inconsistent, or self-contradictory. None of these tactics denies or in any way compromises the assumption of the unity of meaning in a text—of Rousseau's identity, to put it another way. They are rather the poses which this prior assumption makes possible; this is what "interpretive" intellectual history is all about. Because this attitude privileges the *communicative* (and particularly the *referential*, to use the terminology of Roman Jakobson) model of a text, at the expense of other possible facets, it has been accused by recent critics and philosophers of making "an unwarranted presupposition of coherence."[16] Jonathan Culler describes these presuppositions: "The work tries to express an essence which presides over it as its source and its purpose. To capture the truth of the work is to recapture that essence and make it

[15] A notable example of interpretation that systematically questions the possibility of reading is the work of Paul de Man, especially *Allegories of Reading* (New Haven, 1979), in which Rousseau is discussed at length.

[16] Jakobson's influential essay "Linguistics and Poetics" may be found in *The Structuralists: From Marx to Lévi-Strauss*, ed. R. and F. De George (Garden City, L. I., 1972), 85–122. A full discussion of modern trends in literary structuralism is Jonathan Culler's *Structuralist Poetics: Structuralism, Linguistics, and the Study of Literature* (Ithaca, 1975).

present to consciousness."[17] Surely, this "nostalgic desire to recover essences" has been a hallmark of the general anxiety of the intellectual historian. Whether or not we wish to view the nostalgia for essences as a desire for a more secure—that is, prenatal—fantasy state, this presumption of coherence remains the primary historical defense. Indeed, history itself is the existential projection of this anxiety. But challenges have appeared fairly recently which call so much into question that new adaptations and accommodations have arisen, different, but no less anxious.

The questions must inevitably arise: What is a historical treatment of a source? Where may we draw a line to distinguish between treatments of past texts that are historical and those that are not? May the historically trained, those of us who were trained to share historical anxieties, ignore those whose anxieties are different when they confront the texts with which we are, as a group, familiar? If we do not ignore them, what imitative symptoms must be adopted in order to defend ourselves against the dangers they pose, most particularly the striking loss of differentiation and definition which they represent, without succumbing to *their* anxieties?

II

We cease to think when we refuse to do so under the constraint of language; we barely reach the doubt that sees this limitation as a limitation.

Nietzsche, *The Will to Power*

The anxieties about intellectual history's loss of identity, both as a field and as a method, have led its practitioners to pay a great deal of attention to matters that were until recently relatively unproblematic. Language and hermeneutics have become virtual obsessions, although there is certainly no developing consensus about what the proper role of linguistic or hermeneutic studies ought to be. In most cases, to be sure, historians' responses to the "dangers" of language studies or hermeneutic method have been rather cheerful suggestions that aspects of those methods may be profitably incorporated into the ever-flexible methodology of intellectual history, so that the traditional goals may be more effectively pursued.

[17]Jonathan Culler, *Flaubert: The Uses of Uncertainty* (Ithaca, 1974), 17.

Historians' awareness of language as a general focus of interest and as a special and pressing problem is no secret. Nancy Struever notes in her essay "The Study of Language and the Study of History" the "early and brazen case of poaching" on the territory of intellectual history found in Noam Chomsky's *Cartesian Linguistics*, but suggests that Chomsky's "rather threatening humanism" must be confronted in the forms of structural and sociolinguistics by the "modestly equipped historian."[18] Although her treatment is sympathetic overall to the projects and accomplishments of the linguistic tendencies she discusses, Struever notes rather sharply that the most challenging approaches, those of Foucault and Chomsky for instance, have each failed in one way or another. History itself, in her complex recounting of this recent work, is defined as the mediator—that which recognizes the challenge from formal linguistic theory, but which, like Dürer's knight, remains steadfastly on course.

The final tidings Struever brings to historians on the subject of language is: fear not. She writes: "The Humanist portents of contemporary linguistics cited at the beginning of this paper need not be threatening, then, but cheering. And historians should feel not only cheered, but braced."[19] Because of the nice balance found among the range of structuralists, hermeneuticists, sociolinguists, and grammarians, the field has divided itself into "incompatible and inseparable" approaches—the extralinguistic and the endolinguistic—and because historians have long specialized in straddling these aspects, we may cheerfully note that we straddlers are adequate to history, while *they*, despite great descriptive or theoretical virtues, are not. A bit of imitation, protective coloration as it were, will dispel the anxieties provoked by these threatening poachers who fail to respect historical obsessions. However, as often as Struever suggests that historians should be recognized as active participants in the discourse which they form, the thrust of her essay suggests the *re*-activeness of recent thought; it is difficult to determine whom history as a form of thought has threatened, challenged, or even braced in recent years.

Far more formal and less speculative than Struever is Nils B. Kvastad in his essay "Semantics in the Methodology of the History of Ideas." Stressing the need for careful categories of definition (such as narrative, descriptive, or real), and for precise methods of determining such vital issues as synonymity and ambiguity, Kvastad wants to

---

[18]Nancy Struever, "The Study of Language and the Study of History," *Journal of Interdisciplinary History* 4 (1974), 401.
[19]Ibid., 415.

establish historical semantics as a bedrock of interpretation which will attain a formally logical state, a sort of translation to the history of ideas of the "covering law" notions of Hempel and Popper. To his credit, Kvastad repeatedly stresses the importance of ambiguity, a flexibility of interpretation, and the difficulty of establishing definiteness of intention while "dealing mostly with dead authors";[20] nevertheless, he concludes with the familiar apprehensions. Lagging behind general history, "the history of ideas is in its infancy." Semantic studies must become part of the historical discourse. "The reason is that when the foundation of a house is shaky, it does not make much sense continuously to add new stories to it."[21] This rather alarming suggestion of imminent architectural collapse has not prompted, to my knowledge, any widespread cessation of work in historical construction; however, the anxiety that historical writing has been seriously undermined by its inattention to language has not been quite repressed.

Arthur Danto, in an essay titled "Historical Language and Historical Reality," has followed a more philosophical path than Kvastad, but a path toward the same goal. The philosopher quickly trims the sails of his subject by stating at the outset that the "philosophy of history is just philosophy writ small."[22] In the same vein, he writes that the "deep but easily sloganized intelligences of the past, Hegel, Marx, Nietzsche, or Freud" seem destined to live on, reduced to "what men smaller and sillier than they believe them to have said."[23] The "historically real x" decays into the "historically apparent x." Danto proceeds to clarify matters by blasting "shallow naturalism," "stale games" (of continental philosophers, naturally), "dumb oscillations and proto-paradoxes"—in short, he gives a small dose of philosophical salts to purge the small problem of historical reality. Danto's superb philosophical belief in the fundamental triviality of the problem of representation in language and his confidence that the difference between the "historically real x" and the "historically apparent x" disappears when causal and semantical information are analytically distinguished,

[20]Nils B. Kvastad, "Semantics in the Methodology of the History of Ideas," *Journal of the History of Ideas* 38 (1977), 168.

[21]Ibid., 174. The only evidence for the immaturity, inadequacy, or illogic of intellectual history is the absence of consensus in the historical interpretation of texts. The presumption that interpretive agreement is the standard of academic maturity mirrors the general assumption of univocal coherence in the texts themselves. "Textuality," the sensitivity to the way in which texts generate alternate meanings, is ignored.

[22]Arthur Danto, "Historical Language and Historical Reality," *The Review of Metaphysics* 27 (1973), 219.

[23]Ibid., 244.

certainly never address the problem of representation itself, nor the structural slippage of signifieds beneath signifiers, nor any of the other "stale games" played by the perfidious continentals. Nevertheless, he finishes his essay with an evocation of historical anxiety as frightening as any: "our actions lose their point and, in dramatic cases, our lives their purpose," when our belief in *real* history is shattered. "For when the past is in doubt, a question mark blurs the present, and, since we cannot will falsehood, our lives persist unclearly until history-as-science has had its say. The present is clear just when the relevant past is known."[24] Ignorance of the present, we should recall, is the cursed situation of the shades in Dante's *Inferno*, and the anxiety of Danto's.

Language studies seem to have no clear single place in historical methodology. Philosophers want a highly restricted protocol for reading; some semanticists want a formalized understanding of the linguistic processes of definition which lead toward a full semantic dimension; some historians want to use the work of socio- and structural linguistics as broadly as possible in forming models. Even as traditional and antitheoretical a historian as J. H. Hexter sees himself as a student of historical language, of the changing meaning of words, and of the emptiness of most generalizing terms we use. What is shared by these people is an anxiety that the meaning of the past (and with it so much more) is lost (or remains uncaptured) by misnaming or misreading. Whether or not Ranke is to be considered a father of intellectual history—a dubitable paternity, to say the least—we must note that he *was* first of all a philologist, a student of language. However, the nineteenth-century philological concern with authenticity of texts and editions and Ranke's own skills at recognizing the intentions of their creators do not address the modern problems of reading, the density or supplement of meaning created by the reader or the language or the act of writing itself. For this sensitivity, the work of Ranke's contemporaries Schleiermacher, Droysen, and Humboldt seems more to the point. It is hermeneutics, rather than philology, interpretation rather than verification, that defines the anxiety of intellectual history these days.

Quentin Skinner has described the turn from empirical and positivist theories of meaning toward more hermeneutical approaches to texts in an article "Hermeneutics and the Role of History."[25] He cites the

[24]Ibid., 259.
[25]Quentin Skinner, "Hermeneutics and the Role of History," *New Literary History* 7 (1975) 209–232.

revival of a hermeneutical tradition in the work of Gadamer, Ricoeur, and Habermas, as well as the current interest in Wittgenstein's study of language games rather than verification procedures, as signs of a challenge to the traditional practice of intellectual history, which attempts to capture and restate the correct meaning of a text in terms of extrinsic (biographical, social, political, etc.) information. Skinner is nonetheless very much the historian (that is, his anxieties are traditional historical anxieties) in his optimistic conclusion, which greatly softens the confrontation between the two approaches. His tactic uses two standard distinctions. The first and more crucial is between text and context. Once this distinction, which has been severely challenged by recent literary criticism from a number of directions, is granted, a system of reciprocal hermeneutical relationships—the famous "circle"—may be posited, leading to a second distinction between "autonomous" and "heteronomous" texts. Skinner makes the telling point that the interpretive approach based upon contextual study (and this includes most traditional histories of various sorts) "is based on a misleading overstatement which consists (in effect) of assimilating all works of literature to the category of strongly heteronomous texts."[26] The reverse of the contextual approach, however, the privileging of the autonomy of the text and a consequent emphasis on textual or internal interpretive strategies, is only a mirror image of the problem of the first approach. To assimilate all texts into the category of "autonomous" texts fails, in Skinner's view, as much as their assimilation into the category of "heteronomous" texts. While the relationship of autonomous and heteronomous texts derives rather obviously from the prior distinction between text and context, and while these distinctions have been standard among historians for a long time, it is not clear to me how such distinctions can be made except on the basis of prior interpretive decisions. Skinner's sensible spirit, like Struever's, takes the conciliatory position that both approaches should be followed (ritually, as it were), even if "such a process of checking adds little to our original sense of the text."[27] The anxiety about the loss of "text and context," the strong contrast of foreground and background, which has been essential to historical study, is overcome by Skinner through an a priori assumption, which he implies is self-evident, but which is not.

The easy generosity of spirit shown in Skinner's essay is challenged somewhat by Frank Kermode's recent study of the regulation of inter-

[26]Ibid., 227.
[27]Ibid., 228.

pretation by institutions. Using the example of the early Christian fathers as a model of the development of institutional control of texts and their interpretation, Kermode compares the establishment of a canon of sacred books—a long, bitter, and momentous task—with the establishment of a canon of secular, intellectual, and literary texts. It is this canonicity, established by the "profession," which designates what is a "text"—that is to say, what is worthy of foregrounding and study in the first place.[28] To be sure, the canon does change as the institution which designates it and which issues the "licenses for exegesis" that one must possess to enter discussions such as this one, responds to external pressures, enthusiastic movements, and the like. (These comments obtain, of course, only in those places where a reasonably open intellectual life is possible.) Surely, the institutional control of hermeneutic possibility, which Kermode guardedly approves, responds to an anxiety similar to that of the early Church. It is anxiety before these multiple historical interpretations which leads Kvastad to call intellectual history an infant, while Danto merely notes the "smallness and silliness" of some historians. The vision of a similar profusion of sacred texts, a profusion of orthodox readings, and a profusion of accredited interpreters is as academically frightening as it is theologically disturbing, and for similar reasons: both anxieties dread the loss of a truth or meaning necessary to saving something, whether a soul or the past.

Yet the past *is* lost, of course, in the sense of its unrecoverability as present; we recall it not as living memory, but as a series of catalogued signs, the archive, the canon. This loss of living memory is a very old anxiety, but as Paul Ricoeur notes in his essay "History and Hermeneutics," this very loss, and the separation of knowledge and history, may also be taken as opportunity, the hermeneutic opportunity.

> It is still possible to argue with Plato that the perversion of the historical bond begins with recourse to external marks which come to serve as traces for subsequent generations. This primary misfortune is the externalization of memory in such marks. Plato's famous argument against writing in the *Phaedrus* (274e–277a) applies to historical objectification to the extent that it sets in opposition two forms of memory, the one internal and based on the requirements of true reminiscence, the other external and submitted to the condition of marks and imprints. History,

[28]Frank Kermode, "Institutional Control of Interpretation," in *Salmagundi* 43 (1979), 72–86.

after all, is a particularly explicit case of remembrance by means of traces and imprints. Plato's sharp attack against externalization in marks and his ringing defense of reminiscence without external mediation forbid our simply recognizing the fact of temporal distance. It is why we need to introduce a principle of distantiation, which is a form of putting something at a distance rather than the mere fact of being at a distance.[29]

Rather than concede Plato's ancient case against writing, a case which makes our entire tradition and our profession in particular seem diseased in its essence, Ricoeur finds the "distantiation" or "externalization in marks" to be the augmentation of reality, and the mediation which "gives temporal distance its true significance."[30] Because this gap may be seen itself as textual, a hermeneutic arises that may claim ultimately to undermine the text/context dualism of traditional historical method, as well as undermining the distance between past and present. The "paradox of historical methodology" in Ricoeur's view arises from the double interest it serves: the interest for knowledge (which implies a naturalistic, scientific history), and the interest for communication (which implies an evaluative, interpretive history). However, Ricoeur's view of this dualism is as irenic in a practical sense as Struever's or Skinner's; the paradox is not paralyzing, because "the two interests do not exclude each other, but mutually imply each other."[31]

The hermeneutic interest demonstrated by current historiography and philosophy of history, like the interest in language described above, is a symptom, a defense against a primal anxiety—ironically, fear of *the domination of the past by the present*. The traditional defenses against such anxieties, which threaten a loss of identity through a loss of origin, have been a nostalgia for lost essences, the desire to abolish or deny the textual slippage inherent in writing, and the attempt to control the dangerous "intrinsic" of a text by appealing to the allegedly more secure "extrinsic" of its context. These hermeneutics share with semantics and analytical philosophy a desire to rediscover a past-as-reality, without repressing the ever-urgent (almost libidinal) pressure of the present-as-interest. In privileging the past, even in so circuitous a way as suggesting that we cannot know our own present without a dose of the past-as-reality (an ethnocentric suggestion that arrogantly dooms vast numbers of societies and indi-

[29] Paul Ricoeur, "History and Hermeneutics," tr. David Pellauer, *The Journal of Philosophy* 73 (1976), 691.
[30] Ibid., 692.
[31] Ibid., 695.

viduals to self-ignorance), one proves one's loyalties, that one's anxieties are in the right place. The dualisms of text and context, autonomous and heteronomous, endolinguistic and extralinguistic, all of which history is supposed to encompass with humanistic virtuosity by using "distantiation" to overcome distance, are never relinquished, never deconstructed. At most a "transcendence" into a metalanguage is posited, but the cheerful admission of small homeopathic doses of various approaches into the body historical seems to aggravate at least two disquieting matters noted above—the loss of an identity, a differentiation for historical studies; and the ingress of ideas, methods, inspirations, and fads into historical thought without a corresponding egress.

III

> *Historia abscondita.*—Every great human being exerts a retroactive force: for his sake all of history is placed in the balance again, and a thousand secrets of the past crawl out of their hiding places—into his sunshine. There is no way of telling what may yet become part of history. Perhaps the past is still essentially undiscovered! So many retroactive forces are still needed!
>
> Nietzsche, *The Gay Science*

Thus far I have noted that the anxieties inevitably constituent of any formal study have recently been focused upon a loss of identity in intellectual history. The incursion of a powerful movement in literary criticism, which has increasingly chosen to treat all texts as *formally* equivalent and responsive to the same rules of "textuality" had led historical thought, and intellectual history in particular, to study in self-defense the role of language and of hermeneutics to an unprecedented extent.

For the past century, historical method has uneasily faced principles of interpretation which challenged the "common-sense," periphrastic, and antijargon rules that have been the basis of "gentlemanly" history, and has sought to demystify ideological obfuscations, to analyze latent forces, or to excavate deep structures. These hermeneutic tendencies, the traditions of Marx, Freud, and Saussure, do not claim the majority of intellectual historians as party members or even as fellow-travelers. Nevertheless, I believe that Marxism, psychoanalysis, and structuralism create a triangular field of forces, with each point exerting a powerful magnetic pull on all within. To be pulled toward one point is to be pulled away from the others; to "belong" on one point of the triangle creates an ironic sense of loss (for what is "reductionism" if not a loss of scope and flexibility?) that leads increasingly to anxious defenses and adaptations. The new anxieties, which have seemed especially pronounced during the past decade, derive from this triangular field of interpretive strategies. These trends affect the books published in the field, the substance of academic debates, and the vocabulary that all must use in addressing texts.

One significant aspect of the emergence of the hermeneutic movements of the past two decades has been a struggle within each complex of ideas to establish just the sort of power relationships described by Kermode. The issue of canonicity, for example, has come to the fore as the groups scramble to decide the authority of texts. Who, for example, may be admitted into the canon of the Freudian tradition, and who expelled? Who will be assigned to apocrypha or to heresy? Is Foucault a structuralist? How are we to reread Hegel so as to admit the Frankfurt School (both echt and neo-) into a Marxist mainstream? These and innumerable related questions will proliferate in the absence of a professional or an extraprofessional tribunal of judgment or intimidation. Indeed, we may hypothesize that the weakness of the "profession" as a secure, reward-and-penalty-dispensing agency in the past decade has encouraged the creation and collision of new canons. What we are dealing with here is politics—that is, a struggle for power—without much in the way of stakes beyond the profession itself. This creates a great deal of surface movement, and engenders a sort of nervous agility that does not disturb the fundamental shape of things.

Reports of summaries of recent work have become a new genre. Americans, in particular, seem hungry for news of the fortunes of English psychoanalysis after Winnicott, or how the French go about "forgetting" Foucault, or the extent of Habermas's accommodations to liberal democracy. Of course, one of the great practical uses of such reports is to sum up and digest difficult and scattered work in a field. The primers on structuralism and semiotics, or existential Marxism, or French Freud, or the Frankfurt School, all serve to overcome the necessary concern of an American academic audience that it cannot be *sur-le-champ*. But they also carry with them a certain privilege for their authors, who gain from them the right to speak both about the figures within a tradition and about the tradition itself.

A second notable trend in recent scholarship in European intellectual history has been the spate of works on already canonical figures written with the clear intent of rereading them "into shape." Just as a scientist must, in Thomas Kuhn's view, return to nature and "beat nature into shape" after a paradigm shift, so the recent studies of thinker after thinker have reflected the need to reinterpret the canon in the light of Derrida, or Habermas, or Erikson. Freudians write about Freudians, Marxists write about Marxists, and structuralists about structuralists, as well as about their putative intellectual ancestors. The point of this work is not quite to establish the canonicity of these figures, although in some cases (that of Walter Benjamin, for example) the status of the writer has been rapidly elevated. Rather, the interest served by the extensive writing *of* the converted *to* the converted has been that of establishing a right to speak with authority from within the tradition. As such, these works serve the same political purpose as the ones I have discussed above. However, because they are more strictly retrospective, they also serve to reshape the traditions with which they deal. As the post-Derrideans reread Descartes and Kant, as Habermas (and countless others) reread Benjamin and Dilthey, the shape of these figures changes, *their* field of force changes in direction and amplitude. To mention their names is thereafter to invoke a new problematic. The anxious contention of the old canon with the new hermeneutics produces, among other things, a lot of discourse, as it is meant to do.

There is a third element to the hermeneutic wave, however, and it is upon this element that I would like to focus attention here. I refer to the "triangular anxieties" shown in the mutual confrontation of the Freudian, structuralist, and Marxist camps. In general, I should note that anxieties arise in historical thought when something is perceived to be lost or excluded, and that the triangle of hermeneutic camps divides the field—context, intention, and textuality—between them. Freudians will, to be sure, continue to write their form of psychohistory; Marxists, their form of contextual history, and so forth. But, when they begin to desire the "lost" territory of the others, a situation arises in which the Marxist, for instance, can grasp at the desired psychological richness of the Freudian only by imitating or adapting in some way to the problematic or terminology of the other. My use here of the terms "desire" and "triangularity" are borrowed loosely from René Girard; a few examples will suggest what I mean. Girard notes that the desire of a subject for an object is always mediated by a third point, the other who already possesses or also desires the object.[32]

[32]René Girard, *Deceit, Desire, and the Novel: Self and Other in Literary Structure*, tr. Y. Freccero (Baltimore, 1965), 1–52.

Consequently, in the perfect case of triangular desire, the approach of any two points of the triangle must be mediated by the third. Although I suspect that this pure form of triangulation will become more frequent as the virtuosity of hermeneutic rapprochements increases, at the moment most efforts of this sort involve a single encounter, a recognition of the importance of one other part of the triangle.

The amount of attention given today to spelling out these encounters is considerable. I shall mention only a few examples. Russell Jacoby's recent work, which seeks to identify "the radical core of psychoanalysis," and to read out of the true canon those followers of Freud whose writings reflect their "social amnesia"—that is, who are reduced by their failure to navigate the forces of the triangle—certainly may stand for many similar attempts to transcend the long-standing hostility (or at least mutual indifference) of Marxism and psychoanalysis.[33] The French—Althusserians, Lacanians, Girardians, Derrideans—are adept at this sort of triangulation, producing structuralist Marxism, linguistic psychoanalysis, universal structural strategies of desire, and a deconstructive technique that calls into question the basis of meaning itself. Habermas has sought to reconcile an interest-oriented hermeneutic of Marxist tendency with a certain view of the psychoanalytic dialogue in the last section of *Knowledge and Human Interests*; the fact that this reconciliation is brought about by translating both into a rather structural pattern of exchange serves to remind us of the triangular model which these accommodations more or less resemble. When he notes, for example, that "Freudian theory can represent a structure that Marx did not fathom,"[34] he is using the third point of the triangle—the linguistically based structures of communication that he derives from the work of Alfred Lorenzer—to mediate the other two, which appear to be primary for him.

The varieties of triangular anxiety may range from the utter rejection of the real existence of the other approach to its amicable incorporation into one's own methodology. In the first case, which corresponds to a phobia, one may deny the ability of a given hermeneutic stance to confront reality in any adequate way, as when Galvano

---

[33]See Russell Jacoby, "The Radical Core of Psychoanalysis," *Queen's Quarterly* 86 (1979), 105–109, and *Social Amnesia: A Critique of Conformist Psychology from Adler to Laing* (Boston, 1975). See also Robert A. Pois, "Historicism, Marxism, and Psychohistory: Three Approaches to the Problem of Historical Individuality," *Social Science Journal* 13 (1976), 77–91.

[34]Jürgen Habermas, *Knowledge and Human Interests*, tr. Jeremy Schapiro (Boston, 1971), 282. See also Habermas, "History and Evolution," tr. David Parent, in *Telos* 39 (1979), 5–44; and Werner Marx, "Habermas' Philosophical Conception of History," in *Cultural Hermeneutics* 3 (1976), 335–347.

Della Volpe cites the "essential philosophical, *gnoseological* poverty," and the"radical evaluative impotence" of Russian formalist developments in criticism.[35] Literary studies may bear fruit, we are told, only when the literary work is rooted in the "historical humus, with all its ideologies or moral or human ferments—according to the modern materialist conception of poetry."[36] While the ascription of impotence and the concern for fertility reminds us of an anxiety based upon the fear of an event that may call both potency and fertility to a halt, this case is a bit extreme. Other tactics are a good deal more subtle. I have in mind the work of Fredric Jameson, whose *Prison-House of Language* represents a Marxist confrontation with the structuralist tradition that does not fall into Della Volpe's "reductive" strategy of preemptive castration. Jameson laments the loss of diachronic sensibilities in traditional structuralist thought, but never fails to recognize the importance and utility of structuralism's ordering virtuosities. Remarking that the French structuralists "know Marx so well as to seem to be constantly on the point of translating him into something else (the same is true of Freud . . .)," Jameson suggests that the inability of structuralism to overcome the Kantian dilemmas inherent in its static categories has led to the post-structuralist counterpart of nineteenth-century Hegelianism, that is, the Derrideans and the *Tel Quel* group, whom Jameson calls "Left-Heideggerians."[37] Similar confrontations of interpretive systems are becoming frequent. When Benveniste or Todorov reveals the functions of the Freudian dream-work to be essentially psychic versions of the linguistic tropes beloved of the structuralists, or when Hayden White points out that Marx's sketch of the history of commodity forms in the first chapter of *Capital* follows the same pattern, or when we read a book by a literary critic titled *Revolution and Repetition: Marx/Hugo/Balzac*, we must realize that the most urgent anxieties today, as well as the most productive ones, are the triangular anxieties.[38]

---

[35]Galvano Della Volpe, "Settling Accounts with the Russian Formalists," tr. John Mathews, *New Left Review* 113–114 (1979), 139–141.

[36]Ibid., 145.

[37]Fredric Jameson, *The Prison-House of Language: A Critical Account of Structuralism and Russian Formalism* (Princeton, 1972), 176. See also Jameson's "Marxism and Historicism," *New Literary History* 11 (1979), 41–74.

[38]Emile Benveniste, *Problems in General Linguistics*, tr. M. E. Meek (Coral Gables, Fla., 1971), 65–75; Tzvetan Todorov, *Théories du symbole* (Paris, 1977), 285–321 and 361–369; Hayden White, *Metahistory: The Historical Imagination in Nineteenth-Century Europe* (Baltimore, 1973) 287–297; and Jeffrey Mehlman, *Revolution and Repetition: Marx/Hugo/Balzac* (Berkeley, 1977).

IV

I am afraid we are not rid of God because we still have faith in grammar.

Nietzsche, Twilight of the Idols

As intellectual history becomes increasingly hermeneutical, with the erstwhile "annalists of ideas" becoming "analysts of ideas," to cite the title of a recent article by Morton White,[39] a yet deeper anxiety emerges along with the growing confidence in commentary. Because "all commentary is allegorical interpretation," in Northrop Frye's words, the basic structure of historical explanation in the modern period is also allegorical. Allegory, which "says one thing and means another," is the essential genre of interpretation; to speak of hermeneutics is to speak of allegory. To speak of *class* or of *instinct* or of *structure* is to speak allegorically; references to infrastructure, displacement, or liminality are allegorical. In fact, pushed to or at least toward its limit, allegory may be said to encompass the act of reading itself. The distantiation lauded by Ricoeur as the hermeneutical space, the tension of text and context traditionally seen as the space of historical explanation, or the "backward" (rückwärts) reading identified by Nietzsche as the source of the indefinite freshness of the past, all these are the terrain of allegory. The characters of allegory are timeless; when placed in a diachronic narrative—as they inevitably must be—they create, in Paul de Man's phrase, the "rhetoric of temporality" which mediates symbol and time. In *The Transformation of Allegory*, Gay Clifford writes:

> The several strands of the narrative, and the multiplex figures and images which provide texture and meaning locally, anatomize the concepts and emotions and beliefs which concern the author. Particular events or places then provide a culmination to this process. They focus through metaphor and so have the essential open-endedness intrinsic to that figure, but by virtue of providing a culmination, a focus, imply the possibility of perceiving coherence in the world, and the viability of a total conception of life. The values and structures revealed are natural components of an interpreted world.[40]

[39] Morton White, "Why Annalists of Ideas Should Be Analysts of Ideas," *Georgia Review* 29 (1975), 930–947.
[40] Gay Clifford, *The Transformation of Allegory* (London, 1974), 105.

The ability to represent and transmit "values and structures" is the traditional test of historical writing. Without the former, it would be an idle morbidity, a preoccupation with the past for its own sake, which is itself a value of sorts, however useless; without the latter, it would represent a chaos of discrete events (if chaos may be represented), and thus be equally useless either as an explanation of anything or as a stimulus to action in the world. It is the need for value and structure that leads histories to interpret, to generalize, to compare, and to dramatize—all these processes lead toward the allegorical.[41]

The strengths of allegory make it the "natural" mode of historical explanation. The leading authority on allegory, Angus Fletcher, puts the matter as follows: "It allows for instruction, for rationalizing, for categorizing and codifying, for casting spells and expressing unbidden compulsions, for Spenser's pleasing analysis, and, since aesthetic pleasure is a virtue also, for romantic storytelling, for satirical complications, and for sheer ornamental display. To conclude, allegories are the natural mirrors of ideology."[42] The characteristic weakness of allegory, however, is its tendency to "overmanage" events, to know too much.[43] This leads, in turn, to an anaesthesia that incessantly calls attention to our inability to apprehend reality directly. Perhaps it is more accurate to say that the self-awareness of allegorical interpretation *is* merely the apprehension of the inability to apprehend reality directly.

The *anxiety* before allegory comes from the heightened awareness of the distance between what we mean and the texts we produce, or of whether we *can* mean without producing a text, the existence of which always already undercuts the grounds of meaning. The anaesthesia that sometimes accompanies allegory stems from the distantiation necessary to hermeneutic (or allegorical) interpretations. This distance extends to the rupture between our readings of the texts of the past and our "readings" of other times, as well as between our construction of systems of discourse and our desire to signify, or to "mean" (made particularly explicit in French as *vouloir-dire*). Hints of

---

[41]In *Metahistory*, Hayden White stresses the "moral and aesthetic" choices that must be made existentially by the historian, without provable grounds. I believe that these "moral and aesthetic" choices correspond to the "values and structures" transmitted in allegory. For a discussion of White's work, see Hans Kellner, "A Bedrock of Order: Hayden White's Linguistic Humanism," *History and Theory*, Beiheft 19 (1980), 1–29.

[42]Angus Fletcher, *Allegory: The Theory of a Symbolic Mode* (Ithaca, 1964), 368.

[43]Stephen A. Barney, *Allegories of History, Allegories of Love* (Hamden, Conn., 1979), 49.

this anxiety, which I am suggesting here is the deepest and most "affective" of historical anxieties, are to be found in the discussions of "language" or "semantics" in history; and in the simple realization that language possesses its own density, a dimension far more broadly significant than the conventions of past historiography have recognized. Further indications are revealed by the widespread interest in historical hermeneutics, which was not so long ago one of those terms that historians, the last defenders of "common language" against jargon (which usually means words with Greek, rather than Latin, roots), used only at the risk of violating historical decorum. Even the deconstructive "terrorists," and the dread they have inspired among all those who read texts for a living, pale in my judgment before the allegorical anxiety. After all, deconstruction in the by now classical Derridean sense is in my opinion reassuring in the same (allegorical) way that Marxism or Freudianism is reassuring: the goal of the quest is Grail-like, known in advance. It is the quest itself, always renewable, that is the thing.[44]

If we grant that the most notable characteristic of recent intellectual history is its lack of autonomy—that is, its increasing use of ideas and systems borrowed from nonhistorical sources—and that these sources (including the three I have identified as defining the triangle dominating the current scene) rest upon assumptions and vocabularies elaborated long before in other texts but shared by the reader and the historian, the nature of history-as-allegory becomes clearer. The naming of characters is the most familiar aspect of explicit allegory; the Red Cross Knight, or Everyman, or Ahab alerts the knowing reader to the meaning behind the tale even before the tale is told. Similarly, the vocabularies of the Marxist, Freudian, and structuralist place and order the evidence before any full consideration of it is possible. However, allegorization is by no means limited to specific ideologies. The "Annales School" of historical scholarship is a good example of fertile allegorization disguised as quantitative objectivity of the most rigorous sort. A large variety of special terms have entered its vocabulary; these terms have often created (as an object of study) the concepts that they denote. Mentalité, la longue durée, l'outillage mental, conjoncture are among the many terms invested with allegorical

---

[44]Fredric Jameson has pointed to allegorical aspects of Jacques Derrida's philosophical technique, noting that "the very structure of the sign is allegorical, in that it is a perpetual movement from one 'level' of the signified to another from which it is expelled in its turn in infinite regression" (Prison-House of Language, 180).

authority; when we have agreed to deal with these questions, we have acknowledged the same distance from phenomena that we note in the allegorical characters Good Works or Fellowship.

The traditional movement of defense against the claim that allegory is the basis of discourse in intellectual history has been to insist upon the possibility of semantic equivalence (that is to say, paraphrase) as the foundation of an elementary form of intellectual history. If, for example, it is possible to paraphrase Rousseau adequately, then it follows that it is at least possible to assemble a string of adequate paraphrases to form a sort of intellectual biography, or to "place" these paraphrases among paraphrases of Rousseau's contemporaries to form an elementary "life and times." I have cited above the work of the semanticist Kvastad and the philosopher Danto, each of whom, through improved analysis of language, wants to insure more perfect paraphrases. The ability to paraphrase is valued highly among historians. However, even at the most microscopic levels, the possibility of semantic equivalency is questionable.[45] At the level of intellectual history, which involves large corpuses of difficult texts, it is even harder to grant. The only semantic equivalent of a complex text is the text itself. What the allegorist does, and what the historian does as well, is to create a *counter*-discourse which confronts the "evidence" with the real meaning of the latter, a meaning that is different from or presumed to be hidden in the evidence. The counter-discourse is thus dependent upon *both* the evidence *and* the system of understanding that makes a counter-discourse necessary. All forms of historical *explanation* as such thus make use of allegorical devices to mediate between the evidence and the history created from it.

Although the politics of a given allegorical system may be radical, the structure of explanation is not.

Allegory is, in literary terms, conservative because it relies on special knowledge of language and it alludes to old literature. As the poet says, it must be abstract. Allegory loses in coldness and intellectualism what it gains in freedom and knowledge. All fiction works by indirection, but allegory refuses to conceal its artifice and its scheming. After all, allegory may be considered relatively artless.[46]

[45]A discussion of the linguistic problems in the concept of semantic equivalency is found in Oswald Ducrot and Tzvetan Todorov, *Dictionnaire encyclopédique des sciences du langage* (Paris, 1972), 565–567. A different position, offering the necessity of synonymy, is E. D. Hirsch, Jr., "Stylistics and Synonymity," in *Critical Inquiry* I (1975), 559–579.

[46]Barney, *Allegories of History*, 49.

The relative artlessness of the allegorical aspect of historical texts has hidden it from scrutiny until fairly recently; but in various guises, the awareness of the linguistic or allegorical nature of historical writing has become an important anxiety.[47]

Properly speaking, the allegorical anxiety that I believe is emerging as a major theme in writing on history and culture occurs when one unmasks the allegorical nature of a given discourse from within a counter-discourse that is equally allegorical, whether or not it is aware of itself as such. Michel Foucault's work has been a model of this sort of thing.[48] In *Orientalism*, Edward Said notes the tendency of the Orientalist discourse to overmanage reality to the extent that Arabic (an important character in the orientalist's allegorical discourse) "*speaks* the Arab Oriental, not vice versa."[49] Similarly, Said believes the failure of Orientalism to be its inability to recognize human experience in "the Orient";[50] this is an example of the anaesthesia mentioned by Fletcher as allegory's weakness. Yet Said is keenly aware that he himself speaks from within a universe of discourse which sanctions representation (or misrepresentation) only "for a purpose, according to a tendency"[51]—or, in the terms I have been using, allegorically.

Hayden White expresses a version of allegorical anxiety in his recent essay on René Girard, in which he criticizes Girard for assuming that history—as "background" or "context"— affords a secure base on which to stand in the tricky business of interpreting literary texts. Because this tacit claim—that the individual text, which is problematic, may be explained by the allegedly more secure "historical context"—has been essential to critics and historians, the explicitness of White's statement is instructive.

But it must be pointed out that it is one thing to interpret literary texts and quite another to purport to construct a comprehensive philosophy of history and theory of society, laying claim to the authority of science, as Girard has done. This is not because literature inhabits a realm of

[47] The anxiety expressed in scholarly responses to Fernand Braudel's *The Mediterranean and the Mediterranean World in the Age of Philip II* is discussed in Hans Kellner, "Disorderly Conduct: Braudel's Mediterranean Satire," in *History and Theory* 18 (1979), 197–222.

[48] For a discussion of the linguistic and allegorical principles at work in Foucault's writings, see Hayden White, "Foucault Decoded: Notes from Underground," in *Tropics of Discourse* (Baltimore, 1978), and White, "Michel Foucault," in *Structuralism and Since: From Lévi-Strauss to Derrida*, ed. John Sturrock (Oxford, 1979). See also Allan Megill, "Foucault, Structuralism, and the Ends of History," *Journal of Modern History* 51 (1979).

[49] Edward W. Said, *Orientalism* (New York, 1978), 321.

[50] Ibid., 328.

[51] Ibid., 272–273.

fantasy and history is comprised of facts, or because art is one thing and society another. It is because our interpretations of history and society can claim no more authority than our interpretations of literature can claim.[52]

This passage certainly makes plain the illegitimacy of using the *product* of an allegorizing process as the scientific foothold for another allegorizing process. White's point here is not that interpretation is inherently flawed, or utterly without standards of choice; it is rather that Girard has failed to face the consequences of allegory, and instead is trying to escape into a "reality" of "context." In accusing Girard, as well as Freud and Lévi-Strauss, of explaining too much, White has indicated that what they assume to be their secure base is itself an allegorical construction.

Today, theories of "reading," of interpretation, are not only problematic, but are drawn not infrequently from theological sources by writers who call upon us not to believe, but rather to consider and, in considering, to draw an allegorical lesson about matters which are, in René Girard's phrase, *cachées depuis la fondation du monde*. Harold Bloom's excursion into medieval Jewish mysticism in *Kabbalah and Criticism* took Gershon Scholem's history of the kabbalist tradition and made of these ideas an "extended metaphor" of textual creation. Frank Kermode's *Genesis of Secrecy* uses early Christian sources in a similar project, while Edward Said has recently described a dispute between eleventh-century Islamic linguists as anticipating the major critical debates of today.[53] What seems most striking about all this work is the use of theological speculation—which can be presented today *only* as an allegory—as an almost explanatory procedure. That is, if Bloom had ignored Isaac Luria, or if Said had ignored the Cordovan Zahirites, and they had presented their critical stances at once in the language of Freud or Lukács, the allegorical *gesture* would be missing, although the allegory would not. Instead they each chose a metaphorical model that calls attention to its figurative nature; unlike Girard, they self-consciously demonstrated the allegorical base upon which they envision the process of interpretive reading erecting itself.

The need for self-consciousness in recognizing the fundamentally figurative or allegorical nature of our images of history is the explicit

[52]Hayden White, "Ethnological 'Lie' and Mythical 'Truth,'" *Diacritics* 8 (Spring 1978), 9.

[53]Harold Bloom, *Kabbalah and Criticism* (New York, 1975); Frank Kermode, *The Genesis of Secrecy* (Cambridge, Mass., 1979); Edward W. Said, "The Text, the World, the Critic," in *Textual Strategies*, ed. Josué Harari (Ithaca, 1979), 161–188.

theme of Hayden White's *Metahistory* and *Tropics of Discourse*. Whether or not one finds the tropes, emplotments, explanatory procedures, and ideological stances that he plots of interest, one must, I think, address his major assertion, which resides in none of these. For White, the major problem behind historical writing is the question of *will* expressed in the choice of principles of representation; allegory is precisely the existential projection of our will upon the given field of historical artifacts—meaning as *vouloir-dire*, as the will to say. At its most extreme, the focus on allegorization is an awareness of the artificiality of distinctions in the undifferentiated, but indefinitely differentiable, continuum of "reality," in particular the distinctions that lie behind words. When we speak of the Renaissance and give to it both a name and a body in order to enter the lists of historical periods, we are behaving as allegorically as when we speak of the libido (whose promptings, it has been noted, often differ little from those of Aphrodite), or of a social class, rising or struggling, falling or decadent. The canonical tradition in history offers a cast of allegorical characters—the idea of the Renaissance, the notion of class, or *la longue durée*, or anxiety—from which one might choose in interpreting texts. From these and other choices originate the "values and structures" that a history will impart.

V

Every idea originates through equating the unequal.
Nietzsche, *The Will to Power*

This essay has delineated the current state of European intellectual history by stressing the role of anxiety in defining the goals, strategies, and defenses of both the field in general (an increasingly difficult field to identify), and the major trends within the field. The general anxiety has, perhaps, come from the blurring of distinctions among the various traditional ways of dealing with texts and the breakdown of the traditional professional decorum that has in the past decided which kinds of texts were legitimately part of which canon. Intellectual history is no longer merely political, social, and philosophical thought, nor are literary studies now limited to belles-lettres. "Historical discourse," the means by which historians create a verbal icon representing the past, has come under the same scrutiny that has traditionally been applied to novels; and this scrutiny must generate a certain anxiety in a profession whose identity is based upon precisely the distinction between its own prose and that of the writer of fiction. The results of this blurring of the edges of intellectual history have been a growing interest in language study in historical method, and a renewed and explicit interest in hermeneutics.

In effect, the turning of historians toward linguistics and hermeneutics is more than simply an expression of the desire to assume imitatively some of the remarkable powers of modern linguistics and hermeneutic models. It also corresponds, I think, to the breakdown in confidence in semantic equivalency, which is the foundation both of paraphrase and of traditional intellectual history. Synonymy, the ability to say the same thing in other words, has come under attack in literary theory in a number of ways; in historical study, it is giving way to a self-consciousness about the "distantiation" that impedes the attainment of semantic equivalency. As the process takes place, an awareness of the allegorical heart of historical representation emerges.

Hayden White, who has noted in passing the allegorical nature of the forms of representation discussed above,[54] has also signaled for us the psychological faculty to which it corresponds. He suggests in the "Introduction" to *Tropics of Discourse* that the neglected Kantian faculty of *will* should be reexamined as the source both of our decisions about the nature of the past and of our goals for the future. However, this Kantian belief that a chosen, allegorical past is morally necessary for projecting a chosen, better future confronts a problem posed by Nietzsche's *Zarathustra*. "Nicht zurück kann der Wille wollen; dass er die Zeit nicht brechen kann und der Zeit Begierde—das ist des Willens einsamste Trübsal" (The will cannot will backwards; and that it cannot break time and time's covetousness, that is the will's loneliest melancholy).[55] Yet the will can and does will backwards in the form of historical writing itself; this is the "believing backwards" which Nietzsche found to be the "distinctive virtue and disease" of his contemporaries. It is a disease insofar as it serves as a "revenge," "the will's ill will against time and its 'it was.'" It is a virtue insofar as it is a willing forward in the service of a chosen future. The problem of the will to allegory is, in my opinion, the specific anxiety that will in large part define the future of European intellectual history.

[54]White, *Metahistory*, 15n.
[55]*Also Sprach Zarathustra*, Part II, "Von der Erlösung," translation by Walter Kaufmann.

CHAPTER FIVE

The Future According to Foucault:
The Archaeology of Knowledge
and Intellectual History

MARK POSTER

Judged as a discipline with coherent standards, methods, and problems, intellectual history would not come out high on many scholars' lists. The field includes a disparate array of practitioners. Some prefer the style of Arthur O. Lovejoy and search for shifting configurations of eternal ideas as expressed by the most refined philosophical minds.[1] At the other end of the spectrum, historians such as Robert Darnton use quantitative methods to study the diffusion of books.[2] In this case the object of investigation is not ideas at all but the distribution of certain material objects. Between these two extreme definitions of intellectual history, the varieties are inexhaustible. There are studies of individual thinkers, of intellectual movements, of disciplines, of collective consciousness, of elite and popular culture. The object of study may be a philosophical treatise, a novel, a painting, a newspaper, a collection of letters, a political document, and so on. The method of investigation may be philological, chronological, psychoanalytic, Marxist, anthropological, or, in extreme cases, historical. If the future of a discipline is guaranteed by its diversity, one can confidently predict many rosy years ahead for intellectual history.

It is possible to argue, however, that the diversity of intellectual history is more an appearance than a reality. Behind the innumerable

[1] Some of Lovejoy's methodological statements may be found in *The Great Chain of Being* (Cambridge, Mass., 1936), chap. 1, and in "Reflections on the History of Ideas," *Journal of the History of Ideas* 1 (January 1940), 3–23.
[2] A good example of this method is Robert Darnton, *The Business of Enlightenment: A Publishing History of the Encyclopédie* (Cambridge, Mass., 1979).

variations rest a few central themes and assumptions which do constitute the basis for a coherent discipline, even though they are not always acknowledged openly. The main works of intellectual history over the past few decades consistently display the following motifs either explicitly or implicitly. First, there is a Western intellectual tradition that is highly valued, worthy of study, and important for the culture as a whole. Although this tradition contains diverse strains, its unity is predominant. Individuals may disagree about when it began (in ancient Egypt or Greece, Judea or Rome, the Middle Ages or the Renaissance) or about whom or what it includes. But all agree that it must be pursued as an object of study and that it can be disseminated to alert minds in the period of two semesters or three quarters.

Second, the Western intellectual tradition exists in a state of continuous transformation. It is ruled by evolution within continuity. Changes do occur, more or less dramatically, but they only enrich and expand the corpus as a whole, a corpus whose keepers are the intellectual historians themselves. The traits of evolution and continuity assure an enviable epistemological and cultural role for intellectual historians. They embody and recapitulate the entire history. They constitute a vital link between the past and the present whereby the past becomes identical with the present. Because the tradition is characterized by continuity, the past is domesticated by the historian, shorn of all its strange and threatening difference from the present. A good example of the force of continuity may be seen in the intellectual history of the early modern period. Before the 1960s, important Renaissance systems of belief such as witchcraft, alchemy, and astrology were excluded from the tradition. Since the 1960s, when the Self-Realization Fellowship and the Hari Krishna movement became tolerated if not welcomed by the culture, a new interest has emerged in all sorts of previously ignored beliefs of the sixteenth and seventeenth centuries. The Hermetics were discovered and became a tradition, located in a small but not unrespected corner of the greater tradition.[3] Their contestatory potential in relation to Christianity or science was submerged or mitigated, and they joined in the evolutionary parade of great ideas.

Third, the Western intellectual tradition, although it includes some rather bizarre beliefs, promotes a few central values such as reason and freedom. The bearers of these ideas do not remain the same

[3]Frances Yates, *Giordano Bruno and the Hermetic Tradition* (Chicago, 1964).

through the centuries or in the annals of the intellectual historians, but the values persist and grow nonetheless. If intellectual historians once looked to John Locke and Voltaire for manifestations of the value of freedom, now they may turn to Karl Marx and Sigmund Freud. If David Hume and Immanual Kant once defined the difference between reason and unreason, now Georg Hegel and Søren Kierkegaard may displace them. In either case the victor is the Western tradition.

Fourth, texts are interpreted for consistency and viewed as expressions of ideas within the minds of their creators. Intellectual historians discover in texts the conceptual and moral vision of the writer. The Western intellectual tradition goes beyond the materiality of the printed word to the ideality of spiritual states and expressions. In extreme cases there can be problems in locating, for a given author, a consistent, noncontradictory intellectual configuration. Jean-Jacques Rousseau provides an obvious example of the difficulty. Was he a rationalist proponent of Enlightenment values, or an asocial romantic, retreating from social intercourse into his solitary reveries and paranoid delusions? Did he favor democracy or totalitarianism? How could this proponent of maternal breastfeeding and author of a manual devoted to the most beneficent methods of childrearing, dispatch his own children to an orphanage? Was Rousseau an advocate of an advanced form of social organization as outlined in the *Social Contract*; did he favor the primitivism of the noble savage; or was his preference for some stage of development between the two? Intellectual historians have argued each of these positions, but very few have resisted the metier's penchant for reconciling the differences, collapsing the contradiction, erasing one side of the antinomy.

Intellectual history, then, is a discipline characterized by these four traits—the unity of the Western tradition, its evolution as continuity, its core values of reason and freedom, the preference for noncontradiction and for the ideality of the text. It is legitimate to question the basis of this discipline, to ask if its project is defensible, to investigate its role in the cultural totality and to propose alternatives to it. In *The Archaeology of Knowledge*, Michel Foucault, Professor of the History of Systems of Thought at the Collège de France, sets out on just this task. Not since Wilhelm Dilthey and the debate in Germany over the special epistemological value of *Geisteswissenschaften* as distinguished from *Naturwissenschaften* has intellectual history received a more rigorous and relentless review. Yet Foucault's efforts have been greeted with little enthusiasm by intellectual historians, who have tended instead to regard *The Archaeology of Knowledge* as an unwanted intrusion into their domain by a philosopher who is remote from the special considerations of their craft.[4]

In the eyes of some intellectual historians, *The Archaeology of Knowledge* is a reckless and irresponsible rejection of a valuable scientific enterprise. They accuse Foucault of producing new categories, like discourse and archive, which are abstract and inappropriate for use in intellectual history. Those categories, they assert, are incomprehensible, vague, and riddled with contradictions. Far from providing a new basis for intellectual history, Foucault has, in their view, completely abandoned the discipline of history in favor of a form of structuralism that is incapable of rendering the phenomenon of change intelligible.

Needless to say, I do not agree with this assessment of *The Archaeology of Knowledge* or of Foucault's work in general (which often receives similar evaluations). In order to make a proper judgment of the merits, if there are any, of *The Archaeology of Knowledge*, we must place it in the context of Foucault's larger project and that of French post-structuralism in general.

The first task is to determine why Foucault was so dissatisfied with the state of intellectual history that he took the trouble to write a major treatise devoted at least in part to revising it. Could it be that intellectual historians are failing to make progress in the knowledge of the past? Is it possible that their standards are inadequately lofty and their work shoddy? Are the questions they pursue improper or too crudely formulated? Is there, in short, a problem with the methods, theory, or practices within the discipline of intellectual history? Foucault's answer to these questions is simply no. He grants contemptuously that "to seek in this great accumulation of the already-said the text that resembles 'in advance' a later text, to ransack history in order to rediscover the play of anticipations or echoes, to go right back to the first seeds or to go forward to the last traces, to reveal in a work its fidelity to tradition or its irreducible uniqueness, to raise or lower its stock of originality, to say that the Port-Royal grammarians invented nothing, or to discover that Cuvier had more predecessors than one thought, these are harmless enough amusements for historians who refuse to grow up."[5] Foucault does not take exception to

---

[4]Allan Megill, "Foucault, Structuralism, and the Ends of History," *Journal of Modern History* 51 (1979), 451–503.

[5]*The Archaeology of Knowledge*, tr. A. M. Sheridan Smith (New York, 1972) 144.

intellectual history because of inadequacy in the quality of its work, at least not in the first instance.

Instead he seeks to revise the nature of intellectual history because of its cultural and ultimately political implications. Like Jacques Derrida, Jacques Lacan, and Gilles Deleuze, Foucault has taken over the theme of decentering humans from their metaphysically privileged position in the Western intellectual tradition. Galileo, Darwin, Marx, and Freud all argued that humankind was not the center of the universe, be it physical, biological, social, or psychological. Each thinker demonstrated that the dominant world view of the time had given to human beings a special status that was undeserved. That the earth was the center of the universe, that humanity was the apex of creation, a species apart from the rest, that society was a direct reflection of reason and human intention, that the ego was the center of the psyche, the captain of the soul—all of these deeply entrenched intellectual positions were overturned by the great detractors of man.

But this conclusion is well known to intellectual historians, the coin of their disciplinary realm. In fact the theme of the decentering of human kind may be considered part of the Western intellectual tradition. One might think that there is no cause for alarm here. On the contrary, there *is* reason for worry. Foucault and the post-structuralists carry the process of decentering one step further and by doing so they call into question the foundation of the Western intellectual tradition and its historians as well. The post-structuralists begin their critique where the structuralists left off.[6] The latter had introduced into the intellectual debate the notion that language is not a neutral means for the expression of consciousness. Rather than being a tool at humanity's disposal, language contains its own structure, which shapes consciousness as much or more than consciousness shapes it. From this theme came the notorious structuralist proposition that language was the center of culture, and man its object. Literary critics then began to search in novels not for the intention of the author or for his creative expression, but for the play of language, the internal structure of the text. Anthropologists similarly began to search in "primitive" societies not for the variety of human expression but for an unconscious pattern of binary oppositions that was analogous to the structuralist view of language.[7] Language and society were thus constituted by a level of

[6]Fredric Jameson, *The Prison-House of Language* (Princeton, 1972). For the earlier background, see Mark Poster, *Existential Marxism in Postwar France* (Princeton, 1975).

[7]Claude Lévi-Strauss is the best representative of structuralism in anthropology. A good introduction is *Structural Anthropology*, 2 vols. (New York, 1963, 1976).

intelligibility that was out of phase with human consciousness, behind it and inaccessible to it under normal circumstances.

Post-structuralists rejected the formalist implications of these positions. They focused instead on the logic of representation contained within the traditional notion of reason. In his method of deconstruction, for example, Derrida showed how the traditional concept of reason relied on spoken language as a privileged form of communication and implied an identity of reason and reality, an unlimited ability of reason to contain, embody, and represent the real.[8] Using the model of writing, Derrida was able to demonstrate, against the proponents of a logic of identity, that difference pervaded the relation of idea and reality. By the same token, Foucault, in *The Order of Things*,[9] uncovered a level of epistemological ordering in several discourses which constituted the truth beyond the ken of reason. The nature of this episteme was different in different periods of history. Once again reason was dislocated from its immediate continuity with reality. The rational intention of authors had little to do with the constitution of discourses at the level of the episteme.

Our culture, these post-structuralists argue, presumes that reality is available to reason in a direct and immediate fashion, that the Western intellectual tradition continues in a secular form the Judaeo-Christian view of God's relation to the world in which spirit absorbs reality totally and immediately. In the odyssey of reason, from the Greeks to the existentialists, one finds a pervasive myth that reason is continuous with reality, that the former may make itself identical with the latter, and that priests, philosophers, intellectuals, and now scientists are the privileged caretakers of this process. Intellectual historians are the curators of the great museum of reason, redecorating the walls to reflect changing tastes, dusting off long-forgotten productions, in a never-ending effort to preserve and revalidate the precious heritage. By undertaking this task, the discipline of intellectual history, Foucault proclaims, has become an accomplice of logocentrism and must be condemned along with it. Foucault writes in *The Archaeology of Knowledge:*

> Continuous history is the indispensable correlative of the founding function of the subject: the guarantee that everything that has eluded him may be restored to him; the certainty that time will disperse nothing without restoring it in a reconstituted unity; the promise that one day the

[8]*Of Grammatology*, tr. Gayatri C. Spivak (Baltimore, 1976).
[9]*The Order of Things* (New York, 1970).

subject—in the form of historical consciousness—will once again be able to appropriate, to bring back under his sway, all those things that are kept at a distance by difference, and find in them what might be called his abode. [p. 12]

The task of a truly critical science, one that Foucault attempts to define in *The Archaeology of Knowledge*, a new kind of intellectual history which he prefers to call archaeology, will then be "to operate a decentering that leaves no privilege to any center" (p. 205).

It is not Foucault's purpose to destroy history or even intellectual history. He states explicitly: "One must not be deceived: what is being bewailed with such vehemence is not the disappearance of history, but the eclipse of that form of history that was secretly, but entirely, related to the synthetic activity of the subject" (p. 14). His aim instead is to resolve "a crisis that concerns . . . transcendental reflexion." Now that the texts of the past cannot be taken as expressions of the subject because it cannot be assumed that reason is an emanation of consciousness, how can one look at those texts? If one agrees with Foucault and the post-structuralists that the cultural assumptions of the major intellectual tendencies and traditions only preserve and perpetuate an unwarranted celebration of the rational subject, then one must take seriously his effort to redefine intellectual history so that it no longer is the witting or unwitting accomplice of logocentrism. "This book," Foucault writes in *The Archaeology of Knowledge*, " . . . belongs to that field in which the questions of the human being, consciousness, origin, and the subject emerge, intersect, mingle and separate off" (p. 16).

Foucault places his own discussion of the theory of history in the context of the ongoing project of the *Annales* School.[10] Beginning with Marc Bloch and Lucien Febvre, later with Fernand Braudel, and more recently with a third generation of *Annalistes*, this group has labored against the dominant trend of historical writing, which relies on a narration of events characterized by intentional acts of individuals or groups. Writing primarily about politics, traditional historians were oblivious, the *Annalistes* complained, to the underlying, long-term social, economic, and demographic conditions that were the true basis of historical change and continuity. With the writings of Marc Bloch (*Feudal Society*, 1940) and Fernand Braudel (*The Mediterranean*, 1949), the *Annales* School became notorious for its disregard of polit-

---

[10]For an examination of this relationship see Robert D'Amico, "Four Books on or by M. Foucault," *Telos* 36 (Spring 1978), 169–183.

ical events and for developing quantitative, serial methods to study land tenure systems, price indexes, population curves, climatic shifts, and the like. More recently, *Annalistes* turned their attention to the domain of intellectual history and produced the concept of *mentalité* to denote collective forms of consciousness and make them available for their analysis.[11]

Foucault regards the work of the *Annales* School as representative of the current state of the discipline of history. Far from being a disrespectful nihilist berating the historical profession, he sees himself as building on the solid foundation constructed by the *Annales*. In *The Archaeology of Knowledge* his specific task is, given the methods employed by the *Annaliste*, to elaborate a new theory of history that conceptualizes the objects of their research and clarifies the direction for future study. In the area of intellectual history, the dominant tendency in the work of the *Annales* School was to reject the assumption of a continuous evolution of reason and substitute for it notions of discontinuity, ruptures, and breaks. "Thus," writes Foucault, "in place of the continuous chronology of reason, which was invariably traced back to some inaccessible origin, there have appeared scales that are sometimes very brief, distinct from one another, irreducible to a single law, scales that bear a type of history peculiar to each one, and which cannot be reduced to the general model of consciousness that acquires, progresses, and remembers" (*Archaeology*, p. 8). Happily Foucault finds that the *Annaliste* have already moved along the line of a Nietzschean critique of traditional intellectual history. They no longer assume the document or text to preserve, however silently, the voice of subjects, the consciousness of those long dead, the reason of the fathers. Instead, according to Foucault, they acknowledge that "documents" are simply "monuments," inert traces whose decipherment depends on their being allowed to remain as they are during the act of interpretation—on the historian's resisting the temptation to attribute to them a human form, a unity and familiarity that bespeaks needs that are within him or her, not the history. Foucault would have history avoid anthropomorphism, the error of reducing the significance of texts to the intentionality of a constitutive subject.

Foucault's goal in *The Archaeology of Knowledge* is to reconstitute intellectual history along objectivist lines whereby the texts of the

---

[11]The notion of *mentalité* remains poorly defined. For examples of recent work of the *Annales* School see *Faire de l'histoire*, ed. Jacques Le Goff (Paris, 1974), and on the *Annales* School see Traian Stoianovich, *French Historical Method: The* Annales *Paradigm* (Ithaca, 1976).

Western intellectual tradition would be studied as if they were large-scale social phenomena. His aim is not to rob these texts of their humanity, to reify them and treat them merely as things, but to avoid humanizing them falsely. Foucault wants to avoid creating a past in which the historian finds in the world a home for himself—a cozy, domestic place devoid of the strange and the alien. He does not want the historian to look to the past for a justification of himself, for a religious sanctification of his own values, because this diminishes history to the level of ideology.

The strategy of dehumanization initiated in *The Archaeology of Knowledge* attempts a drastic reformulation of the field of intellectual history. It is difficult to grasp Foucault's concepts of monument, discourse, and archive just because they are so unfamiliar, so removed from the normal procedures of the discipline. Yet when the veils of unfamiliarity are stripped away, however briefly, one can see that his project does make sense and does offer a new notion of what intellectual history could be about. The texts of the past can be viewed without resort to the subject and can reveal a level of intelligibility all their own. The problem of reading Foucault is not that his writing is abstract or that his style elusive, or that his intent is suspicious at best and malicious at worst. It is rather that he speaks from a place that is new and strange and perhaps threatening. This is not to say that Foucault's formulation of intellectual history is without difficulties, but only that it offers a compelling alternative that ought to be considered.

Foucault prefers to call his new form of intellectual history "archaeology." Archaeology works against the grain of intellectual history, reversing its disciplinary strategies. In Foucault's definition, archaeology labors "to untie all those knots that historians have patiently tied; it increases differences, blurs the lines of communication, and tries to make it more difficult to pass from one thing to another" (p. 170). Unlike the intellectual historian who moves, as in a continuous current, from the Renaissance to the Reformation, from the Enlightenment to Romanticism, then to Realism, and so on, the archaeologist remains at one site, digging in all directions, unearthing the specificities of a particular discourse. Foucault regards archaeology as "the intrinsic description of the monument," or object of historical investigation. He does not elaborate the notion of archaeology in much detail, leaving it to denote, at a general level, "a possible line of attack for the analysis of verbal performances" (p. 206).

Such an inadequate level of specification is characteristic of *The*

145

Archaeology of Knowledge, and Foucault is quite aware of this limitation. He defends himself by admitting frankly that he took his project only so far and was unable at this point to develop the new form of intellectual history fully and comprehensively. He acknowledges in the conclusion that "this book was written simply in order to overcome certain preliminary difficulties" (p. 210). He warns the reader that he has not yet discovered a satisfactory theory of archaeology but only the rough outlines, the beginning stages of such a theory. Given these remarks, one can dismiss the book as premature, or accept it as a work in progress that invites contributions from others for further development. There is reason enough based on what is presented in *The Archaeology of Knowledge* to select the latter option. If one keeps in mind the caveat that *The Archaeology* is not a finished product, one can review its propositions and evaluate their strengths and weaknesses in an appropriately tentative spirit.

The first theoretical question to be faced by any discipline is the nature of its object. For Foucault the object of investigation for intellectual history is no longer that of the ideas of subjects, rather it is discourse treated as an objective phenomenon. He argues that "discourse is not the majestically unfolding manifestation of a thinking, knowing, speaking subject, but, on the contrary, a totality, in which the dispersion of the subject and his discontinuity with himself may be determined. It is a space of exteriority in which a network of distinct sites is deployed" (p. 55). The object is no longer the minds of individuals expressed in books, which are communicated to others in an endless succession of silent dialogues. The "unities" or points of coherence of discourse are not those of ideas as traditionally conceived by intellectual historians. Instead, radically new rules must be generated, Foucault thinks, to determine the exact nature of the "unities" of discourse. And this, the new object of intellectual history, is the task of the major portion of *The Archaeology of Knowledge*. Now the question is: what kinds of things must historians look for if they intend to study discourses without relying on a transcendental subject?

Once liberated from the subject and all the forms of continuity associated with it (*Geist*, tradition, influence, evolution, book, *oeuvre*), intellectual history can define its object as discourses which are composed of statements, statements that are constituted by rules of formation and that have types of relations with other statements. Foucault suggests that, for the purposes of a beginning only, one may regard the empirical disciplines, such as the human sciences, as the field of discourses. In the final analysis, discourses will not be identical with disciplines, but the latter, Foucault believes, are the the most sensible place to initiate the labor of discursive analysis. The only reason that is suggested—or better, implied—for this strategic choice is that these disciplines are characterized, more than any other possible starting point, by unities that are discontinuous—by limits, boundaries, breaks, nonidentities, features that help to reverse the traditional strategy of searching for continuity.

After deciding on the locus of discourses, Foucault puts forth some hypotheses relating to their analysis. With discontinuity and nonidentity as the guiding threads, he turns to the rules of formation of discourse as the basic unity. Discourse is characterized by a set of rules that allow it to act upon its object. In order for these to constitute a discourse about something, there must exist a set of procedures through which the object may be coherently addressed. The character of such rules is that their nature and effectiveness has nothing to do with spirit, expression, subjects, and so forth. On the contrary, they "define the transformations of . . . different objects, their non-identity through time, the break produced in them, the internal discontinuity that suspends their permanence" (p. 33). In this way Foucault has begun to specify the objects of the analysis of discourse which, if nothing else, do not rely on the rational subject. He then adds three more features to the analysis: one must look for (1) the relations of connection between statements ("the degree to which they depend upon one another, the way in which they interlock or exclude one another" [p. 34]), (2) the stable concepts they depend on, and (3) the themes they pursue.

When intellectual historians go about their business, they begin by picking a topic such as a concept (freedom, for instance), or an individual (Rousseau), or a text (*The Social Contract*). They next look for connections between instances of their topic (different definitions of freedom in *The Social Contract*) and between their topic and other related topics (the Enlightenment, totalitarian states). Foucault avoids this procedure. He begins with a body of texts that have some externally defined unity (medical treatises in the eighteenth century). He then places in brackets the unities of this body of texts that might have been offered by their authors, the general public in the eighteenth century, or anyone else. Instead he peruses these texts for recurrent statements, which he then differentiates from other bodies of texts. He searches for clues that will define the discontinuity of this body of texts from others. Thereby he believes that he can arrive at a form of coherence that defines them in themselves. The discourse will then stand out by itself and not be absorbed by any sweeping historical phenomenology of mind.

At this point one may ask with some legitimacy what possibly could be the purpose of the undertaking that Foucault proposes? For what possible reason would one go to the trouble of poring over masses of obscure, long-forgotten texts and, after great pains, reveal the discourse within them? These texts are not necessarily beautiful or good or true. They are not fine examples of human intellect, likely to arouse awe at the wonders of man's sublime character. Nor are they likely to contain much wisdom that can be passed on to new generations so that humanity's enterprises may be improved, its life elevated, or its motives purified. The texts will permit little enjoyment in the reading; they are not splendid examples of the craft of writing. As likely as not the treatises Foucault would have us attend to will be cramped and cranky, turgid, boring, and uninspired, written by proponents of fanciful projects, by seekers after hopeless delusions, by advocates of ridiculous proposals. Without connecting us to our traditions and with no prospect of improving our future, the archaeology of discourses appears to be much like digging the proverbial trench only to be able to fill it up again.

The Archaeology of Knowledge does contain an important if only implicit agenda. First, there is the stated task, which must not be minimized, of extricating intellectual history from the morass of logocentrism. Beyond that, however, there also is the implied version of the critique of discourses, of discourses as the locus of a kind of knowledge and power that has become a pervasive form of domination in the twentieth century. *The Archaeology of Knowledge* forms a bridge, I would argue, between Foucault's early writings, which attack a process of exclusion wherein power was conceived as a negative force, and his writings of the 1970s, which attack a process of social control wherein power is conceived as a positive force. The journey from one position to the other required the construction of a notion of discourse as practice that eased the passage toward a general critique of advanced industrial society.

In the *Archaeology*, Foucault states that he is attempting to determine how social practices can become the object of scientific discourse. He dismisses the effort to reduce discourse to social practice or to some other referent because his strategy is the reverse of that. He states: "Not . . . that such analyses are regarded as illegitimate or impossible; but they are not relevant when we are trying to discover, for example, how criminality could become an object of medical expertise or sexual deviation a possible object of psychiatric discourse" (p. 48). Foucault wants to determine how discourse is a practice that creates objects and, by creating them, determines their nature. In other words, his position is the opposite of Marx's: he does not believe that the mode of production results in the ideology of political economy or liberalism, but that the Marxist discourse/practice constitutes an object in which men and women become "economic" agents. This reversal is hard to grasp because it is not simply another form of idealism. On the contrary, Foucault began with the premise that discourses are not the expression of ideas. Between historical materialism, which reduces discourse to social practice, and intellectual history, which reduces social practices to an evolution of ideas, Foucault pursues an intermediate level in which discourse/practices have a form of coherence and a mode of effectivity all their own.

In his inaugural lecture at the Collège de France, "The Discourse on Language," delivered shortly after the appearance of *The Archaeology of Knowledge*, Foucault was more explicit about the relation of discourse to power. "I am supposing," he said, "that in every society the production of discourse is at once controlled, selected, organized and redistributed according to a certain number of procedures, whose role is to avert its powers and its dangers, to cope with chance events, to evade its ponderous, awesome materiality."[12] Foucault does not reduce discourse to a material or social referent, but constitutes it within the play of power. The "procedures" of discourse are designed to shape and form social activity. Discourse does not act at the behest of power. It is power. Therefore it must be examined on its own terms, dissected scrupulously to uncover its mode of effectivity.

If the concept of discourse serves as a transition to a new concept of power, and if intellectual history is to assume a new role as the critique of this form of power, Foucault fails to confront adequately a number of questions raised by this project. The impression left on the reader by *The Archaeology of Knowledge* is that traditional intellectual history is flawed because it does not put into question the Western notion of reason. A new discipline is offered in substitution, one that employs the notion of discourse. The justification for the new discipline is made on positivist grounds: that the new categories fit the data better than the old ones. The data, now discourses, are important to study only because they are there. Foucault writes:

[12]Included in *Archaeology*, 216.

149

To describe a group of statements not as the closed, plethoric totality of a meaning, but as an incomplete, fragmented figure; to describe a group of statements not with reference to the interiority of an intention, a thought, or a subject, but in accordance with the dispersion of an exteriority; to describe a group of statements in order to rediscover not the moment or the trace of their origin, but the specific forms of an accumulation, is certainly not to uncover an interpretation, to discover a foundation, or to free constituent acts; nor is it to decide on a rationality, or to embrace a teleology. It is to establish what I am quite willing to call a *positivity*. . . . If, by substituting the analysis of rarity for the search for totalities, the description of relations of exteriority for the theme of the transcendental foundation . . . one is a positivist, then I am quite happy to be one. [P. 125]

This disarming acceptance of the positivist label satisfies no one and obscures the question of the relation of discourse to power.

Foucault does little better in clarifying the issues on the question of the history of science. It would appear that his concept of discourse is best suited to writing the history of the sciences, especially the social sciences. Medicine, psychiatry, criminology, political science, sexology—these have been his dominant concerns and these discourses seem most appropriately related to the notion of power as positive. In each case a discourse is generated which is closely associated with practice. In each case a domain appears in the social context that is defined and shaped by the discourse/practice. But can the same relation be shown to hold in other discourses, such as utopian writings, which make no pretense to scientificity? Foucault speaks to the question at several points in *The Archaeology of Knowledge* and "The Discourse on Language" without coming to any convincing conclusion. At one place, he leans toward limiting intellectual history to the sciences, at another he includes the process of a discourse becoming a science, and at still another he takes a broader view of the domain of his discipline.

The question of scope is significant in particular because, in one reading, Foucault's project appears as that of tracing the rise of certain social science disciplines until they become, in the twentieth century, dominant forms of discourse that constitute a new formation of power. In this reading, discourse becomes the central vehicle of social control, and Foucault provides a means to comprehend it and undo it. Archaeology aspires to replace Marxism as the new critical theory.

A second reading, equally valid, suggests that discourse is not characterized by an evolutionary rise to dominance, but pertains equally to the premodern, modern, and contemporary periods. The seventeenth-century confessional and the twentieth-century psychotherapeutic session are equal examples of the play of discourse. The same would hold for conversations in a fifteenth-century village and in a twentieth-century welfare agency office. In all these instances discourse plays the same role, has the same weight, reveals the same textuality, and unleashes the same kind of power. According to this reading, however, the archaeologist would have to give up any claim to differentiating historical epochs by the form, not just the content, of their discursive practices.

The choice between these two readings of *The Archaeology of Knowledge* is undecidable. Indeed Foucault's treatment of the questions of historical change and his relation to structuralism in the *Archaeology* would favor the second reading. Against the objection that his concept of discourse is ahistorical because it is presented atemporally, Foucault counters flatly that such is not the case. He writes, "I have not denied—far from it—the possibility of changing discourse: I have deprived the Sovereignty of the subject of the exclusive and instantaneous right to it" (p. 209). According to Foucault, discourses do undergo transformations, but these changes pertain to their internal structure, not to the volition of subjects. To the question of the relation of discursive change to political change, he modestly declines to respond on the ground that his thinking has not yet gone that far.

Another charge often made against Foucault—one that emphasizes the ahistoricity of his categories—is that of structuralism. Like the structuralists, Foucault seems to treat only synchrony, not diachrony. Although no informed reader would claim that Foucault is, like many structuralists, a true formalist, ferreting out the binary oppositions of the object with no concern for referents or *signifiés*, one can establish many parallels between Foucault and structuralist thought. He is obsessed with discontinuity and opposes any reliance on the constituting subject. His is adamantly opposed to organicism, teleology, humanism, and expressivism. Foucault acknowledges that the aims of archaeology "are not entirely foreign to what is called structural analysis," but he denies that he is merely transfering a structuralist methodology to a new field (p. 15). His aim instead is to indicate the limits of "the structuralist enterprise" and to restore to history its vitality." I did not deny history," he proclaims, "but held in suspense the general, empty category of change in order to reveal transformations at different levels" (p. 200).

Structuralist or not, Foucault emerges, in this reading of *The Archaeology of Knowledge*, as offering a promising line of development for intellectual history, one that extricates it from an unwanted reliance upon logocentric assumptions. He offers a path beyond the long-standing embarrassment of intellectual history: that in its loving exploration of the elaborate mansions of the Western intellectual tradition it has been unwittingly complicit with that tradition even in its most critical moments. That the *Archaeology* does not get far enough in constructing new foundations for the discipline is a fault Foucault openly admits. Yet there are enough hints and indications of the shape of the new field to license further work, both theoretically and empirically.

Most disturbing to me is not the incompleteness of Foucault's categories and project, but the fact that I have relied, in this essay, most heavily on the old methods in the pursuit of Foucault's new ones. I have examined the discipline of archaeology not as a discourse but as a set of ideas, as the project of an author, as the work of a subject. If I was unable to avoid such retrogression, I can ask if Foucault was the source of the problem. Is it possible to argue without contradiction, as he attempts to do, that discourses are faceless objectivities and, at the same time, attempt consciously to establish such a discourse? Can he create a discipline and yet maintain that disciplines are not created by subjects? For a partial response I turn to Foucault's text: "I am no doubt not the only one who writes in order to have no face. Do not ask who I am and do not ask me to remain the same: leave it to our bureaucrats and our police to see that our papers are in order" (p. 17).

CHAPTER SIX

Archaeology, Deconstruction, and Intellectual History

E. M. HENNING

Increasingly it appears that much of the highly innovative work done by contemporary French philosophers and critics has significant implications for the theory and practice of intellectual history. On first reading, it is true, their undeniable difficulty is frequently discouraging. Yet initial aggravation and dismay have also given way often enough to permit their efforts to acquire considerable influence upon a variety of disciplines. Indeed, it now seems likely that no truly intellectual endeavor will be able to remain entirely indifferent to them.

Michel Foucault and Jacques Derrida are among the most important and controversial of these recent French figures. They are also among the most immediately interesting in the present context, for there is a sense in which Foucault and Derrida are themselves historians. "At the very least," writes Hayden White, Foucault "offers an important interpretation of the evolution of the 'formalized' consciousness of Western man since the late Middle Ages."[1] Similarly, Derrida has described his own enterprise as a critical examination of our entire metaphysical heritage, "within which are produced . . . all the Western methods of analysis, explication, reading, or interpretation."[2] Each, then, is self-consciously involved in a sustained meditation upon the history of Western thinking. Whatever else they may be, both are intellectual historians.

An early version of this essay appeared in *Stanford French Review*, V,2 © ANMA Libri, 1981. Portions of that version are reproduced here by permission of the publishers of *SFR*.
[1]Hayden V. White, "Foucault Decoded: Notes from Underground," *History and Theory* 12 (1973), 49.
[2]Jacques Derrida, *Of Grammatology*, (1967) tr. Gayatri C. Spivak (Baltimore, 1976), 46.

Yet they are seldom perceived as such—largely because each is always at pains to distinguish himself from the methods and goals of most established intellectual history. Each claims, for example, to have rejected the familiar goal of an autonomous "history of ideas" and the formalist-idealist assumptions it involves. Thus, neither aspires to a faithful reconstruction of past events in the Realm of Thought, a genealogy of objectified structures of consciousness, a *Bildungsroman* of the mind. But each has then also criticized what is still often perceived as the only real alternative: the equally familiar and in some ways even more problematic program for a "social history of ideas." For, despite a mutual concern (more readily apparent in Foucault perhaps) with ideology and its institutionalization, neither is working primarily to determine and describe the "larger societal framework" within which specific ideas have been generated and to which they must therefore be related as either symptom or response. Nor are Foucault and Derrida involved in tracing the process of popularization that major thinkers have undergone. Neither has any interest, then, in explaining the particular intellectual as ultimately a function of his or her particular historical context—thus proving that thinking is a product of its times—or in demonstrating how insignificant figures have assimilated a significant one. By the same token, each has always effectively distanced himself from the inevitable attempt at a more synthetic approach: the conception of an integralizing "total history," a unified "whole picture" of the past that would allow for more interaction between ideas and events, the text and relevant contexts. Neither has been in sympathy with this collective effort to reveal the grand, underlying order of the past—the essential continuity beneath apparent chaos—nor with the traditional ideal of comprehensive unity and coherence upon which it relies. Neither, in short, has seen his work in conventional terms at all. Instead, Foucault has proposed an "archaeology of knowledge," and Derrida a "general strategy of deconstruction." How each may be related to more familiar forms of intellectual history will thus depend, to a great degree, on how these two propositions are understood.

In the case of Foucault, much may be gained by inspecting particular aspects of archaeology—certain themes, as it were—that seem specially prominent. Here it may be helpful to single out three. First, an emphasis upon the rule. In his most explicit and extensive accounts of archaeology, this is the theme Foucault stresses most. Its privilege derives from his repeated assertion that human discourse in general, however complex, appears as a "system of statements." Dispersed and disparate as these may be, they are nonetheless related in regular ways. Discursive practice is always structured; discursive "formations" exist (for example, clinical or economic). These evolve over time, but always along definite paths ("vectors of derivation").[3] Together, the rules to which they adhere will themselves constitute a broader network or "archive." This then functions as the "law" that both determines which statements may emerge into discourse and governs their subsequent relations "in accordance with specific regularities." It is, in fact, "the general system of the formation and transformation of statements." "Archaeology," as Foucault employs the term, consequently designates any effort to educe the "general archive system" of a given epoch or age. It describes prevailing discursive practices and, through their analysis, "uncovers" the archive beneath.[4] Simultaneously, archaeology reveals the "lateral relations" that connect in their regularity various modes of discourse. Together these relations form in their turn a distinct "epistemological field" in which, at any given time, the possibility of knowledge is grounded.[5] Along with the archive, it is chiefly the episteme that concerns the archaeologist.

Now, this theory of discursive regularity seems the produce of a valuable insight. There is, says Foucault, something more to discourse than grammar and syntax, matching words to things, or expressing what one thinks. "There is no statement that does not presuppose others." Each can exist at all only as part of a larger order of elements and relations. How all interact is what lends them meaning and value. It is also what calls new statements into play.

Archaeology, by aiming not to interpret but merely to describe discursive practice—the actual disposition and operation of statements—might reveal that "something more." Yet, an insistence upon the "rules" of discourse quickly leads to problems. There is, of course, Foucault's bewildering proliferation of strange scientistic terminology for categorization. More important, there is his evident hope of capturing the elusive "something else" of discourse in a final "enveloping theory." This appears to sustain a certain belief in the possibility of eventually drawing up a "vertical system" or synchronic table of the discursive elements that characterize any single historical epoch.[6]

[3]Michel Foucault, *The Archaeology of Knowledge* (1969), tr. A. M. Sheridan Smith (New York, 1972), 168–169.

[4]Ibid., 129, 130, 131.

[5]Michel Foucault, Preface to *The Order of Things: An Archaeology of the Human Sciences* (1966) (New York, 1973), xxi–xxii; *Archaeology of Knowledge*, 190–192.

[6]Foucault, *Archaeology of Knowledge*, 7–10, 207.

Formulations like these—together with the assertion of each epoch's ultimate epistemic cohesion—suggest that Foucault's distance both from structuralism and from the prevalent conception of a synthetic, "total description" approach to history is, at least in some respects, rather less than he tends to maintain. In addition (Foucault's disclaimers again notwithstanding), the network of relations (or structure) that constitutes his epochal episteme seems to find both origin and basis in the doctrine of the "archive system." The latter not only manages the genesis of particular statements into the world of historical discourse, and then subsequently provides a general "law" for the governance of their behavior; in this capacity, it also remains outside the otherwise pervasive dynamic of discursive relations and transformations. The archive thus functions (at least within the confines of the epoch in question) as a fixed, unchanging principle of regulation, standing above and untouched by the elements whose historical existence it regulates. A critique of Foucault's archive as a metaphysical and even theological concept therefore seems possible. As both origin and basis of an epoch's most general and distinctive characteristics (the episteme), it in any case leads archae-ology back toward its more conventional meaning.[7]

Finally, Foucault's apparently serious belief that the analysis of discursive practice could in fact rise above the supposedly subjectivist "desire to interpret," so as to become itself a matter of pure description, represents a return to the rather naive, positivist ideals of immaculate perception and perfectly objective representation. In the modern context, it strongly suggests a wish to avoid confronting, or even to deny, the problems of interpretation—an aspiration that would link Foucault to an outmoded conception of science that thinking historians have by now almost all felt obliged to abandon. The fact that much even rather innovative historiography, while in principle acknowledging the hermeneutic imperative, nevertheless continues to understand interpretation as, in essence, a reconstructive description, or painstaking effort to re-member the past, seems especially significant in this regard. For it is with such (more or less covert) reassertions of the positivist enterprise that Foucault appears to associate himself most intimately. Consequently, archaeology, as theory, seems to imply a rejection of any belief in the necessity of the practicing historian's intellectual involvement in the relations he or she studies. For the intellectual historian at least, the putative goal of objective

[7]Cf. Jacques Derrida, "Structure, Sign, and Play in the Discourse of the Human Sciences," in his *Writing and Difference* (1967), tr. A. Bass (Chicago, 1978), 279.

description suggests the preclusion or disavowal of any obligation on his or her part to think through, and even to think further, the problems of the texts in question. By lending this degree of support to the reconstructivist ideal that currently dominates the historical profession, Foucault helps to block off the way to any more actively involved and critical approach to the past. That this support and this result, real as they may be, are not in fact in complete accord with archaeology's strongest tendencies should become clear in the course of this essay.

Archaeology's second theme is discontinuity. Foucault stresses it nearly as much as the rule. Again this emphasis seems the effect of a largely valid critical observation. Traditionally, he argues, intellectual history, with its search for precursors and anticipations—its powerful longing for overall coherence—has regarded all difference with suspicion, striving rather to reduce the past to a perfect continuity. In fact, however, discourse is not an evolving unity, but "a distribution of gaps, voids, absences, limits, divisions."[8] Discursive formations are distinct from one another, and the relations between them (the episteme) similarly isolate each epoch. Archaeology therefore rejects established doctrine to focus instead on history's diversity, its "ruptures," "breaks," and "sudden redistributions." Traditional unities and continuities are subjected to a "systematic erasure"; "discontinuity and difference" are revealed as the norm.

It appears, then—and this is something that must be borne in mind as part of any consideration of Foucault's later attempt to associate archaeology with Nietzschean genealogy[9]—that Foucault has gone here to the extreme of taking what may well have been an established imbalance and simply reversing it. He seems to assert, that is, that among all the "others" that every statement "presupposes" there is none whose existence is historically prior. The discourse of any single epoch would literally have no genuine history. A series of epoch-making "ruptures" prevents it.

Accordingly, Foucault must suffer contortions of logic to accommodate history's irreducible continuities. Statements and entire modes of discourse are related through mutual adherence to a particular "law of division." Their "rule of formation" is always at the same time the "principle of their multiplicity and dispersion." Some historical pro-

---

[8]Foucault, *Archaeology of Knowledge*, 119.
[9]Michel Foucault, "Nietzsche, Genealogy, History," in his *Language, Counter-Memory, Practice: Selected Essays and Interviews*, tr. Donald F. Bouchard and Sherry Simon (Ithaca, 1977), 139–164.

gression is grudgingly acknowledged but only in the form of "homogeneous, but discontinuous series." A "theory of discontinuous systematization" is envisioned.[10] Elements that persist over time are said to be altered radically by a new formational rule "substituted" for the old. Foucault occasionally denies that these "general transformations" are sudden or complete, but this is not his overall thrust. For the most part his epistemic eras appear to succeed one another in catastrophic fashion. No attempt is ever made to relate their synchronic structures diachronically. The latter are, on the contrary, always divided by "archaeological breaks." One simply replaces the other. Why or how remains a mystery unexplored. And the problems that result are serious—for each archive and episteme seems now to emerge *ex nihilo*. Yet (as Derrida has observed), the insistence upon rule and system allows no room for accident. Apparently, then, there are grounds for arguing that archaeology ultimately relies on the assumption of an "external teleology," that is, a suprahistorical power engaged in purposeful creation. Once again, Foucault seems to have been insufficiently careful in his efforts to extricate himself from the web of traditional metaphysics and even theology.

The third theme, already apparent, is what Foucault calls his "principle of reversal." Here archaeology assumes an even more openly critical and contestatory stance toward tradition and traditional values, for the principle of reversal means a fundamental "inversion of signs" in the analysis of the past. This has already been suggested by Foucault's somewhat unconventional emphasis upon discontinuity, as well as by what he takes to be his unorthodox insistence upon "exteriority" (objective description) over the usual "subjectivity" (desire to interpret) in historical writing.[11] The point, as Hayden White observes, is that archaeology works against the grain to defamiliarize the past. And the archaeologist therefore risks general condemnation by scholars and public alike for his subversion of cherished truths.[12]

Foucault, of course, enjoys the risk—heightens it, in fact, by the virulence of his critique. For he does not consider inversion a predominantly academic question, as the modern revisionist historian might. Inevitably, he explains, discursive practice "poses the question of power." It necessarily functions as a "system of exclusion," giving place to certain statements and series of statements while refusing to

---

[10]Michel Foucault, "The Discourse on Language" (1971), tr. R. Swyer (Appendix to *Archaeology of Knowledge*), 231; *Archaeology of Knowledge*, 173.

[11]Foucault, *Archaeology of Knowledge*, 120–122.

[12]White, "Foucault Decoded," 50–51.

sanction others. Consequently discourse is always inherently "the object of a struggle, a political struggle."[13] There is an ideological dimension to every discursive formation. That dimension may be institutionalized as part of the dominant overall structure of society, and this is in fact what has repeatedly occurred in the course of Western history. It has certainly been a characteristic feature of the modern era. Forces that challenge the dominant structure may then find their statements denied the very status of coherent discourse. They will seem instead to employ an incomprehensible jargon or a simply nonsensical collection of extravagant formulations. The powerful institution may suggest that self-evident standards and principles of intelligible discourse have been disregarded, and forces of opposition will find themselves deprived of effective discursive access. Their failure to conform to established norms of argumentation and analysis, their failure to employ the officially sanctioned vocabulary and style, will facilitate their dismissal. They may find that their critique simply does not exist, that their challenge has been effectively silenced.

The strategy of critical reversal involves Foucault deeply in this discursive dimension. Archaeology must unmask the relations of power upon which society is based. It must attack repressive institutions by disclosing the ideological implications of their discourse and subjecting these to question. At the same time, archaeology must strive to rehabilitate the repressed—those unconventional, transgressionary elements tradition has heretofore held in subjection. Such reversal, conducted perhaps in semiconventional terms, may then effectively show up the dis-ease over which an apparently tranquil facade has been spread. "In attempting to uncover the deepest strata of Western culture," Foucault explains, "I am restoring to our silent and apparently immobile soil its rifts, its instability, its flaws."[14]

The above makes apparent, however, a further difference between conventional and archaeological history. The one concerns itself almost exclusively with the "main currents" of tradition, the other with what has been checked, stifled, or repressed—with the specific costs that have been incurred as the price of Western development and growth. Here Foucault is openly rejecting and combating the powerful and ever-popular conception of cultural *Aufhebung*: the reassuring, anxiety-forestalling (-dispelling, -containing) thought of continuous historical gain without significant losses. Indeed, he strongly suggests that the loss has even outweighed the gain. Yet this very opposition to

[13]Foucault, *Archaeology of Knowledge*, 120; "Discourse on Language," 220.
[14]Foucault, Preface to *The Order of Things*, xxiv.

convention also reveals again the way a more traditional notion of archaeology is nonetheless preserved in Foucault's peculiar usage, for it is here very much a matter of recovering and (to a degree) restoring what has been torn down and buried during construction of the currently dominant cultural edifice.

More troublesome still, perhaps, is the fact that this effort to rehabilitate what has been covered over actually increases the amount of tension built into the relation between archaeological themes. For there is, on the one hand, a belief that recovery and renewal of transgressionary forces will have positive cultural value. Yet, on the other hand, there is in archaeology the at least equally intense desire to specify the rules and regulations of all discourse. There is, in other words, both a strong commitment (even more striking in certain of Foucault's essays and interviews belonging to roughly the same period as the *Archaeology*) to the idea of "thought as intensive irregularity," as rule-breaking, or the transgression of limits, and an apparently serious interest in a totalizing conception of discursive regularity.[15]

However potentially fruitful such thematic tension might be, it does not always seem well cultivated by Foucault. He seems, on the contrary, only to oscillate between extremes. At one pole stands his vision of the Rule: the most inescapable and decisive feature—the essence, in fact—of what is always, and for every inhabitant, a highly structured world. Here transgression of any sort seems virtually impossible.[16] Even if it were present and recognized, it could still not be accounted for. At the other pole is an understanding of order itself as inevitably domination, and hence a somewhat contradictory vision of freedom from every structure and hierarchy of value.[17] Between the two—between the cold structural scientist of "discursive systematicity" and the antinomian rebel, *outré de colère*—there is apparently little effective mediation. One might hope to relate them only by arguing that Foucault, having understood discourse as, in every respect, a thoroughly regulated, totalitarian system, subsequently implies a total deregulation and escape from discourse altogether as the only viable alternative. At best one faces a choice between equally extreme—though hardly on that account untraditional—positions.

In the case of Derrida, it again seems possible to proceed by asking

---

[15]Michel Foucault, "Theatrum Philosophicum," in his *Language, Counter-Memory, Practice*, 183; cf. "A Preface to Transgression," "Revolutionary Action: 'Until Now,'" and "Intellectuals and Power," also in his *Language, Counter-Memory, Practice*, 29–52, 218–233, and 205–217.

[16]This position is especially explicit in *Archaeology of Knowledge*.

[17]This emphasis appears in, e.g., "Intellectuals and Power" and "Revolutionary Action."

at the outset how, in its most explicit form, deconstruction is described. Here too it is primarily a question of discourse, though (it would seem) of a more specific sort. Derrida is always in some way concerned with "the most powerful, the most extended, the most durable, the most systematic *discursive* formation of our 'culture'": its philosophical tradition.[18] Hence, while that question is indeed more focused, it nevertheless seems difficult on these terms to call it more "limited." And, Derrida continues, "What philosophy (and all that relates systematically with philosophy) thought it was doing, intended to do, in working from the standpoint of life present-to-itself in its logos, of ontological fullness, or of origin: [it is] precisely that against which the deconstructive operation is defined."[19] Thus—like archaeology—deconstruction provides, at one fundamental level, a drastic critique of the Western tradition. An initial grasp of this "operation" may perhaps be gained, then, by examining certain of its aspects or what Derrida refers to as "phases."

The first is a phase of detection or disclosure. Like Foucault, Derrida proceeds on the basis of an insight into the nature of language: that it is, again, a network of relations larger than any single usage and always beyond the complete control of every individual user. As a user of language, one is, on the contrary, inevitably governed to some degree by the system or order of relations one attempts to inhabit and employ: relations both linguistic in a conventional sense, and at the same time more than simply linguistic. Derrida is clearly in agreement with Foucault's understanding of language as inherently political in the broadest possible sense, as well as with his assertion that its investigation raises, more particularly, the question of domination. Derrida differs, however, in being less absolute in his stress upon regularity. He does not, that is, understand discourse as quite the totalitarian system Foucault has described. (And it is no less totalitarian for being a system of discontinuity and dispersion. These elements of difference upon which Foucault insists are, almost by definition, always thoroughly regulated.)

For Derrida, a user of language is not so completely governed by its rules—its regulations themselves are not so perfectly cohesive and comprehensive—that contestation of its established hierarchies becomes impossible to explain. And yet, it is not by means of any subjectivist reference to the individual user—to his or her intentions,

[18]Jacques Derrida, "Positions," (1971), abr. and tr. R. Klein, *Diacritics* 2 (Winter 1972), 39, n. 13.
[19]Derrida, "Positions," 40.

aspirations, or projects—that Derrida wishes to account for such contestatory movements, actual or only potential, manifest or latent. Indeed, it may well be that contestation of established linguistic or
logical structures has often been possible despite, and not because of,
the explicit intent of the individual user of language.

The deconstruction of a text—in an extended or narrow sense
("text" from the Latin verb *texere*, to weave; any network of relations
is "textual") and including the "text" of tradition—will therefore involve striving to reveal that "certain relationship, unperceived by the
writer, between what he commands and what he does not command of
the patterns of the language he uses."[20]

This may of course suggest a conventional effort to uncover the
implicit assumptions upon which a text relies. Such hidden supports
may, however, be more readily detected when, in unconventional
fashion, the entire textual edifice is methodically "solicited," that is,
threatened or shaken in a rigorous, sustained, and systematic manner.
This is to be accomplished largely through a process of double or
"split" writing. The text's crucial terminology and preferred mode of
argument are now put to work as part of its own critique. They are
simultaneously reemployed and probingly reviewed. In short, the text
"in question" is thoroughly rewritten in a spirit of critical irony.[21]

Insofar as it is actually carried out, this process is also perhaps the
most immediately apparent way Derrida avoids the charge of "sterile
formalism." He does not simply theorize about texts. He invariably
elaborates a critical reading of meaningful, "concrete" evidence as
well. This second, more empirical dimension involves, moreover, a
persistent attempt to thematize and then explore the frequently elided
problem of critical reading itself, of what is involved in *its* conventional strategies. As a result, Derrida's reading of, say, Aristotle or
Rousseau represents something rather different from the familiar idea
of a gloss or reconstructive commentary upon them—an idea that
guides much even very good critical scholarship in the hermeneutic
disciplines. Derrida, by contrast, works to provide a thorough testing
both of the text in question and of the process of testing itself.

One can never safely predict everything a complex and relatively
sophisticated text will reveal about itself during the process of interrogation. Typically, however, Derrida distinguishes at least two very
general characteristics: first, that the more fundamentally determina-

[20]Derrida, *Of Grammatology*, 158.
[21]Jacques Derrida, "Force and Signification," in his *Writing and Difference*, 6; "Positions,"
35.

tive aspects of even a rather innovative text are normally inherited or derived from traditional metaphysics; second, however, that the complexity of a sophisticated text is seldom entirely peaceful and harmonious, but tends instead to involve significant amounts of discord or even dissension. The first relates closely to Derrida's conviction that the dominant intellectual tradition in the West (and therefore all of Western culture at least since Plato and Aristotle) is thoroughly metaphysical. This means the West has characteristically understood and still understands the meaning of being as presence. "To be," in other words, means essentially "to be present." Traditional thinking has then sought anxiously in one direction or another to discover and describe at least one entity, phenomenon, element, concept, principle, perspective, etc., that would prove fully present, and hence, in its presence, fully certain, reliable, secure—an "invariable presence" that would rise above the dynamic flux of the world and therefore be able to function as thinking's solid, unshakable basis or foundation, the "fundamental ground" or standpoint for all its activities.[22]

To some it has seemed that this conviction represents nothing more than a simple a priori assumption about the Western tradition. Yet, in a general way, Derrida follows both Heidegger and Nietzsche here, and, possible first impressions notwithstanding, none of the three can fairly be thought to have shaken such provocative interpretations out of his shirtcuff. Different as they may in other respects be, Nietzsche, Heidegger, and Derrida have in common a rather more than average familiarity with the history of philosophy. The frequently expressed opinion that one or another of them offers only simplistic, unsupported, or fantastic assumptions about that history—vague generalizations inadequately related to experience, mere subjective assertions, and the like—is itself something that contradicts empirical evidence and therefore requires some further attempt at substantiation. Critics, however, have been notably reluctant to attempt what would doubtless be a strenuous undertaking. But it should also be noted that, even if this characterization of the Western tradition as predominantly "metaphysical" were in fact an a priori judgment, that would in itself not be sufficient grounds for its rejection. What is a priori is not on that account false. Moreover, it remains the case that Derrida, like Foucault, has gone to lengths to *argue* his judgment, however it may have been derived, forcefully and with extensive reference to the relevant historical "artifacts." This procedure, at least, links both with the

---

[22]Derrida, "Structure, Sign, and Play," 279–280.

tradition each attacks. Consequently, neither can be dismissed simply because one does not happen to like what he maintains. In both cases, the arguments offered—whatever their putative origins—have first to be met in equally and even more compelling fashion.

In a sense, however, Derrida himself provides the most immediately necessary corrective to his sweeping assessment of Western philosophy and culture. For he continues by suggesting that certain texts, despite and against their own largely metaphysical nature, will, when "solicited," also reveal certain less privileged elements. These—though perhaps no less traditional in themselves—may pose a distinctive challenge to their dominant counterparts. Whatever its dominant tendencies, in other words, the Western tradition is not entirely or uniformly metaphysical in every respect and detail, nor even metaphysical in anything like the same ways. Tradition is not a seamless garment, even from a hostile point of view. Of course, mindless mechanical applications of any so-called deconstructive "method," repeatedly uncovering the same "metaphysical" secrets, can easily become tiresome. The mindless and mechanical usually do. But a shallow sort of "deconstructionism" should not be mistaken for the procedure it mimics. In fact, a genuinely deconstructive reading cannot be "mechanically applied." The effective solicitation of complex texts is not so simple and routine a matter as that.

Derrida does maintain, however, that, characteristically, any challenge to a text's dominant, metaphysical tendency is contained and then more or less neutralized through a relation of "binary opposition."[23] This form of repression is to a high degree typical of the Western approach to theoretical problems, and, despite a certain comfortable familiarity—an appearance of being only Reason's right and proper functioning—it is a far from innocuous relation: "in a classical philosophical opposition we are not dealing with the peaceful coexistence of a vis-à-vis, but with a violent hierarchy. One of the two terms controls the other (axiologically, logically, etc.), holds the superior position."[24] Like Foucault, in other words, Derrida finds that discourse is always bound up with the question of power, and that Western philosophical discourse in particular (hence, all of Western culture as well) has proceeded and developed largely as an abuse of that power for purposes of control and domination.

In the second phase of the deconstructive stratagem, the classical dichotomous opposition is "inverted." An informed and demanding,

[23]Derrida, "Positions," 35, 39.
[24]Ibid., 36.

an insistently challenging, reuse of its basic elements slowly undermines the apparently solid stability of their established hierarchical order. Their "simulated repetition" is actually a revised interpretation.[25] Perhaps it is simply a matter of testing the logic of an argument, of uncovering and emphasizing those tense, but often fleeting and even camouflaged, moments in which the text itself cannot account for its own development, or has employed violent means to force a desired conclusion. Even the subtlest dissonance, for example, may have highly unsettling implications. But perhaps it is also a matter of bringing a certain text back into active dialogue with whatever that text may itself have already interpreted, for instance, Aristotle's *Rhetoric* and *Poetics* on the problem of metaphor and language in general, Rousseau on nature, or established art history on Heidegger's *Origin of the Work of Art*, and hence, on Van Gogh's painting. Deconstruction may involve, that is, rereading an earlier "text" or textual problem, then staging a renewed confrontation between it and the text (or tradition) in question.

Clearly, the renewal of such a dialogue means re-lating the text to its most explicit con-text. The fact that the latter is, for Derrida, seldom or never a limited, readily recognizable socioeconomic or political milieu may well (and frequently does) disappoint a more narrowly pragmatic public, but it does not detract from the nature or significance of this relating. To restage the problem of text and context is, moreover, less easily contrived than is often thought. For it involves, necessarily (and whether or not this is recognized), a double act of reading: the context in any sense always requiring at least as much interpretation as the text.

Here the question may initially be (though this is in itself already nothing simple, nor does deconstruction regard it as a matter for mere subjective assertion) whether prior interpretations—and the hierarchy of values and judgments that necessarily come along with them—can adequately justify themselves. To this extent at least, the strategy employed here does not appear as entirely exceptional as is (from one perspective or another) frequently maintained. It is Derrida himself, of course, who has always argued most explicitly and insistently (however often this is overlooked) against the familiar notion of a simple rupture or break with traditional conceptualization and practice—a notion whose own perennial allure makes it a fundamental component of the very thing with which one would supposedly be

[25]Jacques Derrida, "From Restricted to General Economy: A Hegelianism without Reserve," in his *Writing and Difference*, 260.

breaking. More important is the question of exactly *how* more or less conventional means are actually put to work, and of precisely what *results* are thereby generated. It is a question, that is, of whether such means can yet be found capable of achieving something at once meaningful and highly *un*conventional. Whatever its means, however, deconstruction always aims—as Foucault's archaeology aims, albeit in a different and somewhat more ostentatiously radical fashion—to unseat a traditionally dominant element and to resurrect or restore its opposite number, heretofore held in relative subjugation. Derrida insists that this inversion of established hierarchies is always possible and, in any forceful critique of tradition, must be carried out. "To neglect this phase . . . is to forget the conflictual and subordinating structure of the opposition. It is to move too quickly . . . to a *neutralization* which, in *practice*, would leave the previous sphere intact. It is a phase, moreover, that must constantly be renewed, a form of interminable analysis. For "the hierarchy of the dual opposition always reconstitutes itself."[26]

Like archaeology, then, deconstruction relies on a strategy of critical reversal. Two significant differences now emerge, however. For, whereas Foucault stresses the more obviously ideologico-political dimensions of critique, Derrida treats them as only one instance of the more general problem of domination. In a broad sense, of course, that larger problem is intrinsically ideological and political, both in itself and in all its manifestations. Where structures of domination are concerned, there is no apolitical, nonideological stance. Yet Derrida apparently has less interest than Foucault in their more easily recognized manifestations. Certainly the two concur in maintaining that there is no known sphere of human activity "outside" language and linguistic praxis. Certainly, too, they agree that the latter is always bound up with the problem of domination, and that linguistic praxis is therefore always a thoroughly "political" matter. Both are, moreover, intensely and fundamentally concerned to combat the logic of domination that has been institutionalized pervasively within, and as, the Western Cultural Tradition. The most immediately striking difference between them in this respect (and often this seems the only detail whose relevance "politically active" critics are willing to acknowledge) is that whereas Foucault has written at length on the theme of bodily incarceration, Derrida has instead written most on "philosophical matters." Frequently, this difference of focus has been taken as proof that

---

[26]Derrida, "Positions," 36.

deconstruction has to do only with historical "problems of the mind," with purely intellectual difficulties and concerns. Hence, it has seemed to some that where archaeology discusses serious social issues, deconstruction is really for the most part only a proliferation of words about words, mere scholastic gassing.

Now, clearly a judgment of this sort amounts at bottom to an unthinking reassertion of the classical mind/body dichotomy, with a position of superiority awarded (a priori) to the latter. Derrida's more interesting response, however, is a general contestation of the not so obvious corollary upon which many of his "political" critics predicate their hostility, namely, a somewhat backhanded exaltation of the historical problems of philosophy, and of those concerned with them, to a position of (negative) autonomy. He denies, that is, the very possibility of immersing oneself, for better or for worse, in any Pure Realm of Thought. "Not only have I never believed in the absolute autonomy of a history such as the history of philosophy . . . , but I have regularly attempted to restore philosophy to its place upon a scene which it does not control and which classical historians of philosophy, in the university and elsewhere, often have deemed somewhat inflexible."[27] Whatever else it might be, this larger contextual "scene" is also certainly political.

Nevertheless, it cannot be denied that, on this issue, there is a real difference between Foucault and Derrida. Indeed, an important difference exists and must be scrutinized by both critics and defenders alike. In his own behalf, Derrida offers a frank acknowledgment of his acute interest in the history of philosophy, "in its 'relative autonomy.'"[28] This means an interest in the way philosophy has never lived blindly within its more general context(s), has never simply reflected prevailing socio-politico-economic circumstances. On the contrary, philosophy in a broad sense has also been able, as nothing else really has, to reflect in sustained and systematic fashion *upon* its various historico-cultural contexts, thereby succeeding often enough in thematizing and developing their distinctive tendencies, whether hidden, obvious, or somewhere in between. In addition, philosophy has also managed at times (often, indeed, at the same time) to take a certain critical distance upon that "scene" which, all the same, it never controls or escapes altogether. The philosophical text, in other words, has been abler than most to provide a critical reading of given context(s) it may nonetheless be striving simultaneously to bolster or

[27]Ibid., 39.
[28]Ibid.

ground. All this helps explain Derrida's interest in the "relative autonomy" of the history of philosophy.

> That appears to me indispensable: theoretical criticism is also a "discourse" (that is its specific form) and if it must be articulated rigorously on a more general practice, it must take into account the most powerful, the most extended, the most durable, the most systematic *discursive* formation of our "culture." It is on this condition that empirical improvisation, false discoveries, etc., will be avoided, and that deconstruction will take on a systematic character.[29]

And it would hardly be possible to ignore the fact that this uniquely compelling discursive formation has been institutionalized as part of the culture it inhabits. It is precisely this institutionalization of the dominant tendency in Western philosophy, its canonization as a Tradition, that Derrida opposes most insistently. Still, there remains the fact that Foucault mounts a more direct assault upon institutions themselves, while Derrida focuses more upon what has been institutionalized. Which is more effective is still to be decided. In the United States, at least, Foucault appears to have had less impact, though that in itself hardly provides adequate criteria for judgment.

Of course, it might still be objected that, by itself, "theoretical criticism," even when "articulated rigorously on a more general practice," inevitably remains ineffective and that what is really wanted here is practice itself. In one form or another this objection is surprisingly common. In fact, along with exaggerated notions of the form/content distinction, this supposed opposition between "theory" and "praxis"—the fact that special efforts are presumed necessary before they can be effectively related—seems to constitute the most popular modern version of the classical body/soul dichotomy. Thus, it represents the very oppositional logic against which deconstruction is explicitly directed. For one generally does understand this distinction as an opposition, as theory *vs.* praxis. And although it has now become customary to acknowledge their mutual necessity, priority of some sort is still invariably given, overtly or covertly, to one or the other—usually (at least since Marx) to praxis, to the body.

Too often, then, the objection to such a highly theoretical form of criticism is less a response to Derrida than a simple iteration of the position first criticized. More important, however, is the fact that the objection itself does not hold up very well in practice. Theory has,

[29]Ibid., 39, n. 13.

when good, usually been remarkably effective. The case of Marx himself should be sufficient to make this apparent. It would be difficult, that is, to argue that his own political praxis was, all in all, more consequential than his written works. Indeed, "theoretical criticism" of this sort is often a most effective form of "praxis."

Furthermore, the objection is no more appropriate with regard to Derrida than with regard to Foucault. That it is not in fact directed at the latter is in itself somewhat interesting, since both are primarily writers of criticism, while each has also become involved in problems of institutional policy and procedure. One difference here is that Foucault has acted on behalf of existing social outcasts (prisoners, homosexuals, the insane), whereas Derrida has been active in recent struggles over educational reform, particularly where the study of philosophy has been threatened. Another is that Foucault decries more palpable and painful forms of repression. But one may doubt whether such differences provide sufficient grounds for a broadly positive opinion of Foucault and a general condemnation of Derrida. For, to believe they do would frequently require forgetting that, in France and most of Europe, to oppose official educational policy is to oppose, directly, the national government. Of course, it would also require conceding the point that the supposed opposition between theory and praxis is really a matter of circumstance and degree, wherein it is often very difficult to decide which activity is really the more practical or productive. But ultimately it would still mean trivializing the entire theory/praxis problem in unfortunate and unnecessary ways, by once again denying implicitly, without adequate justification, the role of philosophy as a critical force and agent of social change.

It remains, then, only to observe that this objection frequently takes a somewhat more sophisticated form. Derrida is then accused of failing to take his readers "outside the text," meaning that his deconstructive strategy has perhaps produced interesting and even important insights into written works of theory and literature, but that, all the same, there are no indications of any wider, "extra-textual applications of the method." Here, too, the logic of dichotomous oppositions and domination is clearly at work. The "text" is first reduced to its narrowest possible manifestation: the written, bound book. Then this reduced "text" is opposed to the coincidentally exalted notion of context, the problems, value, and influence of which are thereby allotted a position of manifest superiority. Whenever this relation of text to context is postulated, the latter always seems designated, openly or covertly, but usually without argument, as clearly the more important. It is regarded as Life Itself, the text as mere talk about Life. To a certain extent, it seems possible that the modern emphasis on context serves as a means of avoiding the problems of the text, which are, as Derrida has demonstrated, generally more complex and disturbing than one would like to believe. There is a sense in which the now very widely institutionalized esteem for the context has worked toward something like a repression of serious concern with complex texts. This tendency appears most readily in academic disciplines such as sociology, psychology, and anthropology (all founded upon and decisively shaped by highly intricate, problematic texts that those disciplines normally honor and rarely teach), but also in political science, literary criticism (where primarily biographical and contextual studies still play a surprisingly large role), and, not least, in intellectual history.

Yet the relation of text to context remains a valid issue. Directly or indirectly, consciously or unconsciously, every hermeneutic discipline must eventually confront it. What must then be considered is precisely its complexity and uncertainty. Neither text nor context is ever an unproblematic given. Both must always be defined, delimited, "read," and interpreted. Hence, each always poses broader "textual" problems, whether or not one chooses to recognize them.

In its most general and meaningful form, then, the issue cannot be restricted—and neither Derrida nor Foucault attempts to restrict it—to a question of bound books vs. everything else. It is, rather, a question of the particular, but complex and unpredictable, interrelations between work and world in their broadest sense and in specific cases. Such a question lies, in one form or another, but always as a question, at the heart of any sustained attempt, regular and methodical, to "read," interpret, and account for anything made or done. Every such attempt necessarily provides, openly or secretly, and with a greater or less degree of self-consciousness, its response, however provisional. Work and world, insofar as they are each equally built up and evolve as an intricate and dynamic interweaving of elements, are each by definition "textual," and will therefore equally and always raise specifically "textual" problems.

Thus, the objection that Derrida does not lead us "outside the text" could indeed be met by the observation that, on the contrary, the Western philosophical tradition is perhaps the most significant context conceivable. But this will in turn suggest an actually more fitting response: that there is in fact no "outside the text" at all, that text and context are equally "textual" through and through, and that the desire for any "outside-the-text" represents the metaphysical death-wish *par excellence*.

This response does not, of course, solve the problem of relating bound books to their particular context(s). The problem only returns in a more complicated, but perhaps also more adequate, form. Every book has many contexts—economic, political, intellectual, and so forth. The most significant for many important books, however, is often constituted largely by other books. For a writer like Flaubert, for example, the works of Rabelais or Cervantes may be more important than contemporary events or prevailing socioeconomic conditions in rural Normandy. For a Hegel or a Nietzsche, Plato may ultimately be more important than nineteenth-century German politics or family structure and life among the bourgeoisie. This is not to say such things are simply irrelevant for the works that such figures produce. Rather it is only to point out that, for the books Derrida is concerned with, the most relevant context may be *exactly* what he is in one way or another continually referring to. If, moreover, there is one sense in which every text provides a reading of its context(s), there is also (as every social historian knows well) a sense in which every context reads its texts. And one very basic context is therefore always the Western philosophical tradition, "*within which* are produced . . . all the Western methods of analysis, explication, reading, or interpretation."

Clearly, then, deconstruction is a critical reexamination both of the way given texts have understood and explained their context(s), and of the way one very powerful context has at the same time read and interpreted its various texts. This constitutes another reason why deconstruction, as an example of empirical praxis, could never slip into mere formalism. For it will never be limited to the problems of any narrowly intratextual logic or style. Even when focusing upon the specifically philosophical book, deconstruction is still fundamentally a concern with certain broader historical relations as well.

When it is finally recognized, then, that every context is always also a "text" in itself, then perhaps it will be understood that, even as theory, the "deconstructive strategy" is by no means restricted to the criticism of books. Its "applications" are, in theory, as wide as one cares to make them in an inherently textualized world. True, Derrida chooses to concentrate upon what he considers more profoundly challenging and provocative texts, as well as upon their relation to a less immediately perceptible, yet just for that reason more pervasive, context. True, one will not find in his works anything like an explicit call to arms or program for welfare reform. But when one asks to be taken "outside the text," is this really what one has in mind? Even in Marx, where one actually has the call to arms, there is very little that could be called a serious plan for revolutionary action, and nothing at all like a detailed blueprint for the future. Often as not, specific implications for this or that realm of activity remain to be produced by the reader, as part of his or her own interpretive activity.

It might, however, be argued that those implications are indeed distinctly revolutionary, and in an other than conventional sense. For, by refusing to remain at the stage of simple inversion, Derrida ultimately seems to carry his critical enterprise somewhat beyond Foucault's. Deconstruction's third phase involves, that is, a more general "soliciting" of the classical and still predominant mode of conceptualization. A given opposition must now be so radically "dislocated" or "imbalanced," that *neither* opponent can secure a lasting position of repressive dominance. The very idea of dichotomous, hierarchical thinking must finally be itself "problematized."

Now "problematization" is clearly something different from, and more difficult than, any simple decision to give up hierarchical thinking altogether and try something else for a while. Such "decisions" are all too easily and often made with regard to the elements of tradition, and have consequently acquired something of a classical status themselves. Indeed, the desire to leave tradition behind has no doubt served a powerful, tradition-confirming function. For, as Derrida has himself repeatedly observed, it has inevitably proved impossible to effect such a break. A certain mode of conceptualization or approach to problems does not become traditional for nothing. But careful reading will not mistake an effort to *problematize* for the familiar desire to transcend. It will instead proceed by noting that, in the first place, and whatever his popularizers, pro and con, may say, Derrida is here not so much writing about and against hierarchical thinking in all its various manifestations and effects, as he is writing against a certain repressive form thereof: the classical dichotomous opposition—the pervasive either/or formulation—and the deeply embedded logic of identity and difference upon which it is based. This may be called repressive because it works toward the nonrecognition, and ultimate denial, of the difference within identity, and of the similarity between what is different, as well as, more generally, toward the permanent, institutionalized subjugation of one opposed element by the other. Hence, traditional hierarchical thinking may be characterized as excessively rigid and inevitably one-sided. It is a

logic of domination, having definite affinities with absolutist and ex-
ploitationist ideology.

Second, it should by now be apparent that to represent this effort to
"problematize" as a simple, iconoclastic impulse to reject is to remain
within the confines of that traditional, repressive framework. That this
is so often what happens does not make the resulting interpretation of
Derrida any more valid. When one stubbornly persists in evaluating
either his or Foucault's work solely from a position within the perspective each is criticizing, then misunderstanding and distortion are
almost certain. And it is characteristic of ideologically interested self-
mystification that it frequently adopts whatever means appear to hand,
however great the inconsistencies that result. Thus one commonly
finds that, from the same point of view, Derrida is seen both as
merely the latest clever defender of a sterile, academic "elitism"—
hence as a conservative—and, at the same time, as a dangerous
Dionysian wild man, proclaiming an end to all distinctions, value
judgments, and law—a generalized "return to nature"; both, that is, as
an overly intellectual, "scholastic" formalist who merely poses as a
radical, and, simultaneously, as the modern *philosophe à quatre
pattes*. Such extreme, and extremely diverse, cartoonlike images have
been typical of what Derrida calls the "confused and impotent aggressiveness" his work tends to arouse. A better, a fairer and more accurate, understanding requires a less hasty and more conscientious
reading of this third deconstructive phase.

A "problematization" of the dominant and domination-oriented
form of hierarchical logic involves at least three distinguishable steps.
The first concerns attainment of "a certain exteriority" in relation to
the philosophico-cultural tradition, a certain "exorbitant" position in
the face both of its powerfully attractive metaphysics and of the
specific complex of "predicates" that attends and subtends this "powerful historical and systematic unity."[30] A strange paradoxical position,
at once inside and outside the pull of traditional concepts and methodology—for it is not to be construed as a simple transcendence of what
has been and is established, the familiar idealist-formalist dream (or
materialist nightmare) of the mind's escape from history—this "exorbitant" position is perhaps only attained through a rigorous and extensive process of familiarization with the text(s) of that tradition.

Then, with a careful yet more intensive solicitation, involving now
"a *certain* organization, a certain *strategic* arrangement" of the hier-

[30]Ibid., 39.

archical structure in question, a new "concept" may emerge, one that "no longer allows itself, never allowed itself, to be understood in the previous regime."[31] This does not mean dialectics. Derrida is especially cautious here about keeping deconstruction free from any suggestion of the *Aufhebung* and its sublating resolutions of conflict. "In fact," he says, "it is against the incessant reappropriation of a Hegelian type of dialectics . . . that I am attempting to channel the critical enterprise."[32] Foucault, it should be noted, often appears less careful (for example, in the elaboration of his theories of episteme and archive) to avoid that traditional movement of idealizing reconciliation. His explicit definition of the episteme as a "space" or "principle" of "dispersion" is apparently contradicted by the fact that it is precisely this "principle" that functions as the (formal) focus around which a distinct epoch will coalesce. It is what allows each epoch to emerge as such. The participation of all its elements in one unique epistemic complex is what enables each epoch to be. However much it "disperses," the episteme apparently holds all epochal elements nearer to one another than to those of other epochs. In addition, there remains the really more basic concept of the archive as a "general system" of rules for "the formation and transformation of statements" within an epoch, the overall "law" that regularizes historical discursive praxis. The archive, as was suggested above, seems a conflict-resolving metaphysical notion of a specifically formalist character.[33]

Derrida seems more successful here. The new "concepts" for whose emergence he repeatedly "arranges" must thwart all desire for reconciliation. They are therefore to be "polyvalent," each an "undecidable" or merely "simulative unit."[34] They must, that is, reveal how the old oppositional distinctions and categories always overlap, or "supplement" one another, in theory as well as practice. But then, necessarily double, the new "undecidable" will never be able to offer itself as an essential harmonization. It would seem, rather, that its fundamentally *ironic* nature (which the archive does not share) can only heighten the conflict or tension between terms by narrowing their distance, while yet preventing that gap from ever being closed completely, least of all on any arche-level.

Now this latter has been for many a very disturbing suggestion. It has contributed to the widespread feeling that deconstruction must be

[31]Ibid., 36; "Force and Signification," 20.
[32]Derrida, "Positions," 36.
[33]Cf. Foucault, *Archaeology of Knowledge*, 10, 129–131.
[34]Derrida, "Positions," 36–37.

the irresponsible, merely destructive campaign of an intellectual hatchetman. It has encouraged some to conclude that Derrida's occasional use of terms like "regulated play" actually indicates a defense of "absurdist" irrationalism or simple cutting-up. The idea of perpetually reinvigorated conflict between terms has raised in many minds the specter of cultural chaos, or the famous "abyss" of an "infinite regression." The term "nihilist" has even been used.

Conclusions of this sort, the exact economy of which would repay closer study, seem largely the result of superficial reading and willful misunderstanding. Certainly Derrida works to prevent, and endeavors himself to avoid, any reconciliation or harmonizing resolution where particular problems are at issue. But, just as certainly, this does not amount to or imply a call for generalized, indiscriminate conflict in each and every sphere—racial strife, bloodletting, the end of civilization as we have known it. On the contrary, Derrida works equally hard to break down the ingrained tendency to assume, a priori, that one is always in the end faced with a choice between absolute, eternal conflict and its final resolution, between eventual consensus and the jungle, either one or the other. One does indeed always face the choice between relative degrees of conflict and resolution, however obscure those degrees or that choice may in practice be. But it is basically unrealistic and self-deluding to construe such choices in absolutist terms or to pretend the decision between them is ever a final one. Nor would it be at all realistic to believe that one term of this supposed dichotomy (conflict) is essentially negative and the other (resolution) essentially positive—not, at least, unless one is also willing to deny the irreducibly positive dimension of certain forms of conflict (for instance, social criticism).

Derrida, moreover, has dealt extensively with the unavoidable, never finally decidable, problem of that tense relation between conflict and the desire for final resolution and peace: between the always painful impulse to question, criticize, or negate, and the equally irrepressible urge to affirm.[35] The tension between the two is one possible definition of Western culture, and need not, therefore, be seen in exclusively negative terms. It may instead be the most potentially creative aspect of life. Thus, the belief that Derrida opts, in any sense, for conflict pure and simple is largely the result of a failure to perceive or to respect the profound nature of the problem: that it is in itself already a question of the more general conflict between the

[35] See, e.g., Jacques Derrida, "White Mythology: Metaphor in the Text of Philosophy" (1971), tr. F. C. T. Moore, *New Literary History* 6 (1974), 5–74.

desire for affirmation, consensus, conflict-resolution, and unity, on the one side, and the need for challenge and negation, for active, conscious questioning, for conflict-provocation or -prolongation, however painful, on the other.

Furthermore, to maintain that this nevertheless implies the "privileging" of conflict over consensus, of pathos over ethos, Dionysus over Apollo, means ignoring or failing to take seriously the character of deconstruction's final phase: especially the way it involves subverting the logic of domination by privileging inherently "undecidable" or "double" terms. "Conflict" and the suffering it involves are themselves just such terms. Neither can ever be privileged "by itself," least of all where it is a question of conflict between a need for conflict and the longing to resolve all conflicts.

Deconstruction is indeed an attempt at the perpetual reactivation and even heightening of certain sorts of conflict. But it would be empirically unsound to insist that this attempt necessarily leads to or toward a complete rejection of all order, regulation, (self-)discipline, and common decency. Conflict and order are not dichotomous terms. Nor does even perpetual conflict exclude all forms of resolution, though it would very much oppose the traditional idea of the closed dialectic or Day of Final Judgment.

Second, it is crucial to note just what sorts of conflict deconstruction works to perpetuate. Here, much depends upon the valid distinction between genuine problems—where the desire for final harmony is in the long run perpetually frustrated and can be satisfied only temporarily through recourse to more or less forced solutions—and mere puzzles—where such harmony may well be both possible and desirable. Of course, such a distinction may also be highly problematic, since the same situation often involves aspects of each. There are, however, numerous occasions when it seems arguable that more is to be gained by the perpetuation or reinvigoration of a conflict or struggle than might be derived from its final resolution. Hence, "contest," rather than the more general "conflict," might better describe the type of situation under discussion. Certainly the former seems more in keeping with the implications of this dimension of Derrida's work. To suggest, therefore, that his encouragement of conflict (or contest) is in any sense an inducement (perhaps unwitting) to generalized violence, exploitation, scapegoating, or cultural barbarism is simply to invert his extensive and often explicit argumentation.

Finally, suppose one were to accept for a moment the terms of this objection, and agree that, where genuine problems are at issue, there is implied in deconstruction a certain anarchistic impulse. But then the question becomes one of interpretation, that is, of exactly how one understands that impulse. Certainly it is no longer possible to follow the conservatives—whether of the "liberal" humanist or Marxist variety —in their familiar efforts to equate anarchism with nihilism. There is, and always has been, a large difference between the two, however ancient and enduring their confusion. To proceed without being led by any fixed principle, without being ruled by any "central" concept or fully authoritative element—this does not mean proceeding with nothing at all. To deny the *archē* does not imply a desire for *nihil*. One might even argue that, from the perspective of a genuine critique of metaphysics, no two impulses are further apart. At least, it certainly would appear that equating them or maintaining that the one invariably leads to the other carries with it a reassertion of that age-old theological assumption—which all varieties of "absurdism" share—that without God one can have only The Void.

Similarly, even if anarchism does after all imply a certain degree of disorder, it would still be extreme to equate this, in principle and as a general rule, with chaos. It may indeed be that deconstruction, as a specifically anarchistic enterprise, means the reintroduction of some amount of disorder(ing) and disorientation into Western thinking. There are doubtless circumstances in which this might well be the healthiest, most affirmative course to take. And there are always circumstances in which the longing to escape from conflict, the desire for consensus, may be a distinctly unhealthy, culturally deadening impulse. But it does not follow that deconstruction therefore means generalized confusion, or rejection of all that partakes in the established order of things. That is another false equation, and one that again relies upon the simple iteration of precisely the logic and the assumptions that Derrida has questioned. It is, structurally, only a repetition of the long-exhausted argument that without an absolute, eternally valid order there is no order at all; that without an ultimately certain Truth, Value, Purpose, or End, there will be only absolute relativism and general decay. It is only a variant of that powerfully attractive, and thoroughly metaphysical, belief that in the end one always faces a choice between stable foundations and cosmic catastrophe: again, a choice between mutually exclusive absolutes. Historically, this is the exaggerated and fearful reaction to whatever seriously threatens the status quo. It serves a repressive function and always has. For a certain amount of disordering and disorienting has never precluded the possibility of simultaneously establishing and adhering to certain forms of order. Even the refusal to adhere to or espouse any form of order whatever on a permanent basis does not mean rejection of all order in general or of specific varieties of order when offered on other terms. It is not an either/or choice.

In any more detailed exploration of this question, much would hinge upon what Derrida writes about the inescapable necessity of regularization, rigor, and reorientation. Deconstruction, it should be remembered, is itself meant to be "systematic." It seems possible, however, to maintain (provided one does so with great care regarding terminology and formulations) that the difference between Foucault and Derrida is, in certain major respects, the difference between one further attempt at a (secularized) archae-ology, and a sustained, philosophical an-archism. Nevertheless, even at its most anarchistic, deconstruction, while certainly an attack upon the philosophical heritage, is nothing like a program for its simple effacement or demolition. Indeed, Derrida repeatedly warns against the perennial desire to "turn the page" of philosophy. There are no known alternatives to its conceptual formulations. One always employs traditional concepts and methodology, "and all the more when one does not suspect it."[36]

Yet deconstruction obviously does not mean continuing as before, complacently to inhabit established structures of domination. Hence its attack must always have a subversive character. It will necessarily operate from the inside (because one always does), taking its weapons from the very edifice it would unsettle. Deconstruction does indeed continue to inhabit tradition, and thus runs the risk of misunderstanding and non-recognition. But deconstruction inhabits traditional structures "*in a certain way.*" It continues to examine the texts of that tradition, again "*in a certain way.*" The logic of their terminology is repeated and reused, but also re-petitioned. A rigorous working through of their organization and aspirations may uncover possibilities tradition has not explored. That "way" is therefore critical, but never scornful or derisive. And it may lead in the direction of a breach in the "closure" inherited concepts have erected and reinforce. At the limit, this closure itself must be rethought and perhaps resituated. In its final phase, then (which now shows itself the very denial of all finality), deconstruction is also a re-vision of tradition, a "reinscription" of its "text."

Now, the above also suggests a somewhat more general contrast between Foucault and Derrida. For the one, with his vision of history

[36]Derrida, *Of Grammatology*, 14, 24.

as a series of "breaks" between epistemic structures, appears to adhere to a certain, not entirely unprecedented notion of continuity within epochs and discontinuity between them. It resembles the conception of history one finds in Hegel and other formalist theoreticians, in whom the synchronic is stressed over the diachronic, cultural or ideational forms or structures are understood as the distinctive "essence" of an age or epoch, and history is ultimately represented as the successive appearance of dominant structures (like archive and episteme) that simply replace one another with little or no diachronic continuity of significance.

Derrida, by contrast, seems to propose the less familiar idea (though similar in some respects to Heidegger's) of history as a process of continuous revision, of repetitioning the "text" of the past in an effort to find space for an "inscription" of its latent potentiality. Continuity is emphasized, but never at the expense of difference. Indeed, the conventional historian's desire to exalt continuity, especially in the form of the Western tradition, becomes the subject of a sustained and explicit critique at least as unsettling as Foucault's. Neither figure is simply traditional. Both understand the glorified concept of tradition as largely a benign tableau that requires yet conceals systematic and institutionalized forms of repressive domination. Yet Foucault has apparently responded with the more conventional gesture of rejection: simple denial of significant diachronic continuity, return instead to a (reduced) Hegelian-formalist concept of history as synchronic unities broken apart by gaps—and this remains the case however much Foucault may have to say about what are, after all, and by his own account, only surface dispersions and differences. Beneath them there is still the governing "law" of the archive and the (theoretically) unifying episteme. Derrida offers something rather different: a more subtle and genuinely less traditional insistence upon the inextricably interinvolved relations between elements of continuity and discontinuity over time. The repetitioning of a heritage is nothing like continuity within epochs with discontinuity between them, but rather (as it is in Heidegger) a reexamination of the past in the effort to elicit its repeatable possibilities for something different: a form of repetition in which things do not simply remain the same, though they are never completely new. It is an idea of history that is no longer quite so deeply indebted to the traditional time-line model, and hence of a historiography that no longer sees itself as the objective record of either uniformity or rupture, preservation or novelty, or of some dialectical mixture of the two, but as both an understanding of the same within the different, and a creative e-laboration of the different within the same. Thus, deconstruction breaks away from established "reconstructionist" models. In the implication of a critically involved historiography, it consequently provides greater theoretical support to the contestatory impetus it shares with archaeology. The latter, by contrast, can maintain this impetus only despite, and not thanks to, the idea of historiography that it suggests.

Seen in this way, Derrida appears the more radical of the two. His theoretical promise, that is, seems to go further than Foucault's. But then it would also be necessary to consider the question from a slightly different angle, and see how successfully the promises of archaeology and deconstruction are transformed into practice.

In *Madness and Civilization*, Foucault provides an archaeological reading of primarily one historical epoch.[37] By focusing for the most part upon the problem of insanity, he tries to demonstrate the way post-Renaissance Europe's dominant tendency was to exclude from discourse all that could not or would not conform to the prevailing conception of the rational statement. The theme of discursive regularity is sounded here, but only inchoately. There is almost no suggestion of the involved plan for a categorization of discursive formation and practice. There is no example of a "divergence of enunciative modalities," no apparent attempt to locate "the possible points of diffraction of discourse," no concrete "definition of the types of rules that govern discursive events." There is not even the glimpse of a "general archive system." In brief, regularity in a narrow sense is simply not discovered. What does appear is a strong emphasis upon the internal cohesion of the period. Everywhere, Foucault argues, the same "set of relations" prevailed and guided discursive practice in decisive ways. It all "organizes" into a "complex unity," a new "sen-

[37]It bears pointing out, however, that *Madness and Civilization* (1961) appeared somewhat before *Archaeology of Knowledge* (1969), and that Foucault's methodological thinking and vocabulary had in the meanwhile become a good deal more explicit. Nevertheless, his overall position does not appear to have undergone any modifications radical enough to make the two works incomparable in terms of practice and theory. Foucault's first overt appeal to the concept of an "archaeology" appears to come at least as early as his *Birth of the Clinic* (1963) and the appeal is still more insistent in *The Order of Things* (1966). But one should not conclude from this alone that therefore *Madness and Civilization* is not an archaeological work, i.e., that without the word the thing is absent. Rather, most critics have seemed to understand *Archaeology of Knowledge* primarily as Foucault's first sustained attempt at a theoretical explanation and detailed working out of the methodology he had employed to date. In the face of sharp criticism from figures such as Piaget, a retrospective self-definition and self-defense had become necessary. *Archaeology of Knowledge* contains certain criticisms of earlier works, but nowhere does it repudiate *Madness and Civilization*.

sibility" to problems, especially economic, ethical, and medical. It is this unity of perception that gives significance to events. Hence, "throughout Europe, confinement had the same meaning."[38] Later, in *The Archaeology of Knowledge*, Foucault attempts to support such assertions by grounding them in the theory of the archive as a body of "rules" that structures those "relations." At this point, however, the archive itself remains essentially theoretical. In practice it proves an abstract, merely nominal entity. One never sees the "rules" of which it is supposed to consist.

The theory of the epoch's self-consistency, on the other hand, is at times substantiated rather persuasively: for example, when Foucault examines the nineteenth-century asylum and finds it "a kind of microcosm in which were symbolized the massive structures of bourgeois society and its values."[39] Yet, the argument often goes further than this, to insist upon the actual existence of an underlying "principle of cohesion," or unified "structure" of relations, that "operates" to "organize" the sensibility of the age. It is accordingly this hidden but determining structure that "accounts" for the historical experience of madness, its diagnosis and treatment, but without being itself in turn altered by that experience or by anything else Foucault discusses. In practice, then, he seems to have already formulated his idea of the episteme.

The question at this point is how it differs from the once popular belief in a world view or *Zeitgeist*. And indeed, later prostestations notwithstanding, Foucault would be hard pressed for an adequate response. True, he gives a very unconventional degree of attention to institutional structures and life, but only to explain them as ultimately mere empirical manifestations of the epoch's single, inherent, and abstract episteme. He claims his structural unity is nothing like a spiritual totality, governing all thought and behavior. And he does give some substance to this disclaimer by pointing to examples of atypical or incongruous practice: the freedom allowed the mad in Gheel, for example, or in the hospital at Saragossa. Such anomalies are introduced, however, with a notable lack of fanfare, and are only mentioned in passing. In fact, they are never really treated as incongruities at all. This can be no surprise, for all his stress on the theme of structural continuity within epochs does not now allow Foucault to account theoretically for such atypical practice. All significant behav-

[38] Michel Foucault, *Madness and Civilization: A History of Insanity in the Age of Reason*, tr. Richard Howard (New York, 1973), 45–46, 49.

[39] Ibid., 274.

ior is seen in terms of domination and repression. Foucault never provides an understanding of the relation between dominant structures and elements that escape or actively contradict them without simply being silenced. Indeed, except to dismiss it, he never gives the matter consideration in *Madness and Civilization*. Hence, what he actually describes is at times a source of difficulty (though this is never confronted, as one might wish, in *The Archaeology of Knowledge*) for his theory of the episteme, threatening to undercut its occasionally denied, but generally unmistakable, totalizing tendencies.

At the same time that there is continuity within epochs, however, there is also discontinuity between them. This second theme figures strongly in *Madness and Civilization*. For Foucault argues that previous ages had a quite different "experience" of insanity, one that was far from exclusionary. By two distinct stages, the "classical" and modern eras first "muted," then "silenced" the mad. Thus, in their "sensibility" to madness, and in their discursive practice, the ages are divided by "gaps."

And yet, the attempt to substantiate this thesis encounters major problems. It quickly appears, for instance, that the transition between epochs is actually marked by forms of repetition and a measure of continuity. Foucault notes the "strange fact" that certain customs and attitudes persist and even develop over time. Treatments and cures for madness are frequently little changed from the ancient to the modern period. (It will have been noted by now that, despite his explicit hostility to traditional historiography, Foucault accepts without question not only its usual reconstructionist hermeneutics, but also its traditional periodization. In this and other respects, his work often seems to represent only a semi-structuralist reformulation of conventional assumptions.) Archaeological analysis reveals, in addition, that the many symbolic or ritualistic dimensions of mental treatment are often nearly static over time. The madman himself merely steps into the apparently enduring cultural "space" of scapegoat or social beast. And a variety of beliefs "slowly deposited" in a process of "historical sedimentation" have only recently emerged. What Foucault often discovers in the asylum is, then, only a "new use of old therapeutic themes," a "reinterpretation of old methods," a different "meaning" for the "ancient perception of madness." There accordingly takes shape a more complex picture of history than archaeology promises—one in which continuity and discontinuity cannot be segregated rigidly into synchronic and diachronic dimensions, but always appear together—and always as mutually involved—in various and varying proportions, ways, and dimensions of historically relevant activity.

Foucault is aware of this difficulty, though, and offers a number of different replies. All such "quasi-continuity," for example, might be only a "surface appearance," that further research "on the archaeological level" will eventually dispel.[40] On this level, of course, each age must reveal itself (as it did for Hegel) as internally self-consistent but radically distinct from others. Or again, Foucault argues, much supposed continuity is really only anachronism. Figures like Shakespeare, Cervantes, and Corneille, whose works provide room for a healthy confrontation with madness, do not actually belong to their age at all, but instead hark back to the Renaissance.[41] Foucault's most interesting response, however, is to attribute all genuine interepochal continuity to the existence, at a far deeper level, beneath every individual epoch, archive, or episteme, of "a great motionless structure," a "point where history is immobilized" in a "constant verticality." Thus, madness itself is only one historical manifestation of the larger force of "unreason," a force "connecting with itself outside of time."[42] And though the "awareness of madness" must change between epistemic ages, it evidently can do so only within the limits imposed by the nature of unreason, "the world's *contretempo*." This, it seems, must explain those elements of repetition and continuity in the phenomenon of madness and the way it is encountered. It must, that is, explain the unchanging scapegoat function the madman took over from the leper; the symbolic values and images institutionalized mental treatment has always involved; the very fact, indeed, that a "dialogue" with madness has been carried on through the years in any form at all. In practice, then, archaeology itself seems to re-present in modified form the typically metaphysical and even idealist belief that beneath the flux of history lies an unchanging ground or essence, the deeper structurality of human existence itself.

The final theme, critical reversal, turns out, in some ways, to be the most important. It is, in fact, difficult to avoid the impression that the predominant concern of *Madness and Civilization* is to overturn an established doctrine by reevaluating its past. Specifically, it rejects the notion that the mad were abused and oppressed until an enlightened age learned to treat them with compassion. Instead it argues that the

[40]Foucault, Preface to *The Order of Things*, xxii.
[41]Foucault, *Madness and Civilization*, 30–31.
[42]Ibid., xi–xii, 212.

modern asylum eliminated physical abuses, but replaced them with refined and more efficient forms of oppression. Madness is now defined by the fact that its words can have no meaning, while its transgressionary behavior simultaneously threatens the social order. Hence, there is no longer any attempt at a true dialogue with the mad. As inmates, they are observed, controlled, and treated, but also effectively silenced. In the modern era, they are for the first time all but entirely excluded from discursive practice. The modern, "enlightened" doctor, moreover, is not at all their savior, but "a Judge who punishes and rewards." His power derives, not from medicine itself, but from the aura of "quasi-divinity" that surrounds the medical man. The doctor does not really "know" the madman; he is not any longer "familiar" with madness; he "masters" it instead. His admired objectivity is only the other side of this peculiarly modern version of repressive domination.[43]

At the same time the problem of confinement in general seems the real issue here, for the scope of *Madness and Civilization* is sufficiently broad to take in at times all varieties of noncriminal incarceration in "prisons of moral order." The institutionalized mad are just a special case of this. By the same token, confinement itself is just one variety of the still larger question of the degree to which Western culture has evolved as a structure of domination, repression, and exclusion. It is at this level, then, that Foucault has the greatest affinity with Derrida. The difference is, as noted, that the one focuses upon more immediately recognizable forms of institutional discourse and behavior, the other upon institutionalized philosophico-literary practice and norms. In either case, however, it is clearly always a political focus.

The refusal to admit the political nature of that focus—quite common on the more or less official Left—is, for the most part, predicated upon an excessively restrictive notion of politics, one whose constant insistence upon the "specifically" political would go a long way toward excluding from consideration many important works that have a deep political interest and bearing (including some or all of Nietzsche, Weber, Freud, Heidegger, many works of literature, and even a significant portion of Marx). In this case, at least, the apparently laudable concern for "specifics" (often defined arbitrarily, if at all) threatens to become only one further means for avoiding the challenge of figures like Foucault and Derrida, whose more profound and far-reaching criticisms pose unsettling problems that are difficult

[43]Ibid., 271–272, 277–278.

to handle within the limited and overly rigid framework of conventional political theory. One might argue that such figures, far from being "apolitical" (they are thus denied recognition), or "nihilistic" (they are therefore to be silenced, repressed) will frequently, upon closer inspection, be found working toward a generalization of the political problem.

Now, in the case of Foucault, the problems created by a sympathetic concern for transgression of established norms and limits in general, and a simultaneous quest (in theory at least) for the rules and regulations of discourse, itself understood as a temporally unified "system of statements," have also already been noted Here it may be added that the relative stress on themes is such that entire works often appear at odds in this respect. A "regulatory" text, such as *The Archaeology of Knowledge*, must to a certain degree contradict the more "transgressionary" ones, such as *Madness and Civilization*. And, in much the same way, the promise of archaeology must contradict its practice.

The same problem is to a degree characteristic of the style Foucault employs. He seems, in fact, to have two: one more "imaginative"—playful (as in certain essays) or lyrical (as in portions of *Madness and Civilization*)—and a second that belongs to the more serious structural scientist, the seeker after a general system of "discursive regularities." In practice, the tension between them does not appear to have resulted in a productive dialectic or dialogic interchange within or between texts. It seems, rather, to drive each style to extremes. Eventually, as in *The Archaeology of Knowledge*, even the "regular" style acquires a decidedly excessive character. It is worth observing, therefore, that certain of Foucault's shorter works appear to provide a different, more thought-provoking perspective on this problem. In such essays he often seems to be considering more carefully the very nature of regularity and excess, and of the creative possibilities inherent in their active interrelation. He does so, moreover, in a style that itself more successfully accommodates the two. He does not appear any longer to be offering quite the same choice between extremes of order and disorder, between an elaborately structured world of regulated discourse and apocalyptic suggestions of absolute transgression. He argues instead (and in a more measured fashion) that rules and limits are always involved in what transgresses or exceeds them, that each has a necessary function, that each, indeed, depends upon the other for its existence, both specifically and in general.[44]

[44]Foucault, "Preface to Transgression," 34.

Overall, Foucault has been predominantly concerned to provide a critical retrospective of the hidden role that regulation, control, imposed limitation and restriction have played in the development of a supposedly liberal and enlightened cultural environment. He has striven to locate and describe the ways the dream of a rational order and organization has often exercised a negative, reprehensible influence in practice, especially with regard to modern institutions and institutionalized behavior. At times (certainly in portions of *Madness and Civilization*) he has seemed to adopt a position of radical hostility to institutionalization in any form, apparently arguing that all hierarchical organization is, by definition, repressive. Thus, while discourse has seemed to him best described as a "system of statements," institutionalized discourse has been discussed as, inevitably, a "system of exclusion" and domination. Foucault has been concerned, then, to defend whatever transgresses or undermines this stifling order. He has often given the impression that, in such a world, transgression of boundaries—materially, theoretically, stylistically—becomes, *per se*, a positive, a liberating, a creative act. In certain of his shorter pieces, by contrast, he adopts a less extreme, less absolutely combative stance, and comes to consider the more positive role that limits can play. Like Nietzsche, he suggests that certain forms of limitation are in fact required, both so that valuable efforts toward overcoming can occur, and as an inducement to further transgressions of this kind. In some of its manifestations (for example, self-discipline and the semi-imposed discipline implied in the obligation to meet rigorous, demanding standards in one's work), the limit can even be the condition for a genuinely creative act of transgressing other, less desirable, limits. In this respect, Foucault draws nearer Derrida, whose own "problematization" of traditional conceptualization never appears to involve any conviction that all hierarchy is in itself repressive, and whose own brand of critical anarchy appears consistently more restrained, even when it is actually more radical. Foucault's ability occasionally to rethink his position in shorter works, and to draw back a bit from its more extreme implications, is then reinforced by the more carefully organized, more subtly modulated language these works at times employ.[45]

Additionally, Foucault here also appears to consider at last the way a narrow insistence upon categorization—such as one finds in *The*

[45]See, e.g., Foucault, "Preface to Transgression," "Language to Infinity," "Nietzsche, Genealogy, History," and "Theatrum Philosophicum" in his *Language, Counter-Memory, Practice*.

Archaeology of Knowledge—may imply hostility to all forms of difference, discontinuity, and transgression of categorial limits. However much he may proclaim them, Foucault's explicit conception of discourse still appears to check and even deny the possibility of genuinely irregular difference, discontinuity, and transgression within a given epoch. The face and nature of even interepochal difference, must, from the perspective of "discursive regularity," go unexplained and unexplored. Shorter pieces—for example "A Preface to Transgression"—seem at times to approach the problem in more potentially productive ways.

It is precisely such questions of reciprocity and openness, however, that Foucault's more extensive works (and some essays and interviews also) generally fail to evaluate. And this helps account, no doubt, for their often somewhat self-contradictory extremism of argument. Similarly, there are essays that suggest a more cautious and thoughtful perception of the relation to tradition. Some appear to accept the possibility of continuity over time.[46] Others argue for a notion of repetition with difference that is not entirely unlike certain aspects of Derrida's discussion of tradition.[47] It seems, then, that the promise of archaeology—having encountered certain difficulties in practice— might itself be profitably reconsidered in the light of Foucault's "lesser" works, where a greater awareness of the problems that practice generates can frequently be found.

Turning now again to Derrida, the present essay will try to suggest how, in general, the promise of deconstruction, already further-reaching, is also in practice more nearly fulfilled. *Of Grammatology*, for example, actually provides (along with much else) a rigorously deconstructive reading of the traditional understanding of language and, by extension, of the philosophical heritage out of which that understanding has emerged and upon which it relies.[48] The first phase does in fact consist of a sustained effort to detect and disclose, through a carefully managed use of its own terminology and rationale, the specifically metaphysical assumptions upon which modern linguistics has consciously or unconsciously established itself. Among these appears

---

[46]Michel Foucault, "What Is an Author?" in his *Language, Counter-Memory, Practice*, 127; "Preface to Transgression," 40–41.

[47]Foucault, "Language to Infinity," 62; "Theatrum Philosophicum," 182, 195–6.

[48]The deconstructive reading of established linguistics and its understanding of language is contained in *Of Grammatology*, Part One. Part Two of the same work contains a more extensive reading of Rousseau and his relation to subsequent anthropology. For present purposes, however, a discussion of the linguistic question seems more suitable. Derrida's reading of Rousseau would require a substantially longer discussion.

an assumption that the meaning of being is presence, and that "presence" must in turn mean "present to the mind." Tradition assumes, that is, the existence of mental "experiences" that "reflect or mirror things naturally," and that between being and mind is a relation of "natural signification."[49] Then, within the mind is reason or thought, in which the meaning or "truth" of things appears (is received, produced, composed). And this thought subsequently manifests itself in an immediate and natural manner. For Derrida, this amounts to "logocentrism": the word as presence of thought; the thought as presence of the world's truth or meaning. And, he maintains, Western metaphysics—hence the entire cultural history of the West—has always been predominantly logocentric.

Here two further assumptions are involved. The first, a traditional model of the sign itself as the unity of a heterogeneity: signifier and signified. With the one, the other is said to become present to thought. Historically, this too is a fundamentally metaphysical distinction. Indeed, first appearing explicitly in Stoic logic, it constitutes an integral element of scholastic theology, where the signifier always referred to a divinely created entity, that is, one that in fact required no signifier to be what it was. Modern linguistics, says Derrida, agrees implicitly with its history. By considering the signified "a meaning thinkable in principle within the full presence of an intuitive consciousness," it too understands the existence of that signified as independent of all signifiers. This encourages belief in the possibility of a "transcendental signified," one that is not itself a signifier in turn. Somewhere, it is assumed, the chains of signification must end in a final meaning or truth—an assumption whose metaphysical and ultimately theological basis is clear.[50]

Second, a "binary opposition" emerges in the form of the historical privilege allotted by linguistics to the spoken word, and the correlative depreciation—just as traditional—of writing. The two present a contrast: one as the purest, most immediate manifestation of language; the other as something derivative, a secondary order of sign with the task of signifying speech. For Derrida, this hierarchical opposition derives from the ancient belief that the spoken word, infused with the breath, or *spiritus*, sustains a relation of immediate proximity to the mind, or *animus* (the close, even at times synonymic, association of these two Latin words is surely no accident), and hence of proximity

[49]Derrida, *Of Grammatology*, 11.
[50]Ibid., 10–18, 49, 65–73.

to that which, "within 'thought' as logos, relates to 'meaning.'"[51] It is taken for granted, in other words, that speech is the most direct, and therefore most faithful, truest, best way of signifying those "mental experiences" which themselves naturally "reflect or mirror the world." The spoken sign is "closest to the signified," while its graphic counterpart is merely a sign of the spoken word. Thus, in linguistics, the historical logocentrism of philosophy and theology assumes a "phonocentric" guise.

The second deconstructive phase is the attempted inversion of this hierarchy and the awarding of privilege to writing. The attempt involves, on the one hand, unsettling the apparently secure position of speech. This is accomplished in a variety of ways, but primarily through a general critique of the traditional idea of the sign. Here Derrida is specifically concerned to show why no order of signification can ever produce, generate, facilitate, or cooperate in the attainment of a "full presence" of the signified. He argues, for example, that both difference and absence are necessary for the sign to exist at all. The very possibility of signification presupposes, that is, some difference between signifier and signified, and the absence or deferral (however brief) of the latter. If full oneness were possible, there could be no sign of it. Every sign is therefore also in some sense a sign of dearth or death. This is the pathos of signification, of language in general.

At the same time, of course, these "gaps" can never be pure. No signifier, nor any signified, can ever be a "unique and singular reality." The two always come together, and each will be marked by some "trace" (for instance, historical) of the other or, once again, no signifying relation can form. The sign is, then, neither a unity nor a perfect difference of elements. Words and concepts acquire meaning only through their mutual participation in an intricate historical network of (tainted) differences and deferrals. No "full speech" exists or is possible.

On a different level, this act of dethronement gathers support from a deconstructive reading of the linguists themselves. The latter, in the course of arguing phonocentrically, characteristically proclaim the "arbitrariness of the sign," that it is "an unmotivated institution."[52] Derrida treats this as decisive. For, if the sign were truly arbitrary, there could be no natural hierarchy among signifiers or orders of

[51] Ibid., 11.
[52] Ibid., 44.

signification. Speech, in other words, could have no more natural a relation to the signified than writing, and so could claim no privilege. Only by a form of violence, then, can phonocentrism triumph. It must ignore the implications of a point it has itself made, and force a contrary conclusion. The text has thus worked against itself in maintaining an historical hierarchy. Deconstruction makes use of the fact to assist its critical inversion.[53]

On the other hand, however, it must still establish the priority of writing. This is accomplished through an "enlarged" understanding. "Writing" now comes to signify "all that gives rise to inscription in general." It "signifies inscription and especially the durable institution of the sign."[54] But it also means the "regulated play" of difference between inscriptions. "Writing" consequently becomes a name for that inevitably shifting and uncertain process whereby all forms of symbolism are established and institutionalized. All signs function, in fact, only because they have been established and, to a degree at least, institutionalized, that is, because they have been "written" in this enlarged sense. And "writing" is what is always "at work" in both graphic and nongraphic modes of signification. It is what establishes and disestablishes all orders of expression, representation, or meaning in general—that "play of signifying references" that all language is. Derrida thus concludes that writing "*comprehends* language," that all language is actually but one "species of writing," one "mode" or "aspect" of a larger, more or less regulated "play" of instituted signs.[55]

Yet, in the third phase, writing is itself dethroned. Or, rather, it is shown to have never been allowed to attain a truly dominant position. For this new "concept" has been defined with care. It means neither speech nor writing in the conventional sense. It does not even mean language as that term is commonly employed. It is, indeed, highly

[53]Derrida does not, of course, try to argue that *all* modern linguists *always* proclaim *only* the doctrine of the arbitrariness of the sign. On the contrary, he takes Saussure's work as exemplary and is careful to note that this in fact represents only one of several rather contradictory doctrines Saussure advanced. Nevertheless, modern linguistics does characteristically espouse the arbitrariness of the sign, for it has generally been in reaction against an older doctrine of natural, essential links between signifier and signified. This older doctrine's relation to theology is much more direct and readily apparent. The interesting fact here is that modern linguistics has for the most part explicitly rejected the more obvious metaphysical presuppositions of its history, while continuing to accept them implicitly, at least insofar as it continues to accept the conclusions to which those presuppositions gave rise. Modern linguists have continued to accept the doctrine of the special status, the superior, more effective, more natural, the purer and more potent, powers of the spoken Word.

[54]Derrida, *Of Grammatology*, 9 and 44.

[55]Ibid., 6–7.

"undecidable." Derrida calls it "inscription," "institution," and a "regulated play of differences." Further, from his critique of the sign, it appears that "writing" in this larger sense relies upon other "concepts," like "deferral" and "trace." Each of these is equally undecidable. None can honestly be called an entity or essence, a fact or principle, a phenomenon or concept, for none is or strives to be a simple unity. Nor, by the same token, can any be considered the basis for a synthetic reconciliation or resolution. Each is, on the contrary, at once a *relational* term, and an insurmountable roadblock in the path of any dialectical totalization. For, whatever is, by definition, a relational complex (and what "by definition" is not?) can never be resolved into an identity, except by more or less violent means. Dialectical harmonization always involves some amount of repression (denying, forgetting, distorting—"silencing" of any sort). By insisting in a variety of ways upon the multiple, and self-multiplying, nature of his (and perhaps of all) "key" terms, Derrida hopes to avoid reappropriation by a Hegelian dialectics, the subtlest and most powerful force for recuperation in(to) the Western metaphysical tradition.

Consequently, "difference and deferral," "trace," "play," "inscription," "sign," and even "writing"—all must in themselves clearly imply a relation between entities, principles, concepts, and the like. None can itself pose as a unified, internally tranquil presence. Indeed, none is a "presence" at all, but always a relation-between. Each element in a relation necessarily involves the others. Moreover, each relational term involves and/or implies others as well. "Writing," that is, can itself never be understood apart from "difference," "deferral," "trace," and so forth, though no term can simply be reduced to another. To elevate one or another temporarily to a position of prominence—as Derrida repeatedly does—is therefore not to establish a hierarchy based on domination. It is rather to suggest (or even accentuate) the fundamental ambivalence that every dominationist hierarchy endeavors to conceal or deny. Typically, this familiar concealment or denial takes the form of the argument that, where "ambivalence" and "ambiguity" have been successfully managed, mastered, or reduced, they have "for all practical purposes"—hence (sooner or later, explicitly or implicitly), "absolutely and finally"—ceased to exist. Since they are now and then (but generally less often than one might like to imagine) relatively unimportant, they are readily forgotten or denied altogether in the bulldozing drive toward totalizing harmony and consensus.

Totalitarian thinking, in all its many forms, hates and fears any suggestion of ambivalence and ambiguity. Through the usual distorting reduction of meaning, they are generally first said to be synonymous with simple "confusion" or worse. Historically, totalitarian thinking of every kind then strives, more or less consciously, to "eliminate" ambivalence and ambiguity, generally misrepresenting its activity as the course imposed by the sometimes difficult, but always finally imperative, "choice between confusion and order"—the version of classical either/or logic that most often serves, in the "specifically political" realm and elsewhere, to justify repressive measures. Totalitarian thinking senses (correctly, no doubt) the danger ambivalence and ambiguity contain for every "totality" and totalizing aspiration.

To place, however, a relation in the "central" position—as "writing" certainly does—is to undercut, effectively to decenter, the very thought of a unified totality. It is then also to emphasize the fact that no one element can ever claim an absolute privilege, since each relies on others from which it differs, or to which it defers. By arguing for a certain perception of writing, Derrida has indeed attempted to elevate it over speech. But by doing so in the way he has, he also demonstrates the impossibility of its ever playing the domineering role that, historically, phonocentrism has sought for speech. He has tried, in fact, to show why that very dichotomy, or any absolute dichotomy, can be maintained only by ignoring the way its members are always related or even overlap—yet do not simply merge. So the effort to enforce the domination of one can succeed only through the application of a measure of violence and repression to the other. By placing "writing" at the center, Derrida is asserting the existence of the world as "essentially" a relational network in which absence or deferral plays as important a role as presence, and which has therefore no real center at all.

Hence it is now more apparent what Derrida means by the "problematization" of traditional hierarchical thinking: first, to show why there can be no absolute, but only relative, hierarchies; then, to argue for a form of relative privilege that does not, as traditional privilege does, base itself on principles of domination or try to institutionalize itself in permanent and inflexible form. On the contrary, the sort of "hierarchy" deconstruction establishes—for, despite certain popular impressions, this negative strategy does aim to establish something— is one in which reciprocity and mutual involvement are openly acknowledged and allowed for, even institutionalized: a dynamic structure whose "dominant" mode is a form of irony in which every element will find itself implicated. It suggests a renewal and expansion of that vital contestatory partnership between Dionysus and Apollo.

In its final phase, then, the deconstruction of the historically dominant conception of language means its simultaneous re-vision or "re-inscription." It has been suggested why this must be at least a dual operation. There is, on the one hand, a critical retrospective of traditional views and their presuppositions. These are then not so much denied as "problematized." Eventually, this process must involve Derrida, with his assertion of "concepts" such as "difference" and "trace," in the Heideggerian effort to undermine the entire metaphysical tradition through an attack upon its most fundamental characteristics: an understanding of being as presence, and a correlative linear model of historical time.[56] With his "enlarged" definition of writing, moreover, he is denying every idea of a new home for "truth," a new source of absolutist values (including that of absolute relativism), a new transcendental signified. This might all be considered the negative, or rejectionist aspect of revision. The other is a more positive attempt to start thinking on the way toward freeing itself from historically imposed limitations. Not, of course, by trying to leave tradition behind and move on to something else—*Of Grammatology* repeatedly demonstrates the impossibility of such a move, even with regard to those elements it explicitly calls into question. They are all, in fact, required by that very interrogation. Judgments, rational argumentation, the "concept" and logic of the sign—all are involved in the attempt at their own deconstruction. The last above all, as Derrida insists, cannot be given up, for the sign is organized around precisely the thought of tainted difference and deferral that he works to affirm.

Re-vision can proceed, then, only as a simultaneous familiarization with tradition and the struggle to see it in a somewhat different way—a way that will no longer hold thinking captive to history's least justifiable, most limiting or repressive forms. Thus, older conceptions are neither merely discarded nor simply inverted or reversed, but "reinscribed" within a somewhat broader framework. "Writing" cannot now be given true hegemony over speech or understood in any sense as a transcendental notion. It is, rather, to be thought as the infinite play of difference and deferral, of presencing and absence: the affirmative thought of an endless and endlessly various investment and divestment of sense.

[56]It is perhaps here, in his critical understanding of the metaphysical tradition and his opposition to conventional notions of being and time, that Derrida's work relates most obviously to Heidegger's.

This relation to the past and this disturbing conception of writing suggest one further aspect of Derrida's affinity with Heidegger, for at the very least they imply a decision to reexamine the text(s) of tradition, "reading between the lines" with a new openness to what might there be discovered. Elements that have challenged and been more or less repressed by tradition's dominant, metaphysical tendency must now be recovered and reconsidered, their creative possibilities tested and even developed. The intellectual historian's work, his historical retrospective, is thus not only to be a process of destabilization and destruction (though it is definitely to be these), but also an ex-pedition of discovery and regeneration. Deconstruction aims always at a reconstruction, though never of quite what had been so solidly constructed and firmly implanted. Rather, it aims to "establish" that more dynamic, more ironic perception alluded to above—a certain idea of tradition as an ongoing regulated contest, in which prevailing elements do not attempt to evade or eliminate the forces that challenge their predominance, but are instead alive to all the ways the struggle, however great its tensions or pain, can itself prove the most stimulating, revitalizing, and truly creative encounter.

In conclusion, it may be observed that a number of broad similarities exist between Foucault and Derrida. Both are involved in a reexamination of the Western cultural heritage, and each is especially anxious to challenge its conventional interpretations, to bring out what they obscure. Neither is therefore content to associate his work with that of traditional forms of history. Each instead poses a more general challenge to conventional methods of interpretation. Here, the problems of repression or mastery, as they appear in history or operate in its dominant modes of conceptualization, are a vital concern to both. It should be clear, however, that neither archaeology nor deconstruction can possibly result, as some have feared, in the "homogenization" of Western culture, the forgetting of tradition's great internal diversity, the reduction of its history to a series of more or less clever variations upon a single theme. It would seem, on the contrary, precisely such "homogenizing" that each is designed to oppose. Nevertheless, it has at times been argued that one or the other consists only of tiresome attacks upon the same *bête noire*, the established tradition, against which it has only a single significant complaint. Consequently, it is said, each implies an intellectual history that would always come everywhere only to the same essential conclusions.

To be sure, this objection is not simply wrong. Archaeology and deconstruction do involve repeated attempts to demonstrate the respects in which the dominant tendency in the West has been or become both metaphysical and repressive. But to think that making such attempts means always saying "essentially" the same thing, and therefore represents a rather limited understanding of history, is really only possible if one is prepared first to ignore a great deal: most of all that the Western tradition is no simple monolith, and that this is precisely the point Foucault and Derrida have been making. It is therefore not to recognize the fact that discovering, exploring, and exposing the numerous complex ways that it is metaphysical and repressive can hardly amount to an undifferentiated idea of the past in which everywhere the identical sins are found. Hence this frequent objection seems itself predicated upon a willingness to ignore the great differences between the large number of writings the two strategies have produced.

Even regarding single works, the charge itself requires what it complains of, since neither archaeology nor deconstruction can ever be with justice reduced to its most critical, negationist aspects. There is more to both than the desire to undermine the Western tradition. Both entail the effort to rehabilitate tradition's less familiar and often quite deviant elements or tendencies. And these latter have proved equally various. Moreover, both—though especially deconstruction—have involved developing whatever aspects would be neither metaphysical nor repressive, but rather more keenly playful and open to the possibilities of contestation, including self-contestation—aspects whose relations would be eternally supplementary, rather than complementary and resolution-oriented.

Yet there are also major differences between archaeology and deconstruction. First, of course, there is the practical difficulty the former has in adhering to its promise, while the latter seems to manage this relation with greater self-awareness and care. More notable may be the general way Foucault—apparently without acknowledgment—has stayed more within the limits of the tradition that both contest. His theory of archive and episteme, his typically formalist idea of history as a discontinuous series of largely synchronic structures, his tendency to remain at the reversal stage of conventional dichotomies, his theoretical allegiance to the positivist ideal of objective description in historiography—all are thoroughly traditional (if not metaphysical) components of his work. Derrida, by contrast, demonstrates a surer understanding of such problems and appears more consistently to cope with them. His desire for a general displacement and subsequent reinscription of traditional options, his perception of history as a dynamic but regulated relation of similarity and difference, of repetition with change over time, his more actively involved and even ultimately creative conception of historiography—all these seem to give his work a substantially more radical import. Thus, as well, Derrida appears to indicate more successfully than Foucault directions in which intellectual history might itself begin to move if it would become a still more thoughtful, a more genuinely intellectual, enterprise.

Chapter Seven

On the Problem of the Ideological Origins of the French Revolution

Keith Michael Baker

What an ironic position intellectual historians seem to be in. Once under sentence of confinement to the scholastic irrelevance of the superstructure, we are now treated to a neoscholastic debate over its relative independence. Once threatened by the imperialism of behavioral social science among historians, we seem now to be witnessing a reorientation of the social sciences generally toward problems of meaning. Even those who dismissed ideas as the most ephemeral of appearances, and their history as a narrative cobweb to be swept away by the *Annalistes'* broom, seem now themselves to be recreating *l'événement*. Is it surprising that at a point when everyone else is rediscovering mind, the intellectual historian shows some of the disorientation of the ghetto-dweller after the walls have been broken down? Who are we anyway? Where do we go from here? Have we been invaded or liberated?

I think I can best state my own view of the matter by saying that I regard intellectual history as a mode of historical discourse rather than as a distinct field of inquiry with a clearly demarcated subject matter. It is a way of addressing the past, a certain orientation toward history generally, rather than a separate or autonomous branch of historical scholarship in any strict or categorical sense. The intellectual historian analyzing a text, concept, or movement of ideas, has the same prob-

Research for this paper was supported by the Guggenheim Foundation and the time to write it provided by the Institute for Advanced Study. I am grateful for this support, as for the stimulus offered by the organizers of and participants in the Cornell University conference. Helpful critical reactions were offered by Steven Kaplan, William Sewell, Elizabeth Eisenstein, Harry Harootunian, Julius Kirshner, John Comaroff, François Furet, and George Stocking, many of whose doubts and objections remain to be answered.

lem as the historian faced with any other historical phenomenon, namely to reconstitute the context (or, more usually, the plurality of contexts) in which that phenomenon takes on meaning as human action. History, in other words, is a diagnostic discipline: given the scratch, the historian seeks to discover the itch; or, to offer a less behavioristic formulation, given the solution, he tries to reconstitute the problem. I do not think the intellectual historian differs (or, at least, should differ) in this respect from other historians with other concerns. Let us rebuild no walls.

What, then, is the orientation characteristic of intellectual history? I would say that the intellectual historian seeks particularly to attend to the intellective dimensions of social action as historically constituted. This may seem a rather general definition, perhaps even an empty one. But I choose it for several reasons. The first is that I want to set aside from the outset the idea that intellectual history is confined to the history of "intellectuals." This is not to say, of course, that their activities have no place in intellectual history: the nature and definition of cognitive functions in particular societies, the institutional position, social role, and conceptual claims of those who engage in more or less specialized intellectual activities, remain among the most interesting problems with which the intellectual historian is presented. They offer a rich field for comparative research of a kind that intellectual historians have barely begun to consider. However, such problems do not exhaust the domain of intellectual history; nor, indeed, could they be answered adequately if they did. Intellectual history is not simply the history of intellectuals, broad as that history may be. It is the history of "intellection," which (according to the OED) derives from a Latin root that implies "perceiving, discerning, discernment, understanding, meaning, sense, signification." In a word, it is the history of meaning.

But meaning is a dimension of all social action. We can therefore set aside the untenable distinction between ideas and events—and the artificial and sterile problems about the relationship and priority between them—that has so often introduced confusion and absurdity into discussion of intellectual history. The action of a rioter in picking up a stone can no more be understood apart from the symbolic field that gives it meaning than the action of a priest in picking up a sacramental vessel. The philosopher picking up a pen is not performing a less social action than the ploughman picking up a plough, nor does the latter act lack intellectual dimensions. Action implies meaning; meaning implies cultural intersubjectivity; intersubjectivity implies society. All social activity has an intellective dimension that gives it meaning, just as all intellectual activity has a social dimension that gives it point.

I do not mean to assert here that all history is intellectual history. But I think it does follow from this argument that intellectual history can have no precise boundary with other fields. On the one hand, it will seek to elicit the intellective dimensions in those forms of social action which present themselves as stable forms of behavior—those patterns of action constituted by implicit meanings that often seem indistinguishable from a description of the actions themselves. To this extent, it will merge with institutional or social history as the *histoire des mentalités*. On the other hand, it will seek to analyze those more explicit forms of intellectual activity that have been established as specialized kinds of knowledge—recognizing that the more explicit play of ideas that characterizes such activity occurs within a structured field of discourse that defines its purposes and procedures internally and establishes its existence externally as part of a set of social constraints. To this extent, intellectual history will take shape as the history of particular disciplines, genres, theories, or problems: for instance, the history of the sciences, the history of theology and philosophy, legal history, and the history of historiography. Indeed, insofar as the identity of any such discipline depends upon establishing and maintaining an appropriate genealogy, intellectual history merges imperceptibly into the practice of the discipline itself.

I should emphasize here that I am not trying to reinstate the distinction between popular and elite culture, one dominated by habit, custom, passivity, the other by creativity and the "free play" of ideas.[1] Inherited reifications of constituted experience form many dimensions of the consciousness of the elite, no less than those of other social groups; intellectual creativity occurs within the domain of popular culture, just as it does in more specialized cognitive activities. Nor do I regard the distinction between implicit social meanings and explicitly articulated intellectual activities as an exhaustive one. On the contrary, it defines two more or less stabilized limits in the relationship between intellection and social life: two limits between which there exists a complex middle ground where ideas seem neither to merge with the practice of concrete social life nor to separate out as the object of a set of specialized intellectual activities. This is the middle ground—more or less vast in any particular society at any

---

[1] The problems involved in this distinction are discussed by Roger Chartier in another essay in this volume.

particular time—in which there is a consciousness of ideas at play in social life, in which mental sets appear to form and disaggregate, in which domains of experience are claimed for competing fields of discourse, in which the relationship between words and things presents itself as problematic.

In the body of this paper, I shall consider a classic problem that falls within this domain: the problem of the ideological origins of the French Revolution. Before doing so, however, I feel obliged to return to one aspect of this brief initial effort to characterize intellectual history. I said that the intellectual historian seeks particularly to attend to the intellective dimensions of social action as historically constituted. But I have not yet touched on the problem of how one might think of these dimensions as historically constituted. I have not, that is, suggested how one might counter the Faustian bargain we seem to be offered by the structuralists: an offer of the entire world as a domain of meaning, but at the cost of our historical souls.

I can perhaps approach this problem by appealing to the metaphor of *bricolage* offered by Lévi-Strauss.[2] *Bricolage* is the activity of the *bricoleur*, the jack-of-all-trades who is good with his hands, putters around in his workshop, and finds fulfillment in creating (or undertaking) odd jobs. The *bricoleur* does not throw things away. He collects "bits and pieces," "odds and ends," on the assumption that they will eventually come in handy. He uses them for his purposes in an improvisational way, combining objects that had been fashioned for a variety of prior uses. Thus the distinctive features of the *bricoleur*'s stock are finiteness and heterogeneity. He defines his projects in terms of what he has; his activities are preconstrained by the nature of the materials he has collected. These materials are heterogeneous, in the sense that they have no necessary or systematic relationship. They are remains, the end results of previous activities, the remnants of previous constructions. Thus their actual relationship one to another is contingent: they exist in the stock as the result of the occasions the *bricoleur* has taken to extend and renew it. And their potential relationship is unpredictable, in the sense that the *bricoleur* chooses among and combines them in ways, and for purposes, that do not derive from any necessary relationships underlying their coexistence within the stock. In this manner, Lévi-Strauss suggests, the *bricoleur* "builds up structures by fitting together events, or rather the remains of events," while the scientist or engineer (with whom he is contrasted) creates events by elaborating structures.[3]

[2]Claude Lévi-Strauss, *The Savage Mind* (Chicago, 1966), 16–36.
[3]Ibid., 22.

If this is to be a useful metaphor for intellectual history, we must begin by avoiding the temptation to regard the *bricoleur* as a transcendent, suprahistorical subject: *bricolage* is not the Cunning of Reason. But we can perhaps consider the intellectual stock of any society at any particular time as in some ways resembling that of the *bricoleur*. An inventory of that stock—which would look very much like Foucault's "archive"[4]—would reveal a multiplicity of separate discourses constituting separate domains of meaning. Each of these discourses would have its own history; each would have its own "logic"; each would constitute a field of social action by categorizing the world of social actors in accordance with its own terms of reference. These discourses would coexist within the society as a whole, some remaining quite separate one from another, many overlapping in the practice of social life, as well as in the consciousness of individuals. They would be heterogeneous in the sense that they would often involve assumptions and implications that, if elaborated far enough, would contradict the assumptions and implications of others. Their relationship would be contingent in the sense that they could not be integrated into a total system or structure, as parts to a whole, according to a strict enchainment of logical relations. They would be arranged hierarchically in the sense that some would be regarded as controlling and some thought of as controlled, that some would be thought of as more powerful than others. But this hierarchy would be conventional rather than apodictic, political rather than logical.

How, then, could we move from a synchronic view of such an intellectual universe to a diachronic one? If we set aside the *bricoleur* as a transcendent historical agent, how can we think of the process of transformation and change that would correspond to his activity? The answer would seem to lie in emphasizing that the multiplicity of discourses we have been considering are not dead remnants, the archaeological remains of some vanished constructions. On the contrary, they are fields of social action symbolically constituted, social practices, "language games" each subject to constant elaboration and development through the activities of the individual agents whose purposes they define. Coexisting in a given society, often overlapping in social practice and in the consciousness of individuals, they are not insulated one from another in any strict way. Drawing upon common linguistic resources, they will have a greater or lesser degree of interpenetration, so that individual acts and utterances will often take on

[4] Michel Foucault, *The Archaeology of Knowledge* (1969), tr. A. M. Sheridan Smith (New York, 1972), 126–131. The following discussion draws generally on Foucault's approach to what he calls the "historical a priori" (p. 127).

meaning within several fields of discourse simultaneously. Changes in one realm of discourse will redound upon others in unanticipated and unpredictable ways; elements from several discourses will be combined to define new domains of experience and social action. In some cases, these changes will support and reinforce one another. In others, they will create a state of tension and contradiction still negotiable within the conventional hierarchization of discourse. In others, competing claims and implications will be elaborated to such an extent that their resolution will threaten—and eventually force a redefinition of—that hierarchization in more or less radical ways.[5]

Rather than elaborating these considerations further in purely abstract terms, I shall explore the kind of approach they seem to suggest to one of the classic problems of European intellectual history, the problem of the ideological origins of the French Revolution. Why speak of "ideological" rather than "intellectual" origins? At this point, I have two answers to that question. The first is that I think it inconsistent with what I have already said to offer any strong distinction between these terms. In its original sense, "ideology" was concerned with the study of the process by which the world of phenomena is given order and meaning through the activity of signification. For the Idéologues—the fascinating and much maligned group of philosophers to whom we owe the term—that process was to be understood as an essentially individual one, grounded in a universalistic conception of natural human reason.[6] If we understand it as a social—that is to say, intersubjective—process, grounded in a pluralistic theory of discourse, then "ideology" and "intellection," "ideological" and "intellectual," are not strictly distinguishable.

At the same time, it may in another respect be useful to maintain a differentiation between the two sets of terms. The various uses of "ideology" have generally involved some notion of contested mean-

---

[5]For what I take to be an essentially similar view of this process, see J. G. A. Pocock, "Political Languages and Their Implications," *Politics, Language and Time: Essays on Political Thought and History* (New York, 1971), 3–41.

[6]See George Lichtheim, "The Concept of Ideology," *History and Theory* 4 (1964–65), 164–170; Emmet Kennedy, "'Ideology' from Destutt de Tracy to Marx," *Journal of the History of Ideas* 40 (1979), 353–368. As a result of recent work, the Idéologues are now much better understood. See Sergio Moravia, *Il tramonto dell illuminismo. Filosofia e politica nella società francese (1770–1810)* (Bari, 1968), and *Il pensiero degli Idéologues. Scienza e filosofia in Francia (1780–1815)* (Florence, 1974); Georges Gusdorf, *Les sciences humaines et la pensée occidentale*, vol. 8. *La conscience révolutionnaire, les idéologues* (Paris, 1978); Emmet Kennedy, *A Philosophe in the Age of Revolution: Destutt de Tracy and the Origins of "Ideology"* (Philadelphia, 1978); Martin Staum, *Cabanis: Enlightenment and Medical Philosophy in the French Revolution* (Princeton, 1980).

ing, of the process of signification itself as problematic, of a tension between alternative—usually true (objective) and false (subjective)—constructions of the world. For the Idéologues, "ideology" offered a scientific, objective, rational understanding of the logic of the human mind: an understanding of the order of sensations and ideas that would sweep away false reasoning and establish the basis for a rational social order. In appropriating the term, Marxism inverted the relationship between "science" and "ideology," identifying the latter with the false, subjective reasoning to which the Idéologues had opposed it. But Marxism also maintained the sense of "ideology" as a matter of contested meanings—of representations of the world that are either explicitly contested by historical actors in the course of class struggle, or implicitly contested by the philosopher historian in terms of the dichotomy between ideology and science. I would like to retain "ideology" and "ideological" in a related sense, as terms to characterize those activities and situations in which signification itself seems to be at issue in social life, in which there is a consciousness of contested representations of the world in play, in which social action takes the form of more or less explicit efforts to order or reorder the world through the articulation and deployment of competing systems of meaning.[7]

Perhaps I should add, to avoid possible misunderstanding, that I see nothing in this view that commits me to a notion of ideology as the mere reflection of some more objective or real interests of social groups or classes. I think it points toward a conception of a "politics of language" (in the way Pocock has used that term) rather than a sociology of ideas. Group interests are not brute, objective phenomena; they rest on cognitive principles of social differentiation. A community exists only to the extent that there is some common discourse by which its members can constitute themselves as different groups within the social order and make claims upon one another that are regarded as intelligible and binding. The interaction involved in the framing of such claims is constrained within that discourse, which it in turn sustains, extends, and on occasion transforms. Political authority is in this view a matter of linguistic authority: both in the sense that public functions are defined and allocated within the framework of a given political discourse; and in the sense that their exercise takes the form of maintaining that discourse by upholding authoritative definitions of (and within) it. In these terms, then, a revolution can be

[7]See Clifford Geertz, "Ideology as a Cultural System," *The Interpretation of Cultures* (New York, 1973), 193–233.

defined as a transformation of the discursive practice of the community, a moment in which social relations are reconstituted and the discourse defining the political relations between individuals and groups is radically recast. Some such revolution, it seems safe to say, occurred in France in 1789.

Yet there has been relatively little explicit or systematic attention in recent years to the question of the ideological origins of the French Revolution: that is, to the elaboration of the field of political and social discourse—the pattern of meanings and implications—that constituted the significance of the events of 1789 and gave them explosive force. In large part, this problem has been obscured by prevailing approaches to the field, particularly by the Marxist paradigm that has dominated historical interpretation of the French Revolution until very recently. As François Furet has argued very effectively, the Marxian conception of the French Revolution as an "advent"—the rise of the bourgeoisie to power as the expression of an objective historical necessity—has obscured its nature as an "event"—as the invention of a new form of discourse constituting new modes of political and social action.[8] To the extent that competing modes of political discourse have been treated as functions of a sociological infrastructure— parlementary constitutionalism as noble reaction; Enlightenment political theory as bourgeois consciousness—the question of the ideological origins of the Revolution has disappeared as an independent problem. Perhaps not surprisingly, then, one of the most telling symptoms of the weakening of the Marxist paradigm in the study of the French Revolution is the growing interest in the more directly political aspects of the period, in the goals and strategies of the political actors, in the political vocabulary of the French Revolution not as "mere rhetoric" (two words which the last generation of historians welded together almost as inseparably as "rising" and "bourgeoisie") but as a means of transforming the symbolic grounding of the national community, the supremely political act of redefining the body politic. The most pressing task for the historiography of the French Revolution, Furet has rightly argued, is precisely this: "to rediscover the analysis of its political dimension. But the price to pay is two-fold: not only

---

[8]François Furet, *Penser la Révolution française* (Paris, 1978). Further references to this work will cite the English version, *Interpreting the French Revolution*, tr. Elborg Forster (Cambridge, 1981). I have considered the argument of this work more fully in a review essay, "Enlightenment and Revolution in France: Old Problems, Renewed Approaches," *Journal of Modern History* 53 (1981), 281–303. For a brief review of the historiographical collapse of the broadly Marxist consensus regarding the origins of the French Revolution, see William Doyle, *The Origins of the French Revolution* (Oxford, 1980), 7–40.

must we stop regarding revolutionary consciousness as a more or less 'natural' result of oppression and discontent; we must also develop a conceptual understanding of this strange offspring of *'philosophie'* (its offspring, at least, in a chronological sense)."[9] In short, we must understand the language of the French Revolution as an intellectual creation.

But if, as Furet suggests, the revolutionary consciousness is the offspring of *philosophie*, we should be able to draw on the vast body of work on the Enlightenment in discussing the ideological origins of the French Revolution. Efforts to do so, however, are often obscured by a false problematic (which I am tempted to call the "Heath Pamphlet Problematic") which presents itself in terms of "The Influence of the Enlightenment on the French Revolution." To my mind, no very helpful response is likely to emerge from a question posed in these terms. "Enlightenment" and "Revolution" simply become so reified that they face one another as two blocs—or, perhaps more accurately, like two opposing pieces at the end of a game of checkers, which can be manipulated through an indefinite series of relationships without ever making contact. There have, of course, been attempts to break this issue down analytically; but they have tended to take two forms, neither of which seems to pose the question effectively. The most obvious form has been a linear history of doctrines cast in terms of a necessary logic of ideas, usually with an emphasis on the influence of a particular doctrine or thinker. This, I suppose, is what one would call the "C'est la faute à Rousseau" style of interpretation. The most obvious example in relatively recent historiography is probably Talmon's work on the origins of totalitarian democracy, a work that in my view reveals some of the worst excesses of the teleological tendencies in intellectual history so ably criticized by Quentin Skinner.[10]

This kind of approach can be distinguished from a second one (with which it can merge in practice) which might be called the "diffusionist" or "trickle down" approach. Here the issue comes to rest on questions regarding the extent to which certain writings have been circulated or certain ideas diffused, and the extent to which those acting in the Revolution can be regarded as motivated to act by such ideas. I do not wish to diminish the relevance of quantitative studies of the book trade, or of efforts to investigate the circulation of ideas

---

[9]Furet, *Interpreting the French Revolution*, 27–28.
[10]J. L. Talmon, *The Origins of Totalitarian Democracy* (London, 1952). See Quentin Skinner, "Meaning and Understanding in the History of Ideas," *History and Theory* 8 (1969), 3–53.

among particular social groups. They are important for our understanding of the nature of intellectual and social life during any period. But books are not mere objects; nor are ideas isolated units. Texts, if read, are understood and hence reinterpreted by their readers in con-*texts* that may transform their significance; ideas, if received, take on meaning only in relation to others in the set of ideas into which they are incorporated. Thus it is important to insist upon the distinction between examining the circulation of ideas and understanding their meaning to social actors, and to avoid treating ideas as if they were causal, individual agents of motivation and determination. Understanding the ideological origins of the French Revolution is not a matter of establishing a causal chain linking particular ideas, individual or group motivations, and events in a series of one-to-one derivations. It is not necessary, for example, to establish that everyone in the crowd attacking the Bastille in July 1789 was motivated to overthrow despotism, for that event to take on the meaning of an attack on despotism within the field of political discourse created in the course of the earlier events of that year. Nor is it necessary to deny that the Great Fear retained many elements of traditional behavior in order to recognize its significance as revolutionary action. The Revolution of 1789 depended, in effect, on the creation and deployment of a political language that cast many different kinds of behaviors, from aristocratic resistance to popular fears, into the same symbolic order. In order to understand the Revolution as a political—that is to say, public—event, we need to reconstitute the field of political discourse in which it occurred, a field in which certain kinds of actions took on meanings that often went far beyond what particular actors intended.

Yet there has been relatively little effort in contemporary historiography (though there is a body of older historiography to be recovered on this theme) to consider the political discourse of the prerevolutionary period as an object of study in its own terms. If the power of the "social interpretation" of the French Revolution has been one reason for this lack, another seems to have been what I will call the "Tocqueville syndrome": the tendency to identify French political reflection with the activity of men of letters engaged in an "abstract and literary politics" by definition divorced from immediate problems of political and social life.

Tocqueville's characterization of the Enlightenment can be challenged in a number of ways. It can be insisted that much of its thinking, far from being abstract, was intimately related to the immediate social and political issues of the day. It can be pointed out that many of its principal spokesmen were by no means innocent of the practice of public affairs: that Montesquieu, for example, served as a magistrate in the parlement of Bordeaux; that Mably acted as a ministerial adviser on international affairs and wrote one of the standard works on international law; that Helvétius engaged in tax-farming; that Voltaire produced political tracts at request for several ministers; that Turgot was no less a philosophe for all his experience as Intendant. And it can be demonstrated that its principal institutional expression—the provincial academies so ably studied by Daniel Roche—is characterized precisely by "the solidarity of command and power" of a ruling elite united "in a vocation of common service to city, province or State."[11]

But these arguments do not entirely engage the argument of L'ancien régime et la Révolution. Tocqueville in fact acknowledged, both explicitly and implicitly, that the tendency to abstract radical thinking was not simply a function of a lack of practical public responsibilities. On the one hand, he allowed that eighteenth-century French thinkers contemplating the confused and antiquated spectacle of their social order "were *naturally* led to want to rebuild the society of their time according to an entirely new plan, which each of them drew up according to the sole light of his reason;"[12] on the other, he acknowledged that even those in power yielded on occasion to the claims of abstract thinking.[13] The participation in public affairs he found lacking in France was a special kind of participation, the kind that comes only with free political institutions. Ultimately, he explained the central importance of men of letters in French public life, the radical, abstract quality of their language, and its power over the mass of Frenchmen, all in terms of a single factor: "the complete absence of all political liberty."[14] Denied the acquaintance with the nature of public affairs that comes only with free political institutions, the philosophes became even bolder in their speculations than they otherwise would have been. Innocent of the experience of self-government, and lacking any constitutional means to express their concerns, the mass of Frenchmen

---

[11]Daniel Roche, *Le siècle des lumières en province. Académies et académiciens provinciaux, 1680–1789*, 2 vols. (Paris, 1978), 1:206.

[12]Alexis de Tocqueville, *L'ancien régime et la Révolution*, in *Oeuvres complètes*, ed. J. P. Mayer, vol. 2(i), 6 ed. (Paris, 1952), 195, emphasis added. Although I have not followed the Gilbert translation directly, I will also cite relevant page numbers in the standard English edition, *The Old Regime and the French Revolution*, tr. Stuart Gilbert (Garden City, N.Y., 1955), in this case p. 140.

[13]*L'ancien régime*, 200 (*Old Regime*, 147).

[14]*L'ancien régime*, 195 (*Old Regime*, 140).

readily accepted these speculations as a surrogate for the expression of their political passions. Deprived of their traditional authority, even the nobility engaged in the philosophical parlor game, forgetful, owing to their lack of political freedom, of the obvious knowledge "that general theories, once accepted, are inevitably transformed into political passions and reappear in actions."[15] Thus all sections of French society, Tocqueville would have us believe, were mindless of the fact that ideas have consequences.

> But what will seem more extraordinary to us, as we contemplate the debris left by so many revolutions, is that the very idea of a violent revolution never occurred to our parents' minds. No one talked of it, no one even imagined it. The small disturbances which public liberty constantly inflicts on the most stable societies serve as a daily reminder of the possibility of upheavals and keep the public on the watch. But in this French society of the eighteenth century, which was about to fall into the abyss, there had as yet been no warning of danger.[16]

This picture is surely overdrawn. If France lacked English political liberties, it was by no means devoid of the kind of constitutional contestation many contemporaries associated with that turbulent state across the Channel. Acute observers detected revolutionary English weather in the storms that dominated the French constitutional climate in the mid-eighteenth century. "There is a philosophical wind blowing toward us from England in favor of free, anti-monarchical government," wrote the marquis d'Argenson in 1751; "it is entering minds and one knows how opinion governs the world. It could be that this government is already accomplished in people's heads, to be implemented at the first chance; and the revolution might occur with less conflict than one thinks. All the orders of society are discontented together . . . a disturbance could turn into revolt, and revolt into a total revolution."[17] Considered in this context, "liberty" and "despotism," "property" and "representation" were not abstract literary counters: they were ideological claims that Jansenists hurled against oppressive clergy; that parlementary magistrates elaborated in exile and

---

[15]*L'ancien régime*, 196 (*Old Regime*, 142).

[16]*L'ancien régime*, 197 (*Old Regime*), 143).

[17]*Journal et mémoires du marquis d'Argenson*, ed. J.-B. Rathéry, 9 vols. (Paris, 1859–1867), 6:464 (3 September 1751). Impending revolution became a recurrent theme in d'Argenson's journal during the 1750s as the struggle between crown and parlements unfolded: see, for example, 7:23; 7:51; 7:242; 7:271; 7:295; 8:153; 9:294; 9:370. Lord Chesterfield expressed a similar view in 1752: see Charles Aubertin, *L'esprit public au XVIIIe siècle*, 2d ed. (Paris, 1873), 279, n. 2.

circulated in clandestinely published remonstrances; that provincial Estates mobilized against ministerial enemies. As a result of these conflicts, d'Argenson observed, the nature of *nation* and *état* were debated in mid-eighteenth-century France as never before: "these two terms were never uttered under Louis XIV; even the idea of them was lacking. We have never been so aware as we are today of the rights of the nation and of liberty."[18]

Tocqueville, who cites d'Argenson's *Mémoires* for his own purposes, did not entirely disregard the constitutional struggles which the marquis followed with such interest and apprehension. But it was crucial for the political argument of his work to minimize their importance. He therefore relegated them to a relatively unobtrusive chapter of *L'ancien régime et la Révolution* devoted to the "singular sort of liberty" that did still exist amid the institutions of absolutism.[19] Here the constitutional activities of the parlements are praised as "the only part of a free people's education the Old Regime gave us"; and their resistance to Maupeou in 1770 is held out as an action as noble as any in the history of free nations, even though they were "doubtless more preoccupied with their own interests than the public good."[20] Yet several chapters later—in the chapter upon which his entire work hinges—Tocqueville can still insist that Frenchmen had no interest in liberty in the mid-eighteenth century; that they had lost the very idea of it along with the practice.[21] Why the contradiction? The answer becomes clear in Tocqueville's discussion of the physiocrats, whom he in fact cites far more frequently than the philosophes in his consideration of the ideological origins of the French Revolution. The physiocrats, he argues, reveal more clearly than the philosophes the "true nature" of the French Revolution,[22] that combination of the desire for equality with the acceptance of the despotism of centralized public authority which had emerged again in France in his own day with the *coup d'état* of Napoleon III. It was this latter phenomenon (as Richard Herr has ably demonstrated) that Tocqueville set out to explain in *L'ancien régime et la Révolution*. And he did so by maintaining that the French were infected with the egalitarian, centralizing, despotic ideology exemplified by the physiocrats ("false ideas, vicious habits and per-

---

[18]*Journal et mémoires du marquis d'Argenson*, 8:315 (26 June 1754). For a concise general discussion of these constitutional conflicts, see Jean Egret, *Louis XV et l'opposition parlementaire, 1715–1774* (Paris, 1970).

[19]*L'ancien régime*, 168–177 (*Old Regime*, 108–120).

[20]*L'ancien régime*, 174–175 (*Old Regime*, 116–117).

[21]*L'ancien régime*, 214 (*Old Regime*, 165).

[22]*L'ancien régime*, 209 (*Old Regime*, 158).

nicious tendencies" contracted by long exposure to absolute authority) *before* they reacquired their taste for liberty.[23] Ideas of equality as implemented by centralized authority established themselves first; ideas of liberty as an alternative to centralized authority appeared only as a weaker (and ultimately incompatible) second.[24] To buttress this argument, Tocqueville was therefore obliged to set aside the actual political conflicts of the mid-eighteenth century (in which the conflict between liberty and despotism became clearly defined as the central issue) despite the quite compelling evidence of their importance in the development of French political consciousness. Later historians have tended to follow his lead in minimizing the importance of these constitutional struggles or writing off the political language of the parlements as a mere guise for the defense of particular social interests.

Thus it was the effect of Tocqueville's analysis to emphasize the gap between philosophical thinking and immediate realities of political life on the one hand, and to divert attention from the ideological significance of the actual political conflicts that occurred in eighteenth-century France on the other. Both of these issues need to be re-examined. The philosophes need to be considered within the spectrum of political language existing in their own day, not artificially insulated from it; the nature of eighteenth-century French political culture needs to be reconsidered in its own terms, rather than denied by comparison with English political liberties. Neither of these suggestions is new.[25] Yet oddly enough, there has been no systematic effort to reconstitute the discourse of French public life in the decades preceding the French Revolution; nor has there been a full-scale attempt to recover the competing representations of social and political existence from which the revolutionary language ultimately emerged.

[23]*L'ancien régime*, 213–216, 190 (*Old Regime*, 163–167, 137). See Richard Herr, *Tocqueville and the Old Regime* (Princeton, 1962), passim, esp. 56–63.

[24]"It was this desire to introduce political liberty in the midst of ideas and institutions that were incompatible with it but that had become ingrained in our tastes and habits—it was this desire that has, over the last sixty years, produced so many vain attempts to create free government, followed by so much effort, by such disastrous revolutions. Finally, tired by so much effort, disgusted by such a painful and sterile undertaking, many Frenchmen abandoned their second objective [political liberty] in order to return to their first [efficient administration and social equality] and found themselves welcoming the realization that to live in equality under a master still had, after all, a certain attraction. Thus it is that we resemble much more today the economists of 1750 than our fathers of 1789" (*L'ancien régime*, 216 [*Old Regime*, 167–168]. In this case, I have followed the translation by Herr, *Tocqueville and the Old Regime*, 61–62, including his interpolations).

[25]See, for example, Peter Gay, *Voltaire's Politics* (Princeton, 1959), and *The Enlightenment: An Interpretation*, vol. 2. *The Science of Freedom* (New York, 1969); Furio Diaz, *Filosofia e politica nel Settecento francese* (Turin, 1962).

Despite the wealth of material available (though perhaps, in part, because of it) there is no equivalent for prerevolutionary France of Bernard Bailyn's *Ideological Origins of the American Revolution*.[26]

Daniel Mornet's classic work is a particularly interesting contrast in this respect. *Les origines intellectuelles de la Révolution française* is presented as "a history of the intellectual origins of the Revolution and not a history of revolutionary ideas."[27] Since these latter (liberty, equality, fraternity, the social contract, and so on) have existed more or less confusedly in all human societies, Mornet argued, a history of revolutionary ideas would require an endless genealogical regression into the history of political doctrines. But what then does Mornet mean by the "intellectual origins" of the Revolution? Can one, indeed, write such a history without also writing a history of ideas? The effort to do so seems to me one explanation of why Mornet's erudite and far-ranging work is yet so concrete in some respects and so elusive in others. Something is being diffused in Mornet's prerevolutionary France, but it is difficult to say precisely what it is. It seems to be a critical attitude of mind or habit of thinking, subversive of authority in all aspects. Mornet's favorite term for it is *intelligence*.[28] Yet, in an odd way, he appears to offer us a story of the growth of a habit of thinking, without any sustained analysis of its categories of thought.

This lack is particularly noticeable in relationship to political thinking. In this respect, Mornet suggests another distinction that is quite revealing: a distinction between "intellectual causes" of the Revolution and "purely political" causes. Purely political causes involve "situations or events intolerable enough to inspire the desire to change or resist, without any other reflection than the sentiment of suffering and the search for immediate causes and remedies." This latter search is revealed in "purely political works . . . limited to setting out these situations and events, these causes and these remedies without ever seeking to generalize, or to base themselves on principles and doctrines." By contrast, purely intellectual causes express themselves in

[26]Bernard Bailyn, *The Ideological Origins of the American Revolution* (Cambridge, Mass., 1967).

[27]Daniel Mornet, *Les origines intellectuelles de la Révolution française (1715–1787)*, 6th ed. with preface by R. Pomeau (Paris, 1967), 1.

[28]"Our study proposes precisely to examine this role of intelligence in the preparation of the French Revolution," Mornet explains by way of introduction (*Les origines intellectuelles*, 2). In his conclusion, he speaks of "this vast, active, passionate awakening of intelligence [which] was not limited to Paris or some large towns" (475). See also below, text to note 31.

"the study of these principles and doctrines without concern, at least in appearance, for the political realities of the present time."[29] Of course, Mornet insisted that this dichotomy was more theoretical than real, particularly in relation to eighteenth-century France: "the purely political actor [le politique pur] will seek to fortify his claims by appealing to philosophical justice and reason; the philosopher will construct his doctrine to resolve the problems that real life and contemporary politics have posed."[30] Yet what is missing in this formulation—or, more properly, precluded by it—is exactly the sense of politics as constituted within a field of discourse, and of political language as elaborated in the course of political action. This is perhaps the reason for the striking absence in Mornet's work of any sustained discussion of the constitutional conflicts that were so central a feature of French public life after the middle of the century, and of the conflicting representations of the social order that were elaborated in response to them. "It is intelligence," Mornet insists in the very last words of his book, "that produced, organized the consequences, and gradually came to demand the Estates-General. And from the Estates-General, but without intelligence suspecting it, would come forth the Revolution."[31] Unfortunately, Mornet offers us a history of that intelligence without providing us with the language in which it was articulated. It is difficult to imagine how from an intelligence so inarticulate so profound an utterance could spring.

This does not mean that we must resort to the endless genealogy of revolutionary ideas that Mornet regarded as the logical alternative to his own approach. On the contrary, we should aim not to write the history of particular unit ideas, but to identify a field of political discourse, a set of linguistic patterns and relationships that defined possible actions and utterances and gave them meaning.[32] We need, in short, to reconstitute the political culture within which the creation of

---

[29]Les origines intellectuelles, 431.

[30]Ibid.

[31]Ibid., 477.

[32]For a suggestive move in this direction, informed by a sophisticated linguistic analysis, see the work of Régine Robin: "Fief et seigneurie dans le droit et l'idéologie juridique à la fin du XVIIIe siècle," Annales historiques de la Révolution française 43 (1971), 554–602; "Polémique idéologique et affrontement discursif en 1776: Les grands édits de Turgot et les remontrances du Parlement de Paris" (with Denise Maldidier), in J. Guilhaumou, D. Maldidier, A. Prost, R. Robin, Langage et idéologies. Le discours comme objet de l'histoire (Paris, 1974), 13–80; Histoire et linguistique (Paris, 1974). The cahiers of 1789 have also been the subject of an important study by George Taylor, "Revolutionary and Non-Revolutionary Content in the Cahiers of 1789: An Interim Report," French Historical Studies 7 (1971–72), 479–502.

the revolutionary language of 1789 became possible. I would argue that this political culture began to emerge in the 1750s and 1760s and that its essential elements were already clear by the beginning of Louis XVI's reign. While I am unable here to offer a full demonstration of such an argument, I can perhaps suggest some aspects of the process of ideological elaboration that I think was involved.

Contemporaries were very well aware of the transformation of French political culture that began to occur in the 1750s. D'Argenson was by no means alone in this respect. Gilbert de Voisins, the acute administrator who was later among those charged to draft the vigorous defense of royal authority set forth during the celebrated *séance de la flagellation*, offered a no less grave appreciation of the situation in 1753:

> This is a kind of intellectual revolt [révolte des esprits] which, without opposing authority by force, gradually undermines it. The habit of obedience is lost and the acts of authority defend it without reestablishing it. A no less dangerous consequence of this situation in the public is that it becomes a habit to be seriously concerned with affairs of State. There has always been frivolous and inconsequential reasoning in France about the conduct of government: but today the very foundations of the constitution and the order of the State are placed in question. The different degrees of authority and power, the rules and the measure of obedience, the mysteries of the state are indiscreetly debated under the eyes of the vulgar.[33]

Less apprehensive in his reactions, the abbé Mably responded to this situation with nothing less than a script for a revolution. Apparently written in 1758, his little work entitled *Des droits et des devoirs du citoyen* took the form of a dialogue between an Englishman and a Frenchman set in the luxurious gardens of the palace of Marly, here a symbol of the despotism and luxury that threatened to extinguish political life in France. "Agree that in the past few years you have been roused to indignation against despotism," the English visitor tells his French interlocutor; "that you desire to see the end of its abuses; and that in the current state of intellectual fermentation [*fermentation des esprits*] you today express yourselves, even publicly, in discourse that is much more daring than your most secret thoughts were twelve

[33]Quoted in Philippe Godard, *La querelle des refus de sacrements (1730–1765)* (Paris, 1937), 277, from Archives nationales, K698. On the *séance de la flagellation*, see "Le discours de la flagellation (3 mars 1766)," *Recueil de travaux offerts à M. Clovis Brunel*, 2 vols. (Paris, 1955), 1:33–37.

years ago."[34] This fermentation is of particular interest to the Englishman, who is unmistakably recognizable as one of those English Commonwealthmen for whom contestation is the condition of all healthy political existence. Delighted at the growth of political consciousness he sees in France (and the appetite for English political works in translation that it is fostering) the Commonwealthman goes on to lay out a strategy for ideological contestation and constitutional confrontation—a strategy for a *révolution ménagée* that would overthrow royal despotism and reestablish the rights of the nation—that bears a remarkable similarity to the events that led up to the calling of the Estates-General thirty years later. This revolution would occur when the parlements, recognizing that they could not remain free amid the ruins of despotism, withheld approval of tax edicts and suspended their judicial functions until the Estates-General were called. A monarch forced by sustained opposition to call that body, Mably maintained, would be in no position to control the outcome of the elections to it or to subvert the integrity of its representatives. And the very act of forcing the convocation of the Estates-General would, in itself, constitute the political education of the nation. Its passions engaged and its political consciousness developed, "it will not be imbecile enough to accept a sham representation."[35]

This script for a French revolution in 1758 offers a genuine puzzle to historians. We have accustomed ourselves not to expect such language thirty years before the event, particularly from a writer usually counted among the most abstract of eighteenth-century utopians. Indeed, it is hard at first encounter with this work not to credit the suspicion expressed when it was published at the end of 1788, that the text had been revised after Mably's death to meet the circumstances of its publication. Yet there appears to be no textual evidence to support this suspicion and abundant contextual evidence to render it unnecessary. Certainly, by the end of a decade of constitutional struggle that was far more intense than we often assume, Mably was not alone in laying plans for ideological contestation. One of the most interesting is a confidential memorandum circulated within ministerial circles in 1759 by Jacob-Nicolas Moreau, later historiographer royal, who de-

[34]Gabriel Bonnot de Mably, *Des droits et des devoirs du citoyen*, ed. Jean-Louis Lecercle (Paris, 1972), 183. (For a fuller discussion, see K. M. Baker, "A Script for a French Revolution: The Political Consciousness of the abbé Mably," *Eighteenth-Century Studies* 14 (1980–81), 255–263.) The phrase *fermentation des esprits*, which Mably uses here, appears frequently in contemporary accounts of the political troubles of the period.

[35]Mably, *Des droits et des devoirs du citoyen*, 173.

voted a lifetime to the defense of monarchical principles.[36] This memorandum, entitled *Principes de conduite avec les parlements*, was a program for ideological confrontation, or, more precisely, for the recovery of ideological initiative by the crown.[37] The argument of the *Principes de conduite* rested on the conviction that the 1750s marked a turning point in French political life. Before that date, conflict between the magistrates and the government had been sporadic and the parlements divided by their individual pretensions and claims. In Moreau's judgment, Jansenism and the issue of *billets de confession* had changed all that; the monarchy was now faced with concerted parlementary action based on a systematic ideology of opposition to royal power that threatened to make the French constitution even less favorable to monarchical authority than the English.[38]

Moreau recognized that the strength of the parlements' resistance depended on several factors: the power of their appeal to public opinion; their skill in mobilizing the symbolic resources of French history against the monarchy; the weakness and inconsistency of government policy. He recognized, perhaps more clearly than anyone else on the government's side, that the crown had lost control of the central symbols of monarchical authority—that recourse to principles of law, justice, and reason without which any act of royal will could

[36]On Moreau, see Dieter Gembicki, *Histoire et politique à la fin de l'ancien régime: Jacob-Nicolas Moreau (1717–1803)* (Paris, 1979).

[37]"Recueil de pièces concernant le Parlement," Bibliothèque du Sénat (Paris), ms. 402, ff. 27–135. On the composition of the *Principes de conduite avec les parlements* (which was included by Moreau in a catalog of his works) see Jacob-Nicolas Moreau, *Mes souvenirs,* ed. Camille Hermelin, 2 vols. (Paris, 1898), l:xxvii, 109–110. I thank the director and staff of the Bibliothèque du Sénat for their courtesy in permitting me to consult this collection. Another copy of the "Principes de conduite" (transcribed by the Jansenist barrister and polemicist Adrien Le Paige, but attributed by him to the magistrate and intendant Bourgeois de Boynes) has been identified in the Bibliothèque de Port Royal, Collection Le Paige, 569(7), by Martin Mansergh, "The Revolution of 1771, or the Exile of the Parlement of Paris" (Oxford, D.Phil., 1973). Mansergh considers aspects of Moreau's political activities not discussed in Gembicki's work.

[38]*Principes de conduite*, ff. 27–33. On the significance of Jansenism as a political issue during this period, see Godard, *La querelle des refus de sacrements*; Dale Van Kley, *The Jansenists and the Expulsion of the Jesuits from France, 1757–1765* (New Haven, 1975), and "Church, State, and the Ideological Origins of the French Revolution: The Debate over the General Assembly of the Gallican Clergy in 1765," *Journal of Modern History* 51 (1979), 629–666; René Taveneaux, *Jansénisme et politique* (Paris, 1965); E. Préclin, *Les jansénistes du XVIIIe siècle et la Constitution civile du clergé* (Paris, 1929); Pierre Rétat et al., *L'attentat de Damiens: Discours sur l'événement au XVIIIe siècle* (Paris 1979); J. M. J. Rogister, "The Crisis of 1753 in France and the Debate on the Nature of the Monarchy and of the Fundamental Laws," in *Herrschaftsvertäge, Wahlkapitulationen, Fundamentalgesetze* ed. Rudolf Vierhaus (Göttingen, 1977), 165–120. D. Carroll Joynes has taken a fresh look at Jansenist political theory in "Jansenists and Ideologues: Opposition Theory in the Parlement of Paris (1750–1775)," (Ph.D. diss., University of Chicago, 1981).

be construed as the exercise of arbitrary and despotic authority. He recommended and devoted his career to promoting an ideological offensive that would recapture public opinion on behalf of traditional monarchical principles, a project that ranged from the production of preambles for acts of royal authority to the composition of multi-volume treatises on the history and underlying principles of the French monarchy. Perhaps more striking, however, were his efforts to create a massive historical arsenal for ideological purposes.[39] This effort to comb public and private collections throughout France, in order to "amass the materials which can perfect our history and finally substitute the truth of well-established facts for the uncertainty of opinions and the dangers of systems,"[40] became a virtual obsession for Moreau for thirty years. It represented nothing less than an effort to control French history on behalf of the monarchy: to control it at an archival level, by gathering together the entire body of sources related to French constitutional law; to control it at the level of collective representation, by offering authoritative interpretations of the meaning and significance of the historical materials thus gathered and hence of the nature of the political community whose history these materials represented; and to control it at the political level, by mobilizing these interpretations in order to determine the outcome of the constitutional struggles of the time. Moreau was still building this archive, which then amounted to hundreds of cartons and thousands of pieces, when it was taken over on behalf of the nation in 1789.

While it is impossible here to make the case definitively, these examples are perhaps enough to suggest the emergence of a radically new political culture in France in the two decades separating the outburst of constitutional conflict over *billets de confession* in the early 1750s and the ideological contestation surrounding Maupeou's attempt at "revolution" in the early 1770s. In the course of these two decades, politics broke out of the absolutist mold. "Opinion" became "opinion publique": not a social function but a political category, the "tribunal du public," the court of final appeal for monarchical authority as for its critics.[41] "Droit public"—the nature of the political order

[39]See Gembicki, *Histoire et politique*, 85–173.

[40]"Circulaire aux intendants des provinces pour leur demander de favoriser le développement du Dépôt des Chartes" (25 January 1765), printed in *Le comité des travaux historiques et scientifiques (Histoire et documents)*, ed., Xavier Charmes, 3 vols. (Paris, 1886), 1:91.

[41]On the "tribunal du public," see Edmond Jean François Barbier, *Chronique de la régence et du règne de Louix XV (1718–1763)*, 8 vols. (Paris, 1885), 6:512 (March 1757), citing the denunciation of unauthorized writings concerning the Damiens affair by Joly de Fleury, avocat général of the parlement of Paris. On the emergence of the term "opinion publique"

and the conditions under which the nation existed as a collective body—became the ultimate question upon which that tribunal was called to decide. And the "publiciste" as learned authority on the nature of "droit public" began to give way to the publicist as man of letters whose ambition it was to define the language of the court of public opinion by laying down the meaning of terms.[42]

The various efforts to reconstitute the meaning of "droit public" and redefine the nature of the social order in France were remarkable in their number and complexity. But I think they can be understood in terms of three basic strands of discourse. These strands represent a disaggregation of the attributes traditionally bound together in the concept of monarchical authority—reason, justice and will—and their reconceptualization as the basis of competing definitions (or attempted redefinitions) of the body politic. According to the traditional language of absolutism, monarchical authority is characterized as the exercise of justice, that justice by which each receives his due in a hierarchical society of orders and estates. Justice is given effect by the royal will, which is preserved from arbitrariness by reason and counsel. In the second part of the eighteenth century, this cluster of attributes seems to separate into three strands of discourse, each characterized by the analytical priority it gives to one or the other of these terms. What I shall call the judicial discourse emphasizes *justice*. What I shall call the political discourse emphasizes *will*. What I shall call the administrative discourse emphasizes *reason*. These three competing vocabularies structure the language of opposition to monarchical authority, just as they define the efforts and claims of its defenders.

The idea that royal power is essentially judicial remains a constant theme of monarchical theorists throughout the eighteenth century. At the same time, it provides the essential topos in the parlementary constitutionalism that becomes so important in focusing the attack on royal despotism in the 1750s and afterwards. It finds its clearest expression in the argument for a traditional constitution, a historically constituted order of things which both defines and limits royal power,

more generally, see Jürgen Habermas, *Strukturwandel der Öffentlichkeit* (Neuwied, 1962), pp. 104–118.

[42]On the term "publiciste," see Ferdinand Brunot, *Histoire de la langue française dès origines à 1900*, new ed., 13 vols. (Paris, 1966–1972), 6(i):36; Walther von Wartburg, *Französisches etymologisches Wörterbuch*, 21 vols. (Bonn, 1928–1965), 9:508. Malesherbes offered an interesting historical view of this process in the *Remontrances* of the Cour des Aides in 1775: see K. M. Baker, "French Political Thought at the Accession of Louis XVI," *Journal of Modern History* 50 (1978), 279–303.

and which it is the function of royal authority to uphold. The essential notions in this discourse are justice as the recognition of that which is fitting and proper (giving each his due in a hierarchical society of orders and Estates), social order as constituted by prescription, tradition, and continuity, public power as adjudication, public participation as *représentations* (in the traditional sense of making representations, that is, framing particularistic claims). This is the prevailing language of parlementary remonstrances. It is still perceptible in the more liberal constitutionalism of figures such as Malesherbes, and it informs much of the resistance to monarchical reform in the immediate prerevolutionary period.

Alongside this discourse of justice, however, and increasingly in tension with it, there emerges a discourse of will. Again this remains a characteristic of defenses of royal sovereignty in more or less traditional terms. But it also becomes the central feature of a vocabulary of opposition to monarchical authority that is couched in explicitly political, rather than quasi-judicial/constitutional terms. In this discourse, social order is defined not in terms of justice, law, prescription, adjudication, but in terms of will, liberty, contingency, choice, participation. If in the judicial discourse will is opposed to justice as the arbitrary and contingent to the lawful and constituted, in the political discourse will is opposed to will. Royal power is despotic, not because it is the exercise of will *per se*, but because that will is royal or particular, not national or general. The discourse of will provides the dominant language in Rousseau and Mably, in some of the works of the radical parlementary propagandists, and eventually in Sieyès's famous pamphlet *What Is the Third Estate?*

This discourse of will can in turn be distinguished from a third discourse, a discourse of reason. In its terms, the ancient constitution has become a present contradiction, of which the arbitrariness of royal will is but one expression. The contingency of royal will must give way, not to the assertion of the political will of the nation, but to the exercise of reason and enlightenment. The social order must be reconstituted on the basis of nature—which is to say property and civic equality—in order to transform political contingency into rational order, arbitrary government into rational administration, law into education, and representation into a theorem for rational choice. Elements of this language pervade much of the political thought of the Enlightenment, as well as the thinking of some of the enlightened administrators of the period; it is at its clearest in the discourse of

Turgot and the physiocrats, whose aim is to transpose the problem of social order into the language of social science.

The emergence, elaboration, and interpenetration of these three discourses, I think it can be argued, defined the political culture that emerged in France in the later part of the eighteenth century and provided the ideological framework that gave explosive meaning to the events that destroyed the Old Regime. The origins of the political language of 1789, the language that came to constitute the grounding of the new order, cannot be found solely in any one of them. Instead, it seems to have been created from the competition among them. The revolutionaries replaced the historical jumble they characterized as feudalism with a rational social order grounded in nature; in doing so, they based their reconstitution of society on such principles as property, public utility, and the rights of man. To this extent, they achieved the goals and accepted a language defined within the discourse of reason. At the same time, they established responsible government subject to the rule of law, and insisted that public authority be limited constitutionally in a system of representative government. To this extent, they fulfilled the purposes and accepted some of the language of the constitutionalism I have associated with the discourse of justice. But all of this was construed as an act of will, as an expression of the general will of a nation that declared itself one and indivisible in the assertion of its inalienable sovereignty. All of this was bracketed, in short, within the discourse of will. The result was a transformed political discourse with its own tensions and contradictions, which in turn played their part in patterning the history of the Revolution after 1789.

CHAPTER EIGHT

Popular Dimensions of Modernist Elite Culture: The Case of Theater in Fin-de-Siècle Munich

PETER JELAVICH

The 1970s, like the 1960s, saw an expansion of the thematic field and the methodological complexity of the historical sciences.[1] Two topics that increasingly have gained the attention of social and cultural historians—albeit not the same historians—are the rise and development of modernism in the arts, and the relationship of popular and elite culture in the early modern period. On the one hand, a small but growing number of scholars are studying the political, social, and economic determinants of the break-up of nineteenth-century elite culture and the rapid proliferation of new styles in the arts between 1890 and 1930.[2] On the other hand, scholars of the early modern period are seeking to describe (often in anthropological terms) the

This essay is part of a larger study of the political, social, and economic origins of modernist theater in Munich from 1890 to 1924. The author wishes to thank the Council for European Studies at Princeton University, the German Academic Exchange Service (DAAD), and the Society of Fellows at Harvard University for their financial support of this research.

[1]For historiographical developments in the 1960s and the 1970s, see, respectively, *Historical Studies Today*, ed. Felix Gilbert and Stephen Graubard (New York, 1972); and *The Past before Us: Contemporary Historical Writing in the United States*, ed. Michael Kammen (Ithaca, 1980).

[2]Modernism has, of course, long been a subject of interest to literary critics and art historians; a good introduction to the subject, primarily from a literary perspective, is the collection of essays edited by Malcolm Bradbury and James MacFarlane, *Modernism 1890–1930* (New York, 1976). Historians concerned with pre–1914 modernism have tended to focus on Vienna: cf. Allan Janik and Stephen Toulmin, *Wittgenstein's Vienna* (New York, 1973); William McGrath, *Dionysian Art and Populist Politics in Austria* (New Haven, 1974); William Johnston, *The Austrian Mind: An Intellectual and Social History* (Berkeley, 1976); and Carl Schorske, *Fin-de-Siècle Vienna: Politics and Culture* (New York, 1980).

contours of elite and popular culture, and to examine their interaction.[3]

The purpose of this essay is to suggest that these two thematic concerns may be productively combined, that the interaction of popular and elite culture in the formation of modernism is worthy of separate and systematic study. Many of the specific themes and forms of modernism were the products of an elite-popular dialogue that occurred at the end of the nineteenth century. Especially in the non-literary arts—theater, painting and graphics, music—producers of elite culture relied increasingly on what they considered the themes and forms of popular culture. Elements of puppet shows, pantomimes, vaudeville, and circus acts—genres associated with a peasant or lower-class urban public—appeared in the works of playwrights, directors, and stage designers: one thinks of Wedekind, Reinhardt, and Brecht in Germany; Jarry, Léger, Artaud in France; Blok, Meierhold, Evreinov, Tairov, El Lissitzkii, and Maiakovskii in Russia. Similarly, the style and content of popular woodcuts and devotional pictures, of peasant art and painting on glass influenced modernist painting (Kandinsky and the Blue Rider group; Gauguin, Matisse, and Picasso; Larionov, Goncharova, the Burliuks, and Malevich). Modern music, too, saw the incorporation of European folk melodies and American jazz (Weill, Krenek, Hindemith, and Orff; Bartok; Stravinsky).

In addition to explaining some of the specific themes and forms of modernist theater, visual art, and music, a study of the elite-popular interchange should help the social historian of culture to define more accurately the social space of the producers of modernist elite culture. The conscious and unconscious attitudes of elite artists concerning their social class, their social function, and their relations to the populace at large can often be inferred from their appropriation of popular artistic themes and forms. By focusing on a specific art in a specific city—theater in Munich from 1890 to 1924—this essay will attempt to present a case study of the influence of popular arts on modernist elite culture.

In his comprehensive survey, *Popular Culture in Early Modern Europe*, Peter Burke has asserted that all classes of society originally participated in various aspects of popular culture. After the Reforma-

---

[3]Much of this scholarship has been summarized in Peter Burke, *Popular Culture in Early Modern Europe* (New York, 1978); this is the best (albeit a controversial) introduction to the subject, and it contains an extensive bibliography. Another good introductory work, which includes essays on the modern period, is the collection edited by Jacques Beauroy, Marc Bertrand, and Edward Gargan, *The Wolf and the Lamb: Popular Culture in France from the Old Regime to the Twentieth Century* (Saratoga, 1976).

tion, though, the upper classes, who had always possessed their own literary, classical, scholastic, or courtly culture, began to withdraw from the practices that they shared with commoners. Their segregation, which was inspired by new notions of religious purity and secular "good taste," was supposedly complete by 1800. Whether or not one accepts Burke's contention that the eighteenth century saw the culmination of the withdrawal of the elites from popular culture,[4] it is hard to deny that the same century witnessed the origins of new forms of cultural interchange across classes. Previously, the upper estates had participated in popular culture in a spirit of play; after 1750, however, their perception and definition of popular culture became an increasingly serious concern.

Initially, it was German intellectuals, such as Herder and the Grimm brothers, who contended that "genuine" culture originated among the Volk. This notion was inspired by both aesthetic and political concerns. Hoping to free the German elites from the domination of French culture and to create a consciousness of German national identity, such writers argued that neoclassicism, which had been imported from France and codified by Gottsched, should be rejected in favor of the more elemental, natural, and "untainted" culture of the Volk. Modern folklore and modern nationalism thus originated from the combination of an aesthetic revolt against classicism and a political desire to forge a national consciousness.[5] As will be seen below, the modernists' appropriation of popular culture was likewise an attempt both to reform elite culture and to establish new models of community.

With the outbreak of popular upheavals during the Revolutionary and Napoleonic period, popular culture ceased being merely an interest of German intellectuals, and became an issue of deep concern among elites throughout Europe. Members of the upper classes rapidly became convinced that the "people" would have to be integrated actively into the changing political and socioeconomic frameworks; failure to do so on terms dictated by the elites might result in radically

[4] Burke's scenario of an eighteenth-century cultural divorce of elites and populace has been challenged by, among others. Robert Isherwood, "Entertainment in the Parisian Fairs in the Eighteenth Century," *Journal of Modern History* 53 (1981), 24–48. Despite its relative novelty, the study of the relationship between popular and elite culture in the early modern era has already generated heated debates, beginning with definitions: the way one perceives the problem is, of course, fundamentally affected by one's conceptions of "popular," "elite," and "culture." Some of the issues involved in the bifurcation of "elite" and "popular" culture are discussed in the essay by Roger Chartier in this volume.

[5] Burke, chap. 1 ("The Discovery of the People"), discusses the origins of elite interest in folk culture in the eighteenth century.

new social systems commanded by the populace. The elites were, however, politically divided, and their ideological proclivities determined how they perceived the lower classes. A progressive tradition, expressed in the works of writers ranging from Michelet to Marx, approvingly depicted "the people" as a conscious and active historical force, though one that needed at least a modicum of "guidance" from liberal or radical elites. Other liberal and many conservative theorists, who argued for a pacific cultural hegemony of the elites, viewed "the people" as an essentially traditional body that valued stability above change, order above unrest, and subordination above pretension. In contrast, authoritarian writers believed that "the people" would degenerate into anarchic mobs if they were not controlled by direct tutelage and cowed by fear of force.

These divergent views of "the people" coexisted among that diffuse class which was rapidly becoming the major social component of the elite, namely the bourgeoisie. The ambivalence of the bourgeoisie toward the lower strata of society was a function of its own social and cultural ambiguity. Certainly, the bourgeoisie aspired to participate in older elite culture; and this desire, recognized and reluctantly appreciated by the traditional ruling orders, was institutionalized in official forms such as the German Gymnasium and unofficial forms such as the salon. But the bourgeoisie also maintained many ties, both social and affective, with nonelite culture. Upwardly mobile bourgeois often had popular roots; successful families might make the transition from rural villagers to urban bourgeois within two or three generations. Moreover, as was the case with early modern upper classes, middle-class people continued to participate in popular culture in various direct or indirect ways, especially during childhood. The stories told to children by their nursemaids or read to them by their parents (bowdlerized Grimm) were popular in origin. For entertainment, bourgeois children attended the puppet shows and other amusements of local fairs.[6] Whereas previously the elites had taken part in traditional popular culture as adults, by the nineteenth century they participated mainly as children—a significant change of attitude, and one none too flattering to the populace. Yet even as adults, the middle classes attended music halls and vaudeville, where popular culture had acquired the guise of incipient mass culture.

[6]Among the modernist writers who utilized in their mature works elements of popular culture experienced during childhood were Flaubert, Nerval, and Proust; see Robert Mandrou, *De la culture populaire aux 17ᵉ et 18ᵉ siècles: La bibliothèque bleue de Troyes* (Paris, 1964), 168–170.

The rise of "mass culture" from popular culture is one of the most important developments of the modern period; mass culture has created a greater degree of homogeneity of culture, information, and opinion across class lines than popular culture was able to achieve in its heyday.[7] In the nineteenth century, nationalism and capitalism—the transformation of all people into citizens and consumers—laid the basis for the mass culture of the twentieth. This broad perspective should not blind one, however, to the continuing vitality of popular culture in the nineteenth century. Members of communities, provinces, and social classes whose identities and livelihoods were threatened by national consolidation and modernization clung consciously and tenaciously to their cultural traditions. Urban workers maintained contacts with their rural relatives, and often formed voluntary associations to sustain their local customs amid their urban "exile." And many artistic members of the elite, dismayed by the direction of social and cultural change, saw value in the persistence of popular culture.

The century that saw the embourgeoisement of the elite and the beginnings of mass culture was also a time of dislocation for producers of elite culture. Bourgeois artists—and most artists were of bourgeois origin—were in a doubly ambiguous position: they were an unstable subgroup within an amorphous and changing class. Their political attitudes ranged across the full spectrum of those of their own class; accordingly, they viewed the populace as progressive, creative, docile, or destructive. But artists also harbored ambivalent feelings toward their native bourgeoisie. With the relative decline of princely and aristocratic patronage, they became increasingly dependent upon the middle classes for personal commissions or anonymous purchases. This financial dependence was exacerbated by a relative surplus of artists, whose impoverishment and "proletarianization" aroused feelings of déclassement and hostility to the bourgeoisie.[8]

Even successful artists often disliked catering to the middle classes. Even though there was a distinctively "bourgeois spirit"—often associated with logic, rationality, calculation, cerebrality, and the "culture

---

[7]An exemplary work that describes the development of a society characterized by a popular/elite cultural split into one dominated by mass culture is Maurice Crubellier, *Histoire culturelle de la France: XIXe–XXe siècle* (Paris, 1974). It is important to recognize, of course, that mass culture is "received" by different social classes in different manners, and that alternate cultural forms persist, sometimes even as subcurrents within the mass media themselves: cf. Herbert J. Gans, *Popular Culture and High Culture: An Analysis and Evaluation of Taste* (New York, 1974).

[8]An interesting and useful schematization of the social and political stances of alienated artists in the modern period is presented in Helmut Kreuzer, *Die Boheme* (Stuttgart, 1971).

of the word"—the middle classes also required a culture of representation, material life, and entertaiment; and this culture was still very much in the making in the nineteenth century. In keeping with the amorphous nature of the middle classes, bourgeois culture was largely a bricolage of earlier elite and popular forms. Elite bourgeois culture was generally historicist: styles and stories of previous ages were imitated or recreated in architecture, interior design, painting, literature, "classical" theater, and opera. "Popular" bourgeois culture acquired shape in *Trivialliteratur*, domestic farces in commercial theaters, vaudeville, and the music hall. Many artists deplored these alternatives. On the one hand, even though historicism in the arts allowed great room for innovation, it remained essentially imitative. On the other hand, the bourgeois variants of popular culture, unlike traditional popular culture, tended toward noncritical, nonparticipatory, and nonregenerative banality. Artists who sought to escape these alternatives could proceed along two routes: the withdrawal and escapism of art-for-art's-sake, or the engagement of social, political, and cultural criticism. Both paths led directly to the rise of modernism.

Followers of both routes tended to be antibourgeois, and they felt affinities with the "prebourgeois" classes; but whereas the escapists were attracted to aristocratic social and cultural values, the critics turned toward popular culture. In general, artists who felt estranged from their native bourgeois class turned to popular culture for any of three reasons: (1) they saw popular culture as a source of antibourgeois sentiment, which could be used to combat elite bourgeois culture; (2) they utilized aspects of popular arts to transform and revitalize elite culture; and (3) popular forms were appropriated as means of forging new types of community among both the elite and the populace at large, thus giving artists a socially reconciliatory role. These three contentions need elaboration.

(1) The increasing alienation of artists from their native bourgeois class made them view "the people" and popular culture as embodiments of non- or antibourgeois sentiment; they saw both "the artist" and "the people" as victims and opponents of bourgeois society. Some artists thus extracted from popular culture those elements which were antagonistic to the elite and used them to "unmask" or criticize bourgeois society. Specifically, they highlighted the aspects of popular culture that Mikhail Bakhtin has labeled "carnivalization" and "grotesque realism". According to Bakhtin, popular culture—epitomized in carnival—is participatory culture, in which all people take part as

equals. All notions of social and spiritual hierarchy are parodied, inverted, or annulled; ruler and ruled, sacred and profane, spirit and body, actor and spectator become confused and commingled. This "carnivalesque" spirit, which, according to Bakhtin, has been incorporated in undercurrents of elite literary culture since the Renaissance, played a prominent role in the antibourgeois revolt of the modernists, beginning with Flaubert and Manet.[9]

(2) Whereas some alienated artists used popular culture in a purely adversary manner in order to discredit bourgeois moral or aesthetic values, others saw the popular arts as a means of revitalizing, redirecting, or revolutionizing the culture of the elite. Popular culture was generally seen as being, on the one hand, more vital and emotional than bourgeois culture, and, on the other, formally more simple and abstract. These two dimensions allowed popular culture to serve as a catalyst in a conscious move away from a nineteenth-century culture that was literary and mimetic to a "modern" one that was gestural and abstract.

Nineteenth-century European civilization was a culture of realism and, even in its nonliterary manifestations, very much of the word. Mimesis and narrative were the dominant aesthetic principles in academic art. The viewer was encouraged to forget the two-dimensionality of the medium by means of illusory, three-dimensional shading of forms. Pictures were supposed to tell a story, the highest genre being history painting, which depicted historical, mythological, or biblical events recognizable to those who had received the proper literary education. Similarly, theater had lost many of its specifically "theatrical" elements. The European stages of the latter half of the nineteenth century were dominated by "classics" and history plays on

---

[9]Mikhail Bakhtin's theory of popular culture is presented in *Rabelais and His World* (Cambridge, Mass. 1968), 1–58, and *Problems of Dostoevsky's Poetics* (Ann Arbor, 1973), 100–108. The concept of "carnivalization" is applied to Flaubert in Arthur Mitzman, "Roads, Vulgarity, Rebellion, and Pure Art: The Inner Space in Flaubert and French Culture," in *Journal of Modern History* 51 (1979), 504–524. The related concept of *blague* is applied to Manet in Linda Nochlin, "The Invention of the Avant-Garde: France, 1830–80," in *Avant-Garde Art*, ed., Thomas B. Hess and John Ashbery, (New York, 1968), 19–21. Other studies concerned with the impact of popular arts on the rise of modernism have likewise tended to focus on mid-century Paris. Cf. the works on Courbet: Meyer Shapiro, "Courbet and Popular Imagery: An Essay on Realism and Naïveté" (1941), reprinted in his *Modern Art* (New York, 1978), 47–85; and T. J. Clark, *Image of the People: Gustave Courbet and the Second French Republic 1848–1851* (London, 1973). On Manet, see the two essays by Anne Hanson: "Manet's Subject Matter and a Source of Popular Imagery," in *Museum Studies* (Art Institute of Chicago), no. 3 (1968); and "Popular Imagery and the Work of Edouard Manet," in *French Nineteenth Century Painting and Literature*, ed., Ulrich Fink, (Manchester, 1972), 133–163.

the one hand, and salon pieces on the other. Productions of classical works or their imitations were pretexts for incorporating on stage texts or tales canonized by the regnant aesthetics and ostensibly known exclusively to the educated classes. Salon pieces were conversational plays that depicted the life of the elite; the emphasis lay on dialogue, for it was through verbal exchanges that ideas were expounded, feelings expressed, relationships delineated, and plot advanced. Actors strove increasingly to imitate "natural" speech and "natural" gestures (or rather, the *lack* of gestures in bourgeois life)—a tendency that culminated and was codified in the productions of André Antoine in Paris, Otto Brahm in Berlin, and Stanislavskii in St. Petersburg. By 1900, realistic illusion and the predominance of the spoken word were the hallmarks of the elite stage. Truly theatrical—gestural, ritual, or mimic—elements were lost.

Practitioners of modernist theater sought to overcome this situation by moving in two directions: toward ritual abstraction, or toward gestural vitality. Writing in the period 1915–1920, the Russian director Alexander Tairov noted: "True theatrical action moves repeatedly between two poles—mystery and harlequinade."[10] The same view was held by Oskar Schlemmer, who presented, in his essay on the Bauhaus theater, a diagram that placed theater between the poles of religious cult and folk entertainment. The central line of this diagram—with the keywords "theater of illusion," "actor," "Shakespeare," "Mozart," and "ballet"—designated the theater favored by the elites of the nineteenth century; the rest of the field described the paths that advocates of modernist theater sought to travel.

Though they were schematically polarized, both religious cult and folk entertainment were associated by the modernists with popular culture. The majority of the population came into touch with theater (broadly defined) in two forms: as church ritual, and as the spectacles of the fair and the marketplace (circus, puppet show, jugglers, clowns, moritat singers). This was especially true in the nineteenth century in those lands that contributed significantly to theatrical modernism—Bavaria, Austria, France and Russia, where the Catholic and Orthodox churches maintained theatrical ritual in religious celebration, and indigenous peasant cultures were still vital. This fusion of sensuous

[10]Cited in Joachim Fiebach, *Von Craig bis Brecht: Studien zu Künstlertheorien in der ersten Hälfte des 20. Jahrhunderts* (Berlin, 1977), 63. Fiebach's work is an excellent analytic introduction to the rise of modernist theater. For surveys of modern and modernist theater, see also Paul Pörtner, *Experiment Theater* (Zurich, 1960), and Oscar Brockett and Robert Findlay, *Century of Innovation: A History of European and American Theatre and Drama since 1870* (Englewood Cliffs, 1973).

SCHEME FOR STAGE, CULT, AND POPULAR ENTERTAINMENT ACCORDING TO:

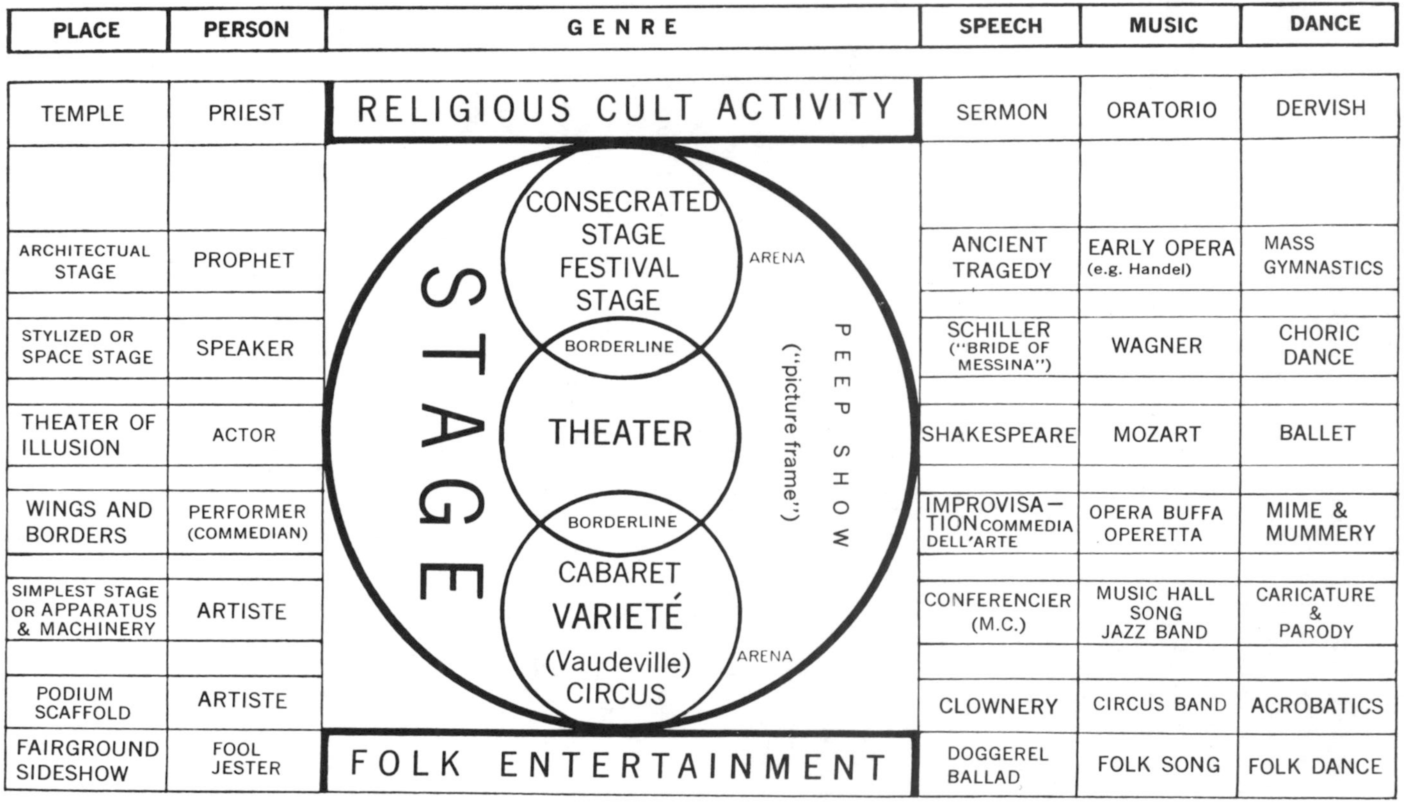

PLACE	PERSON	GENRE	SPEECH	MUSIC	DANCE
TEMPLE	PRIEST	RELIGIOUS CULT ACTIVITY	SERMON	ORATORIO	DERVISH
ARCHITECTUAL STAGE	PROPHET		ANCIENT TRAGEDY	EARLY OPERA (e.g. Handel)	MASS GYMNASTICS
STYLIZED OR SPACE STAGE	SPEAKER		SCHILLER ("BRIDE OF MESSINA")	WAGNER	CHORIC DANCE
THEATER OF ILLUSION	ACTOR		SHAKESPEARE	MOZART	BALLET
WINGS AND BORDERS	PERFORMER (COMEDIAN)		IMPROVISATION — COMMEDIA DELL'ARTE	OPERA BUFFA OPERETTA	MIME & MUMMERY
SIMPLEST STAGE OR APPARATUS & MACHINERY	ARTISTE		CONFERENCIER (M.C.)	MUSIC HALL SONG JAZZ BAND	CARICATURE & PARODY
PODIUM SCAFFOLD	ARTISTE		CLOWNERY	CIRCUS BAND	ACROBATICS
FAIRGROUND SIDESHOW	FOOL JESTER	FOLK ENTERTAINMENT	DOGGEREL BALLAD	FOLK SONG	FOLK DANCE

Central diagram (GENRE column):

PEEP SHOW ("picture frame")

STAGE — three overlapping circles: CONSECRATED STAGE / FESTIVAL STAGE (ARENA) — BORDERLINE — THEATER — BORDERLINE — CABARET VARIETÉ (Vaudeville) CIRCUS (ARENA)

Diagram by Oskar Schlemmer, copyright © 1961, reprinted from *The Theatre of the Bauhaus*, ed. Walter Gropius, tr. Arthur Wensinger, by permission of Wesleyan University Press.

and spiritual elements in popular culture seemed to the modernists to harbor a vitality and a sincerity that could be transmitted to elite culture through the adoption of popular forms, through the theatrical use of vital or ritual gesture.

(3) The third reason why alienated artists appropriated popular culture was to forge a new sense of community in an increasingly atomized society. The projected community could consist of the upper classes alone or of society at large. In either case, popular theatrical culture, in its ritual as well as its vital forms, was considered a means of creating community. On the one hand, religious ritual had perfected symbolic communal experience. On the other, there was an implicit anti-individualist spirit in popular entertainment. Popular theater portrayed not the individualized (and eventually psychologized) bourgeois man or woman of salon drama, but rather "eternal" stock types: the peasant, the rogue, the miser. The tendency of both religious ritual and popular theater toward generality, typicality, and hence abstraction, had a great influence on the rise of formalism in modern theater. Yet it also allowed the alienated artist to attribute to himself a potentially redemptive role: he could use forms of religious ritual and the eternal types of popular theater to create performances that encouraged communal values, that stressed behavioral generality over individuality. The rejected artist sought social acceptance and, indeed, political power by claiming to be able to produce an affective sense of social and spiritual harmony across class lines.

Whether as opponents of bourgeois society, proponents of a transformation of elite culture, or potential forgers of community, modernist artists turned to popular culture to define their social space and social role and to refashion forms of elite art. The remainder of this essay will examine the development of theater in Munich at the turn of the century, in order to present specific cases of these developments as exemplified in the highly varied works of Oskar Panizza, Frank Wedekind, Georg Fuchs, Max Reinhardt, Vassily Kandinsky, and Bertolt Brecht.

The German naturalist movement, which arose in Munich in the early 1880s and spread to Berlin and other literary centers by the end of the decade, was the first of the modern (though not yet modernist) oppositional cultural movements in Germany. Artistically it criticized historicism, while thematically it attacked bourgeois morality and capitalism. The rise of this movement and the specific forms it took can be explained in large part by the disenchantment of young writers in the Wilhelmine Empire. The system of classical education taught young middle-class men that elite culture embodied the highest ideals of humanity, and that theater was the greatest of cultural manifestations. This educational advertisement was complemented by a great expansion of the culture market, inasmuch as many new publishing houses, newspapers, journals, and theaters were established after 1870. Education and an expanding market combined to persuade numerous young men to become writers. Their numbers soon exceeded the market demand, however, so that a large literary proletariat came into existence.[11]

With no prospects of attaining the scarce cultural sinecures offered by the courts, court theaters, and academies, and facing low income and uncertain prospects on the glutted culture market, the young generation turned against the historicist styles and the capitalist practices of the day. Their own proletarianization, rather than any real prior contact with the laboring population, made the impoverished writers feel an affinity with the working classes. Naturalist dramatists thus wrote conversational plays critical of bourgeois culture and sympathetic to the artists' plight and the struggles of labor, and they founded theatrical societies to produce these works before a wide audience. The naturalists' flirtation with the working class ended by the early 1890s, however, owing both to the mutual suspicion of Social Democratic politicians and bourgeois (albeit critical) naturalists, and to the preference of the laboring classes for popular theater and entertainment (as opposed to the essentially literary style of naturalist drama).[12]

The collapse of naturalism heralded the rise of modernism for two reasons. First, recognition of their total social isolation—their rejection by aristocratic, bourgeois, and proletarian publics—induced some writers to adopt that attitude of permanent opposition to society at large which has come to characterize much of the modern avantgarde. Second, flirtation with "the people" introduced other writers

[11]For the problem of the literary proletariat after 1870, see Manfred Brauneck, *Literatur und Öffentlichkeit im ausgehenden 19. Jahrhundert. Studien zur Rezeption des naturalistischen Theaters in Deutschland* (Stuttgart, 1974), 7–15; and Wolfgang Martens, *Lyrik kommerziell. Das Kartell lyrischer Autoren 1902–1933* (Munich, 1975), 15–18.

[12]For the political dimensions of German naturalism and its relation with Social Democracy, see Brauneck; Georg Fülberth, *Proletarische Partei und bürgerliche Literatur* (Darmstadt, 1974); *Naturalismus. Bürgerliche Dichtung und soziales Engagement*, ed., Helmut Scheuer, (Stuttgart, 1974); and Vernon Lidtke, "Naturalism and Socialism in Germany," in *American Historical Review* 79 (1974), 14–37. These works tend to focus on Berlin; naturalist theater in Munich is the subject of Rainer Hartl, *Aufbruch zur Moderne. Naturalistisches Theater in München* (Munich, 1976).

and artists to genuinely popular cultural forms, which contrasted markedly with the literary and realistic styles of historicism and naturalism, and laid the basis for the stylistic innovations of modernism.

The first two postnaturalist playwrights in Munich to sense the socially and artistically subversive nature of popular culture were Oskar Panizza and Frank Wedekind. Panizza (1853–1921) saw that popular culture harbored elements that could be used against the political powers and cultural ideals dominant in Bavaria.[13] Throughout the nineteenth century and into the twentieth, Bavarian politics was dominated by a struggle between liberal (usually Protestant) royal bureaucrats and conservative Catholic politicians over the kingdom's social and cultural future. The liberal bureaucracy claimed that it was trying to forge a modern state and rational economy out of a rural society, while the Catholic church and the Center party claimed that the rural population should be protected from social disruption and spiritual secularization. Panizza argued that neither group genuinely knew "the people," and that popular culture expressed values that stood opposed to both. He was the first German to stress the critical spirit of *Haberfeldtreiben*, or charivaris, whereby the peasantry protested infringements on their local rights and customs by the state bureaucracy, and maintained the moral order of their communities on the basis of ethical codes different from those of the church. The songs of the *Haberer*, which were censored from some of Panizza's publications, used a crude and sometimes obscene language to chastise sexual infractions, yet to laud sexuality itself.[14]

Panizza made extensive studies of all such popular expressions of hostility to the Bavarian state and Catholic morality. He admired in popular culture precisely those two elements that Mikhail Bakhtin considered its major characteristics: an opposition to social hierarchy

---

[13]Panizza's life and work are discussed in Friedrich Lippert and Horst Stobbe, *Im memoriam Oskar Panizza* (Munich, 1926); "Nachwort" by Hans Prescher in Oskar Panizza, *Das Liebeskonzil und andere Schriften* (Neuwied, 1964); and Peter Brown, "Doghouse, Jailhouse, Madhouse: A Study of Oskar Panizza's Life and Work" (Columbia University, Ph.D. diss., 1971).

[14]Panizza's works on *Haberfeldtreiben* include: "Die Haberfeldtreiben im bayrischen Gebirge," in *Neue deutsche Rundschau* 5 (1894), 37–56, "Haberfeldtreiben. Uber einen internationalen heidnisch-christlichen Kern in der 'Haberfeldtreiben,'" in *Wiener Rundschau* 1 (1897), 261–267; and *Die Haberfeldtreiben im bayrischen Gebirge—Eine sittengeschichtliche Studie* (Berlin, 1897). Panizza's views were challenged by an opponent of charivaris in Georg Queri, *Bauernerotik und Bauernfehme in Oberbayern* (Munich, 1911). Lately, charivaris have become a subject of increasing interest to early modern historians: see the influential essays of E. P. Thompson, "The Moral Economy of the English Crowd in the Eighteenth Century," and N. Z. Davis, "The Reasons of Misrule," both in *Past and Present*, 50 (1971).

and a carnivalesque spirit in which sacred and profane commingled. Panizza saw the latter principle manifested in popular enactments and representations of Christ's Passion, from medieval mystery plays to contemporary rural Stations of the Cross. He noted in these works a juxtaposition of pain, sincere religiosity, sexual excitement, and crude jesting. In popular representations such as those of Mary Magdalene —"pressing her largely décolleté breasts together in intense pain, sobbing with open mouth and looking up to the cross with tear-drenched eyes"[15]—religious devotion and sexual longing seemed to coalesce. Panizza considered such juxtapositions "a tendency of the people to place the great, the meek, the gruesome, and the pitiable close together."[16] Such "ability to weave together the heavenly with the earthly"[17] was not only an expression of a genuine popular belief in the conformity of the sacred and the secular, but also a statement of the people's "superclever roguishness and know-it-all attitude":[18] by treating the sacred in a human, all-too-human fashion, by portraying the saintly in familiar, all-too-familiar terms, popular culture not only incorporated the divine into its own realm, but also parodied elite, hierarchical, and spiritualized notions of religiosity.

Although he perceived the carnivalesque elements that Bakhtin attributed to popular culture, Panizza also committed what the Soviet scholar considered the fallacy of most elite writers attempting to imitate that culture: he reproduced only its negative and destructive elements.[19] In his major play, The Council of Love (Das Liebeskonzil, 1894), Panizza attempted to satirize the Catholic church by dramatizing the sexual excesses at the court of the Borgia Pope Alexander VI in 1495. Half of the play's scenes take place in Heaven, where the members of the Holy Family are travestied: God is an old, dottering fool; Jesus is weak and simple-minded; the Virgin Mary is highly sensual; the Holy Ghost appears as a rocket streaking across the stage; and the Devil is by far the most vital character in the cast. Although these creations bear superficial resemblances to some products of baroque and popular culture,[20] the total absence of religious

[15]Panizza, "Der Klassizismus und das Eindringen des Variété. Eine Studie über den zeitgenössischen Geschmack," in Die Gesellschaft 12 (1896), 1273.

[16]Panizza, notebook 25 (1886), 77; in the Handschriften-Abteilung der Stadtbibliothek München. The author would like to thank Richard Lemp, the curator of that collection, for permission to examine and quote from the Panizza archives.

[17]Panizza, Dialoge im Geiste Huttens (Zurich, 1897; reissue Munich 1979), 91.

[18]". . . superkluge Schalkheit und Allerweltsweisheit": Panizza, "Der Klassizismus, 1273.

[19]Cf. Bakhtin, Rabelais, 36–45.

[20]Cf. Burke, Popular Culture, 122–124, on religious parodies. Panizza's notebooks reveal great interest in medieval and postmedieval satires of religious customs and beliefs.

devotion made them alien to the popular spirit. Therefore, when Panizza was brought to trial in Munich on charges of blasphemy, he was sentenced by a lower-class jury to a year in jail. A juror noted after the trial: "If that dog had been tried in Lower Bavaria, he wouldn't have gotten away alive."[21] Panizza's case illustrates well the disjuncture between enthusiasm for popular culture and distance from the popular spirit typical of many elite modernist artists.

Panizza was the first German to use elements of popular culture in a modernist mode, but it took the dramatic genius of Frank Wedekind (1864–1918) to begin a true revolution in German playwrighting and stage practice.[22] Like Panizza, Wedekind was keenly aware of the sensuous aspects of popular culture, and he hoped to make use of them to revitalize a moribund classical tradition. He both admired and condemned the classical education that he had received as a youth, contending that the cerebral dryness of such education, its philological emphasis on grammar and texts (which he pilloried in *Spring Awakening*, his first major play), masked a corpus of highly charged sensuality. Whereas the classical education of the nineteenth century sought to exalt the spiritual at the expense of the sensual, Wedekind perceived that both Greek and German classicism in their original states saw no disjuncture between body and spirit: both were to be developed and allowed expression so that the individual could fashion himself into a harmonious whole.

Wedekind initially believed that this goal found a concrete (and to some extent also a metaphorical) expression in forms of popular entertainment, especially the circus and vaudeville. The use of formal principles of the spirit to harness the vital energies of the body led to a spiritualization of the body and a sensualization of the mind, so that in circus acts, "the barriers between the bodily and the spiritual are momentarily forgotten."[23] Wedekind proceeded to use elements of circus and other forms of popular culture to reform stage practice. Already in his early plays (*Art and Mammon*, 1886; *Fritz Schwigerling*, 1891), he was moving away from conversational salon pieces

---

[21]Cited in *Kritische Stimmen über Das Liebeskonzil* (Zurich n.d.; 1895?), 6.

[22]The most complete biography of Wedekind is Artur Kutscher, *Frank Wedekind. Sein Leben und Werk*, 3 vols. (Munich, 1922–1931). An excellent recent study that concentrates on Wedekind's social criticism is Hans-Jochen Irmer, *Der Theaterdichter Frank Wedekind. Werk und Wirkung* (Berlin, 1975).

[23]Wedekind, "Im Zirkus" (1888), in *Werke* (Berlin, 1969), 3:168. Wedekind's relations to the circus are discussed in Robert A. Jones, "Frank Wedekind: Circus Fan," in *Monatshefte*, 61 (1969), 139–156; and Hector Maclean, "Wedekind's *Der Marquis von Keith*: An Interpretation Based on the Faust and Circus Motifs," in *Germanic Review* 43 (1963), 163–187.

by adopting elements of the defunct but once-popular commedia dell'arte, which utilized pantomime and slapstick. His decisive turn to popular theatrical forms came during his years in Paris (1891–1895), where he regularly attended the numerous circuses, vaudevilles, and cabarets that the metropolis had to offer.

Wedekind saw in circus and vaudeville sensuous elements that could eventually undermine the dominance of literary theater. Popular theater relied only minimally upon words; communication took place by physical means, ranging from gestures and "body language" to acrobatics, where the whole body was transformed into a disciplined and abstract work of art. Wedekind believed that gestural and bodily elements were important dimensions of theater not only for their vitality but also because he questioned the ability of language to communicate much about anything at all. As early as *Spring Awakening*, he sought to transcend the expressive poverty of conventional conversation by means of a breakdown of syntax, frequent use of verbal imagery, and explosive vocal outbursts that culminate in outright screams.[24] In his later plays, he developed the style of *Aneinandervorbeireden*, or "speaking past one another," whereby conversations were shown to be nondialogues among individuals lost in their own concerns. According to Wedekind, the atomization and cerebrality of bourgeois society left the individual isolated and emotionally impoverished, and he believed that if people did not soon recognize and cultivate their senses and emotions in a healthy, natural manner, then violence and insanity would ensue. Increasingly, Wedekind integrated elements of popular theater into his plays as a means of expressing emotions in a predominantly nonverbal manner; dance, pantomime, acrobatics, and especially song became prominent in his works. Indeed, he even wrote scenarios for four pantomimes, with indications of the type of music to be played in each scene.

Wedekind also came to believe that popular forms should be introduced into elite theater to grant them a haven before they themselves lost their vitality and spontaneity. Although he initially thought that circus and vaudeville were loci of a balanced bodily and mental training, he soon learned—through his friendships with performers, and through his own problems in the culture market—that institutions of popular entertainment were, in reality, exploitative enterprises: as in any other profession, entertainers underwent a one-sided develop-

---

[24]For the breakdown of language in *Spring Awakening*, see Peter Jelavich, "Spring Awakening"; in *Passion and Rebellion: The Expressionist Heritage*, ed. Stephen Bronner and Douglas Kellner (New York, 1982).

ment, were forced to specialize, and were financially subservient to managers.[25] Although the theatrical forms presented in circus and vaude-ville might have had a genuinely popular origin, their integration into a commercial nexus meant that their spirit was slowly dying. Just as classicism had been strangled by the educational system, popular culture was being stifled by the increasingly commercial institutions that diffused it. The role of the elite artist was thus to create new aesthetic forms that would keep alive the libertarian spirit of both classicism and popular culture.

The problematic nature of such an enterprise was made explicit by the rise of vaudeville and its elite outgrowth, the cabaret. Panizza's "Classicism and the Infiltration of Vaudeville" (1896) was the first major German essay to point to the significance of vaudeville for elite culture.[26] The last half of the nineteenth century had seen the increasing popularity in Germany of vaudeville shows that included a concate-nation of popular arts: jugglers, tightrope walkers, trapeze artists, clowns, comedians, mimes, and folk singers. Although such enter-tainment was originally spurned by the "respectable" bourgeois public, a taste for such spectacles spread up the social ladder, so that by the end of the century, vaudevilles were seriously competing with conventional theaters for both lower and upper middle-class audiences. Panizza believed that classical theater would soon be destroyed by vaudeville, which harbored three principles inimical to it: physical and sensual vitality; a love of artistic forms for their entertainment value, regardless of aesthetic canons or the strictures of "good taste"; and a parodistic spirit, which imitated elite cultural forms in order to submit them to ridicule. Panizza's dire predictions for conven-tional theater were soon brought home to dramatists in Munich, where the *Duetsches Theater* opened in 1896 as a haven for elite drama, went bankrupt within a year, and was turned into a vaude-ville theater.[27]

Wedekind, like Panizza, welcomed the destruction of literary the-ater implicit in vaudeville, but he objected to the overthrow of clas-sicism per se, and he viewed the future of vaudeville with great misgivings. Not only did he now consider vaudevilles exploitative

[25]Wedekind's concern with the deleterious effects of commercialization upon culture is the subject of Peter Jelavich, "Art and Mammon in Wilhelmine Germany: The Case of Frank Wedekind," in *Central European History* 12 (1979), 203–236.

[26]Cf. note 15 above. A good historical introduction to the history of vaudeville is Ernst Günther, *Geschichte des Varietés* (Berlin, 1978).

[27]The *Deutsches Theater* affair is described at length in Hartl, *Aufbruch zur Moderne*, 106–534.

institutions: their audiences, failing to perceive the unity of bodily and spiritual expression that Wedekind imputed to popular entertainment, saw either nonregenerative satire or sexually titillating (but not fulfilling) acts.[28] Although he perceived only vaguely where the road was leading, Wedekind was one of the first writers to criticize what was to become the mass culture of the twentieth century. Commercial vaudeville, forerunner of film, radio, and television, was the first step in the development of a mass culture whose characteristics were the fusion of the cultural tastes of the lower classes and the elites, and the catering to, and manipulation of those tastes by commercial means of cultural diffusion to large and passively receptive audiences. The development of a cross-class culture was predicated upon the demise of the values formerly characteristic of the separate classes: classicism for the elite and carnivalesque "grotesque realism" for the populace at large. With the turning of both elite and popular audiences to a manipulated mass culture, critical artists such as Wedekind saw themselves as bearers of the spirit (and sometimes the forms) of both classicism and popular culture. Thus arose one of the paradoxes of the modernist avant-garde: while the lower and middle classes were becoming culturally fused by mass culture, popular culture and classicism were being creatively appropriated by a small group of artists who felt themselves alienated from all social classes. It was thus that a self-proclaimed avant-garde could declare itself—despite its extreme social isolation—the sole bearer of a culture that was at once truly popular and truly classical-elite.

Such was the goal of the first wave of the cabaret movement in Germany, which flourished briefly between 1901 and 1903. By far the most famous cabaret of the period was *Die Elf Scharfrichter* in Munich.[29] Many participants, including Wedekind, its most prominent member, were driven into the venture in part by financial pressure: the *Deutsches Theater* debacle, which Wedekind dramatized in his play *The Marquis of Keith* (1900), taught playwrights that the middle classes had begun to prefer vaudeville to literary theater. Young artists hence sought to use the vaudeville format and to maintain at the same

[28]See especially Act 3 of Wedekind's *Erdgeist* for a portrayal of vaudeville and its lascivious public.

[29]For the history of cabaret, see Heinz Greul, *Bretter, die die Zeit bedeuten. Die kulturgeschichte des Kabaretts* (Munich, 1971); and Rainer Otto and Walter Rösler, *Kabarettgeschichte: Abriss des deutschsprachigen Kabaretts* (Berlin, 1977). For a history of the *Scharfrichter*, see the appropriate chapters of these two works, as well as Peter Jelavich, "'Die Elf Scharfrichter': The Political and Sociocultural Dimensions of Cabaret in Wilhelmine Germany," in *The Turn of the Century: German Literature and Art 1890–1915*, ed. Gerald Chapple and Hans Schulte (Bonn, 1981), 507–525.

time the spirit of both popular and classical culture which was being lost in the emergent mass culture.

The cabaret movement integrated for the first time on an elite stage a myriad of popular theatrical forms. The *Elf Scharfrichter* presented pantomimes, puppet shows, shadow plays, songs, dances, and skits. Sometimes genuinely popular works, such as folk songs, were performed. At other times, the forms of popular theater were used to satirize either contemporary politics or elite literary culture. The *Scharfrichter* group also recited or staged the more "pagan" works of the German classicists. They even sought to capture some of the spirit and spontaneity of popular festivity by having writers and artists themselves perform the works they wrote, and by asking members of the audience to participate.

Despite its popular format, however, the cabaret addressed only the upper bourgeoisie. The entrance fee alone (three marks) assumed the exclusion of the lower classes. Indeed, genuine *Volkssänger* and entertainers who performed for laboring audiences were openly hostile to the cabaret's elitist imitation of their art.[30] Thus although the cabaret reproduced the forms of popular entertainment, it was nondemocratic both in its socially restricted appeal and its specific concern with elite cultural and political issues.

The cabaret movement fizzled after two years for political and artistic reasons. The *Scharfrichter* was forced to close in November 1903 after the Bavarian government, under mounting pressure from Catholic politicians to put an end to the critical and supposedly amoral venture, subjected the programs to severe censorship. By that time, however, many of the writer/performers were already weary of the cabaret: they felt burdened by the pressure of performing every night, and of composing a new repertory every six to eight weeks. The fact that the writer/performers were mainly imitating popular arts or satirizing elite culture, rather than creating a new cultural synthesis, caused dissatisfaction among those with higher artistic aspirations. The feeling became prevalent that the cabaret was merely a transitional phase: it mocked the limitations of literary drama and showed the potentials of popular theater, but it could not itself provide the right format for generating a new theatrical culture. The task was now to create a novel synthesis of popular and classical theater.

The significance of the cabaret movement lay in stimulating a reform of the conventional stage and precipitating a move away from

[30]Cf. Michael Schneider, *Die populäre Kritik an Staat und Gesellschaft in München (1886–1914)* (Munich, 1975), 96–97.

literary to gestural elements. The year 1903 marked the beginning of widespread experimentation with "theatrical" theater in Central Europe by people who had been connected, directly or indirectly, with the cabaret movement. The result was soon visible. At the *Ausstellung München 1908*—a large exposition held to display the commercial and cultural achievements of Munich to an international public—all three "model" theaters exemplified the appropriation of popular forms by elite artists: the *Marionettentheater Münchener Künstler*, for which many of Munich's major artists produced puppets; the *Schwabinger Schattenspiele*, at which shadow plays were presented; and the *Münchener Künstlertheater*, which sought basic changes in concepts of theater space and stage practice and in the relation of the artist to society. Three men of the theater involved with, or influenced by, the *Künstlertheater* between 1908 and 1914— Georg Fuchs, Max Reinhardt, and Vassily Kandinsky—exemplified different modalities of the relationship of modernist artists to both popular culture and "the people."

Georg Fuchs (1868–1948), the primary moving force behind the *Künstlertheater*, was also its most politically conscious director. Throughout the nineteenth century, public festivals had been used to instill patriotism in Germans, who were becoming politically unified but at the same time socially and economically more differentiated. In the face of increasing class divisions, Wagner and the young Nietzsche, among others, advocated the use of ritual theatrical experiences to restore an emotive sense of unity and cohesion among the populace at large. The notion that culture could unite what economics had sundered was especially appealing to artists, inasmuch as it attributed to them a potentially powerful and socially redemptive role. In conformity with the increasingly virulent nationalism of the Wilhelmine era, Fuchs gave this concept an aggressive (and somewhat totalitarian) turn: he believed that artists had the duty to instill a uniform mode of sense, perception, and thought in all Germans in order to unify and strengthen the nation for the expansionistic "world-historical tasks" that lay in its future. He believed that this spiritual homogenization of the Volk could be achieved by means of a popular theater conceived as an ecstatic communal experience.[31]

[31]Fuchs presented his political views most explicitly in *Der Kaiser, die Kultur und die Kunst* (Munich, 1904). For further discussion of the political implications of his artistic reforms, see Peter Jelavich, "Marché culturel, radicalisation idéologique, et innovation esthétique dans le théâtre munichois fin de siècle: Thoma, Wedekind, Fuchs," in *Le Mouvement Social*, no. 109 (October–December 1979), 35–65. The most complete study of Fuchs's life and ideas is Lenz Prütting, *Die Revolution des Theaters. Studien über Georg*

To achieve this goal, Fuchs contended that a total reform of theater was necessary, a "revolution" that would refashion theater architecture, stage practice, and dramatic writing. Since he desired to transcend class divisions, he opposed architectural elements that had arisen in the princely courts of the early modern period and had persisted through the nineteenth century, notably the horseshoe-shaped auditorium that focused the spectators' attention as much on the princely box as on the stage and the use of loges and balconies as means of upholding hierarchies and maintaining class divisions. Fuchs proposed instead an amphitheatrical auditorium without loges, in which the attention of all spectators would be focused exclusively on the stage. This theatrical space symbolized not only the equality of all spectators, but also their collective subordination to the stage—and thus to the artist.

Fuchs believed that the theatrical experience emanating from the stage should evoke *Rausch*, a feeling of ecstatic excitement, among the spectators. Such an experience could not, however, be generated by the literary theater that dominated the nineteenth-century stage. Fuchs believed that theater would have to return to its original and essential elements, as expressed in both early Greek and popular culture. He contended that drama originated from ritual dance, which, with its rhythmic bodily motions, was a sublimated and communal form of sexuality. The addition of choral songs, then soloists, then individual spoken roles, eventually led to the creation of drama proper, but also to the preponderance of the spoken word and rational, realistic action. This tendency culminated in the divorce of a literary theater for the elite from the popular community at large.

According to Fuchs, only a reintroduction of rhythmic, gestural, and sensual elements could lay the basis for a truly communal theater. The genuine popularity of such elements was demonstrated by the fact they were kept alive by popular culture—at the Oberammergau Passion Play, in popular dances and festivities, and especially in vaudeville. "Drama in its simplest form is the rhythmic movement of the body in space. Vaudeville is the place where drama is still cultivated in its simplest form, as dance, juggling, tightrope-walking, boxing and wrestling, animal training, *chanson*, masques, etc."[32] In spite of his enthusiasm for these forms, Fuchs did not encourage an imitation or

---

Fuchs (Munich, 1971). Fuchs presented his plans for reform of the theater—summarized below—in *Die Schaubühne der Zukunft* (Berlin, 1905), and *Die Revolution des Theaters* (Munich, 1909).

[32] Fuchs, *Revolution*, 179.

artificial revival of popular dance and theater among the elite, which would have been incongruous. Instead, he believed that elite culture should creatively appropriate the essential formal elements of popular theater, fuse them with classical traditions, and thus evolve a totally new, "modern" theatrical culture under which existing popular and elite culture could be subsumed.

The main element of the "modern" theater space created by Fuchs was the relief stage. This shallow stage sought to imitate the non-perspectivist two-dimensionality of pre-Renaissance, popular, and modern (*Jugendstil*) art. Such a stage, which negated the three-dimensional perspectivist realism of nineteenth-century painting and set design, was meant to underscore the essential unreality of the theatrical experience: art was to be seen as a sphere both different from and higher than everyday reality. Moreover, such a nonrealist stage would force a rejection of realistic acting in favor of a highly stylized form in which gestural, rhythmic, and dancelike elements would predominate.

Fuchs declared that at first only a minority of the classically educated elite would appreciate the significance of his projects; but ultimately the general public would flock to his theater, once the popular essence of his proposals was recognized under its "modern" garb. He hoped that the symbolic space and the rhythmic, gestural acting would evoke a strong sense of rhythm and form, which would not only produce a mesmerizing experience for the immediate audience, but also, over time, engender a unified and instinctive mode of perception, thought, and emotion in the German nation at large.

Fuchs could not achieve many of his goals during the summer of 1908, the only season he had charge of the *Künstlertheater*. Commercial factors put an end to some of his more drastic nationalist and artistic aspirations. Because the exposition where the theater was located was to be a drawing point for foreign tourists, Fuchs's aggressive chauvinism was hushed up as much as possible by the exposition directors. Moreover, they granted only limited funds and a small plot of land to the theater, which, when finished, seated only 642 spectators, in contrast to the 1500 seats Fuchs had wanted. Limited seating necessitated high prices, and this antipopular dimension was compounded by the Bavarian court's insistence that loges be built at the back of the theater, against Fuchs's expressed wishes.[33]

[33]Compare Fuchs's theater project of 1905, as proposed in *Die Schaubühne der Zukunft*, with the actual theater, as described in Fuchs, *Revolution*, and Max Littmann, *Das Münchner Künstlertheater* (Munich, 1908). For a history of the theater itself, see W. Grohmann,

The main barrier to Fuchs's success lay, however, in his artistic principles. Although the relief stage proved that, in certain scenes of certain plays, elimination of props, symbolic use of light, and employment of rhythmic and ritual speech could heighten the dramatic effect, such a style was ludicrous when doggedly applied to the existing dramatic literature. Not reduction to imaginary theatrical first principles, but rather an eclectic employment of different forms, was needed to create a theater that was at once classical, "theatrical," and popular. Such a formula was provided by Max Reinhardt, whose Berlin troupe took over the *Künstlertheater* from 1909 to 1912. Fuchs and Reinhardt chose similar repertories—mainly Shakespeare, the Greek and German classics, and some contemporary works; but whereas Fuchs forced them into the mesmeric rhythms of ritual speech and gesture, Reinhardt tended toward the opposite end of Schlemmer's spectrum, inasmuch as he preferred the vital and unruly forms of popular entertainment.

Reinhardt (1873–1943), originally an actor from Vienna, had rapidly gained fame in Berlin after 1900 as an innovative director. He was the first person to make "art" theater truly popular among the broad segments of the middle classes through the creation of mass-cultural formats for traditional elite culture. This achievement was a product of his familiarity with the wide range of conventions of popular and festive theater. Significantly, his style grew out of the cabaret movement. His Berlin cabaret *Schall und Rauch* (1901–1902), which marked his turn from acting to directing, was second only to the Munich *Scharfrichter* in fame and quality. He subsequently directed increasingly large theaters until finally, in 1910, he produced *Oedipus* in a large, arenalike assembly hall in Munich.

Reinhardt's success in popularizing high cultural theater was based upon three principles. First, Reinhardt conceived of theater as spectacle, rather than as literature: the text of the drama was but a skeleton around which a multimedia experience was to be realized. He applied the principles of vaudeville—emphasis on mimic and gestural elements, and constant variation—to classical works. The major precept of his directing style was to keep actors in perpetual motion; he added pantomimes, music, song, dance, and acrobatics to classical and modern works even when they were not called for in the scripts. Second, Reinhardt was fully aware that marketing was an integral part of

Das Münchener Künstlertheater in der Bewegung der Szenen- und Theaterreform (Berlin, 1935).

success in the cultural world of his day. He engineered press campaigns to advertise his projects, and he built up a theater empire by persuading investors that his productions were money-making enterprises. Third, he conceived of theater exclusively as entertainment and diversion: he had no desire to transform society or his public in any practical way. Personally opposed to the politics of both the Left and the Right, he saw art as a realm divorced from "the misery of daily existence":[34] theater was a place of refuge and escape, which could provide a sense of thrill and community as long as the performance lasted, but no longer. This nonagonistic and apolitical notion of theater proved attractive to Reinhardt's financiers and the broad middle-class public.

The financial managers of the *Künstlertheater*, disappointed at the reception of Fuchs's productions, were drawn to Reinhardt, and allowed him to use the *Künstlertheater* for four summers. Even though Reinhardt, like Fuchs, rejected literary in favor of "theatrical" theater, he believed that the relief stage was spatially too constricting. Nevertheless, he made the best of a bad situation. Not only did he modify his Berlin productions to fit the dimensions (although not the Fuchsian acting style) of the relief stage; he also experimented with new theatrical forms. In 1910, he produced for the first time an entirely pantomimic work (Friedrich Freska's *Sumurûn*). *Oedipus* was the first of his numerous arena or theater-in-the-round productions, which culminated in 1919 in his acquisition of the Schumann circus hall in Berlin, where 3500 spectators could be seated. There the revitalization of classical drama through the introduction of popular theatrics was complemented by the use of a popular stage-space.

The Reinhardt recipe, which has been imitated in various ways throughout the Western world, has remained the basis for whatever success "art" theaters catering to a broad middle-class public now enjoy. Nevertheless, many of his truly "modernist" contemporaries opposed his practices for three major reasons. First, it was claimed that his eclecticism did not constitute, strictly speaking, a "new" or "modern" style; as in the cabaret, he simply amalgamated the more popular theatrical conventions of previous centuries. Second, he was accused of suppressing the socially critical dimensions of both popular

[34]Letter from Reinhardt to Arthur Kahane, shortly after 1900, cited in Heinrich Braulich, *Max Reinhardt. Theater zwischen Traum und Wirklichkeit* (Berlin, 1969), 66. This book is a fine introduction to Reinhardt's life and work. For his productions in Munich, see Grohmann, 64–108; and *Max Reinhardt. Ausgewählte Briefe, Reden, Schriften und Szenen aus Regiebüchern*, ed., Franz Hadamovsky, (Vienna, 1963), 42–48.

and classical culture by purposely separating the world of the theater from the "real" world. As in mass culture, the elements of play, spectacle, and escapist entertainment were upheld at the expense of the analytic and socially critical dimensions of much classical and popular theater. Third, Reinhardt was accused of being too enslaved to market considerations, which supposedly encouraged his noncritical and ostentatiously "theatrical" predilections.

The truly "modern" dramatists who criticized Reinhardt perceived two radically different directions in which the artist could travel in order to remain free from subservience to, yet still have an impact on, modern society. These directions were, on the one hand, that of the self-consciously independent avant garde, and, on the other, socially directed grotesque realism. In the Munich context, these positions were respectively maintained by Vassily Kandinsky and Bertolt Brecht, whose works embody some of the most creative and "modern" appropriations of popular arts.

Although Kandinsky (1866–1944) is known primarily as the major originator of abstract art within the Russo-German cultural sphere, theater was for him a concern second only to the visual arts. Between 1909 and 1914 he wrote four plays, one of which, *The Yellow Sound*, might have been performed at the *Künstlertheater*, had not war closed that institution in the summer of 1914.[35]

Throughout his formative years, Kandinsky maintained an interest in popular culture and folk art. Like Wedekind, whose father intended him to be a lawyer, and Fuchs, who originally studied to become a Lutheran pastor, Kandinsky was initially very much a part of the culture of the word: he began as a lawyer in Russia, and his turn to art was a revolt against the legalistic spirit. Indeed, it was a confrontation with peasant law that helped undermine Kandinsky's confidence in his formal legal training. In the 1880s, he received a government commission to study peasant customary law in the courts which peasant communities had been allowed to form in the 1860s to handle local cases. He discovered in these courts the prevalence of what he considered a truly Christian spirit, which he contrasted with the "pagan Roman law" in which he was trained. The peasants had a flexible notion of justice, which took social position, motives, and personality into account; the spirit of justice, rather than any written code, took

---

[35]Kandinsky's interest in the *Künstlertheater* is discussed in Peg Weiss, *Kandinsky in Munich: The Formative Jugendstil Years* (Princeton, 1979), 92–103. *The Yellow Sound* was first published in W. Kandinsky and Franz Marc, *Der Blaue Reiter* (orig. 1912; Munich, 1965), 209–227.

precedence.[36] Contact with the peasantry also gave Kandinsky a new appreciation of art: the peasants' *"Wunderhäuser,"* where all objects were covered with colorful ornamentation, taught him to "move" and "live" in painting.[37] The genuineness of peasant religion, justice, and art, all of which were divorced from the historical and literary traditions of the elite, deeply impressed Kandinsky, who continually turned to folk culture for inspiration in later years.

In 1896, Kandinsky declined a professorship of law in Russia and settled in Munich, where he began a new career as an artist. In his major theoretical treatise, *On the Spiritual in Art* (1912), he deplored the rampant materialism of the nineteenth century, which stifled the "inner resonance" from which he felt all true artistic creation must spring. He rejected the visual realism and narrative content of academic painting, which reproduced only the appearance of objects and events, and applauded instead the arts produced by European peasants as well as non-Western "primitives." The latter works displayed an authenticity of artistic feeling that used form, color, and object primarily to express emotional and spiritual states, rather than to reproduce "reality" or narrative events.[38]

Kandinsky did not, however, believe that a mere imitation of peasant and "primitive" art would reintroduce the desired spirituality to elite culture. He contended that the present, the darkest hour of human history, when values and perceptions were wholly material, would give birth to a new religion, a "Third Testament," an "epoch of the great Spiritual."[39] A new artistic style was needed to herald this age, since in this apocalyptic vision the artist was cast in the role of a messiah who, by laying bare his own "inner resonances," would provide a model for others to uncover their spiritual essences. More explicitly than any other artist of the time, Kandinsky enunciated a theory of the avant-garde whereby the solitary artist, unbeknownst to his contemporaries, created values upon which future civilizations would be built.[40] Whereas Fuchs believed that the artist could be a recognized leader in his own day, Kandinsky portrayed him as a hidden legislator of future generations.

[36]Cf. Wassily Kandinsky, *Rückblick* (orig. 1913; Baden-Baden, 1955), 14, 44, 46.

[37]Ibid., 19–20.

[38]Cf. Kandinsky, *Über das Geistige in der Kunst* (orig. 1912; Zurich, 1952), 21–22, 41–42. See also the juxtaposition of peasant, "primitive," and modern art in *Der Blaue Reiter*, passim. The influence of non-Western and folk art on modern art is the subject of Robert Goldwater, *Primitivism in Modern Art* (New York, 1938).

[39]" . . . *Epoche des grossen Geistigen*"; Kandinsky, *Über das Geistige*, 143.

[40]Ibid., 27, 29–30, 33–34.

Kandinsky sought to attract at least a small following for his art among the elite during his lifetime, as well as to lay the basis for a future appreciation by the populace at large. Thus for reasons of both aesthetic and public reception, he utilized themes and forms of Bavarian and Russian peasant art in his path to abstraction from 1909 to 1914, as Rose-Carol Washton Long has demonstrated.[41] From 1908 on, Kandinsky lived intermittently in the Bavarian village of Murnau, where *Hinterglasmalerei*, or painting on glass, was practiced by the local population. The bright colors, use of strong line, and religious imagery appealed to him, and he started to paint works in the same medium. He chose for his paintings themes of Bavarian and Russian popular art which he thought expressed the coming cultural upheaval and the messianic role of the artist—the Deluge, the Apocalypse, or Saint George. Over the course of a few years, these images, initially painted in a style imitative of folk art, were successively modified and transformed into Kandinsky's first abstract pictures. In these later works the popular religious imagery served only as a residual sign of the pictures' meaning, which received more powerful expression through abstract form, line, and color. Kandinsky had, in essence, freed the strong linear and coloristic elements of folk art from their mimetic function, and had them evoke religious feelings in an expressively abstract manner. Hardly discernible yet still recognizable, popular Christian imagery drawn from folk art was retained to allow a traditional public to step into the picture.

Similar principles were operative in Kandinsky's plays. He believed that nineteenth-century drama, like visual art, had been reduced to narration and a depiction of "external life"; both "the life of the soul" and the "cosmic element" were "completely absent."[42] It was no wonder, he wrote, that people turned "to vaudeville, to the circus, to cabaret, to movie theaters."[43] From such forms, a new theater would arise that would greatly surpass all previous theatrical experience. This was to be brought about by unleashing the essential elements of

[41]Rose-Carol Washton Long, "Kandinsky and Abstraction: The Role of the Hidden Image," *Artforum* 10, (June 1972), 42–49; and "Kandinsky's Abstract Style: The Veiling of Apocalyptic Folk Imagery," *Art Journal*, 34, (Spring 1975), 217–228. The remainder of this paragraph draws heavily on these articles. See also Hans Konrad Röthel, *Kandinsky: Painting on Glass* (catalogue, Guggenheim Museum, New York, 1966); E. Roters, "Wassily Kandinsky und die Gestalt des Blauen Reiters," in *Jahrbuch der Berliner Museen* 5, no. 2 (1963), 201–206; and Hideho Nishida, "Genesis of the Blaue Reiter" in *Homage to Wassily Kandinsky*, ed., G. di San Lazzaro (New York, 1975), 18–24.

[42]Kandinsky, "Über Bühnenkomposition," in *Der Blaue Reiter*, 194–195.

[43]Kandinsky, "Über die abstrakte Bühnensynthese" (1923), in *Essays über Kunst und Künstler* (Teufen, 1955), 69.

theater and using them for purely expressive purposes. The liberation
of form, line, and color from the object in painting was matched in
Kandinsky's plays by a liberation of what he considered the three
elements of theater: color, sound, and motion.[44] The very title of *The
Yellow Sound* evoked the first two elements, which were utilized
in "pure" forms: sometimes a play of light alone was called for on
stage, and nonsense words and syllables were used at certain points as
"pure" sound and voice.

As for motion, Kandinsky employed those forms of popular theatrics which he believed were expressive without being narrative.
"Clowns, in particular, build their composition on a very definite
illogicality. Their action has no definite development, their efforts
lead nowhere and, indeed, they're not meant to. But at the same time
the spectator experiences impressions with total intensity."[45] Some of
the actors in *The Yellow Sound* were dressed in colored tights, or had
painted faces, or otherwise looked like characters from circus or popular entertainment. They were supposed to act in the manner of,
alternately, puppets, acrobats, and dancers. In addition, huge mari-
onettes were required, to portray giants. These elements combined in
a way analogous to Kandinsky's abstract paintings: although there
was no narrative plot-line, certain symbolic scenes and gestures made
clear that the play concerned the evolution of human society to a
popular utopian community of the future. Color, sound, and motion
were used to evoke the spirit, rather than narrate the history, of these
events.

Kandinsky's work stands at the beginning of an extreme strand of
modernist theater that rejected narration and, ultimately, the human
actor; the stage becomes a place for a play of color and form. To a
certain extent, this development restored a participatory element to
modern culture. Kandinsky, like other modernists, sought to awaken
the active involvement of the spectator in the creation or re-creation of
the meaning of his nonnarrative paintings and plays.[46] However, unlike
traditional popular culture, where participation was physical and collective, Kandinsky's art and theater required a manner of involvement
that was mental and individual. Such art and theater could, at best,
teach the spectator to liberate his or her artistic imagination and sub-

[44]Ibid., 72; and "Uber Bühnenkomposition," 206.

[45]From an article by Kandinsky published in Moscow in 1920; cited by John Bowlt,
"Vasilii Kandinsky: The Russian Connection," in Bowlt and Rose-Carol Washton Long,
The Life of Vasilii Kandinsky in Russian Art (Newtonville, 1980), 27.

[46]Kandinsky, "Über Bühnenkomposition," 192.

conscious visions, to reveal and express his or her self on an individual basis.

The socially critical and collectively regenerative spirit of popular culture underlay the other pronounced variant of modernist theater which found its fullest expression in the works of Bertolt Brecht (1898–1956). Brecht recognized both the critical and the entertaining dimensions of popular theater, and he combined them in novel forms in order to address a popular audience. He realized that "the people" were now the urban laboring population, and thus he sought to create a theater that could dramatically present the problems of advanced capitalist societies.

Brecht's early years, before his move to Berlin in 1924, were divided between his native Augsburg and Munich. As a youth in Augsburg, he assiduously attended the side shows of the local fairs; while in Munich, he admired the performances of the popular clown-comedian, Karl Valentin. Like Panizza and Wedekind, whom he idolized, Brecht sensed a critical and adversary spirit in popular culture.[47] Not only could collective festivities such as carnival—which he later depicted in scene 10 of *Galileo*—be highly political events; much humbler forms of popular culture were evidence of what Brecht called the "dialectic" nature of popular thought. "Even in the panoramas of the side shows and in folk ballads, the simple people, who are hardly simple at all, love the stories of the rise and fall of great men, of eternal change, of the cunning of the oppressed, of the potentialities of mankind. And they look for truth, for 'what is behind it all.' "[48]

Two of these elements—the notion that society is amenable to change, and the desire to depict "what is behind it all"—were the underlying principles of Brecht's own work. In order to demonstrate his beliefs, Brecht developed a style of theater that was realistic, but not illusory or naturalist. "Realism" implied portraying people as they

---

[47]A comparison of the works of Wedekind and the young Brecht is the subject of Gerd Witzke, *Das epische Theater Wedekinds und Brechts. Ein Vergleich des frühen dramatischen Schaffens Brechts mit dem dramatischen Werk Wedekinds* (Tübingen, 1972).

[48]Bertolt Brecht, "Studium des ersten Auftritts in Shakespeares *Coriolan*" (1953), in *Schriften zum Theater. Über eine nicht-aristotelische Dramatik* (Frankfurt, 1957), 196–197. Brecht refers to popular culture and theater throughout his writings. For a short description of the influence of Bavarian popular theater on his early works, see Martin Esslin, *Brecht: The Man and His Work* (Garden City, N.Y., 1971), 110–115. For Brecht's use of song in his plays, see Zbigniew Slupinski, *Die Funktion des "Songs" in den Stücken Bertolt Brechts* (Poznan, 1971); Bernwald Thole, *Die "Gesänge" in den Stücken Bertolt Brechts* (Göttingen, 1973); and Sammy K. McLean, *The Bänkelsang and the Work of Bertolt Brecht* (The Hague, 1972).

"actually" were, rather than as they appeared. Such an endeavor required the use of the "grotesque realism" that Bakhtin attributed to, and Brecht perceived in, vestiges of popular culture: willful distortions were means of depicting the essence (rather than the surface appearance) of a person or situation. Moreover, an inherent didacticism could be seen in the fact that fairground actors and moritat singers constantly interrupted and commented on the action or narrative of their shows or songs, so that the "moral" would not be lost. The destruction of illusion through distortion and the interruption of the narrative from a perspective outside of the story itself became major principles of Brechtian *Verfremdung* (estrangement). Even such a primitive form of popular entertainment as moritat singing, which Brecht especially enjoyed and made use of, employed many of the distance-creating devices that he used in his mature plays (such as songs, illustrative pictures and diagrams, and direct addresses to the audience).

Such trademarks of Brecht's style, like those of Reinhardt, were a product of his openness to and command over popular theatrical forms. Yet whereas Reinhardt encouraged social escapism, Brecht strove for an entertaining didacticism that would change the audience's perception of society. The destruction of illusions on stage was to have modular value for the destruction of the illusions that masked the reality of capitalist life. Conversely, the vitality of the entertainment, the element of play, was intended to demonstrate the human creativity upon which a new social order could be based. "The theater of the scientific age can make dialectics a pleasure. The surprises of development, proceeding logically or in leaps, the instability of circumstances, the humor of contradictions, and the like, these are amusements caused by the vitality of man, and they enhance the art of life as well as the joy of living."[49]

This ebullient element in Brecht's theater is what distinguished it from that of the naturalists before him and the "socialist realists" with whom he had intermittent battles toward the end of his life. Indeed, Brecht's combination of criticism and laughter, of seeing the comic and hopeful dimensions in a world of constant change (and change often for the worse), brought him very close to the spirit of popular culture described by Bakhtin.[50]

Whether Brecht's works ever, to a significant degree, spoke di-

[49]Brecht, "Kleines Organon für das Theater" (1948), in *Schriften*, 173.
[50]Bakhtin explicitly mentioned Brecht as a latter-day exponent of popular "realist grotesque": see *Rabelais*, 46.

rectly to the modern "people," the proletariat, is, however, a different matter. The eclecticism and vitality of his works could appeal, despite their social criticism, to many of the same people who enjoyed Reinhardt. The great success of *The Threepenny Opera* among bourgeois audiences is a well-known fact, and the "repressive tolerance" of capitalist societies has guaranteed his dramas repeated performances on both sides of the Atlantic. Brecht's works have also become showpieces for socialist countries, especially the German Democratic Republic; yet his persistent conflicts with the emerging German socialist state suggest that there too, his social aspirations were far from being fully realized.

The paradox of the reception of Brecht's works was ultimately no different from that of other modernist dramatists. All were of middle-class background; all were antibourgeois; and all were condemned to be appreciated by bourgeois audiences, if by anyone at all. Bourgeois culture remained essentially an in-house affair. But it was a house divided against itself; and in this struggle, the familial outcasts, whether involuntary or self-proclaimed, turned to popular culture to undermine or transform their home.

Within the short span of at most forty years—1890 to 1930—an influx of popular themes and forms had led to a discrediting of the literary and realist theater of the nineteenth century and the creation of Panizza's satirical caricatures, the circus style of Wedekind, the ritual theater of Fuchs, Kandinsky's abstract dramas, the spectacular eclecticism of Reinhardt, and the grotesque realism of Brecht. Theatrical modernism was not, of course, limited to southern Germany; other countries—notably France, Italy, Austria, and Russia—saw a proliferation of new styles of dramatic writing, staging, and design. Allowing for national differences, all of them witnessed similar processes of incorporating popular culture into elite contexts. At the turn of the century, each of these countries had, to varying degrees, the proper ingredients for an elite/popular mixture: a still vital, though often threatened, peasant and popular culture; a Catholic or Orthodox tradition of ostentatious religious ritual; producers of elite culture alienated from their native middle class; and the beginnings of a culture industry that sought consumers in all sectors of society.

Seen from the production angle, this mixture was highly conducive to experimentation; but few modernist artists could find large numbers of consumers among either the "people," whose traditional arts they appropriated, or their native bourgeois elite, which they ostensibly despised. Audiences remained generally small, and always middle-class—with the important exception of the proletarian-oriented modernist theater movements in northern Germany and the Soviet Union in the 1920s. From the turn of the century to the present, spectators from all social strata have gravitated increasingly to a mass culture industry, about which Adorno wrote: "Culture industry is the deliberate integration of its consumers from above. It forces together the realms of high and low art. . . . To both their detriments. High art is deprived of its seriousness by playing to the gallery; the harness of civilization deprives low art of the unruly resistance which it embodied as long as there was not complete social control."[51]

Except for Reinhardt, who accepted and contributed to the noncritical nature of mass culture, all of the figures discussed in this essay hoped to preserve both the seriousness of elite art and popular culture's "unruly resistance" to the social and cultural trends of their day. Their ideologies ranged from the Marxist Left (Brecht) to the prefascist Right (Fuchs) to religious utopianism (Kandinsky); yet they all shared the ability to look beyond their native bourgeois horizon, and to appropriate, preserve, and creatively transform elements of popular culture.

[51]Theodor W. Adorno, "Résumé über Kulturindustrie" (1963), in *Ohne Leitbild. Parva Aesthetica* (Frankfurt, 1967), 60.

CHAPTER NINE

Reading Freud's *Civilization and Its Discontents*

DAVID JAMES FISHER

Your letter of December 5, 1927, containing your remarks about a feeling you describe as "oceanic" has left me no peace.
>   Freud to Romain Rolland, 14 July, 1929

I can at least listen without indignation to the critic who is of the opinion that when one surveys the aims of cultural endeavor and the means it employs, one is bound to come to the conclusion that the whole effort is not worth the trouble, and that the outcome of it can only be a state of affairs which the individual will be unable to tolerate. My impartiality is made all the easier to me by my knowing very little about all these things.
>   Freud, *Civilization and Its Discontents*, 1930

Civilization and Its Discontents can be viewed as a starting point for the student of modern Western cultural and intellectual history. This relaxed, imaginative, and discursive essay combines tightly reasoned passages with lyrical flights, speculative leaps with qualifying statements, literary with nonliterary forms of writing. The text also contains some dead ends, some nonsense, and some anachronistic and problematic assertions, which can be jettisoned or radically revised without damaging the richness of the essay. The art of reading

This paper is dedicated to my father, Martin M. Fisher, M.D.

I am grateful to Louis Breger, Peter Gay, Steven L. Kaplan, Dominick LaCapra, Peter Loewenberg, and Ruth B. Shapiro for having criticized an earlier version of this paper. I also thank Sigmund Freud Copyrights., The Institute of Psycho-Analysis, the Hogarth Press, and W. W. Norton & Company, Inc. for permission to quote from Volume 21 of *The Complete Psychological Works of Sigmund Freud* translated and edited by James Strachey.

Freud is not to take every word as revealed truth; let us follow his insistence on analytic interpretation and on desacralization by viewing his own works in a critical spirit.

Foucault has asserted that Freud began the modern medical and psychological dialogue with unreason; he accomplished this linguistic breakthrough by systematically investigating the physician-patient relationship.[1] Freud was also an "initiator of discourse"[2] on society and culture, employing psychoanalytic perspectives to diagnose the psychological roots of cultural trends, to unearth archaic patterns in "civilized" behavior, and to illuminate the relationship of the individual to society.

In *Civilization and Its Discontents*, we confront an author who writes without precautions, sometimes without apparent transitions, who leaves things out, and who does not always explain his premises.[3] His narrative structure is not linear or focused around one central theme.[4] This places a burden on the reader. To comprehend these absences, these nonlogical juxtapositions, the mixed nature of the style, to grasp the multiple meanings of the text, the reader is well advised to be familiar with psychoanalytic theory, to have a knowledge of Freud's revolutionary works, including the seminal books on dreams, infantile sexuality, jokes, the psychopathology of everyday life, and the case studies, in addition to his social, anthropological, and religious writings. Knowledge of Freud's correspondence, his biography, and the political and cultural history of his era help to situate him and this text in its historical framework.

Psychoanalysis focuses on intrapsychic conflict. Freud conceptualized the mind in dualisms, in binary opposites. I have used the method of deciphering contradictory forces to understand the structure

[1]Michel Foucault, *Madness and Civilization: A History of Insanity in the Age of Reason*, tr. Richard Howard (New York, 1973), 198, 277–278; Foucault, *The History of Sexuality*, tr. Robert Hurley (New York, 1978), 53, 56, 150, 158–159; see my review of Foucault's *Histoire de la sexualité*, in *The Journal of Psychohistory* 5 (Winter 1978)), 481–486.

[2]Michel Foucault, "What Is an Author?" in *Language, Counter-Memory, Practice: Selected Essays and Interviews*, tr. and ed. Donald F. Bouchard (Ithaca, 1977), 131–136; Foucault, *The Order of Things: An Archaeology of the Human Sciences* (New York, 1970), 373–376.

[3]Provocative readings of Freud's texts can be found in Jacques Lacan, *Ecrits: A Selection*, tr. Alan Sheridan (New York, 1977), 114–178, 292–325; Lacan, "Desire and the Interpretation of Desire in *Hamlet*," tr. James Hulbert, *Yale French Studies*, no. 55–56 (1977), 11–52; Samuel Weber, "It," *Glyph*, 4 (1978), 1–31.

[4]Roy Schafer, "Narration in the Psychoanalytic Dialogue," *Critical Inquiry* 7 (1980), 29–53; Leo Bersani, "The Other Freud," *Humanities in Society* 1, no. 1 (1978), 33–49; Peter Brooks, "Freud's Masterplot: Questions of Narrative," *Yale French Studies*, no. 55–56 (1977), 280–300; Peter Brooks, "Fictions of the Wolfman: Freud and Narrative Understanding," *Diacritics*, (1979), 72–81.

and hidden components of *Civilization and Its Discontents*. Unraveling these oppositions enables the reader to see invisible connections in the text, thus assisting him to make mediations and to fill in the gaps between manifest and latent relationships, which Freud only hints at.

In this paper I shall discuss the various strategies Freud employs in coming to grips with Romain Rolland's postulation of the "oceanic sensation." I will map out and explain Freud's appeal to his audience and his rhetorical maneuvers in Chapter I of *Civilization and Its Discontents*; his alternation between a polemical, defensive, and disputatious voice, and one that indicates his warmth, vulnerability, modesty, erudition, and creative audacity. I will examine his mixed feelings; his theoretical and speculative passages that link the oceanic feeling to narcissism; his use of jokes, irony, literary devices, quotations, and humor to evade the issue; and his imaginative but abortive attempt to set up explanatory analogies from other disciplines. The creative ambiguity of Freud's thought will be accounted for in terms of his tolerance for his own theoretical inconsistencies and gaps in knowledge or method; that is, his own certainties coexisted with undecidability and plurality of meaning.

Freud's introduction of Romain Rolland, particularly in Chapter I but also throughout the text, allows him to scrutinize culture from a highly subjective point of view, in addition to one which appears disinterested. I will indicate how Rolland figures in Freud's analysis of the Judeo-Christian commandment "Love thy neighbor"; how one can extend psychoanalytic cultural criticism to see the oceanic sensation as a reaction-formation, a benign desire disguising the sadistic wish for the total annihilation of mankind. I will show the way Freud's ambivalence toward Rolland takes the form of bipolar oppositions in the text: Freud sees Rolland's world view as prophetic and saintly but poses psychoanalysis as a therapeutic tool and an instrument to desacralize religious and mystical modes of thinking. Rolland is present throughout the text as Freud's Double and Other, an object of irresistible attraction and aversion, someone with whom Freud is deeply identified and from whom he felt unalterably different. Rolland simultaneously represents the achievements of Western civilization, and the dangers of excessive sublimation. In short, Freud condenses his ambivalent feelings for the French writer into his meditations on civilization as a whole. I view the addition of three footnotes and a one-sentence conclusion to the 1931 second edition as a continuation of the oceanic sensation controversy, a displacement of Freud's double feelings toward Rolland onto a parallel text, and Freud's last word on the significance of this intellectual encounter.

After the appearance of the second edition, Freud sent Rolland a personally inscribed copy with a dedication: "From the Terrestrial Animal to his Great Oceanic Friend."[5] This ironic dedication goes to the heart of the debate that the two carried on and gives us a view of Freud's method of thinking and his style of intellectual life. Foucault has specified that, in analyzing discourse, knowledge of the speaker's identity and of his situation is often as important as the text itself or omissions in the text. The terrestrial animal/oceanic friend dichotomy condenses the mixed feelings and the almost unbridgeable divergences of Freud and Rolland. It also suggests that their controversy, which flows into the entire fabric of *Civilization and Its Discontents*, into their letters, into Rolland's three-volume study of Indian mysticism,[6] and Freud's 1936 paper on the Acropolis,[7] was not conducted in the same conceptual context. The debate ended in an impasse, each participant holding to his original position.

Freud, the terrestrial animal, saw himself—possibly too rigidly—as a scientific psychologist, identified himself with the material world, with the biological and earthly realm of drives, with concrete and observable data. He attempted to speak the language of the reality principle, and evolved a methodology which worked on the level of the conscious. Freud's methodology relied on the application of logic to seemingly illogical phenomena. His intelligence was comfortable in the analytic register, and his skepticism moved toward critical inquiry, not toward resignation or despair. Furthermore, his characteristic mode of thinking is analytic. He was authentically self-critical, extending his radical doubt toward himself and toward his own theoretical perspective. The terrestrial animal took seriously Charcot's ironic injunction to combine theory-building with close observation of reality; it was a protective measure against his own speculative in-

[5]For a full discussion of this debate, see my "Sigmund Freud and Romain Rolland: The Terrestrial Animal and His Great Oceanic Friend," *American Imago* 33 (Spring 1976), 1–59; also see David S. Werman, "Sigmund Freud and Romain Rolland," *International Review of Psycho-Analysis* 4 (1977), 225–242; Irving B. Harrison, "On the Maternal Origins of Awe," *The Psychoanalytic Study of the Child* 30 (1975), 181–195; Irving B. Harrison, "On Freud's View of the Infant-Mother Relationship and of the Oceanic Feeling— Some Subjective Influences," *Journal of the American Psychoanalytic Association* 27, no. 1 (1979), 399–421; and J. Moussaieff Masson, *The Oceanic Feeling: The Origins of Religious Sentiment in Ancient India* (Dordrecht, Holland, 1980), 33–50.

[6]Romain Rolland, *Essai sur la mystique et l'action de l'Inde vivante: La vie de Ramakrishna* (Paris 1929), and *Essai sur la mystique et l'action de l'Inde vivante: La vie de Vivekananda et l'evangel universel*, 2 vols. (Paris 1930).

[7]Sigmund Freud, "A Disturbance of Memory on the Acropolis: An Open Letter to Romain Rolland on the Occasion of His Seventieth Birthday" (1936), *Standard Edition of the Complete Psychological Works of Sigmund Freud*, (London, 1964), 22:239–248.

clinations. Nor did Freud ever propose that his writings were definitive on any subject. His humility is closely related to his method of problem-solving. The derogation of his own work was not merely ceremonial, not just a disarming mode of speech, but an essential part of the quest for truth, accuracy, and perpetuation of the process of understanding. Here is Freud's ironic comment upon the completion of *Civilization and Its Discontents*; it reads almost as a paradigm of self-deprecation:

> Anna has already told you that I am working on something, and today I have written the last sentence, which—so far as is possible without a library—finished the work. It deals with civilization, sense of guilt, happiness and similar lofty topics, and strikes me, no doubt rightly, as very superfluous—in contrast to earlier works, which always sprang from some inner necessity. But what else can I do? One can't smoke and play cards all day, I am no longer much good at walking, and most of what there is to read doesn't interest me any more. So I wrote, and in that way the time passed quite pleasantly. In writing this work I have discovered afresh the most banal truths.[8]

Rolland, the oceanic friend, swam in the boundless waters of eternity and universal love—his mind retained access to primitive emotions; he valued the images, symbols, affects, and subjective experiences that were derivatives of the primary process. He was a mystic and a religious believer, and his imagination worked intuitively, introspectively, and synthetically; he emphasized similarities, not differences, between people, groups, nations, past and present forms of religious and cultural life. Moreover, his need for transcendence was linked to a search for totality, the goal of which was for the individual to achieve a symphonic balance of competing psychic and social forces.

In his controversy with Rolland, Freud had moved from an analysis of the common person's religion to a theoretical evaluation of the foundations of humanistic mysticism—to what Rolland alleged was the deepest and most universal source of the religious impulse. Rolland had touched a sensitive nerve in pointing out that Freud had not analyzed ecstatic states or deep introspective feelings in *The Future of an Illusion* (1927). Rolland subsequently described and coined the term "oceanic sensation" in an eight-paragraph letter written to Freud

[8]Letter from Freud to Lou Andreas-Salomé, 28 July 1929, in *Sigmund Freud & Lou Andreas-Salomé Letters*, ed. Ernest Pfeiffer, tr William and Elaine Robson Scott (New York, 1972), 181; for an interesting reply to Freud's analysis of the oceanic sensation, see letter from Lou Andreas-Salomé to Freud, 4 Jan. 1930, ibid., 182–183.

in December 1927, in which he pressed Freud for such a scientific evaluation.[9]

Spontaneous religious sensation, he told Freud, was a prolonged intuitive feeling of contact with the eternal, a direct feeling of vastness, of living in or among immense forces. Rolland insisted that the oceanic feeling be researched and understood as an energy which surpassed traditional categories of time, space, and causality. It had nothing to do with organized or institutionalized religion or promises of personal salvation. This "free vital gushing" (*jaillissement vital*) promised to be a spontaneous source of action and thought that might have regenerative powers for the undeveloped nations of the world and for decadent Europe. Because he was an accomplished critical realist, Rolland could not be dismissed as a mindless or crackpot mystic. In his writings he never opposed reason or scholarly and scientific investigations. He asserted, on the contrary, that the oceanic sensation could exist side by side with one's critical faculties, that the oceanic did not give rise to a world of illusions.

Rolland proposed that the oceanic feeling was a sensation of the individual's identity with his surroundings, of sublime connection to objects, to one's entire self, and to the universe as an indivisible whole. It ended the separation of the self from the outside world and from others and promised the individual participation in higher spiritual realms. It resisted traditional Western scientific and empirical explanations, and Rolland attributed the sensation to a primeval force in all people. The oceanic was nothing less than the divine inner core of existence; it had the quality of perpetual birth. The oceanic feeling was an idea-force, a benign form of energy, which could mediate between man as he was now and man as he could become. Since the sensation fostered relatedness among individuals, it could potentially break down the barriers of class, ethnicity, nationality, sexuality, culture, and generation, and could possibly lead to universal fraternity in the distant future. For Rolland the oceanic sensation represented an indestructible moral aspect of man's spiritual nature. It was nothing less than the basis of religious experience: spontaneous, innate, omnipresent, the force responsible for the individual's amorous bonds with other humans and the environment. The French writer also felt that the oceanic contained enormous imaginative possibilities; that it

[9]Letter from Romain Rolland to Freud, 5 Dec. 1927 in Romain Rolland, *Un beau visage a tous sens. Choix de lettres de Romain Rolland (1886–1944)*, Cahiers Romain Rolland, No. 17 (Paris, 1967), 264–266; for an English translation, see Fisher, "Sigmund Freud and Romain Rolland," 20–22.

provided the artist with reservoirs of inspiration, instinctive sources of creativity. It was the force that unified the works of literature, music, and humanistic mysticism. It was a centering and harmonizing emotion. Exploration of the oceanic feeling could lead to new forms of self-discovery and self-mastery, to the purification of ideas, and to insights about the nonrational foundations of being. Not simply a fantasy, mysticism was a form of knowledge and cognition that operated through the emotions. If he practiced on a daily, methodical basis, as in meditation or in yoga, the mystic could expand the oceanic sensation into another mode of discourse, a new spiritual discipline, another way of reaching higher truths.

Freud's treatment of the oceanic sensation in Chapter 1 of *Civilization and Its Discontents* deserves careful scrutiny. Freud was obviously not exaggerating when he wrote to Rolland that "your letter of December 5, 1927 containing your remarks about a feeling you describe as 'oceanic' has left me no peace."[10] There is a combination of praise and slight blame in this chapter, a touch of self-conscious reserve toward Rolland, and a complex repertoire of rhetorical and analytical strategies.[11] In fact, throughout this chapter Freud is unusually evasive and tentative.

He disarms the reader with his humility, his modesty, his candor, and his admission of personal limitations. He opens by mentioning the difficulties in treating a reputedly universal feeling that is absent in himself: "I cannot discover this 'oceanic' feeling in myself" (*Civilization*, p. 65).[12] With understatement, the father of psychoanalysis admits how problematic it is to deal with emotions: "It is not easy to deal scientifically with feelings" (p. 65). He states the inadequacies of his insights and his method: "I have nothing to suggest that would have a decisive influence on the solution of this problem" (p. 65). Before beginning to set up linguistic resemblances, he warns the reader to beware of his analogies: "This analogy may be too remote" (p. 68). He

[10]Letter from Freud to Romain Rolland, 14 July 1929, in *Letters of Sigmund Freud*, ed. Ernst L. Freud, tr. Tania and James Stern (New York 1960; hereafter cited as *Freud Letters*), 388. It may not be accidental that Freud wrote Rolland on Bastille Day, the most important secular holiday for the French, and also the title of one of Rolland's most celebrated plays, *Le Quatorze Juillet* (1902).

[11]Robert R. Holt, "On Reading Freud," *Abstracts of the Standard Edition of the Complete Psychological Works of Sigmund Freud*, ed. Carrie Lee Rothgeb (New York, 1973), 3–73; also see Roy Schafer, *A New Language for Psychoanalysis*, (New Haven, 1976).

[12]All citations are to Sigmund Freud, *Civilization and Its Discontents*, tr. James Strachey, vol. 21 of *The Standard Edition of the Complete Psychological Words of Sigmund Freud*, (London: Hogarth Press, 1961).

refers to the absence of research and reliable knowledge on the issue: "The subject has hardly been studied as yet" (p. 69). He briefly takes on Rolland's role, becomes the imaginative writer, the lyricist, the man who gives expression to the fantastic, the unthinkable, and the dreamlike: "There is clearly no point in spinning our phantasy any further, for it leads to things that are unimaginable and even absurd" (p. 70). As his writing becomes dialogic, he anticipates the reader's criticism and attempts to counter the expected rebuttal: "Our attempt seems to be an idle game," "We bow to this objection," and "Perhaps we are going too far in this" (p. 71). He signals the reader to beware of spurious arguments: "To me this claim does not seem compelling" (p. 72); and he refuses to speculate on the unknown and perhaps the unknowable: "There may be something further behind that, but for the moment it is wrapped in obscurity." (p. 72). And he states his inability to analyze diffuse emotional constellations: "Let me admit once more that it is very difficult for me to work with these almost intangible quantities" (p. 72).

It is meaningful that in *Civilization and Its Discontents*, Freud's discourse on culture begins and ends with himself. The first-person point of view—"I," "me," "my,"—is used sixteen times in the second and third paragraphs. Conspicuously, he concludes the essay with thirteen first-person references in the last paragraph of Chapter 8. By opening and closing on a personal note, the author indicates his subjective involvement with the questions. In such studies, pseudoscientific aloofness or value-free detachment is inappropriate.

In the text, disclaimers, qualifications, understatements, and use of the personal idiom run counter to Freud's sweeping generalizations, his universal interpretations, and his *ad hominem* arguments. Within the first chapter, Freud reiterates, but does not prove or demonstrate, the main thesis of *The Future of an Illusion*. "The derivation of religious needs from the infant's helplessness and the longing for the father aroused by it seem to me incontrovertible" (p. 72). A skillful rhetorician, Freud knew how to use adjectives for emphasis. Yet emphatic statements are not substitutes for sustained argument, well-documented evidence, and convincing proof. A nonjudgmental reader, working without a priori limitations on what he is permitted to discover, is not persuaded that the oceanic is by necessity a secondary manifestation of the mind.

Let me mention other evasions and rhetorical strategies in this chapter. Freud deals with the ideational content of the oceanic sensation rather than with the feeling itself or with its physiological signs

(p. 65). (Rolland had asked for an empirical inquiry into the feeling, and had described the physiological transformations resulting from yoga.) Freud paraphrases but does not quote Rolland's letter on the oceanic, compressing eight paragraphs into one, even after Rolland had twice granted his permission to use the material from their private discussion. Freud's summary, while accurate, does not precisely convey the tone or the substance of the original document. The scientific language Freud uses is different from the metaphorical and imagistic language of Rolland's letter; Freud's version corresponds to a free-floating transcription, an adaptation of vitalistic ideas into a psychoanalytic vocabulary and conceptual framework. Freud's refusal to name Rolland as the friend in the first chapter (of the first edition) also suggests some feeling of hostility toward Rolland's views or possibly toward Rolland himself. The emphasis on Rolland's humaneness and on Freud's friendship for him may mask unfriendly feelings. Philip Rieff has observed that Freud was unable to separate men from their ideas;[13] something about Rolland's critique of psychoanalysis and his tenacious defense of mysticism left Freud unsettled.

Moreover, Freud does not always use irony to deflate pretentious ideas or to disrupt the reader's received notions. In this essay irony camouflages his personal limitations, becomes a form of self-defense, and occasionally a technique to mock opposing philosophical or methodological orientations. The irony often works against the spirit of critical inquiry, against the authentic search for a solution to the problem. I suggest that Rolland's account of the oceanic sensation caused Freud to take refuge in a variety of verbal subterfuges—jokes, self-laceration, cynicism, and finally a graceful form of literary dismissal.

In letters debating the oceanic sensation, Freud joked about Rolland's defense of Indian mysticism: "I shall now try with your guidance to penetrate into the Indian jungle from which until now an uncertain blending of Hellenic love of proportion, Jewish sobriety, and philistine timidity have kept me away."[14] The joke acknowledges Freud's consciousness of his differences from Rolland; Freud employed self-mockery to reassert his individuality, his own wide cultural erudition, and his serious commitment to use psychoanalysis to understand nonclinical materials. The ethnocentric labels incongruously placed side by side, the clever name-calling aimed at himself, all suggest defensiveness on Freud's part. Freud was unwilling to

[13]Philip Rieff, *The Triumph of the Therapeutic: Uses of Faith after Freud* (New York, 1960), 80.
[14]Letter from Freud to Romain Rolland, 19 Jan. 1930, *Freud Letters*, 392.

make his way through his friend's Indian jungle; perhaps he feared it would be too primeval, too amorphous to yield to analytical interpretation. His collision with Rolland in their correspondence reminded him of his own personal limitations and blind spots. This made him reiterate the fact that psychoanalytic methods had not illuminated all realms of knowledge and that the science was not an integrated world vision.

One way of dealing with the debate over mysticism was to state candidly, as Freud did, "that it is not easy to pass beyond the limits of one's nature."[15] "Nature" implies his background, intellectual formation, age, character structure, and theoretical bent. Freud, good tactician that he was, knew when to call a truce in a polemic, also when to retreat. He gracefully ends his discussion of the oceanic feeling in *Civilization and Its Discontents* not by moving into a detailed analysis of parapsychology, trances and ecstasies but by citing some lines from Schiller: "Let him rejoice who breathes up here in the roseate light!" (p. 73). By implication, Freud breathed better on other terrains, felt uncomfortable "above," more at ease in lower, or "Infernal Regions."[16]

Employing maneuvers of classical rhetoric to disarm the reader, admitting that his subject was intangible and puzzling, and warning the reader to beware of analogies, metaphors, and lyricism, Freud used all the devices that he warned against. Before publishing his interpretation, he wrote to Rolland with customary self-deprecation: "But please don't expect from my small effort any evaluation of the 'oceanic' feeling. I am experimenting only with an analytical diversion of it; I am clearing it out of the way, so to speak."[17]

Freud was nonetheless able to develop a compelling analysis of the oceanic sensation. He denied Rolland's hypothesis that the oceanic feeling was at the root of religious beliefs. In illustrating the genetic fallacy, Freud showed that he was nonreductionist in wielding his own theory. Nodal points in psychological development do not automatically derive from the earliest stages of infancy; and the oceanic, while remote, is not primary in the individual's psychosexual development; nor is it the foundation of his religious faith. For Freud, the oceanic sensation is related to a pre-oedipal period of ego development. The sublime feeling of fusion with the universe reflects sensa-

---

[15]Ibid.

[16]Freud cited a passage from Virgil's *Aeneid* for his epigraph to *The Interpretation of Dreams*: "If I cannot bend the Higher Powers, / I will move the Infernal Regions."

[17]Letter from Freud to Romain Rolland, 20 July 1929, *Freud Letters*, 389.

tions of early childhood when the infant distinguishes imperfectly between the self and the external world. With the ego's boundaries with the universe blurred or incorrectly drawn, the infant experiences an indissoluble bond with his surroundings. This feeling of the ego's omnipotence corresponded to the child's merger with the mother, or more specifically with the mother's breast. Freud conjectures that the infant experiences unpleasurable sensations as outside the self. Eventually, through experience the child is forced to distinguish the internal from the external, the self or ego from that which is outside the self. "Our present ego-feeling is, therefore, only a shrunken residue of a much more inclusive—indeed, an all-embracing—feeling which corresponded to a more intimate bond between the ego and the world about it"(p. 68).

The oceanic refers to a symbiotic fusion between mother and infant; it is the feeling of being harmoniously unified with the mother, or perhaps the memory of this experience, reinforced by the child's longing for warmth, closeness, protection, and security. The oceanic sensation recaptures the soothing feeling of being enveloped by a benevolent maternal guardian, of being caressed, fed, warmed, and rocked. The infant's nondifferentiation from his mother includes all of her parts and attributes, from her voice, gestures, and clothing to her gaze and her language. The infant's lack of separation from the outside world is related to his feeling of being afloat in his surroundings, of swimming in the waters of pleasurable stimuli.[18]

Freud suggested that the oceanic sensation recurred in adult life as a wishful fantasy, reassuring the individual about such disagreeable features of existence as mortality, the harshness of everyday life, and the compromises and accommodations necessary for survival. Thus oceanic feelings were powerful forms of consolation for the precariousness of human existence.[19] Freud also connected the oceanic to the

[18]Margaret S. Mahler, Fred Pine, Anni Bergman, *Psychological Birth of the Human Infant* (New York, 1975), 44, state: "From the second month on, dim awareness of the need-satisfying object marks the beginning of the phase of normal symbiosis, in which the infant behaves and functions as though he and his mother were an omnipotent system—a dual unity within one common boundary. This is perhaps what Freud and Romain Rolland discussed in their dialogue as the sense of boundlessness of the oceanic feeling."

[19]Erik H. Erikson, "The Life Cycle: Epigenesis of Identity," *Identity, Youth, and Crisis* (New York, 1968), 102–103, 106. Post-Freudian etiological criticism avoids reductionism by seeing the oceanic feeling as more than an infantile experience; ego psychologists argue that the sensation can also generate hope and trust in the future. The experience may encourage an adolescent or adult to persevere in adverse circumstances, to struggle assiduously to bring his efforts to fruition. Erik Erikson links faith to the development of trust, which stems from the "attainability of primal wishes," and he incisively suggests that these wishes are attained in the child's earliest trust in his mother.

process of introjection, the ability to incorporate dangerous or fearful aspects of reality, which was likewise comforting because absorption countered the given menace. In *Civilization and Its Discontents*, Freud associates the oceanic feeling with masochistic drives, more specifically with the defense against self-destructive rage or self-mutilating impulses. Narcissistic rage and self-devaluation can frequently take the form of suicidal feelings. As if to balance Rolland's cosmic propensities, his urge toward flight and transcendence, Freud cites a literary source, Christian Dietrich Grabbe, to remind his readers that escape from conflict in suicide is not a viable option: "'We cannot fall out of this world'" (p. 65).

In the final analysis Freud viewed the oceanic sensation as largely a regression to a childlike state in which the individual had no conception of himself as differentiated from objects or from the environment, and in which he experienced an ecstatic feeling of well-being. It was related to the narcissistic function of the ego whereby the self could be extended to embrace all of the world and humanity; thus it was, as Freud put it, the self enlarged to "limitless narcissism" (p. 72). Ultimately, he rejected mystical and idealist positions, seeing them as irrational retreats from external reality; they might endanger the ego's capacity to respond to internal assaults from unconscious impulses and to threats and obstacles encountered by the individual in social life. From the point of view of Freud's psychology and his value system, mysticism was a mystification. He wrote to Rolland:

> We seem to diverge rather far in the role we assign to intuition. Your mystics rely on it to teach them how to solve the riddle of the universe; we believe that it cannot reveal to us anything but primitive, instinctual impulses and attitudes—highly valuable for an embryology of the soul when correctly interpreted, but worthless for orientation in the alien, external world.[20]

Notwithstanding this dialectically complex analysis of the oceanic, Freud, in the first chapter of *Civilization and Its Discontents*, deploys his repertoire of rhetorical and critical skills to elude the oceanic sensation. Just as he is speculative and open-ended in his theorizing, so, too, is he mobile and inconclusive in his suggestions for further research. Emphatically stated and firmly grounded psychoanalytic ideas coexist with more fragmentary and problematic interpretations. The result is multiple significances attached to the oceanic, not one

[20]Letter from Freud to Romain Rolland, 19 Jan. 1930, *Freud Letters*, 393.

final solution. These fragmentary interpretations, in the form of wandering associations, ironic and pictorial juxtapositions, inversions and role reversals, and a dissemination of analogies, show us Freud's mind at work on a particularly baffling issue. Freud blends theoretical speculation and other rhetorical maneuvers in *Civilization and Its Discontents*; I attribute this blend partially to the speed with which the work was written. Freud completed the first draft of it in one month without having access to a library; at seventy-three, he wrote easily, fluently, densely, and with remarkable versatility. His competence as a problem solver was intact.[21] The very speed of the composition underscores his adherence to the psychoanalytic rule: the writer, like the patient, is willing to say without censorship and restriction whatever comes to mind. In short, I see this work as autobiographical, and as one in which Freud constantly employs the device of free association.

To illustrate how the mind is structured and to show how past memories are preserved in mental life, Freud ingeniously borrowed an analogy from another field, archaeology. The psychoanalytic approach to culture is akin to the excavation of ancient sites where layers of buried material and ruins are often preserved next to more modern and restored parts of a city. It is not accidental that Freud selects Rome as his exemplary ancient city. Rolland's first name was Romain, which is French for Roman. To follow the internal logic of Freud's associations to Rolland, we should remember that *roman* is the French word for novel, romance, fiction, and romanesque; moreover Rolland had written two *roman-fleuves (Jean-Christophe* and *L'âme enchantée)*, which in French is a novel saga, a novel constructed like a river, which flows into the sea. Freud may have been reminded of the Eternal City by the putative eternal quality of the oceanic feeling. He may also have known that Rolland spent a "Roman Spring" in the Eternal City from 1889 to 1891,[22] doing work in the Vatican Archives for his doctoral dissertation on the history of the opera.[23]

Freud's Rome analogy has a tripartite structure: it begins as a historical discourse, glides into archaeology, and concludes with a

[21]Ernest Jones, *The Life and Work of Sigmund Freud: The Last Phase 1919–1939* (New York, 1957), 148, 339–342, 345–348.

[22]Romain Rolland, *Printemps Romain. Choix de lettres de Romain Rolland à sa mère (1889–1890)*, Cahiers Romain Rolland. No. 6 (Paris, 1954); Romain Rolland, *Retour au Palais Farnèse. Choix de lettres de Romain Rolland à sa mère (1890–1891)*, Cahiers Romain Rolland, No. 8 (Paris, 1956).

[23]Romain Rolland, *Les origines du théâtre lyrique moderne. Histoire de l'opéra avant Lully et Scarlatti* (Paris, 1895).

biological comparison. All three analogies are fragmentary, tentative, and discontinuous; the transitions are not readily apparent or logical. They are linked to Rolland by Freud's free association, and by his assuming the public and professional roles of the French writer.

First, Freud reveals his competence and charm as a historian, mixing vignettes with bits of erudition about ancient and contemporary Rome. Rolland had been trained as a historian at the University of Paris. Here Freud temporarily displaces him as an archaeological historian. The positive pole of Freud's ambivalence toward Rolland corresponded to his exceptional fondness for Rome.[24] The verbs, "admire," "grace," and "bequeathed," reveal Freud's affection for the city (pp. 69–71).

Second, Freud shows how identified he is with Rolland's pursuits by usurping Rolland's vocation as a writer. The Rome analogy is written in exquisite and lyrical prose. We should remember that Freud's literary and stylistic genius was recognized in his lifetime; he was awarded the Goethe Prize for Literature in 1930. On two occasions in Chapter 1 of *Civilization and Its Discontents*, he interrupts his scientific narrative with these artistic digressions: "Now let us, by a flight of imagination, suppose that Rome is not a human habitation, but a physical entity" (p. 70). And, "There is clearly no point in spinning out our phantasy any further" (p. 70).

After anthropomorphizing ancient Rome, Freud suddenly abandons his historical and archaeological analogies as inappropriate and introduces an embryological one. His point is to show that the different stages of mental development are preserved, absorbed, or effaced in mature mental structures; or, put more cautiously, are "not *necessarily* destroyed" (p. 71), despite the exigencies of the life cycle and the processes of amnesia. Yet, here too, Freud is frustrated. He knows that his analogy is weak and imprecise. Once again he stops trying to conceptualize the mind in spatial or pictorial terms.

Why did Freud try out and then relinquish the biological analogy? One reason may be his association of Rolland with pictorial or naturalistic forms of representation. Rolland had written several books on painters, including a well-known biographical study of Michelangelo. Many of Michelangelo's most sublime creations are, of course, housed in Rome. Freud admired Michelangelo's work and wrote an essay on his Moses.[25] In their letters, Freud once referred to Rolland's mystical

[24]See Carl E. Schorske, "Politics and Patricide in Freud's *Interpretation of Dreams*," *Fin-de-Siècle Vienna: Politics and Culture* (New York, 1980), 189–193, 199, 202–203.

[25]Romain Rolland, *La vie de Michel-Ange* [1906] (Paris 1964); Sigmund Freud, "The Moses of Michelangelo," (1914), *Standard Edition of the Complete Psychological Works of Sigmund Freud*, ed. James Strachey, (London, 1953), 211–238.

knowledge as "highly valuable for an embryology of the soul when correctly interpreted."[26] His own approach to embryology tended to be traditionally scientific, empirical, and ontogenetic. Yet Freud was also quite conscious of the finite parameters of pictorial forms of representation. The psychoanalyst, in short, conceives of the mind with a knowledge of the limitations both of writing and of nonverbal forms of representation.

The first chapter of *Civilization and Its Discontents* effectively shows how inconclusive analogies are, even the most ingenious. The Roman associations Rolland's oceanic sensation triggered in Freud in turn gave rise to three abortive analogies and assorted discontinuous attempts to represent his concepts historically, archaeologically, imaginatively, and pictorially. All partially failed. Moreover, the back and forth movement, the offering and relinquishing of the analogies, disrupts the narrative and theoretical flow of Freud's own discourse, muting the definitive impact of the oceanic discussion. Freud both recognized and gave expression to the difficulties involved in conveying psychoanalytic insights about the layers of the mind. This problem was particularly acute in describing overlapping layers of the mental apparatus where old and new cohabit, where fragments and condensations and displacements often become the only evidence of earlier content and structures. Freud's own language here is remarkably mobile and shifting. His form of expression seems to reflect the form and content of his material, which is fluctuating, overdetermined, erratic, and cannot be pinned down with one comprehensive picture or one overarching theoretical model.

Various disguised allusions to the question of the oceanic sensation pervade the text. In Chapter 8, Freud rejected the Judeo-Christian commandment "Love thy neighbor as thyself," as an unrealistic injunction, which is not only nearly impossible to fulfill, but once fulfilled, caused more injury and stress than the aggressiveness against which it is a defense. Freud perceived Rolland to be an advocate of universal love: "Because for us your name has been associated with the most precious of beautiful illusions, that of love extended to all mankind."[27] We also know that Freud read Rolland's biography of Gandhi, in which the French writer updated and popularized the Tolstoyan (and Kantian and Christian) notion of neighborly love, in addition to linking it to the political philosophy of nonviolent re-

[26]Letter from Freud to Romain Rolland, 19 Jan. 1930, *Freud Letters*, 393.
[27]Letter from Freud to Romain Rolland, 4 March 1923, *Freud Letters*, 341.

sistance. "Mahatma Gandhi," Freud wrote to his friend, "will accompany me on my vacation which will begin shortly."[28]

In debunking the imperative to love one's neighbor uncritically, Freud is directly replying to Rolland's world vision. The commandment, in his view, contains a self-serving component, for its only practical value is to reinforce the ethical person's sense of self-righteousness. "'Natural' ethics, as it is called, has nothing to offer here except the narcissistic satisfaction of being able to think oneself better than others" (*Civilization*, p. 143). Psychodynamically, the good conscience of the Christian stems from bad faith. The precept of universal love presupposes a neglect, or a glossing over, of distinctions between the ego and the real world (p. 102).

From a psychoanalytic view, Freud objected to the notion of universal love on practical as well as on theoretical grounds. Nondiscriminating love offered to humanity is egalitarian and nonreflective, disregarding differences in the behavior of human beings. Love extended to humanity in general tends to devalue the love directed toward the particular individual. This is an obvious injustice to the one who is loved (p. 102). Freud also held that most people were unworthy of love, that it was foolish to love those who were power-hungry or ambitious for success, or who sought material wealth with no authentic desire to serve others. Love and friendship ought to be reserved for the deserving, for those who can reciprocate, and not wasted on the multitudes of people who are hostile, malicious, and impotent, and who crave domination over others. It is in this context that Freud asserts that people are wolves, not gentle creatures; most people, he observes, are unlovely and unlovable (pp. 102, 109–111). Furthermore, Freud posits that the idea of universal love is rooted in narcissism—that people are thus motivated to seek out and love idealized aspects of themselves in others, that sharing common values, common interests, and a common cultural orientation also can be traced back in part to a deep need to love a mirror of oneself (pp. 84, 118).

In Chapter 5 of *Civilization and Its Discontents* Freud shows that the Judeo-Christian (and Rollandist) precept "Love thy neighbor" is an extension of the feeling of oneness with the universe, of the non-discerning feeling connected with an amorphous love of humanity. The oceanic sensation and Christian moral injunctions ultimately stem from the same psychical source. To deflate these absolutist moralistic ideals, Freud used unusual images:

[28]Letter from Freud to Romain Rolland, 15 June 1924, cited in Fisher, "Sigmund Freud and Romain Rolland," 10.

But if I am to love him (with this universal love) merely because he, too, is an inhabitant of this earth, like an insect, an earth-worm or a grass-snake, then I fear that only a small modicum of my love will fall to his share—not by any possibility as much as, by the judgment of my reason, I am entitled to retain for myself. What is the point of a precept enunciated with so much solemnity if its fulfillment cannot be recommended as reasonable? [P. 110]

He states rhetorically that realization of the precept is palpably absurd, and he jokes about the commandment to drain away its pretentiousness. Finally, he cites a hilarious tale by Heinrich Heine about loving one's neighbors only after they have been murdered: "'One must, it is true, forgive one's neighbors—but not before they have been hanged'" (p. 110 n. 1). Freud is casting Heine's modernistic, ironic parable against Rolland's idealism. He is also illustrating how literary performances can give expression to, can legitimize with humor, forbidden sadistic wishes.

As a diagnostician of civilizational malaise, Freud searched for hidden phenomena in cultural and ideological modes of expression. He pointed out how manifestations of love and forebearance often disguised feelings of deep intolerance. He recalled, for instance, how the love preached by organized Christianity was often offset by the disastrous history of Christian persecutions, massacres, and hostility toward non-Christians (p. 114). I would like to extend the Freudian interpretation of the oceanic sensation by arguing that the feeling which is described as the deep source of religion and of human relatedness on a grand scale is actually a reaction-formation. That is to say, the limitless narcissism of the oceanic conceals or counters a feeling of universal hatred for humanity.

I think that individuals who proclaim love for humanity secretly have powerful feelings of aggression and contempt for humanity, that feelings of eternity actively spring from unbounded feelings of repressed rage, of unsatisfied oral cravings. Rolland's oceanicism conceals a strong sadistic impulse, a monumental fury against humanity, a drive to destroy civilization. The openly proclaimed affection for and overidealization of humanity hides a devaluation of it. The oceanic sensation comforted Rolland by wiping out his recurring feelings of despair and loss of direction; monumental feelings of connection opposed his feelings of unconnectedness. The reactions took the form of feelings of omnipotence, grandiosity, optimism, and the pattern of attaching himself to strong, admired father figures to reestablish his self-esteem. The philosophical idealist may incorporate grandiose objects as a defense against infantile feelings of anxiety, shame, guilt, and lack of self-worth. The person who feels universal love may paradoxically be the one with the harshest and most primitive superego. To defend himself against his own self-punishing conscience, Rolland emerged as a public man of virtue, self-sacrifice, and penance. Thus the narcissism associated with the oceanic sensation does not fundamentally spring from self-love or self-admiration; it may embody an elaborate defense against aggressive impulses.

For Rolland then, and by implication for all humanistic mystics, total love of humanity may be unconsciously fused with the impulse to annihilate humanity totally. This fusion of opposites generated powerful tensions in his art, his cultural criticism, and his engagement with contemporary society. Psychoanalysis can lay bare the psychical roots of metaphorical and idealist modes of expression, such as oceanic feelings. It shows how these apparently benign attitudes are diametrically opposed to repressed wishes, how these attitudes become constituted as reactions to these impulses. Under the cloak of universal pity, compassion, virtue, and humane contact, the oceanic sensation may function to counter sadistic and immoral impulses, wishes that are incompatible with conscious and civilized outlooks.

> In consequence of this primary mutual hostility of human beings, civilized society is perpetually threatened with disintegration. The interest of work in common would not hold it together; instinctual passions are stronger than reasonable interests. Civilization has to use its utmost efforts in order to set limits to man's aggressive instincts and to hold the manifestations of them in check by psychical reaction-formations . . . hence too the ideal commandment to love one's neighbor—a commandment which is really justified by the fact that nothing else runs so strongly counter to the original nature of man. In spite of every effort, these endeavors of civilization have not so far achieved very much. [P. 112]

From an examination of their correspondence, a discourse analysis of *Civilization and Its Discontents*, and an interpretation of Freud's 1936 paper "A Disturbance of Memory on the Acropolis: An Open Letter to Romain Rolland on the Occasion of His Seventieth Birthday," I have concluded that Freud viewed Rolland as one of the special few, marked off from the masses by his sensibility and his gifts. Freud considered him a man of encyclopedic knowledge and wisdom, who had a powerful commitment to research and learning. Moreover, Rolland posed tough and significant questions; he knew what questions really mattered. Rolland represented those men who did the work of civilization, who knew how to discipline their imaginations, who worked steadily, who led a regular life, who kept visitors and diversions away, and who appreciated the psychological necessity of intellectual work.

Rolland was Freud's unnamed friend in the first edition of *Civilization and Its Discontents* who saw a gap in the psychoanalytic explanation of religion, a gap which perplexed Freud enough to rethink his previous position. In his life and work Rolland refused to be parochial, self-serving or narrow-minded. He was an exceptional man, whose sincerity and tolerance never interfered with his courageous articulation of dissenting opinions (he took public stances in favor of the doctrines of pacifism, Gandhism, and antifascism, and was known to be sympathetic to communism). In the first paragraph of *Civilization and Its Discontents*, Freud refers to Rolland in glowing terms as someone who does not use false standards of measurement, who does not seek power, success, or wealth for himself or admire them in others. The tenderness of this description underlines Freud's esteem for the French writer, whom he viewed as an exemplary figure. The reverential tone and substance of *Civilization and Its Discontents* is congruent with the opening paragraph of "A Disturbance of Memory on the Acropolis."[29]

For Freud, Rolland had evolved into more than a famous man of letters. He had become a contemporary idealist and prophet, in short a writer with a priestly world view. Conceiving of his role and mission with arch-seriousness, Rolland offered inspiration and consolation to his countless readers, presenting them with strong culture heroes (Michelangelo, Beethoven, *Jean-Christophe*, Gandhi) upon whom they could attach themselves. Rolland had moved beyond the confines of being novelist, critic, and historian to make universalist pronouncements to his audience, to speak on all issues in the name of higher wisdom. He conceived of the writer in a sacerdotal manner, as if he had a divine authority and a highly moral agenda.

However, Freud's veneration for Rolland covers a repressed tendency to compete with and devalue his friend. As early as the first paragraph of *Civilization and Its Discontents*, Freud qualifies his admiration for Rolland with sentences which soften, check, and self-criticize (p. 64). The full nature of Freud's ambivalence toward Rol-

---

[29]Freud, "A Disturbance of Memory on the Acropolis," 239.

land is revealed in the third paragraph: "The views expressed by the friend who I so much honor, and who himself once praised the magic of illusion in a poem" (pp. 64–65). To praise illusion is tantamount to defending self-deception. In a letter to Rolland, Freud wrote: "A great part of my life's work (I am ten years older than you) has been spent [trying to] destroy illusions of my own and those of mankind."[30] Age, experience, maturity, world-weariness, and psychoanalytic insights all encouraged Freud to be wary of the bad faith and blind alleys connected with wishful thinking.

On the last page of the essay, Freud announces his firm refusal to play the role of prophet, sage, revolutionary or religious leader (*Civilization*, p. 145). In brief, he rejects the full spectrum of Rolland's public roles. All he can be is what he is: an impartial man of science, a theory-builder, committed to the search for and the expression of the truth. Freud saw himself as a demystifier of magical and metaphysical explanations about man and his relationship to the world. In contrast to Rolland, he refused to offer his audience consolation or easily digested images of themselves. In opposition to Rolland's tendency to sacralize the intellectual, Freud assumed the therapeutic stance of desacralization. The psychoanalytic critic of culture, he tells us explicitly, offers interpretations, not fixed meanings. This is a responsible posture, for interpretations can be modified, revised, and reassessed, while grandiose claims of omnipotence persuade by their appeal to our need for faith, hope, grandeur, and happiness. Rather than bestow upon his readers a lofty system of moral teachings, linked to a transcendent realm, Freud presents them with a critical method of inquiry, and with a model which demands that they proceed with their inquiry in a nonjudgmental, analytically neutral, detached, and empathic manner.

In all of Freud's writings to or about Rolland, there is a pronounced tension, a wavering between affection and genuine esteem on the one hand, and strain, envy, and bitterness on the other. This tension stemmed from Freud's oscillation between uncanny feelings of familiarity with Rolland and his sense of unalterable separation from him. On an unconscious level, Rolland may have represented a rival, a ten-year-younger, gifted sibling, a contentious but private opponent of psychoanalytic theory and practice, an object of competition, envy, and hostility—someone, in brief, to be replaced, argued with, or to be cleared out of the way.

Rolland was Freud's Double. Freud felt a kinship with Rolland for his capacities as a realistic writer, as a novelist and playwright with psychological probity; he identified with the French writer's ability to penetrate beneath social conventions. Freud felt attracted to artists who handled language deftly and who playfully tapped the imagination. Rolland had provided his readers with moments of pleasure, comfort, and exaltation. He was an artist with a vast public, with enormous contemporary resonance; that is, he was a maker of high culture who spoke a language accessible to the masses.

Rolland's capacity to communicate with and move the masses was highly problematic in Freud's eyes, however, especially given Freud's view of the mass public as uncritical, lazy, careless, unreliable, easily deflected by the pleasure principle, easily manipulated by intoxicating substances and religious sedatives and narcotics. Moreover, Rolland's ability to mediate between high and popular culture reminded Freud of his own isolation, unpopularity, and vulnerabilities. Freud, the scientific investigator, had reached his insights only after long and laborious effort, after detours and a lifetime of investigations. As founder of psychoanalysis, he had given expression to disturbing and unwanted truths about the human mind. Humanity had often repaid him for his labors by treating him unkindly or by totally ignoring him.[30]

What I am suggesting here is that Freud tended to make invidious comparisons between Rolland and himself, that he tended to overestimate Rolland's popularity, and that he subtly made a distinction between varieties of sublimation. As the Other, Rolland had gifts that Freud lacked. If we examine the ambivalence of this relationship, we can infer that Freud valued scientific sublimation as more reliable and more prudent than the substitute satisfactions of the artist. Despite his sensitivity to literary, plastic, and representational forms of artistic expression, Freud was disturbed by, and distrustful of, artistic creations that had their origin in the realm of the id.[31]

To be sure, Freud's admiration for Rolland as a creative writer, humanitarian, pacifist, and conciliator of mankind existed side by side with envy and distrust of him. What is attractive in Rolland is highlighted by Freud's perception of their dissimilarities: "I may confess to you that I have rarely experienced that mysterious attraction of one human being for another as vividly as I have with you; it is somehow

[30]Letter from Freud to Romain Rolland, 4 March 1923, *Freud Letters*, 341.

[31]Lorin Anderson, "Freud, Nietzsche," *Salmagundi*, No. 47–48 (Winter-Spring 1980), 3–29; Françoise L. Simon-Miller, "Ambivalence and Identification: Freud on Literature," *Literature and Psychology*, 28, no. 1 (1978), 23–39, 28, no. 3–4 (1978), 151–167; Lionel Trilling, "Freud: Within and Beyond Culture" (1955), *Beyond Culture: Essays on Literature and Learning* (New York 1965), 77–102, and "Art and Neurosis" (1945, 1947), *The Liberal Imagination: Essays on Literature and Society* (New York, 1976), 160–180.

bound up perhaps, with the awareness of our being so different."[32]

Rolland, then, represented both Freud's Double and the Other.[33] As Freud's Double, Rolland was a brother in the cultural enterprise: he was irrepressibly honest, had the courage of his convictions, understood individual psychology and the role of instincts, defied social conventions, and combined his individual integrity with artistic ability. As Freud's Other, Rolland was the unreachable love-object, a symbolic object of temptation and seduction, a desire that remained eternally unfulfilled. His differences from Freud were striking. It is quite possible that Freud saw in Rolland, as Double and as Other, long suppressed aspects of his own personality, such as a susceptibility to mystical ideas, a craving for success and recognition, creative aspirations, and a desire to serve humanity.

In *Civilization and Its Discontents*, the scientist, artist, and intellectual are the prototypes of the sublimated man. Freud delineates sharp oppositions between artistic activity and the work of science.[34] I would like to suggest that Rolland is one of the principal, but invisible representatives of artistic and intellectual sublimation in the essay, and that Freud approaches him with a characteristic double-edged sword: with appreciation on the one hand; and with a consciousness of the risks involved in too much sublimation on the other hand—the inference being that Rolland could no longer serve as a realistic model for emulation.

Freud recognized the self-discipline and years of self-sacrifice that went into the creation of literary masterpieces. Rolland was an "Unforgettable Man"[35] because he knew how to suffer, how to endure hardship, how to give altruistically to humanity, and he not only embodied will power, but also channeled his psychic drives in constructive directions. In his relationship and debates with Rolland, Freud was forced to revise his earlier a priori views of the artist as passive, given over to fantasy, slightly feminine, out of touch with the

---

[32]Letter from Freud to Romain Rolland, May 1931, *Freud Letters*, 406.

[33]See letter from Freud to Arthur Schnitzler, 14 May 1922, *Freud Letters*, 197–198, for Freud's thoughts on his doubleness with a prominent Viennese writer. For a psychoanalytic reading of the problem of otherness, sée Lacan, "Desire and the Interpretation of Desire in Hamlet," 11–52; Jacques Lacan, "The Function of Language in Psychoanalysis," in *The Language of the Self*, tr. Anthony Wilden (Baltimore, 1968), 3–87; Anthony Wilden, "Lacan and the Discourse of the Other," ibid., 137–311; Herbert I. Kupper and Hilda S. Rollman-Branch, "Freud and Schnitzler—(Doppelgänger)," *Journal of American Psychoanalytic Association* 7 (1959), 109–126.

[34]J. Laplanche and J.-B. Pontalis, *The Language of Psycho-Analysis*, tr. Donald Nicholson-Smith, (New York, 1973), 431–433.

[35]Letter from Freud to Romain Rolland, 29 Jan. 1926, *Freud Letters*, 364; this is the opening line of Freud's tribute to Rolland on his sixtieth birthday.

reality principle—a dreamer and romantic. Rolland had demonstrated that cultural work emanated from the artist's self-mastery. Unless the impulses were tamed, the cultural products themselves could not be transformed into vehicles for the transfer of energy between the artist and his public. Committed to the creation, reinvention, and interpretation of beauty, Rolland's life and work took on meaning in the production of useless yet highly prized artistic objects and ideas (*Civilization*, pp. 82–83). The word "useless" is intended neither to denigrate culture, nor to confer meaning on cultural objects; rather, Freud is referring to a biological and material concept of necessity. Artists like Rolland had to survive through compensatory forms of gratification. They derived sustenance from the pleasure of steady mental work, from the narcissistic pleasure of giving birth to beautiful creations, a joy not unlike those which parents derive from their children; and from the mild intoxications that come with solving mental problems or perfecting one's craft.

Freud reasons in *Civilization and Its Discontents* that too much sublimation can result in grave dangers to the artist himself. To deprive the instincts of direct gratification is to court the possibility of frustration and mental disorder; it may even warp the perspective of the artist, or impair his ability to complete projects. According to Freud's theory of the economics of the libido, the life of regiment and restriction can give rise to a severely stunted personality. Overly sublimated artists like Rolland lived like horses without oats;[36] they ignored or obliterated instinctual demands. They often loved ideas or humanity in an abstract and disembodied sense; they withdrew from the cities and from social relationships; they lived a hermit's existence; they mortified the flesh; they craved rest, isolation, and solitude; and they were unable to achieve or to sustain mutual, intimate, heterosexual love relationships (*Civilization*, pp. 79–81, 102).

Thus the poignant situation of the makers of civilization is that those who apparently gave the most to society and to posterity received very little in return. According to Freud's perception, Rolland was a perfect symbol of the overly sublimated, ascetic, self-abnegating man of culture, the martyr who knew how to give gifts, yet who seemed constitutionally or psychologically incapable of permitting human reciprocity. Within the Freudian conceptual framework, Oedipal man is guilt-ridden, while narcissistic man is tragic. Rolland thus served Freud simultaneously as a symbol of the achievements of civilization and an example of the dangers of excessive sublimation.

---

[36]Sigmund Freud, *Five Lectures on Psycho-Analysis* (1910), *Standard Edition of the Complete Psychological Works of Sigmund Freud*, ed. James Strachey (London, 1957), 11.55.

For the second edition of *Civilization and Its Discontents*, Freud added several footnotes, one sentence to an existing footnote, and the concluding line to the text. I suggest that these seemingly trivial editorial corrections refer directly and indirectly to Rolland, that they are a parallel text that reflects Freud's continual ambivalence toward the French writer, and that they require interpretation. They are part of the debate on the oceanic feeling, and they continue the polemic, further illustrating Rolland's presence throughout the text of *Civilization and Its Discontents*.

After mentioning but discretely not naming his "friend" four times in the text (five if we include the reference to "another friend of mine" who experiments with yoga, who is also Rolland), Freud abruptly ends the confidentiality, identifies Rolland by name, and then cites three of his works: "*Liluli*. Since the publication of his two books, *La Vie de Ramakrishna* and *La Vie de Vivekananda*, I need no longer hide the fact that the friend spoken of in the text is Romain Rolland" (p. 65, n. 1). The word "hide" is striking; one wonders about Freud's mixed motives in concealing this information, especially given his methodological interest in exposing latent psychological relationships and meanings.

While discussing the mental satisfactions of concentrated intellectual or artistic activity, Freud adds the following note on narcissistic forms of self-sufficiency: "No discussion of the possibility of human happiness should omit to take into consideration the relation between narcissism and object libido. We require to know what being essentially self-dependent signifies for the economics of the libido" (*Civilization* (p. 84, n. 2). This passage shows that to Freud there was a real, if not fully articulated, connection between Rolland's radical isolation from society and from others and Freud's theoretical speculations about narcissism. We watch Freud opening up a path for further research, urging the psychoanalytic researcher to investigate narcissistic disorders from the point of view of object relations, that is, by analyzing how the individual relates to significant others, beginning with his mother.[37]

To link the concept of virtue and a punitive conscience, Freud adds a footnote in Chapter 7. In citing Mark Twain's story "The First Melon I Ever Stole," Freud is once again casting one literary sensibility against another, siding with Twain against Rolland. His purpose is

---

[37]This suggestion has recently led to creative results in the psychoanalytic works of Heinz Kohut, *The Analysis of the Self* (New York, 1971), and of Otto Kernberg, *Borderline Conditions and Pathological Narcissism* (New York, 1975).

to signal the dangers of overly strict moral stances. To answer Rolland's righteousness, to refute the French moralist's defense of a severe conscience, Freud juxtaposes Twain's light, sarcastic musings on melon stealing. The melon is a sexually evocative symbol, and to engage in melon stealing is to fulfill a proscribed but universal wish. Twain wonders out loud: "*Was* it the first?" And Freud replies: "The first melon was evidently not the only one" (p. 73, n. 2). Thus Freud himself steals the metaphor to indicate in a gentle way that virtue often cloaks underlying sadistic tendencies. Like Heine's, Twain's honesty is refreshing and funny; Freud was delighted by Twain's ability to lift the censorship which surrounds pilfering and other "immoral" acts. He viewed this admission as a disruptive activity which carried an important psychological significance.

Finally, the last sentence of the second edition of *Civilization and Its Discontents* can be viewed not as an afterthought, not simply a presentiment of the rise of Nazism, but rather as a deliberate effort to counter the optimism connected with the supposed return and victory of Eros in the perpetual struggle between life and death: "But who can foresee with what success and with what result?" (p. 145). This interrogative mode suggests that Freud's metapsychology is fundamentally dissimilar to Rolland's oceanic metaphysics. Freud's technique and conceptual apparatus do not necessarily lead to wisdom, progress, happiness, or optimistic conclusions. To end the second edition on a measured note is to restate the cautionary stance of psychoanalysis. Enlightening man about his unconscious processes and his psychosexual development may take generations. Nor is Freud more sanguine about the tangible results of his own methodology in analyzing cultural patterns, in providing answers to man's "ultimate concerns," or in guaranteeing the triumph of Eros over Thanatos. It may also be that he wanted to reply to Rolland's oceanic sensation one last time: by criticizing oceanic optimism, Freud ends his most synthetic essay poignantly, with modesty and uninhibited skepticism.

The history of the psychoanalytic movement is intimately related to Freud's personal and intellectual history. In a dramatic way Freud was his own most persistent patient. And throughout his life, he continued to interpret his dreams, to free-associate, to analyze jokes, slips, memory disturbances, in short to apply his techniques to himself with the evenly suspended attention he called for in the treatment of patients. Rieff has described Freud's directness and candor, and his adherence to the ethic of honesty in psychoanalytic theory and practice; the overriding psychoanalytic rule, after all, is to say what comes to mind. Freud's discourse on culture in *Civilization and Its Discontents* does precisely this: and with results that are stunning, surprising, and majestic.

As a diagnostician of culture, Freud is not always logically consistent, conceptually precise, or philosophically rigorous. His arguments are not always crystal clear, his mediations are often insufficiently elaborated. In reading him we have to beware of his sloppiness, his occasional use of nonreferential material, and his unhistorical tendency to rely on poorly defined temporal and spatial categories. This early pioneer in the psychohistory of culture often lacks historical specificity.

Freud's restless, curious mind is perpetually searching for significations; he could not tolerate meaninglessness. If Freud errs in any direction, it is in his tendency to overinterpret, which, in turn, reflects his desire for closure, for posing solutions to problems. Frequently these solutions are tentative, speculative, and shifting, while the issues being scrutinized seem pressing and urgent. But if he overintellectualizes, he also displays remarkable ease with contradiction, ambiguity, and mixed meanings. He not only appreciates the process of delay involved in building theory and in conducting research, but he also calls for periodic reassessments of working hypotheses in the light of new data.

In initiating psychoanalytic discourse on culture, Freud brought to his researches a militantly atheistic and secular point of view. This is totally opposed to the world view of Romain Rolland. For Freud the accent is always on man himself, as he is, without metaphysical or sentimental embellishment. Psychoanalysis is not formulated as a religion; it neither provides a fully integrated world vision, nor offers answers to the riddles of the universe. We have seen how Freud sets up psychoanalytic constructs as a stable, scientific theory differentiating them from less reality-bound endeavors, such as literature, music, mysticism, or revolutionary politics, which are likely to instigate or perpetuate illusions. Yet his own writing is often literary, metaphorical, evocative, mobile, and wandering. Freud tapped his own fantasy life in his writings, and his very best writing is playful. In *Civilization and Its Discontents*, he even played with the notion that civilization itself might be overvalued, that cultural production may not be worth the sacrifice and demands it entails for the individual creator.

Extending the psychoanalytic stance of technical neutrality toward the patient, Freud remains neutral toward past and present forms of culture. Such neutrality allows both for empathic understanding and for self-reflexive interpretations. Freud thus consciously avoids speculating about the value of human civilization. Unlike Rolland, he deliberately refuses the role of prophet, makes no predictions about the future of mankind, presents no coherent scale of values or particular set of priorities to his public.

Instead of mindless hope or religious consolation, instead of ecstatic fusion with humanity or narcissistic fantasies of amorous bonding, Freud offers the qualified program of an irreligious education to reality, informed by psychoanalytic insights and methods. In the twentieth century, only the ignorant can afford to bypass psychoanalysis. Such an education aims at subverting naive or antipsychological prejudices, at eroding rigid ethical codes and outdated moralisms, in order to establish a more sober approach to the perennial question of freedom and necessity.

The psychoanalytic outlook on culture stresses how society, through language, symbol, ritual, institutions, and the family, imposes itself on our drives. Freud's point of view in *Civilization and Its Discontents* mirrors his therapeutic posture: both the analyst in the clinical setting and the psychoanalytic culture critic endorse the voice of the reality principle, opposing simultaneously the unrelenting demands of the id and the false idealism and destructive demands of the superego. In contrast to oceanic forms of merger, the reality principle presupposes that the self can keep distinct the line where the self ends and the external world and the world of objects begins; that is, it requires paying attention to the real world. The ego needs to be both protected and fortified; it is fragile, easily ensnared, easily decentered. Part of the condition of being neurotic in modern society means the impossibility of achieving mental synthesis. The ego develops defensive and adaptative tendencies to cope with this absence of psychic and social harmony. Paul Ricoeur argues that for Freud the reality principle is closely linked to an ethical idea of prudence. The individual learns how to endure pain, loss, separation, lack of success, unpleasure, without giving way to despair or destructive deflections, and without "acting out."[38]

Writing neither as an indignant enemy of nor as an apologist for civilization, believing neither in imminent social apocalypse nor in some static model of the individual's conflict with society, Freud refrained from a priori ethical judgments and prescriptions. He is a

[38]Paul Ricoeur, *Freud and Philosophy: An Essay on Interpretation*, tr. Denis Savage (New Haven, 1970), 279, 302–309, 326.

system builder who appreciated the inconclusive quality of lived experience, of disruptions that could not be circumscribed by systems. He is a moralist who refrains from moral preaching, a teacher who eschews didacticism. Truth-seeking is elevated into a process of comprehending the individual's situation in society. The suspension of value judgment is thus a step toward self-knowledge, toward truly critical forms of cultural inquiry, for it liberates the mind from infantile modes of thought. It is also a way of releasing the individual from violence and self-destructiveness, without imitating or internalizing the aggression. Ethical neutrality makes it possible for the reality principle to dominate the pleasure principle in the development and deployment of human consciousness. Consciousness—"de-emotionalized reason"[39]—becomes indispensable in Freud's view of cultural continuity and rupture; it, alone, provides the individual with the tools by which he can master nature and move gropingly toward control of aggression, guilt, and his own self-destructiveness. Consciousness becomes crucial in lifting the censors, in moving toward self-fulfillment in one's work and in one's love life. Freud, then, presents psychoanalysis as more than a synchronic discourse which comments on other discourses in an artifical and ahistorical manner. Psychoanalytic culture criticism integrates theory and practice, while working at the points of convergence of the individual's life in society; it is oriented toward the individual's mastery of infantile modes of thought and behavior without denying the complexities of lived experience.

To read *Civilization and Its Discontents* is to recognize that the psychoanalytic interpretation of culture may be as fundamentally interminable and enriching to the reader as psychoanalytic treatment is to the patient. The book's own self-reflexive form and ambiguous meaning prepare us for the long process of remembering, repeating, and working through that is involved in the mastery of the Freudian instrument of liberation. The ideal reader and teacher of *Civilization and Its Discontents* would be one with a tolerance of delay, detour, and postponement in the search for answers to meaningful questions. Such a reader would be open to psychoanalytic culture criticism as a research strategy, or at least would be willing to suspend his disbelief. An audience of such readers would be unafraid to draw on their reservoir of personal emotions as well as on their intellectual facul-

---

[39]The term is taken from Frank E. and Fritzie P. Manuel, *Utopian Thought in the Western World* (Cambridge, Mass. 1979), 791; the Manuels read *Civilization and Its Discontents* as "the most trenchant and devastating attack on utopian illusions—what he [Freud] called the lullabies of heaven—that has ever been delivered" (788).

ties. Such an audience would, above all, try to emulate Freud: in using one's own psychic conflicts and ambivalences creatively in order to fertilize one's relationship to the cultural process—as a both creator and recipient of that culture.

CHAPTER TEN

Method and Ideology in Intellectual History: The Case of Henry Adams

HAYDEN WHITE

My first impression, after I had read through these richly suggestive essays on the present state and possible future condition of intellectual history, was one of surprise. I was surprised, first of all, by the general air of buoyancy and self-confidence expressed in them—a pervasive sense that a renaissance of a field that had been, to say the least, recessive with respect to that social historiography which has predominated in our discipline in the last two decades, was in the offing. Second, I was impressed by the freshness of the ways of conceptualizing the field shown by most of the papers here presented, a freshness that marks them off rather sharply from the conventions and presuppositions that prevailed in an older generation of intellectual historians, both in this country and in Europe. I discern a wish to rethink the basic issues of intellectual history, to reexamine governing concepts and strategies of interpretation, not out of any feeling of beleagueredness, but on the contrary, in response to new methodologies that have arisen in philosophy, literary criticism, and linguistic studies and that offer new ways of conceiving the tasks of historical hermeneutics. I sense that the older authorities of the field—Hegel, Marx, Nietzsche, Dilthey, and Freud—are still present to the consciousness of this group of intellectual historians, but more as ancestral shades or sanctioning grandfathers than as models and guides to specific research tasks. New models, represented by Benjamin, Gadamer, and Ricoeur, by Habermas, Foucault and Derrida, Barthes, and possibly J. L. Austin, appear to be moving to the center of the scene, to authorize new ways of looking at texts, of inscribing them within "discourses" (a new term to intellectual historians of the current generation), and of linking them to their contexts. One senses a conviction that the social historiography of the past generation has, temporarily at least, reached a limit in its incapacity to speak meaningfully about what might be called "consciousness," and that the *explanatory* procedures of that historiography are giving way to *hermeneutical* practices which have their origins in phenomenology, analytical philosophy and speech-act theory, deconstruction, and discourse analysis.

The themes that recur in these essays touch the principal topoi of the field, since its modern inception in (whom?): Hegel (?), Dilthey (?), Cassirer (?), the *Annales* group (?)—it hardly matters to a generation of scholars who have become suspicious of the problem of "origins" as an ideological trap fraught with metaphysical preconceptions and even political *partis pris*. At the center of this set of themes is the crucial one, not only for intellectual historians but for any historian of anything, that of the text-context relationship. What is this relationship? What, indeed, is a text—an entity which used to have a reassuring solidity and concreteness, which lay before the scholar in a comforting materiality, and which possessed an authority that the "context" in which it had arisen and to the existence of which it attested could never have? *Where* is this context, which literary historians used to invoke as a matter of course to "explain" the distinctive features of the poetic text and to anchor it in an ambience more solid than words? *What* are the dimensions and levels of this context? Where does it begin and end? And what is its *status* as a component of the *historically real* which it is the historian's purpose to identify, if not explain? The text-context relationship, once an unexamined presupposition of historical investigation, has become a problem, not in the sense of being simply difficult to establish by the once vaunted "rules of evidence," but rather in the sense of becoming "undecidable," elusive, uncreditable—in the same way that the so-called "rules of evidence" themselves have become. And yet this very undecidability of the question of where the text ends and the context begins and the nature of their relationship appears to be a cause for celebration, to provide a vista onto a new and more fruitful activity for the intellectual historian, to authorize a posture before the archive of history more dialogistic than analytic, more conversational than assertive and judgmental.

And if the text-context distinction is now problematized, so too is the distinction *within* the domain of historical artifacts between the so-called "elite," high-cultural, "classic" text and the common, derivative, or merely "documentary" text. Not all of the essays in this collection problematize this relationship. Some, Marxians and Freudians especially, continue to suggest, when they do not argue it outright, that certain texts, in this case, those by Marx and Freud, provide models of especially insightful analytical techniques, and so enjoy a privileged status among the artifacts coming down to us from an earlier time. But most of the essayists here represented imply that even works by Marx and Freud are not *self-interpreting* and cannot serve as interpretative or explanatory models without stringent limits being put upon their adequacy. Not even Marx and Freud can any longer escape the charge of ideological distortion which they once brought against their opponents in the methodological and theoretical disputes of their own times. They too must be "deconstructed," their "blindness" specified, and their places in the "epistemes" of their epochs determined before they can enter the lists as possible models of historical reconstruction and analysis. And as it is with Marx and Freud, so too is it with every other "classic" text that once served as a "representative" text of the best thought of an age: Homer and Plato, Tacitus and Augustine, Machiavelli and Erasmus, and so forth. Their very "representativeness" is brought under question, their status as both "evidence" of a "spirit of the age" and as the privileged interpreters of their own time and place is placed in doubt. And this because "representativeness" and "interpretation" are no longer taken as unambiguous *possibilities* of texts. Or rather, since every text, grand or humble, is seen to be equally representative, equally interpretative of its proper milieu, the notion of a text that might serve as an especially privileged interpretative model is set aside.

And if the classic text is problematized, so too is the distinction, which is of the same order, between reliably transparent texts or documents and "ideologically" distorted, unreliable, or opaque texts. Considered as historical *evidence*, all texts are regarded as being equally shot through with ideological elements or, what amounts to the same thing, as being equally transparent, reliable, or evidential in what they can tell us about the "mental climate" (here variously construed) in which they arose. To the historian equipped with the proper tools, it is suggested, *any* text or artifact can figure forth the thought-world and possibly even the world of emotional investment and praxis of its time and place of production. Not that any given text can alone call up the whole world of its origin or that any given set of texts can reveal its world completely. But in principle, it seems to be held that we today possess the tools to probe texts in ways only dimly perceived or, if perceived, not fully utilized by earlier intellectual, as well as other kinds of, historians. And these tools, it is suggested, are generally *linguistic* in nature.

This is not the uniform opinion of these essays, of course, and for obvious reasons. For some historians, a linguistically oriented approach to the study of history raises the specter of a Whorfian kind of relativism. A specifically structuralist-linguistic approach to historical texts raises the threat of "ahistoricity" for which structuralism is ritualistically denounced by many historians. And a specifically post-structuralist linguistic approach to historical texts holds out the prospect of an infinite "freeplay" of interpretative fantasy that takes one further and further from, rather than closer and closer to, the origin and subject of the texts studied. It is for reasons such as these, I surmise, that our essayists divide rather evenly into those who (1) take their stand on one or more of the classical hermeneutics of the nineteenth century (Hegel, Dilthey, Marx, Freud) or their twentieth-century avatars; (2) adopt the neo-Humboldtian, philological theory of language lately revived and refined by Gadamer and Ricoeur; or (3) openly advert to the post-Saussurian theory of the linguistic sign, of which both Foucault and Derrida, though in different ways, are exponents.

And here arises a division between the historian who wishes primarily to "reconstruct" or "explain" the past and one who is interested either in "interpreting" it or using its detritus as an occasion for his own speculations on the present (and future). Nineteenth-century systematic hermeneutics—of the Comtean, Hegelian, Marxist, etc., varieties—was concerned to "explain" the past; classical philological hermeneutics, to "reconstruct" it; and modern post-Saussurian hermeneutics, usually laced with a good dose of Nietzsche, to "interpret" it. The differences among these notions of "explanation," "reconstruction," and "interpretation" are more specific than generic, since any one of them contains elements of the others; but they point to different degrees of interest in a "scientific" enterprise, an "object of study" (the past), or the investigator's own powers of composition and invention, respectively. And this question of the domain to which the historian is responsible is, of course, a crucial issue in any effort to determine what an "appropriate" performance in the discipline of history will consist of. On this question turns what might be called the "ethics" and possibly the "politics" of the discipline. To what is the historian responsible, or rather, to what *should* one be responsible?

There can be no answer to this question, I should think, that is not value-laden and normative, prescriptive and judgmental, rather than obvious, self-evident, or objectively determinable. To be sure, the field of linguistics is, in the human sciences, *the* principal new field of investigation opened up in the twentieth century in the West, surpassing in its importance even the field of ethnography (which, in a way, has finally found *its* favored hermeneutical models in this very field of linguistics). And to expect that historians would not find linguistics at least as attractive as investigators in other fields have found it would be naive. Historians have always had to draw upon theories from other fields in the humanities and social sciences, when they have not credited current common sense or traditional wisdom, for their analytical strategies. And indeed modern historical method was, in its Rankean formulation, little more than the philological method carried over to the investigation of documents of a nonliterary sort. Historians have always used some version of a theory of language to assist them in their work of "translating" meaning across the historical continuum, in order to "make sense" of their documents. It would appear, therefore, that the question confronting contemporary historians is not whether they will utilize a linguistic model to aid them in their work of "translation," but what kind of linguistic model they will use. And this is especially crucial for intellectual historians who, as the essayists in this volume seem to agree, are concerned above all with the problem of meaning and that of translating between different meaning-systems, whether as between past and present or between the documents and those readers of history books who wish to know what these documents "really mean."

But which linguistic theory will be used, or might be used, or even should be used to help us in this work of translation?

Well, there are at least four ways of construing the relationship between language and the world of things. Language can be taken to be a *manifestation* of causal relationships governing the world of things in which it arises, in the mode of an *index*. It can be taken to be a *representation* of that world, in the mode of an *icon* (or *mimesis*). It can be taken to be a *symbol* of that world, in the mode of an *analogue*, natural or cultural specific, as the case might be. Or it can be taken simply as another thing among those that populate the human world, but more specifically a *sign system*, which is to say a code that bears no necessary or (more technically) "motivated" relationship to that which it signifies.[1]

[1]For a general survey of modern theories of the sign, see Roland Barthes, *Elements of Semiology*, tr. Annette Lavers and Colin Smith (New York, 1968), chap. 3; Oswald Ducrot

Marxists—and social determinists in general—tend to think of language as an *index* of the (or rather *its*) world, being rather like a symptom or an effect of causal forces conceived to be more basic, residing in the "infrastructure" or at least in the "social relations of production." As one lives, so one speaks. A weaker version of the same idea, but usually unattended by the theoretical apparatus of the Marxist notion, holds that language does not so much "indicate" as "represent" a world, and does so as much in its grammar and syntax as it does in its lexicon, such that the kinds of meanings that a given cultural configuration can generate are reflected in the formal features of its modes of discourse, grammatically defined. This is the basis of the faith in the philological method espoused by an older generation of intellectual historians or historians of ideas, of whom Spitzer, Auerbach, Cassirer, and so on were representative. The *iconic* fidelity of language—if not of texts—was taken for granted, and one had only to know the structure of the language to penetrate to the real meaning of texts or historical documents.

A third way of construing the nature of the relationship of language to its world was to regard language in general as a *symbol* of that world, that is to say, by viewing it as a natural analogue of that of which it was a representation. This was the Hegelian view, and it underwrote the whole enterprise of *Geistesgeschichte* which presupposed a "Zeitgeist" manifested in all aspects of a culture, but in language especially, such that a proper analysis of *any* artifact deriving from the culture would reveal the "essence" of the whole, "microcosmically," as it were, in the mode of a synecdoche.

It can be seen that all these notions of language presuppose some "natural" relation between it and the world of which it is a representation: causal, mimetic, or analogical, as the case may be. And one or another of these notions of language has underwritten different approaches to intellectual or cultural history in the modern period. What is notable at this moment in the evolution of language theory is that, for most intellectual historians, it is one or another of these versions of the nature of language that still informs their conceptualizations of the text, textuality, discourse, and evidence for their field of study. This point is interesting because it reflects the extent to which even those intellectual historians enlivened to the implications of modern language studies for their field have not yet fully assimilated the

---

and Tzvetan Todorov, *Encyclopedic Dictionary of the Sciences of Language*, tr Catherine Porter (Baltimore, 1979), 84–90; and *Language Thought and Culture*, ed. Paul Henle (Ann Arbor, 1972), chap. 7.

Saussurian theory of language as a sign system, the theory that stands at the basis of both structuralism and post-structuralism, and that offers, in my view, the best immediate prospects for a fruitful revision of the central problem of intellectual history, the problem of ideology.

I call ideology the central problem of intellectual history because our field has to do, as Keith Baker asserts, with meaning, its production, distribution, and, so to say, consumption in different historical epochs. But in the West at least, the question of meaning, or more precisely that of the meaning of meaning, has evolved against the background of a conviction of the irreconcilable opposition between science (conceived as *some kind* of objective view of reality) and ideology (conceived as a distorted, fragmentary, or otherwise deformed view, produced to serve the interest of a specific social group or class).[2] This distinction regenerates most of the earlier epistemological conflicts of our culture, those between reason and faith, philosophy and theology, secular and sacred learning, and so forth, but with this difference: whereas earlier conflicts of this sort had envisioned a resolution in the form of the establishment of one or the other of these pairs as an *organon* of or propaedeutic to the *other*, the science-ideology conflict took on, in the course of the nineteenth century, the aspect of a manichaean struggle that could end only with the extirpation of ideology and its replacement by a scientific view of reality. From the standpoint of the intellectual historian who viewed his enterprise as a part of the cause of science, his own conception of his discipline required that he assume the role of arbitrator as to what counted as a more or less "objective," "realistic," or "reliable" representation of reality and what had to be identified as primarily "ideological" in nature. Underlying and authorizing this critical activity was—as I noted above—a tacit theory of language, of discourse, and of representation in general by which to sort out the distortions of reality present in any text under analysis and a presupposition of the concreteness and accessibility of a text's original historical context by which a given distortion could be verified. But once it was realized (or conceded) that this context was itself accessible only through the medium of verbal artifacts, and that these were subject to the same distortions by virtue of their *textuality* as the evidence of which it was to serve as a control, the problem of identifying ideological elements in a given text was extended to the concept of the context as well. Therewith, the very enterprise not only of the intellectual historian but

[2]See now the comprehensive survey of modern theories of ideology by Fredric Jameson, *The Political Unconscious: Narrative as a Socially Symbolic Act* (Ithaca, 1981), chap. 1.

of other kinds too was opened up to the dangers of ideologism. For if the context represented to one in the documents was subject to distortion, by virtue of its being represented or being accessible only by way of verbal artifacts, the same could be said of that "science" which one invoked as organon for guiding one's own investigations.

Of course, one could still moot the whole question of language and continue to act as if the problem of its opacity did not exist, but this became increasingly difficult to do in the wake of structuralism and post-structuralism and *especially* the problematizing of the whole task of textual interpretation by literary scholars, hermeneuticists, and even such neo-Marxists as Althusser and Habermas, under the press of a new sensitivity to the problem of language itself. And here it is possible to specify the nature of a crucial split, not only among intellectual historians, but among cultural analysts in general, between those who continue to use a linguistic theory of the text and those who embrace a specifically semiological conception of it.

By a linguistic theory of texts I mean one that takes specifically lexical and grammatical categories as elements in its analytical model and, on the basis of this model, seeks to establish rules for identifying a "proper" as against an "improper" instance of language-use—after the manner of Russell, Wittgenstein, Austin, or Chomsky. By a semiological conception of texts, I refer to the tradition of cultural analysis which builds upon the theory of language as a sign (rather than a word) system, after the manner of Saussure, Jakobson, and Benveniste, and distinguishes between those sign systems that are extrareferential, on the one side, and those that have as their referents some other sign system, on the other. This provides the basis for a methodologically significant distinction between a linguistic inquiry and a specifically semiological one that has important implications for the way we might conceptualize the problem of characterizing the ideological aspects of a given text, discourse, or artifact.

As Paolo Valesio, the student of Jakobson who has given his work a distinctively Marxist turn, puts it: the ideological aspects of a text are specifically those "metalinguistic" gestures in it by which it substitutes another sign system for the putatively extralinguistic referent about which it pretends to speak or of which it pretends to be a straightforward, objective, or value-free description.[3] A semiological

---

[3]Paolo Valesio, "The Practice of Literary Semiotics: A Theoretical Proposal," in *Working Papers and Pre-Publications* of the Centro Internazionale di Semiotica e di Linguistica (University of Urbino), No. 71 (February 1978), Series D, 1–23. And for a more comprehensive theoretical statement and application, Valesio, *Novantiqua: Rhetorics as a Contemporary Theory* (Bloomington, 1981), chaps. 1, 3.

approach to the study of texts permits us to moot the question of the text's reliability as witness to events or phenomena extrinsic to it, to pass over the question of the text's "honesty" or "dishonesty," its objectivity or subjectivity, and to regard its ideological aspect less as a product (whether of self-interest or group interest, whether of conscious or unconscious impulses) than as a process. It permits us, more precisely, to regard ideology as a process in which different kinds of meaning are produced and reproduced by the establishment of a mental set toward the world in which certain sign systems are privileged as necessary, even natural ways of recognizing a "meaning" in things and others are suppressed, ignored, or hidden in the very process of representing a world to consciousness. This process goes on in scientific discourse no less than in fictional or legal-political discourse. Indeed, a discourse could not *appear* scientific if it did not, in the process of its own elaboration, substitute a specific sign system (the "code" of science) for the referent ("nature," "atoms," "genes," and so forth) that is its manifest object of representation and analysis. This has implications not only for the way we read historical texts, but for the ways we read the works of other historians as well.

When historians analyze and criticize the work of their colleagues or predecessors, in order to identify the ideological elements in their work, as in Fisher's reading of Freud or Poster's reading of Foucault, they are inclined to present the points at issue in terms of "contents": "themes," "concepts," "arguments," "judgments," and "values" or the like. The conventional procedure is then to characterize these contents as being either distortions of the "facts" or deviations from the "truth"—as these "facts" and "truths" are given in some other corpus of works, either the "documents" which the investigator regards as having been correctly analyzed by himself, or some interpretative canon, such as Marxism, which the investigator regards as the ultimate court of appeal for the authority and rectitude of his own interpretations. What is offered as a *description* of the text under analysis, in this case Freud's or Foucault's writings, usually turns out to be a set of quotations, paraphrases of passages in selected texts, or condensed summaries of positions which function as synecdoches of the works in question. The question of why or in what manner Foucault's or Freud's work is authoritative is dealt with by simply assuming that they appeal to coprofessionals because *these* share *their* respect for Freud or Foucault. This amounts to a *petitio principii* which assumes the existence and nature of what is supposed to be analyzed and explained.

But we should take this as given: a bourgeois historian will of course make sense to other bourgeois historians and not to Marxist ones, just as the Marxist will make sense to other Marxist historians and not to bourgeois ones. That is less in the nature of a problem than an assumption which all ideologically oriented analysis must presuppose even to enable its heuristic quest. The more interesting question would be to ask: not *what* do Freud, Foucault, etc., assert, allege, argue, and so on, but *how* do they establish, through the articulation of their texts, the plausibility of their discourse by referring the "meaning" of these texts, not to other "facts," or "events," but rather to a complex sign system that is treated as "natural" rather than as a code specific to the praxis of a given social group, stratum, or class? To ask this question is to shift hermeneutic interest from the *content* of the texts being investigated to their *formal* properties, considered not in terms of the relatively vacuous notion of "style," but rather as a dynamic process of overt and covert code-shifting by which a specific subjectivity is called up and established in the reader, who is supposed to entertain this representation of the world as a "realistic" one in virtue of its congeniality to the *imaginary* relationship that the subject bears to his own social and cultural situation.[4]

All of this is of course highly abstract and would require not only a wealth of illustrative exemplifications but also considerably more theoretical exposition than space here permits, to gain even minimal plausibility for its claims. Such a theoretical exposition would require, however, at least detailed reference to the work of Jakobson, Benveniste, Eco, Barthes, and so on, as well as to that of Lévi-Strauss, Althusser, Lacan, the neorhetoricians and theorists of discourse analysis, and so forth, on which its authority as a theory would in many ways depend. Moreover, such an exposition would itself be able to escape the charges of tautology and *petitio principii* which I have leveled against the "content" method of analysis, only if it plainly displayed and drew explicit attention to the code shifts by which *it* provided a "meaning" for phenomena that it might pretend only to "describe" and objectively "analyze."

To be more specific: such an exposition would have to draw explicit attention to the *problem of exemplification* itself, the *semiological significance* both of the *text* it had chosen as a specimen for illustrative purposes and of those *portions* of the text on which it had

[4]The formulation is, of course, that of Louis Althusser, "Ideology and Ideological State Apparatuses (Notes towards an Investigation)," in *Lenin and Philosophy and Other Essays*, tr. Ben Brewster (New York, 1971), 127–186.

chosen to lavish its hermeneutical attention. Nor could it obscure the fact that the very distinction on which the analysis is based, that between linguistic and semiological analysis, is hardly a universally agreed upon protocol, but is rather in the nature of an enabling pre-supposition, the utility of which is to be assessed solely in terms of a quantitative criterion, namely, its capacity to account for *more* of the elements of any given text, of whatever length, than any contending "content"-oriented method could match. Beyond that, this approach would demonstrate its "objectivity" above all in the methodological tolerance and patience it lavished on texts that are *opposed* to the investigator's own consciously held political, social, cultural, and scientific values, one of the universally agreed upon criteria for as-sessing any hermeneutic being its capacity to entertain sympathetically not only those texts that the hermeneut values and regards as "clas-sic," but also and especially those texts that represent other, opposed positions, projects, and the like. But now that I have said all this, an example by way of illustration *is* called for, and here it is.

Suppose we are interested in characterizing the ideological status, and thereby the historically evidentiary nature, of a work like *The Education of Henry Adams*.[5] The conventional approach would be to try to identify certain generic elements of the text, themes, arguments, and so forth—this in the interest of establishing what the text is *about*, what *point of view* its author represents, and its importance *as evidence* of some aspect of early twentieth-century American social and cultural history. We might say that the text sets forth views and arguments with respect to politics, society, culture, ethics and moral-ity, epistemology, and so forth, and we would then proceed to assess the validity of the positions assigned to the author or the text, to determine the extent to which they were prophetic, prejudiced, fore-sighted, reflective, sapient, antiquated, and so forth, much in the way that D. W. Brogan did in his introduction to a 1961 edition of the *Education*.

Here, for example, we find such statements as:

> It is, indeed, on the surface, the story of one who failed. . . .
> For Adams is a child of Rousseau, of the romantic movement. . . .
> . . . the *Education* . . . illuminat[es] . . . American history, seen
> sometimes from the inside, sometimes from an exceptionally good posi-

---

[5]The standard edition is that of Ernest Samuels, *The Education of Henry Adams* (Boston, 1973), with indispensable notes. For reasons that are obvious I have used the earlier edition, with an introduction by D. W. Brogan (Boston: Houghton Mifflin, 1961).

tion on the sidelines. . . . And it is a statement of the predicament of modern man in the late nineteenth century. . . .

. . . the book can only be appreciated if it is realized how American the book is and yet what an exceptional American Adams, merely as an Adams, was bound to be. . . .

The *Education*, briefly summed up, is the story of a lifelong appren ticeship to the fact that the world could ignore the standards, the ranks, the assumptions of Boston, that nothing was stable, not even the natural precedence of the Adams family. . . .

From one point of view, this [the first twenty chapters dealing with Adams' formal education and service in the American ministry in London during the Civil War] is the most successful part of the book. . . .

Brogan continues:

It can be held (I hold this view) that the most important part of the *Education* is the record of disillusionment with the victorious Union. . . .

Adams was an artist and an anarchist. . . .

Adams was not a scientist or a philosopher but a historian, and he had shown in his writings a mastery of the techniques of historical scholarship. . . .

Henry took a . . . pessimistic point of view . . . [but] this pessimism is partly "an act.". . .

There was in his correspondence with [his brother Brooks] an unattractive and rather stupid strain of anti-Semitism. . . .

For the background of our present perplexities, the *Education* is an indispensable document.

But it is more than that; it is a great work of art and in its first half, at any rate, a nearly perfect work of art. . . .

Adams . . . fell more and more under the influence of French ways of thinking and writing. The stylistic effects are beneficial.

And finally:

He [Adams] speaks to us as mere Presidents and millionaires cannot and he speaks for an American attitude that we tend to ignore, for that critical side of American life that knows how much more the human heart needs than mere material goods and the vulgar success that Henry Adams, to our profit, escaped."

Now, I want to stress that this kind of mixture of thematic description and assessment (the two are hardly distinguishable) is a perfectly legitimate kind of commentary, and even when only impressionistic and unsystematic, as this example is, can be illuminating to the reader when the commentator is a shrewd, knowledgeable, and eloquent impressionist, as Brogan was. But it can serve in no way as a *model* of analysis, which students might emulate and apply to other texts (unless they became versions of Brogan himself), and provides absolutely no criterion, either explicit or implicit, for assessing the validity of the various generalizations offered in the commentary. We may intuitively credit certain of the generalizations and reject others (but this would be a matter of personal taste on our part); we can also imagine a commentary on this text that might take the negative of every one of Brogan's predications as the real truth about the text or Adams and, probably, find some passage in the text that would justify this reading rather than the one offered by Brogan (also on the basis of personal taste, inclination, or ideological commitment), and arrive at an utterly different account of what the text *really* means. The "authority" of Brogan's reading is simply assumed, rather than argued for, and the picture it gives of the text, no less than the assessments it makes of its various aspects, is utterly arbitrary—by which I mean a matter of the psychology of the commentator rather than the results of a theoretical position vis-à-vis the nature of texts and the problem of discriminating between what they *say* and what, in an ideological sense, they might *mean* or *do*.

From a semiological perspective, by contrast, we can provide a theoretically generated reading of this text, which would give *an* account for every element of it, whether as large as the book's gross organization (with Editor's Preface, [Author's] Preface, its thirty-five chapters and their curious pattern of entitlement, the concluding chapter's title, "Nunc Age," and so forth) or as small as a single paragraph, sentence, or phrase. Not an account in the sense of providing a causal explanation of why Adams says what he says wherever he says it, but one that would help identify the patterns of code-shifting by which ideological implications are substituted for the straightforward representation of a social life or meditation on a single life which the text pretends to be. Such an analysis would begin with a rhetorical characterization of the text's elements, after the manner of Barthes's *S/Z*,[6] by which to identify the nature of the authority claimed by the text as a perspective on the reality it purports to represent; would proceed to the disclosure of the modality of code-shifting by which a particular mental set is specified as necessary to the proper reception of the text by an ideal reader; and thence to a detailed analysis of the

[6]See Roland Barthes, *S/Z*, tr. Richard Miller (New York, 1974), 16–21; *Structuralism and Since*, ed. John Sturrock (Oxford, 1979), pp. 52–80.

metalinguistic elements of specific passages where a particular kind of social code is invoked as the standard for assessing the validity of *all* social codes in the reader's purview.

Here the rule is "begin at the beginning," in this case, with the title of the book, which does not feature reference to an author, except indirectly or inferentially: *The Education of Henry Adams [An Autobiography]*.

The title appears to be nothing other than the product of an act of nomination, although on reflection the idiosyncrasy of the locution (why not: "The Autobiography of Henry Adams: An Education"? Or any number of other possibilities? Why "education" for "life"? And so on) should alert the hermeneut to other rhetorical moves having to do with the manipulation of the genre of autobiography specifically. One notices that, although the author of the work is also its subject, the subject is featured at the expense of the reader's sense of the author. The work is not offered as being "by" Henry Adams. It is only by the device of labeling the genre to which the work belongs—the label was affixed by the Massachusetts Historical Society, not Adams—that we can infer that it was written by its subject. And it is "an" autobiography, not the "the" autobiography, which, as the text will confirm, is specifically the case: it is a version of a life that, because it can be said hardly to have existed at all, would presumably bear many more versions than only a single, definitive one. No matter that the title replicates a conventional formula of entitlement, for there were any number of alternative formulas that might have been followed. The choice of this convention, along with its peculiar twists of locution, immediately locates us in a thought-world more like that of Henry James than that of Thoreau (cf. *Walden or, Life in the Woods* "by" Henry David Thoreau) or Jean-Jacques Rousseau (cf. *The Confessions* "of" Jean-Jacques Rousseau). With this title, the text already signals the reticence of the author, that denial of authorial ego which Adams himself justifies in his own "Preface," and that "dissolution of the ego" which remains a theme throughout the book.

Next we would comment on the number, subject matter, and above all the titles of the thirty-five chapters given in the Table of Contents (titles with place names, proper nouns, and subjects indeterminable from the title alone) and the curious gap which the "Contents" indicates, that of the years 1871–1892, in which, so it would appear, "nothing happened." This, we would learn from extratextual sources, comprises the period of Adams's marriage and the suicide of his wife, and other events which, ordinarily, we would expect to be included in an "autobiography." The fact that they are *not* included suggests to us that we should be prepared for anything but an "ordinary" or "conventional" autobiography and that we should attend with especial care to what has been left out of the account and try to determine what other rules of exclusion *systematically* operated in the construction of the text.

We would next attend to the "Editor's Preface," which is signed by "Henry Cabot Lodge," seemingly acting as the spokesman for the Massachusetts Historical Society, under whose auspices the text is being offered to the public. We would not realize, unless we had other evidence to tell us, that this "Editor's Preface" was written not by Lodge, but by Adams himself, for Lodge's signature—another example of the author's reticence, duplicity, humility, desire for control, or what? I am not sure. But what strikes our eye, especially once we have read the author's "Preface," is the seeming equivocation, deferral, or ambiguity with which the author viewed his own text, and the pains he took to assure that his readers (if they attended to these opening gestures especially) would read the work in the "proper" spirit or frame of mind. In both prefaces, the author seeks to characterize his own book, assign it to a genre, identify its specificity within the genre, and bracket, as it were, the whole problem of the sincerity, authenticity, veracity, or literalness of a text which, because it is an autobiography, *should* have all these qualities.

The "Editor's Preface," for example, likens the work to Saint Augustine's *Confessions*, only to qualify the supposed similarity between them by stressing their differences and, implicitly, to suggest the superiority of Adams's work over that of his Christian prototype. In the author's "Preface," by contrast, the work is likened to the model provided by Rousseau's *Confessions* and, in an aside, Franklin's *Autobiography*, only, again, to stress the differences between them and, by implication, the superiority of Adams's work. We might, from a semiological perspective, regard all this as a working of the code of literary genres, in such a way as to foreclose any impulse to compare Adams's work with similar examples of the genre, thereby *establishing* the author's originality, on the one side, and locating the reader in the appropriate domain of critical response for assessing his product (in this case, the aesthetic domain, rather than that of religion, psychology, or ethics), on the other.

In fact, this intention had already been explicitly suggested in the preface by "Lodge" when he stated that the author's dissatisfaction with his own work had been so strong that he had decided *never* to have it published; and that this dissatisfaction had to do, not with the content of the work, the matters of fact or judgments rendered in it, but what "Lodge" calls "the usual [problem] of literary form." This was "the point on which the author failed to please himself" and it was the one point on which he "could get no light from readers or friends"—all of which suggests the topos of the isolated artist struggling to express a truth too deep to be rendered in mere words and which refers us not so much to an actual fact or condition (since Adams's sense of his own stylistic capability was as inflated as that of Henry James or any other mandarin writer of the time), as to a specific ideology of a certain *kind* of artist—not a romantic one at all, as Brogan suggests, but rather more like Oscar Wilde, to whom Brogan *does* liken Adams but only to dismiss the comparison as inappropriate (Introd., vii).

The location of the artist's persona in the precious, however serious, world of Oscar Wilde and Swinburne (whom Adams professes to admire) is further effected by a passage in the author's "Preface" which turns upon a reworking of another literary topos, that of the "philosophy of clothes" which was dominantly represented in nineteenth-century Anglo-American literary culture by Carlyle's influential *Sartor Resartus*. This passage is crucial for the semiologist because it is one in which the author comments on his own work, less in a metalinguistic than a metageneric intervention. Ironically, almost to the point of malign satire, he signals the literal "emptiness" of his text as a fit vehicle for the representation of the emptiness of his own ego; and then sketches what might be called a "mannikin" theory of the literary work which makes of it not a product of a dialectic between form and content, but rather a relationship between two forms equally evanescent: the *clothes* in which the tailor's dummy is garbed and the *surface* of the dummy's body which feigns the form of a man but has no interior.

But no sooner is the mannikin model invoked than it too is distanced and brought under question by being characterized in the second sense in which the term is conventionally used, that is, as a model only, which "must be taken for real, must be treated as though it had life," in order to serve as a "measure of motion, of proportion, of human condition," and the like. But this new characterization is itself dissolved in the rhetorical question that forms the last thought of the preface. This question is: did the mannikin ever have any life?

And the answer given is: "Who knows? Possibly it had!" A rhetorical question, followed by an ambiguous answer—which might very well serve as an emblem of the "style" of Henry Adams.

But alongside of the rhetoric of aestheticism and evasion, by which Adams locates his work within a particular domain of the writer's code of his time and place, there is another important topos that is more social-class specific and that surfaces right at the beginning of the pseudonymous preface signed by "Henry Cabot Lodge." The first words of this first preface are:

> This volume, written in 1905, as a sequel to the same author's "Mont-Saint-Michel and Chartres," was privately printed, to the number of one hundred copies, in 1906, and sent to the persons interested, for their assent, correction, and suggestion.

Not only does this passage attest to the author's scrupulousness concerning the factual "content" of his text; the phrase "privately printed" summons up a special kind of writerly condition and a notion of this writer's potential public that is at once patrician or aristocratic and seemingly solvent of any aspiration to the attention of the general public. This topos of privacy-publicity recurs in the third paragraph of "Lodge's" preface when he mentions that "The 'Chartres' was finished and privately printed in 1904." The publicizing of both of these texts, their projection into the public domain, is explicitly characterized by "Lodge" as having happened beyond the author's "control." "In 1913," "Lodge" reports, "the Institute of American Architects published the 'Mont-Saint-Michel and Chartres'"—a phrase that leaves unspecified how the Institute claimed the right to do so (it is almost as if Adams had had nothing to say about the matter). But the placement of the text under the auspices of a professional institution has the effect of signaling the kind of authority as a scholarly work to which it can lay claim, as well as suggesting that the book was, as it were, "fated" to see the light of day, whatever the author's "private" wishes on the matter.

This motif is repeated in the next sentence following that just quoted, when "Lodge" reports that: "Already, the 'Education' had become almost as well known as the 'Chartres,' and was freely quoted by every book whose author requested it." So much for "privacy"— quality will out! But so will fate: "The author," we are told, "could no longer withdraw either volume; he could no longer rewrite either, and he could not publish that which he thought unprepared and unfinished, although in his opinion the other was historically purposeless without its sequel." In the end, therefore, he preferred to leave the "Education" unpublished, "avowedly incomplete, trusting that it might quietly fade from memory," thereby confirming a precept he had long believed, namely, that "silence next to good-temper was the mark of sense." Since this was made an "absolute" rule after midsummer, 1914, the intervention of the Massachusetts Historical Society alone was able to overcome the author's express wish to ignore his book, and so, as "Lodge" tells us: "The Massachusetts Historical Society now publishes the 'Education' . . . not in opposition to the author's judgment, but only to put both volumes equally within reach of students who have occasion to consult them."

Now, a preface is, by its very nature, an instruction on how to read the text that follows it and, by the same token, an attempt to guard against certain misreadings, in other words, an attempt at control. In his masterful meditation on the preface as genre in Western writing, Derrida notes that the preface is always a narcissistic enterprise, but of a special kind, that in which a proud parent looks upon and praises, excuses, or otherwise prepares the way for its child, the text which he has at once sired and given birth to. If we might consider the matter in this way for a moment, what do we make of an *autobiographical* text that has *two* prefaces (both written by the author but one of which is offered over the name of a friend who is a representative not only of the Boston patriciate, but also of the Massachusetts Historical Society)?

The double preface is at best redundant and, as such, symptomatic of an excessive solicitude for the future of the progeny for whom it obviously wishes to smooth out the way. The shadow of the author casts itself over the work, not only as one presence seeking to guide the reader's approach to the text, but as two, the first of which wishes to guide the reader's approach to the text *and* the author. The repetitiveness of the pretextual gesture already puts it in the domain of obsessive concern which, from a psychoanalytical perspective, we might refer to some traumatic experience in the life of the text's author. Not only does the double preface (one counterfeit, the other "genuine") suggest an especial concern about the fate of the text (a concern explicitly stated in "Lodge's" account of the text's reluctant "birth", it also suggests a kind of fear of being muffled by prejudicial misreading which is repeated in the text proper by the theme of the burden of an inherited tradition that *misfitted* the author for a proper "life" in the twentieth century.

All this is, I believe, clear enough; but clear enough from what perspective(s)?

From a psychoanalytical perspective, concerned as it would be with moving from the text to a determination of the author's unconscious and conscious intentions in writing the text (and the conflicts between them), this excessive concern is to be regarded as a symptom, that is to say, an *index* of the writer's "state of mind" and stance vis-à-vis his world as *he perceives it*. This state of mind is to be referred, in turn, to the sociodynamics of the author's family experiences as the cause of the neurotic fixations in response to which both the text and the activity of writing are to be regarded as sublimations. The typicality of the text, then, its status as evidence of the social world in which it takes its rise, resides in the extent to which it reveals something about the psychoeconomics of a particular kind of family structure. And this is one way to proceed, as long as it is realized that, in order to carry out the analytical operation, one must *presume* the adequacy of some version of Freudian doctrine to such an analysis.

From a Marxist perspective, the text will also be treated as an *index* of a structure (a contradictory one by definition), that of a specific class consciousness and practice and, in the degree to which it is self-consciously a representation of that consciousness and practice, an *icon* as well. If, beyond that, the text is treated as an especially apt manifestation of this class consciousness, one that systematically offers itself to its public in such a way as both to mask its class nature and to defend it surreptitiously, it will be elevated to the status of a *symbol* of it. This leads the investigator from the text through the postulated consciousness of the author to the social context, of which the text is then supposed to be a highly complex, but still perfectly decodable, reflection. And this too is a way to proceed, provided that, as with the Freudian tactic, it is recognized that one must simply *presume* the adequacy of the Marxist doctrine to explicate the double relationship between text and author, on the one side, and between the author and the "superstructure," on the other.

A semiological perspective, on the other hand, treats the text less as an effect of causes more basic or as a reflection, however refracted, of a structure more fundamental, than as a complex mediation between various codes by which "reality" is to be assigned possible "meanings," and seeks, first of all, to identify the hierarchy of codes that is established in the process of the text's elaboration, in which one or more emerge as seemingly "self-evident," "obvious," "natural" ways of making sense of the world. In the dynamics of a complex text such as that represented by the *Education*, various codes are, as it were, "tried on," rather in the way that one tries on various sizes and styles of suits, before finding the one that "fits" more or less adequately—one that appears to have been *especially tailored* for the thing it is meant to clothe, adorn, warm, and protect from the elements. In the *Education*, the codes of history, science, philosophy, law, art, and so on, as well as various social codes, cultural codes, etiquettes, protocols, and so forth, are all "tried on" only to be rejected as "unsuited" to the needs of a "sensitive" intelligence asked to come to terms with the "real" forces governing life in the twentieth century. These are systematically reduced to the status of a "patchwork" or "motley," to the status of dispersed "fragments" or "sherds," to harlequinade—the utility of which for life is adjudged to be nil. What is revealed to be operative in the new world is power, or rather brute force, represented as an "energy" that has no end or purpose beyond pure process itself (in the animal world, the symbol of this force is represented by the shark *pteraspis*, in the physical world by the "dynamo," and in the cultural world by the "Virgin"). Standing over against this impersonal, blind, undirected force, as a last refuge of *sensitivity* (itself seen as a kind of "sport" of nature) that is itself rapidly disappearing in response to powers it can not begin to resist, is the "personal" gesture of the exemplary autobiography whose "authority" is contained in its status as mere "literature," and whose "integrity" is confirmed by its aspiration to a *stylistic* consistency which the author himself adjudges not to have been achieved.

The code-switching involved here is from a postulated social consciousness inherited from the eighteenth century, to a putatively more "realistic" perception of "the way things really are" in the nineteenth century, on the level of formal argument; and from a putative historical and scientific knowledge to a hypostatized, but purely local or personal, aesthetic consciousness, on the level of affect or valuation. The form of the discourse, that of the autobiography, enacts a similar switching of codes. Its manifest message is that it is impossible to write an autobiography like any of the traditional types (religious, psychological, ethical) on the basis of the *modern* experience; second, by virtue of the stated incompleteness of the effort on Adams' own part, it is asserted to be impossible to write an autobiography at all (this in evidence of the dissolution of the "ego" which modern society and culture are seen to have effected); and third, it is suggested that the only possible justification even of the *effort* to write an autobiography would be the consistency of style with which the enterprise was undertaken by a person like Adams—a criterion that is a purely aesthetic one, although it is represented in the text as having *moral* implications.

The strategy consists in taking what one considers to be the defects of one's own culture or historical moment (in this case, its dissolution of "the ego") and turning them into, first, a *method* of observation, representation, and assessment and, second, a protocol for orchestrating the introduction of the text so as to limit the kind of audience it will find—that complex ballet of approach-avoidance which we have seen manifested in the two prefaces of the work. In the two prefaces, the triple irony that pervades the text is given direct embodiment. And the form of the whole text can be seen to figure forth the precise nature of the value attached to the messages contained in the text proper.

Indeed, in a way quite different from Saint Augustine and Rousseau, not to mention Franklin, the *form* of this work can be seen, from a semiological perspective, as the specifically *ideological content* of the text as a whole. And our assent to the form of the text as something given, in the interest of entertaining, assessing, and otherwise responding to the thematic content, representations, judgments, and so forth contained in the narrative levels of the text, is the sign of the power of this text considered as an exercise in *ideological* mystification.

Once we are enlivened to the extent to which the *form* of the text is the place where it does its ideologically significant work, other aspects of the text which a criticism unsensitized to the operations of a *form-as-message* will find bewildering, surprising, inconsistent, or simply offensive (such as the "gap" in the account of the years 1871–1892 or the shift from a narrative account in the early years [which Brogan and most modern commentators like] to the so-called speculative discourses of the last fourteen chapters [especially offensive to historians by virtue of their supposedly "abstract" or a priori or deductive method]) themselves become meaningful as message.

In fact, the formal differences between the account of the earlier years and that of the later ones involve a code switch from a putatively "empirical" record of social and political events, of which the author was more or less a witness, to a manifestly "speculative" and deductive meditation on processes, a switch that is required by the supposedly different "natures" of the matters dealt with. But since this change of scale, scope, and content is not mediated by any *theoretical* necessity that the author can envisage (he has rejected Hegel, Marx,

Darwin, etc.), and since it is authorized by a canon of "taste" and "sensitivity" rather than of method or formal thought, the "gap" in the account of the years 1871–1892 is not only fully justified from an aesthetic standpoint, it is a necessary element of the message of the text as a whole.

To say that Adams left this hole in his text, this rupture in his account, because of the pain he suffered during those years, that these experiences were too personal for recounting, given the fastidiousness of his patrician nature, is to acquiesce in the fiction of "taste" as epistemic criterion which informs the work and is consistently invoked to validate its judgments.

All this talk about Adams's suffering may be true, but how could we be sure of it? The textual *fact* is the gap in the chronicle of the narrative. The reasons for or causes of this gap we can only speculate about. But the textual *function* of the gap is clear enough. As message, it reinforces the thesis of the emptiness of life that Adams adumbrates in the figure of the "mannikin" throughout the book. Adams cannot account for this emptiness, ontological in nature as he envisions it, either by historical-empirical-narrative methods (the methods of the first part) or by aprioristic, deductive, and speculative methods (those used in the second part). It is like the gap between the first, pseudo-editor's preface and the second, author's preface. These may reflect a kind of schizophrenic condition in Adams's psyche, but to explain or interpret a rupture in a text by referring it to a rupture in the author's psyche is merely to double the problem and to pass off this doubling operation as a solution to it.

The two parts of the text are manifestly not intended to be viewed as *phases* of a continuous narrative or as *stages* in the elaboration of a comprehensive argument. They are, as Adams himself suggests at the opening of his penultimate chapter, to be apprehended as aspects of a complex *image*. Here he writes:

> Images are not arguments, rarely even lead to proof, but the mind craves them, and, of late more than ever, the keenest experimenters find twenty images better than one, especially if contradictory; since the human mind has already learned to deal in contradictions. [P. 489]

But this image—as we can expect from reading almost any other part of the text—has a hole in its center, conformable to the text's explicit assertions that the depths of the individual personality are as unplumbable as the mysteries of history and nature. This sense of unplumbable mystery more than adequately justifies, in the terms of the text itself, the structure of the last chapter, ironically entitled "Nunc Age" (meaning both: "Now, depart" and "Now act") and ending with a meditation on Hamlet's last words: "The rest is silence." Before the enormity of the mystery of death, Adams suggests, we are capable only of either commonplace or silence. And, as he had said in the "Editor's Preface," "silence next to good-temper was the mark of sense."

All of this places the reader firmly within a social domain specifically *literary* in nature, not only in a society inhabited by such figures as Henry James, Swinburne, Wilde, and Carlyle, but also in a world in which meaning is conferred upon experience not by reference to some empirically discernible reality, social or natural, but rather by reference to other literary works, artistic monuments, and similarly encoded "texts."

It was, Barthes has argued, the supreme achievement of nineteenth-century realism, whether in literature or in social commentary, to substitute surreptitiously an *already textualized image* of the world for the concrete reality that it feigned iconically to represent. We can locate Adams within this tradition as another representative of realism's imminent unmasking, and of the writer's surrender to the free-play of language itself as the true function of literature, along with James, Proust, Virginia Woolf, Joyce and other heralds of what we have come to call "modernism" (as John Carlos Rowe has persuasively argued), if we wish to do so. But Rowe's suggestion that Adams's art, which "uses its artifice to question the nature of all signification," summons us to return once again "to the human dialogue that we ought to be renewing"[7] seems more a pious hope on Rowe's part than a conclusion justified by either the explicit messages of the text or that implicit message given in its form. Rowe's concluding suggestion returns Adams to that favored domain of the traditional humanist, the realm of the timeless "classic" which always shows us that "some beauty and nobility lurk in the anguished burden of human consciousness."[8]

But as an antidote to the arbitrarily hopeful reading of the *Education*, let us look at the last sentence of the text, which reports a fantasy in which Adams imagines himself returning to the world in 1938, the centenary of his own birth, with his two best friends, John Hay and Clarence King (not, be it noted, with his wife), "for a

---

[7] John Carlos Rowe, *Henry James and Henry Adams* (Ithaca, 1977), 242.
[8] Ibid.

holiday, to see their own mistakes made clear in the light of the mistakes of their successors; perhaps then," the wish continues, "for the first time since man began his education among the carnivores, they would find a world that sensitive and timid natures could regard without a shudder" (p. 505). "THE END."

It is of course possible to read any text as a meditation, more or less explicit, on the impossibility of representation and the aporias of signification, just by virtue of the fact that any text attempting to grasp any reality through the medium of language or represent it in that medium raises the specter of the impossibility of the task undertaken. But Adams's text is anything but an invitation, explicit or implicit, to a renewal of any *dialogue*. Its suppression of the expected voice of the dialogistic mode of discourse, that "I" which *implies* the existence of a "you" to participate in the verbal exchange by which meaning is to be dialectically teased out of the words used as a medium, is enough to suggest as much. This alone is sufficient to mark its essential difference from a work such as Thoreau's *Walden*, with which it might be profitably compared, in semiological terms; *Walden* can be shown to be intended as implicitly dialogistic in spite of its manifestly egoistic *form*. Adams's autobiography is a monologue, and if we can speculatively summon up the elements of dialogue in it, we must insist that the other party in the exchange can only be imagined to be some fragment or sherd of Adams's own fractured persona. He speaks of himself in the third person singular—as "he," "Adams," and so forth—splitting himself into both the speaker who is hidden behind the anonymity of the narrative form and the referent or subject of the narrative, who occupies center stage, around which (and in the fiction of the book, *for which*) the events of both nature and history occur—just as, in the prefatorial matter, he splits himself into two speakers, "Lodge" and "Adams," and assigns them slightly different things to say about his book.

This splitting, unraveling, or doubling of the persona of the author is, to be sure, a function of authorship itself, in which every writer is both the producer and consumer of his own discourse. The narcissistic or, if you wish, onanistic nature of this function is manifest. And on one level at least, texts differ by virtue of their respective efforts to transcend the narcissism inherent in the author-function and move to what a Freudian might call that *anaclitic* relationship which sociality presupposes as its basis. Not that we would follow Freud in regarding this as a qualitatively (morally) superior condition to the narcissistic one, for we could do that only by moving outside the text and affirming another ideology that regards the anaclitic form of love as more human, that is, more natural, than its narcissistic counterpart. Far from being an "egoless" text, the *Education* is—in spite of (because of?) the suppression of the authorial "I"—a supremely *egoistic* one; moreover, an egoistic one that is explicitly class-based. Thus, in the second paragraph of the *Education*, in which Adams likens his christening to a "brand" as burdensome as that laid upon any Jew in the synagogue, he says:

> To his life as a whole he was a consenting, contracting party and partner from the moment he was born to the moment he died. Only with that understanding—as a consciously assenting member in full partnership with the society of his age—had his education an interest to himself or to others.
>
> As it happened, he never got to the point of playing the game at all; he lost himself in the study of it, watching the errors of the players; but this is the only interest in the story, which otherwise has no moral and little incident. [P. 4]

The *Education*'s manifest announcement and demonstration of the end of the ego in the modern age has to be viewed as a message both personal and subjective, on the one side, and as social and historical, on the other. Insofar as Adams identifies his own ego with that of his class, the announcement of the dissolution of one is also the announcement of the dissolution of the other.

The seeming depersonalization of Adams's autobiography, the use of the objectivizing voices of the third-person narrative, of an author who distances himself from himself and writes the history of his (mis)education, is another sign of the fusion of the subjective ego with that of a specific social class. And the theme of (mis)education is simply another way of speaking about the (mis)fortunes of the latter in terms of those of the former. As for the further identification of "Henry Brooks Adams" with world history, which is also explicitly (however much on its surface it is ironically) made—this means that, far from being a mannikinlike counterpart of Saint Augustine's *Confessions*, the *Education* is intended to provide a superior alternative to that work. The *Education*'s superiority consists, it is suggested, not so much in its worldliness (in contrast to the Christian mythology of Augustine's *Confessions*) as in its egotism (a quality that Augustine seeks to erode in his own text as much by precept as by discursive example).

I could go on indefinitely this way, seeking to identify the various codes, psychological, social, metaphysical, ethical, and artistic by which the complex fabric of the text could be said to emit messages, more phatic and conative, to use Jakobson's terminology, than referential or predicative. The aim would not be to reduce all of these messages to a single seemingly monolithic position that could be neatly condensed into an emblematic paraphrase, but rather to show the myriads of different messages and different *kinds* of messages that the text emits. The aim would also be, however, to characterize the types of messages emitted, in terms of the several codes in which they are cast, and to map the relationships among the codes thus identified, both as a hierarchy of codes and as a sequence of their elaboration, which would locate the text within a certain domain of the culture of the time of its production.

How, then, *does* a semiological approach to intellectual history contribute to the resolution of the specific problems arising in that field of inquiry? How does it help to resolve the problem of the text-context relationship, the classic text–documentary text relationship, the interpreter text–interpreted text relationship, and so on?

The crucial question for any historical investigation is the evidential status of any given artifact, more precisely, its *referential* status. Of what is the artifact evidence? To what does it refer, or put another way: what referent does it permit us, however indirectly, to perceive? As long as the object to which an artifact gives access is conceived to exist *outside* the artifact, these questions are irresolvable, at least when it is a matter of historical perception. And this because, by definition, we might say, a datum is *past* only in the extent to which it is *no longer* something to which I can be referred as *a possible object of living perception*. The historically real, the past real, is that to which I can be referred only *by way of* an artifact that is textual in nature. The indexical, iconic, and symbolic notions of language, and therefore of texts, obscure the nature of this indirect referentiality and hold out the possibility of (feign) direct referentiality, create the illusion that there is a past *out there* which is directly reflected *in* the texts. But even if we grant this, it is the reflection that we perceive, not the thing reflected. By directing our attention to the reflection of things that appear in the text, a semiological approach to intellectual history fixes us directly before the process of meaning-production that is the special subject of intellectual history conceived as a subfield of historical inquiry in general.

It goes without saying that not all historical inquiry is concerned with the production of meanings. In fact, most historical inquiry is concerned less with the production of meanings than with the *effects* of such productive processes—what we might wish to call the exchange and consumption of meanings within a given socio-cultural configuration. Wars, alliances, economic activity, exercises of political power and authority, anything involving intentional creation and destruction, aim-oriented activities entered into by individuals and groups—these are what I have in mind. If intellectual history, which takes as its special subject matter the ideas, *mentalités*, thought systems, systems of values and ideals of particular societies in the past, simply treats these as data that *reflect* processes in some way more "basic" (such as economic, social, political, or even psychological processes), then intellectual history is supererogatory in relationship to the historical reconstruction of these other processes. For in that case, it can only double the accounts provided by specialists in these other fields of study, tell the same story, with slightly different material and in a slightly different register, as the story told about these other fields.

Manifestly, however, the data of the intellectual historian are different from those with which political and economic historians work, and their differentness consists in the fact that these data *show us directly* the processes by which cultures produce the kinds of meaning systems that give to their practical activities the aspect of meaningfulness, or value. Groups engage in political activities for political purposes, to be sure, but these activities are *meaningful* to them only by reference to some other, extrapolitical aim, purpose, or value. This is what permits them to imagine that *their* political activities are qualitatively different from those of their opponents or represent a higher value than those of their enemies—who are enemies or opponents precisely in the extent to which they envision *other* aims, purposes, values, specifically different though generically similar to those of the first group. And so too for economic, religious, or social activities. Historical events differ from natural events by virtue of the fact that they are meaningful for their agents and variously meaningful to the different groups that carry them out.

Economic activity no doubt has to do with economic aims, the production, exchange, and consumption of goods, but different modalities of economic activity (feudal, capitalist, socialist, and all mixtures thereof) exist because this activity is regarded as serving other ends than those of mere production, exchange, and consumption of goods. Food, clothing, and shelter may be basic "economic" necessities, but what is considered the *proper* kind of food, appropriate clothing, and humanly adequate shelter varies from culture to culture. Moreover, the provision of these necessities in any given culture is governed by rules and laws which have their justification in an extra-economic domain, specifically that in which the meaning of what is to be considered as proper, appropriate, and adequate is produced.

Put this way, it immediately becomes obvious why intellectual historians take their inspiration from Hegel, Marx, Freud, and Nietzsche —and their modern avatars, Lévi-Strauss, Habermas, Foucault, Derrida, Ricoeur, Gadamer, J. L. Austin, and so on. For every one of these is concerned with the problem of *mediation*, which we can construe as the deflection of basic impulses (economic, social, sexual, aesthetic, intellectual, whatever) from their putatively immediate aims by considerations that are culture-specific in nature. And here "culture-specific" means specific to a historically determinate system of meaning.

The intellectual historical artifact viewed semiologically permits us to see the system of meaning-production operating directly in a way that other kinds of historical artifacts do not—and this because these other kinds of artifacts (weapons, treaties, contracts, account books) inevitably appear to us more as the *effects* of such operations or at best as instruments of them, rather than as *causes* of them. This is why a content oriented, history-of-ideas approach to intellectual history is perfectly appropriate for the analysis of certain kinds of documents in those situations in which we are interested more in the effects of culture on its members than in the ways that culture produces those effects. And this way of formulating the matter points to a way of resolving the classic text–documentary text relationship.

The classic text *seems* to command our attention because it not only contains ideas and insights about "the human condition" in general, but provides an interpretative model by which to carry further our investigations in our own time, or indeed at any time. In reality, however, the classic text, the master-text, intrigues us not because (or not *only* because) its meaning-content is *universally* valid or authoritative (for that is manifestly impossible, and in any event, is a profoundly *unhistorical* way of looking at anything), but rather because it gives us insight into a *process* that is universal and definitive of human species-being in general, the process of meaning-production. To be sure, even the most banal comic strip can yield some insight into this process, especially when submitted to semiological analysis—and in a way that it could not do, incidentally, under investment by a conventional history-of-ideas approach. And in the interest of a scientific responsibility which must inform our work, if it is to claim an authority any larger than that of virtuoso performance, we must be prepared to grant that the comic strip cannot be treated as *qualitatively* inferior to a Shakespeare play, or any other classic text. From a semiological perspective, the difference is not qualitative but only *quantitative*, a difference of degree of complexity in the meaning-producing process (complexity, I assume it will be granted, marks a qualitative difference between two objects only for those for whom complexity itself is a value). The difference in degree of complexity has to do with the extent to which the classic text reveals, indeed actively draws attention to, its own processes of meaning-production and makes of these processes its own subject matter, its own "content."

Thus, to return by way of conclusion to *The Education of Henry Adams*, the text serves us especially well as an intellectual-historical document, in a way that his diaries, letters, and other documents relating his daily life would not, precisely in the extent to which it contains all those evidences of self-concern and fear of failure that we have indicated as aspects of its ideologizing function. What might be regarded as its flaws from the standpoint of a naive expositor, which is to say, anyone wishing to assess its logical consistency or to assign points for its stylistic proprieties in its various parts, becomes for the semiologically oriented commentator its very virtue as a "document" of intellectual history. The differences between the first part of the *Education*, so beloved by diplomatic historians for its observations of the diplomatic scene and by those with a conventional notion of what a "narrative" should be, and the second part, with its metahistorical speculations and tone of pessimism, which offends those who have a conventional notion of what a proper "autobiography" should be; the mandarinlike pickiness and preciosity of the diction of the whole work; its hesitancies and duplicities; the thematic obsessions; the pervasive irony—all become equally valuable for the analyst concerned with meaning-production rather than with meaning produced, with processes of the text rather than with the text as product. It is precisely these "flaws" that point us to what makes of the *Education* a classic work, an example of a self-conscious and self-celebrating creativity, *poiesis*.

As for the text-context problem—the extent to which the *Education* was a product of causal forces more basic than itself, whether these are regarded as social, psychological, economic, or what have you, the extent to which Adams's work either "reflects" his own time or "reflects on" it perspicuously, as Brogan praises it for doing—I have suggested that this problem becomes resolvable from the semiological perspective to the degree in which what conventional historians call the "context" is *already* in the text in the specific modalities of code-shifting by which Adams's discourse produces its meanings. For surely, when we inquire into the context of a work such as the *Education*, we are interested above all in the extent to which that context provided resources for the production of the kinds of meanings that this text displays to us. To have information about this aspect of the text's context would not illuminate the operations of Adams's work *in their specificity*, in their details as we follow or track the text's narrative. On the contrary, it is the other way around: the context is illuminated in its detailed operations by the moves made in Adams's text.

Of course, Adams drew upon his society and his culture for the kinds of operations he carries out in his text, by which to endow his experiences, his "life," with a meaning, even if the meaning provided is only the judgment that life itself is meaningless. What Adams does is show us one example of how the cultural resources of his historical moment and place could be fashioned into a plausible justification for this kind of nihilistic judgment. In wedding the general notion of nihilism with the particularities of his life, Adams produces an *individual* version of the nihilistic credo, which is to say, a *type* of this credo (type being defined as a mediation between particulars and real or merely feigned universals). It is the *typicality* of Adams's discourse that makes it translatable as evidence of his own age which a reader in our age can comprehend, receive as message, *understand*.

Typicality is produced by the imposition of a specific form on an otherwise wild content. The imposition of this form is carried out in the discourse materialized in Adams's text. It is the enactment of this discourse that attests to Adams's status as a "representative" of the culture of his age. And it is the product of that enactment, the text entitled *The Education of Henry Adams*, considered as a finished *form*, that gives us insight into the type of meaning-production available in the culture of Adams's time and place.

This notion of the typicality of the text permits us to deal with the problem of the hated "reduction" of the complex text which hermeneuticists lament endlessly. In saying that a given text represents a type of meaning-production, we are not reducing the text to the status of some causal force conceived to be more basic than that of meaning-production in general. We are pointing, rather, to what is both obvious and undeniable: namely, that Adams himself has "condensed" his life into the form that it displays in the *Education* and, moreover, transformed that life into a *symbol* of the sociocultural processes of his own time and place *as he perceived them* thereby. This is not a reduction but a sublimation or transumption of meaning, which is a *possible* response of human consciousness to its world everywhere and at all times. By unpacking the rich symbolic content of Adams's work we desublimate it and return it to its status as an immanent product of the culture in which it arose. Far from reducing the work, we have, on the contrary, enflowered it, permitted it to bloom and caused it to display its richness and power as a symbolizing process.

Notes on Editors
and Contributors

KEITH MICHAEL BAKER is Professor of History at the University of Chicago and editor of *The Journal of Modern History*. He is the author of *Condorcet: From Natural Philosophy to Social Mathematics* (1975) and editor of *Condorcet: Selected Writings* (1976). In his most recent work, he has been exploring aspects of the problem of the ideological origins of the French Revolution.

ROGER CHARTIER is a member of the Ecole des Hautes Etudes en Sciences Sociales, whose Center for Historical Research he directs. He is a frequent contributor to the *Annales*, and the *Revue d'Histoire Moderne et Contemporaine* and the co-author of *La Nouvelle Histoire* (1978) and *Histoire de la France urbaine*. He is now working on problems of education, popular culture, and the book trade in old-regime France.

DAVID JAMES FISHER, Assistant Professor of History at the University of Southern California, is an associate editor of the quarterly journal *Humanities in Society*. Currently he is completing a book called *Intellectual Politics: Romain Rolland and Engagement between the Wars*. He is a Research Clinical Associate at the Los Angeles Psychoanalytic Society and Institute.

E. M. HENNING is a graduate student in the Department of History at Cornell University. He is preparing a dissertation on the problem of Nietzsche's critical "reception" in the West.

MARTIN JAY is Associate Professor of History at the University of California, Berkeley, the author of *The Dialectical Imagination: A History of the Frankfurt School and the Institute of Social Research, 1923–1950* (1973), and a senior editor of *Theory and Society*. He is at work on a book on Western Marxist concepts of totality.

PETER JELAVICH, Assistant Professor of History and Social Studies at Harvard University, is completing a book on the rise of the modernist theater in Munich.

STEVEN LAURENCE KAPLAN is Professor of European History at Cornell University, where he directs the Western Societies Program. He is the author of *Bread, Politics, and Political Economy in the Reign of Louis XV* (1976), and *La Bagarre: Gabani's "Lost" Parody* (1979). He is currently making studies of the bakers of Paris and the grain and flour trades of the Paris area in the eighteenth century.

HANS KELLNER teaches in the Department of Humanities, Michigan State University. Among his essays on historical writing are "Time Out: The Discontinuity of Historical Consciousness," *History and Theory* (1975); "Guizot and the Poets," *Journal of European Studies* (1977); "Disorderly Conduct: Braudel's Mediterranean Satire," *History and Theory* (1979); "A Bedrock of Order: Hayden White's Linguistic Humanism," *History and Theory* (1980); and "The Inflatable Trope as Narrative Theory: Structure or Allegory?" *Diacritics* (1981).

DOMINICK LaCAPRA, Professor of History at Cornell University, is author of *Emile Durkheim: Sociologist and Philosopher* (1972); *A Preface to Sartre* (1978); and *"Madame Bovary" on Trial* (1982). He is currently working on a collection of essays addressing problems of theory and method in intellectual history.

MARK POSTER is Professor of History at the University of California, Irvine. He is the author of *Existential Marxism in Postwar France* (1975), *Critical Theory of the Family* (1978), and *Sartre's Marxism*. He is now writing a study of the social thought of Michel Foucault.

HAYDEN WHITE is Professor and Chairman of the Program in the History of Consciousness at the University of California, Santa Cruz. He is author of *Metahistory* (1973) and *Tropics of Discourse* (1978).

Index

Modern European
Intellectual History

Designed by Richard E. Rosenbaum.
Composed by Eastern Graphics
in 10 point Linotron 202 Times Roman, 2 points leaded,
with display lines in Times Roman.
Printed offset by Thomson/Shore, Inc. on
Warren's Number 66 Antique Offset, 50 pound basis.

Library of Congress Cataloging in Publication Data

Main entry under title:
Modern European intellectual history.

"Most of these papers were first presented at a conference held at Cornell
University on April 24–26, 1980"—Pref.
    Includes bibliographical references and index.
    1. Europe—Intellectual life—Congresses. I. LaCapra, Dominick, 1939–
II. Kaplan, Steven L.
D1055.M59   306′.094   82-7418
ISBN 0-8014-1470-9   AACR2
ISBN 0-8014-9881-3 (pbk.)